SUMMERHILL, WARRENPOINT

A Memoir

by
Barney Carr

Published by Barney Carr 2012

Copyright © Barney Carr 2012

Designed by
Apex Design, Newry

Printed by
W.G. Baird

I.S.B.N
978-0-9572383-0-5

Edited by
Michael J McCann
and Anne Holland

DEDICATION

To my parents Hugh Carr and Mary (Minnie) Tumilty who gave me life and a set of values and to those who made that life such a wonderful experience; my darling wife Anne (Polley), my children, Hugh, John and Louise and to Susan (Connolly), my daughter-in-law and mother of my grandchildren

ACKNOWLEDGEMENT

I wish to record my appreciation to the townspeople who shared 'The Point' with me over the years; many of their names appear in the pages of this book. Writing a book at my time of day meant I needed some good advice and assistance. I wish to thank Frank McCorry of Lurgan (my earliest reader and the author of a number of fine books) for pointing me in the right direction. My sincere thanks also to my former Summerhill neighbour, Cathal McCabe, a literary professional who introduced me to my co-editors Michael McCann and Anne Holland who have transformed my script into a readable book. I wish to record my appreciation to the staff of the various libraries which I frequented over the years, Warrenpoint, Newry, Armagh, the Newspaper section of the Central Library in Belfast and the Public Records Office. Summerhill has been captured with accuracy and sensitivity by my grandniece Jenny Jenkins who is responsible for the cover picture and I offer her my thanks and congratulations. Thanks also to Noel McAllister of Apex Design, Newry who has made me a publisher in my ninetieth year. Overseeing the entire process was my daughter, Louise, whose encouragement and judgement as well as her IT skills were vital components.

PROLOGUE

Barney Carr was born on Summerhill, Warrenpoint in 1923 and has lived there at three different addresses for all but seven of his eighty-nine years. He was the fifth of ten children born to Hugh and Minnie Carr (née Tumilty). He with his brother, Paddy and sister, Noreen are the only surviving members of the family. He attended St Peter's Primary School in Warrenpoint and then Carrick Primary School in Burren before enrolling at The Abbey Christian Brothers' Secondary school in Newry where he would say he became a 'dropout' before completing his third year.

Like many Point boys, he had a seagoing experience during the summer holidays on the Warrenpoint–Omeath ferries but his first real job was as a grocery assistant in the Vitamin Stores in Church Street. In the early forties, he left this to join the Northern Ireland Road Transport Board as a conductor and later became a driver when one-man bus operations became the norm.

In the mid-sixties he was appointed Education Welfare Officer with the Down Education Committee and, after the reorganisation of education administration in 1974, he became senior officer in the Newry area. Later in the eighties he became Chief Welfare Officer with the Southern Education and Library Board at its Armagh headquarters.

In his early years he had been an enthusiastic footballer, first as a soccer player and later in the Gaelic code. He began playing with his local St Peter's Club in 1940 and was a member of their three senior county championship winning teams in the 1943–53 period. His Inter-County career began in 1941 when he represented Down minors. His senior career commenced in 1943 and he became a regular for the next ten years.

From a young age he had an interest in politics first in what came to be called 'the Old Nationalist Party' from which he resigned to form the local branch of the SDLP in the early seventies. He resigned from that party too in 2000 when he failed to get some internal structures changed.

He is best known for his association as manager with the great Down team which won All-Ireland titles in 1960 and 1961, and in the process brought a new dimension to Gaelic football. Much has been written about that team and that period but there is a fuller story which has never been told. Barney Carr would have been happy not to have it told, but in its telling, his own life story has emerged and he feels he should share it with the world.

Barney married Anne Polley of Dundrum on 8 September 1953. They had three children Hugh, John and Louise. Anne died on 11 September 2001, just hours before the sun rose in the American sky.

CONTENTS

Introduction

Many times over the past 50 years, individuals have expressed their surprise that I had never come up with a book or two. As recently as September 2004, at a book launch in Newry by Frank McCorry of Lurgan, Seamus Gorman, a man from Mayobridge and a lifetime acquaintance, asked, in what I thought was a serious tone of voice, 'Are *you* not writing anything?'

'Why would you ask a man in his eighties a question like that?' I queried back, and got a measured response in the same serious tone, 'I think you have a good story to tell.' The truth is that it is nearly 50 years since I said to my wife—at a function celebrating Down's first All-Ireland success—'If I ever write a book I will write about this night.' And now I have done so.

Despite the thought on that occasion, it was many years later that I repeated the 'if I ever write a book' threat. This was at Christmas 1990, after reading Denis Donoghue's version of Warrenpoint in his book of that name. At the time some people expressed their views in the local and national newspapers, but newspapers are burned the next day, whilst books sit on shelves for evermore. I have written about Warrenpoint and Denis Donoghue's view of it at some length in this memoir, though it was years later before another literary expression became the catalyst that drove me to the keyboard.

I have good reason to remember the last Tuesday in August 1996, the day Maurice Hayes, a former Secretary of the Down Gaelic Athletic Association (GAA) Board, launched his book *Minority Verdict,* though not for any reason relating to Maurice or his book. I had been invited to the launch and had expected to be there, but an earlier engagement on the day overran by a considerable period and ruled me out. I wish I had gone to the book launch, for I am still experiencing the 'fall out' from that earlier engagement.

For whatever reason, in *Minority Verdict,* Maurice chose to disparage the GAA, and worse, questioned the integrity of one of its most distinguished members. On this occasion my reaction was not, 'if I ever write a book,' but rather 'I need to write a book'. Four years later I still had not made a start on it, and probably never would have, but for a function in November 2000 commemorating Down's first All-Ireland win over Kerry. Among the guests were Paddy McFlynn, a former president of the Association, and his wife, Kathleen. Paddy is 'the distinguished member' I have referred to above. When I met them during the evening I started the conversation with a jocular, 'You never went to law,' referring to Maurice's book, for many were of the opinion that Paddy had been 'hard-done-by' in it. Paddy laughed it off, but it was no laughing matter for Kathleen. She did not conceal the hurt she felt for 'her man,' even though she was never into the GAA as some women might be. I felt for her that night, and I regret that she has not been spared to experience Paddy's integrity being upheld.

The next day, I sat down and wrote the first paragraph of this memoir. That paragraph sat on its own until January 2001; I then resumed writing in a more structured fashion for a couple of months, during which time my dear wife's ill-health was becoming apparent. The writing stopped completely at Easter.

11 September 2001, or 9/11 as it is called in America, changed the world, and me in particular. My darling wife died just hours before those thousands in the Twin Towers in New York and other parts of America. Many times since, I have contemplated the beauty and wonder of her death in Daisy Hill Hospital in Newry, caressed and comforted by three pairs of loving hands and three prayerful tongues in the earliest hours of that fateful day, contrasting it with the awfulness of the American holocaust that was unleashed hours later. The suicide bomber had made the nuclear bomb obsolete, for this generation at least.

When writing resumed in January 2002, I had the shape of the book in my head and very little else, but I have to confess this is not the book I sat down to write, and while I have written at length about Warrenpoint and the views of Maurice on the GAA, they have become a secondary part of the story. While Richard Dawkins was just a name that cropped up in the news from time to time, I was nearly three years into this book when he crossed my path for the first time. I relate the details of his visit to Dublin in 2003 and how Professor William Reville, who writes on science in *The Irish Times,* described him as 'pompous'. That same year when I read, probably in *The Irish Times* too, that Dawkins was considered to be among the ten best intellects in the world, I muttered to myself (remembering the professor's assessment), 'pompous fool,' for by this time I was aware of the gospel he was proclaiming.

Long before I had the book finished I knew I had a problem with it, so I renewed a slight acquaintance I had with a man in the publishing business in Dublin, Michael Adams, who was the controller of Four Courts Press. I took a few chapters down to him and his verdict was, 'You would need to write two books, you would lose your readers with some of that.' I knew he was right, but I also knew that I did not have the capacity for two books, so I am prepared for a loss of readers. Sadly, Michael Adams, a comparatively young man of great integrity, died rather suddenly a few years ago. He has been greatly missed. The risk of losing readers does not deter me from making do with one book for I cannot divorce any single chapter of my life from its entirety.

I suppose it could be said it has taken me a long time to complete this book; and while the pace of doing anything tends to slow when one gets into the eighties, time itself moves even faster. One other consideration which might have slowed the pace of writing was the fact that I had taken a decision not to publish during the lifetime of a couple of individuals for whom I have great respect. One of these was Síle Nic an Ultaigh (Sheila McAnulty), the author of *Ó Shíol go Bláth*, the story of the Down GAA—a massive work. Síle died in July 2004, and while the other person concerned is some years older than me and might well outlive me, I feel it is time to tell my story.

In telling it, I am conscious of the defects that are bound to be in it, and for the most serious of these I would claim a degree of critical immunity on grounds of age. I am conscious, too, that like many writers of autobiography, I 'have been forced to be egotistical only in order to be sincere'.

PART I

1 — THE EARLY GAMES

Conscious memory begins for me on what I have always taken to be a pleasant September Sunday, when I was being hoisted by the armpits into the well of a jaunting car by a man with a black moustache. I knew I was bound for a football match in Rostrevor with my father but I have no memory of leaving home. My father and three other men climbed on to the jaunting car, two on each side, and when the man with the black moustache got himself into the driving seat, we set off up Church Street at a gentle trot. Settled as I was between two walls of humanity, I had my first experience of delayed vision as the physical world came into view long after I had passed it. The Baths registered with me for the first time when I was a hundred yards beyond them, as did a solitary sailing boat and the Gunnaway Rock.

It was the same all the way to Rostrevor. As people walking the road spied the little figure in the well of the car, a wave of the hand or handkerchief signalled recognition. If there was any other traffic on the road (and I'm sure there was) I have no memory of it, but the sound of the tinkling harness bell and the smell of tobacco smoke also registered for the first time. I remember the sharp left hand turn we made as we entered Rostrevor village. For whatever reason, the field in which the game was played made a very definite impression, something that could not be said for the match itself. One team had green jerseys but the dress of their opponents, the quality of the play or the result itself, did not impact on me at all. Indeed, the action that closed the day for me on that occasion was being re-hoisted, by my father this time, into the well of the jaunting car for the return journey. I must have slept all the way back for I have no memory of ever arriving home. It is fair to say that this was the only sporting occasion in which The Point and Rostrevor were in opposition that failed to raise my temperature.

My next football outing was slightly more vivid though neither team wore jerseys, but every individual on the pitch was known to me by name. It was a Saturday morning, the venue was Shanaghan's Hill and the contestants were St Peter's School and Dromore Road School. The latter establishment would never have got its official designation in those days but would have been called Jameson's School, named after its principal William Jameson, whose father had been principal before him. Needless to say, he was known to all and sundry as 'Billy' but addressed by all as master or mister.

I am not sure that I had commenced school myself, but I was conscious of my commitment to St Peter's, by virtue of the fact that some of my older brothers were playing. The match was not what could be called an official fixture, but had been arranged by the boys themselves, which explained the absence of jerseys, goal posts or any field markings. Two stones set at agreed distances apart at each end of the pitch were all that was needed for the occasion. I cannot recall disputes about line balls, offsides or throw-ins, nor do I recall if there was even a referee. Dromore Road won the game which probably was unique for it was the only occasion the two schools met in a football match in my schooldays. Until July 2002 there were two survivors of the team that represented St Peter's that Saturday morning, John Crawford, who played in goal, and John (Corney) O'Hare who was an outfield player.

The John Crawford I refer to was Bishop John Crawford, OP, a Dominican priest, who died suddenly that year in Australia even as he was making preparations for his annual visit to the homeland. The sole survivor, John O'Hare, lived in retirement in Dublin after spending his working life, marrying and raising his family in the fair city. He died in 2006. On the last occasions I spoke to both men they recalled playing often on Shanaghan's Hill but neither could recall the game in question.

I know of no survivors from the Dromore Road team though one in particular has survived uniquely in my memory, Alex Toombs by name. He lived at the Orange Hall where his father was the caretaker and he, along with Mickey Kelly, would have been my earliest heroes. Mickey was a real stylist, a good dribbler and a good passer of the ball, while Alex, a half back of firm resolution, wore a trademark in the shape of shin guards and padding on both legs which would have turned a bullet, never mind the boot of an opponent. How he got stockings over them I do not know.

It strikes me that the venue, Shanaghan's Hill, would raise an eyebrow on any present resident of Warrenpoint under the age of 75, so I should explain that in The Point of that time, Slieve Foy Place was for the most part a greenfield site. Some houses had been built on the shore side of the avenue but the town side was still a green hill. The proprietor of the property that became the Balmoral Hotel was a Mr Michael Shanaghan, and his holding included the football field which was to bear his name for many years after. By all accounts, Mr Shanaghan was a well-remembered name and deserves more than a passing reference. He was a Tipperary man who married a local girl, a McCartan from Aghavilla. He took a great interest in local affairs and for a period was chairman of the Town Council. He had a great interest in Gaelic games and provided a trophy, the Shanaghan Cup, which was of historic significance in the fledgling GAA of the time.

After birth, the next marker on most chronological clocks is the day one begins school, but if I have doubts about being registered at St Peter's when the football match took place, I certainly have a clear recollection of the first day I entered the door of that establishment. A year or two ago, I was amazed to hear a well-known female novelist declare in a radio interview that she remembered nothing of her primary school days. I find that hard to take in, for to this day I have clear mental pictures of my arrival and reception on the occasion I crossed the door with my elder brother, Hugh. Coinciding with my arrival was the arrival of a new teacher, a Miss Eithne McDonald, who in time became known as 'Sandy'. Miss McDonald was replacing a retiring teacher, Miss Connolly. I am almost certain it was Miss McDonald's first appointment, and Miss Connolly was back at school that first morning to welcome her and 'to show her the ropes' so to speak.

The reality was that St Peter's was a two-roomed school and Miss McDonald was sharing the room, as Miss Connolly had done for how many years I know not, with Master Crawford. He had the responsibility of three classes, second, third and fourth. My first impression of school was that it was a very crowded place.

Miss Connolly left after an hour and my academic career got under way. Lunchtime came and with it some very heavy rain. So heavy in fact, that Miss McDonald told my brother, who was in the same room, to tell my mother that I would have my lunch in school with her.

Home he went and Miss McDonald proceeded to take her flask and sandwiches from her bag. She had a cup for herself and she unscrewed the aluminium top of the flask and put it in front of me. She put sugar and milk in and set one of her sandwiches beside it before proceeding to pour the tea. It is likely that this was the first time I had ever taken tea out of the top of a flask, but the second I grasped the cup it was so hot, I let it go immediately, with the contents over table and sandwich; my earliest public mortification. Despite my discomfort and protests, Miss McDonald insisted on giving me her cup and another sandwich and proceeded to take her own tea out of the aluminium cup. She won a friend for the rest of her life.

I relate the detail of my first day at school for two reasons. The first is to confess that while some of what happened to me yesterday or even this morning might already be beyond recall, the important events of 75 years are stored in the album of the heart. The second is to dismiss out of hand a view expressed a few years ago by a classmate of my own vintage, and a life-long friend, in a magazine celebrating 150 years of St Peter's School. This was his comment: 'Poor Sandy McDonald just didn't seem to excel in anything, except teaching us morning prayers, hymns and catechism.'

'Poor Sandy' spent her entire career in St Peter's. Among the hundreds of pupils she guided in their earliest days were his son and mine and until I read that magazine I had never heard the slightest suggestion of any inadequacies in her work. In relation to her teaching of religion I would suggest that if she convinced one pupil (and she did) of the reality of Christ in the Eucharist, her teaching career would have been fulfilled.

Within weeks of commencing school and without voicing my complaint about the overcrowding, we arrived there one morning to find Carvills' men working on the foundations of an additional classroom. Carvills was a local building firm who had their base at the foot of our back lane. Most of those engaged in the work were known to me, and 'young Carr' received a few admonitions from Owen Woods and Joe Trainor as he jumped over the holes they were digging. In a matter of months we were installed in a fresh new classroom and the learning process got under way in earnest.

The most memorable event in the early lives of that first intake of pupils had nothing to do with school and it didn't even take place in the school environs. Almost the entire school population went home for lunch and on a particular day when we were returning a diversion, in the shape of an aeroplane, appeared overhead. For most of us it was the first sighting of a mechanical bird. When I saw it disappear behind the church I thought it was about to crash into the sea, but in fact it was a seaplane capable of landing on the lough, which it did just off the

Baths. It taxied round to a spot the locals would have called 'The Beach,' watched by most of the boys in the school. The bell sounded for the restart of lessons after the lunch break and quite a few answered the call to learn, but the unheeding majority was much too concerned about the dinghy and its occupant who was coming ashore from the plane. By two o'clock it dawned on everyone that we were going to be in trouble with Master Thomas Glancy, the headmaster, but a defiant shout went up, 'We'll not go back today,' a shout which got general acclaim from all on the beach except a few faint-hearts like myself. Nevertheless, I was not going to go back to school on my own at that time of the afternoon. I joined the rebellion. Most of the school spent the rest of the afternoon on the Gas Road and Campbell's Pond, which was an adventure playground generations before the term was coined. I will immortalise Hugh Campbell, not the Campbell of The Pond, but father of John on the Burren Road, by declaring him to be the leader of the first education rebellion in The Point.

All rebellions are paid for in one form or another, so next morning there was an air of expectancy, if not suspense, as we took our places in our respective classrooms. Not a word was uttered about the happenings of the previous day through the first three half-hour periods. The toilet break came and an air of optimism was apparent. It was felt that there was such a number of offenders that it would be impossible to punish all of us; plus it was felt that this being the first aeroplane that was ever seen about The Point made the event so exceptional that no understanding principal could be anything but sympathetic.

Alas, once we settled back in class, we soon knew that the hour of retribution was at hand. There was obvious movement in the porch which served as a common cloakroom for all three classrooms. Master Glancy's voice was audible, though the message he was delivering did not reach our ears. Then it began, swish, swish, swish, swish, until every man in his room who had defected—and that was most of them—received two thumpers on each hand, with the odd howl of pain testifying to their severity.

Then it was the turn of Master Crawford's class, also in the porch. Two of the best, on each hand was their entitlement also, and doubtless, for younger boys, it would have been their first taste of real punishment. With the second instalment duly delivered, Master Glancy entered our room showing no signs of his exertions and addressed the pupils.

'Would the boys who did not return to school yesterday, come to the front of the class.' When we did not get the call to the porch I thought we were going to get away with a stern warning. Probably the nine or ten boys who joined me at the front of the class were of the same opinion, but there was no reprieve. To be fair to Master Glancy, he did take into consideration the fact that all of us were under seven, and we got away with two whacks, one on each hand. It must be recorded that I heard no complaints from any of my classmates, nor do I recall any complaints from irate parents. It was the general view that we got our just desserts.

While life is all sport in the formative years, I have only referred so far to the occasions football touched on my experience, though the reality is that my earliest sporting passion was engendered by a game which now seems obsolete, the game of billiards or, as the framed rules of the game described it, 'The Game of English Billiards'. My uncle, Hugh Tumilty, was the caretaker in the Irish National Foresters Club and he lived with grandmother Tumilty on the top floor of the building. I lived with them in the third year of my career at the nearby St Peter's. On Saturdays, as well as doing messages for Granny, I performed a range of tasks particularly in the billiard room which was in the basement of the building. I soon learned the rudiments of the game and, by the time the winter competitive season got under way, I was an enthusiastic supporter of the club teams.

Bessbrook, Rostrevor and Warrenpoint would have been consistently the top performers and needless to say when Rostrevor met The Point, the intensity of the rivalry on the green beige equalled anything I experienced in later life on the green grass. For those not acquainted with the format of competitive billiards it should be explained that a team comprised of four players. Their names were written on slips of paper and placed in two small heaps of four and it was a straight draw, no seeding. The best of one team could have met the least accomplished of the other, though the top teams mentioned would have four top-class performers. Certainly as far as Rostrevor were concerned, the top man was Tom Sloan. He had great back-up from Michael Murphy, Barney Cole and John McCartan.

When Michael Murphy left to work with *The Irish News* in Belfast, he was replaced by a young fellow called Jim Curran. For The Point, it was Billy Burns who probably would have been number one, though the other team members John Magee, Hugh McGuigan and Billy's brother, Johnny, were all players of very high quality. I am the only man alive who travelled to Bessbrook on Nesbitt's bus when we beat St Columban's four nil, and I recall being encouraged by my father to go and congratulate each winner in turn. A chap called Paddy Quinn was the great Bessbrook player of the time and later in life I got to know him very well. But it was the matches with Rostrevor that drew the crowds. One could hardly cough during the games for fear of being ejected.

My father Hugh Carr played on the B team and while he was a competent enough shot-player he lacked the ability to build good breaks, says I, the experienced seven-year-old. But the player I distinctly recall from that era is none of those mentioned. It is Paddy Burns, who played mostly on the B team with my father. Only a handful of people would have known Paddy by name, but everybody in the town would recognise him as 'Laddie Da' and quite wrongly, for his proper nickname was 'La-Di-Dah,' a name he made for himself on the billiard table—though it is only experts like myself and millions of others who would appreciate the use of 'side' in billiards and snooker, which was rarely played at the time. Laddie would use tremendous side on occasions and, when his shots were successful and drew applause from the spectators, he would turn to the crowd and exclaim, 'It took the la-di-dah for that one.' So Paddy became 'La-Di-Dah' which in turn became 'Laddie Da'. If one was speaking to him he would be addressed as 'Laddie,' but if one was speaking about him he would be referred to as 'Laddie Da'.

For whatever reason, the skills and the sensitive touch the game demanded all seemed to run in a number of families; the Magee, Burns, Dinsmore and

McGuigan families all seemed naturally gifted on the billiard table. Does anyone play billiards today? Walter Lindrum, rest easily in your grave.

Golf is probably the most popular one-to-one game of the modern sporting era, for even without an opponent the course will always present its own challenge. I never got into it properly and I put that down to a bad experience early in my career. It was towards the end of the Easter holidays that Johnny Delahunt and I went up to Thomas O'Hare's fields, now Pinewood Hill, on the Bridle Loanin. The Bridle was not the racetrack it is today. The only house on it was O'Neill's slaughterhouse and because the Loanin was comprised of loose stones and deep tracks it was imperative that horses were led up it rather than driven, hence the name, Bridle Loanin.

Johnny owned all the golfing equipment that we carried, one driver, two golf balls and one tee. I was first to drive (probably the first time I had a golf club in my hand) and surprised myself by hitting the ball dead centre and dead straight to a reasonable distance. Next to the tee comes Johnny, a boy four or five years older than me and not even in my room at school. He addressed the ball a couple of times and swung. At the same time he half-jumped forward and while he hit the ball, his follow-through hit me straight on the forehead and down I went, though not completely out. I would describe it now as the most uncoordinated golf shot of all time. With Johnny's help I struggled to my feet and staggered across the field to the Loanin, already feeling the bump rising on my forehead.

At that stage in my life, I had scarcely heard of the Good Samaritan, but there, coming up the Loanin, I met him in the person of Mickey Ruddy, an older boy in the school. Mickey took one look at my forehead, surprisingly not bleeding, but a lump the size of an egg was in the process of forming. He knew immediately what to do. Over to the ditch he went searching until he got a reasonably flat stone which he applied to my aching skull. The cold stone and the earth still clinging to it was a soothing poultice, and it gave some ease to my throbbing head. 'Hold that on till I get another one.' I held the stone to my head and in a matter of seconds Mickey returned with another instalment of his magical healing potion. I thought, 'How could Mickey know to do all these things?'

Not only did Mickey render first aid, but he turned back and accompanied Johnny and myself to my home on Summerhill. I can remember his parting words to my mother, 'Don't worry, Mrs Carr, he'll be all right.' Ever since, whenever I have heard the parable of the Good Samaritan preached, I have always thought of Mickey Ruddy.

O'Hare's garden was a vacant piece of ground at the bottom of Summerhill, opposite the O'Hare family homes and contracting business. At the time I am writing about, the first modern intrusion on the garden, the Electricity Board's sub-station, was not in place. We were still in 'the gas age'. The garden was used by the children of the area, including the O'Hares, as a playground and while it was a bit bumpy, boys played football on it. A couple of Saturday mornings after my golfing incident, I was in the garden kicking a ball with a few companions when we realised there was a commotion at the Masonic Hall at the top of Duke Street, adjacent to the top of the garden. Up we ran to investigate, and saw a small four-seater car with driver, passenger and a policeman on board, surrounded by a score of laughing, shouting and cheering schoolboys of my own age and upwards, all of them known to me. To the background of cheering and jeering, we soon learned what was happening and instantly joined the unruly chorus. To my amazement and even consternation, Mickey Ruddy was being taken to Belfast to the reformatory (the first time I had ever heard the word) for his poor attendance at school.

We were soon filled in on the events of the morning, which began when the car arrived at the police Barracks with the driver and the man from the reformatory on board. They collected one of the local policemen before proceeding to Post Office Street, where Mickey lived with his two older brothers and his grandmother, an elderly grey-haired lady who was hard-of-hearing and could be very excitable. Trauma was not a word that was in common usage then, but one can imagine the scene in the Ruddy household that morning as that posse arrived to take Mickey into custody. Eventually Mickey was hustled into the back seat of the open car beside the man from the reformatory.

With Mickey deposited in the car, the policeman headed down Post Office Street on foot heading for the Barracks, thinking his job was done, but as the car moved off Mickey jumped out, flew up what we called the Big Lane into Church Street, turned left down to Tommy Cunningham's Corner, up King's Lane, another left turn into East Street and past O'Hare's garden where we, unaware of the chase, had been blissfully kicking a ball. Mickey flew past unobserved, to the freedom of the open fields on the Bridle Loanin.

Within minutes of our arrival on the scene, the posse was joined by another policeman and after a short discussion the two policemen set off on foot up The Bridle. The car turned and slowly made its way down Duke Street to the condemning chorus of what was at this time the entire school population. Into The Square it went, down Newry Street and on to the Lower Dromore Road, past the golf club and Ward's slaughterhouse to stop near Smyth's, the barber's residence.

After a lengthy interval, a shout went up, 'They caught Mickey,' and as the assembly raised their eyes to the hills that stretched up to The Bridle, there was a communal groan as the small figure of Mickey descended with his two captors. As the trio reached ground level, the dismay turned to real anger as the raiding party moved off in the car to a storm of boos, shouts of, 'Good man Mickey' and a sod or two.

I cannot say just how long Mickey spent in the reformatory, but in due course he returned and became an integral part of the Warrenpoint environment that fashioned my formative years and indeed my life.

2—THE NATIONAL QUESTION

I had a run-in with the police myself earlier in my young life when I answered an early morning knock on our door at 18, Summerhill. Our knocker had a very distinctive knock and, being a light sleeper, I was the only one in the house to hear it. It was just after five o'clock in the morning and in bright daylight, when the rat-tat-tat wakened me. No one else stirred and when the rat-tat-tat came a second time, and as I was sleeping at the floor side, I slid out of bed and descended the stairs in my nightshirt. To my utter astonishment, my opening of the door revealed two policemen who were as surprised to see me as I was them.

'Is Thomas Tumilty at home?' one asked politely.

'My Uncle Tommy doesn't live here.' I answered.

The policemen exchanged glances and then the same man asked, 'Where does he live then?'

I pointed to a house almost directly opposite. 'He lives over there with my Aunt Kitty and Uncle Jack.' They turned from the door and went across the street.

My banging the front door wakened my parents in the back room and my brothers in the front. When I reached the landing and told them what happened I had a volley of questions from some of the brothers.

'Where are the police now?' one asked.

'I sent them over to Aunt Kitty's.' I replied and immediately there was a rush to the front windows to view the two constables on Aunt Kitty's doorstep.

It was she who opened the door and after a comparatively short conversation the two policemen went off down the hill. At this my brothers turned to me with disapproval.

'You shouldn't have told them anything about Uncle Tommy,' they said. I had only told them where he lived, but the command from my father, 'Get back to your beds and no more talk,' ended my harassment.

There was no sleeping in the Carr household after the rude awakening and my father was on the first train as usual at 7.20 A.M. It was when we were all at our breakfast sometime later that my education on the national question began, with more criticism of my telling the police where my Uncle Tommy lived.

'Did you not know Uncle Tommy was in the IRA[1] during the Troubles?' asked my eldest brother, John, with more than a note of censure in his voice.

I was mystified, for while I certainly had heard of the Troubles, I doubt if I had heard of the IRA and certainly nothing at all about Uncle Tommy's involvement. I was a puzzled little boy going to school that morning.

I was well beyond the use of reason when I got the full story of that morning from my mother, and it revolved around the fact my uncle Jack Moran had been a Sergeant in the Royal Irish Constabulary (RIC), stationed in Dundalk, where he met Kitty who worked both at the Railway Station tea rooms and the Great Northern Railways Hotel (GNR) in Greenore. At the disbandment of the force, they settled in Warrenpoint, though not at Summerhill. Initially Jack spent some years in Chicago, probably earning enough to buy the house on Summerhill where

---

1   Irish Republican Army

they resided for the rest of their lives. He and the local Sergeant Donoghue, also a former RIC man who had come to the town a year or two before, had known each other and the bold Donoghue tipped Jack off about the impending arrest of Tommy. Duly warned, Tommy slipped off to his cousins in Newry and stayed there for a couple of weeks until the dust settled.

The reality of the situation at the time was that those who had been active in the War of Independence were likely to be taken into custody at the drop of a hat under the Special Powers then operating and held for months on end. Tommy would never have put Jack in the embarrassing situation of housing 'an active rebel' and I'm sure Jack would have made that clear to Sergeant Donoghue.

If that was my introduction to the revolutionary side of the national question, the constitutional side was not far behind, for on a Sunday morning some time later, as we were leaving for Mass, my mother warned us, 'Be home early for your dinner, your Daddy is going to a meeting in Castlewellan.'

Now Daddy was secretary of the local branch of the Irish National Foresters (INF) and would often have meetings on a Sunday, but never in Castlewellan. After dinner he went upstairs and when he came down wearing a bowler hat we all went into hysterics for I don't think any of us had seen the bowler hat before. Apparently, he had it from his wedding day, 15 or 16 years before.

'Where did you get the hat, Da? Did you borrow that from Jimmy Dowd?' Jimmy was one of our Protestant neighbours. 'You'll look well on the Twelfth, Da,' was the opening part of the humorous barrage under which we put him until a car came to collect him and end the torture. He went out with a broad smile on his face.

In the evening, when he returned, someone called, obviously to discuss the meeting and in the conversation that ensued I heard the name National League mentioned for the first time. It was years later before I heard it mentioned again. In due course, when he stood as a candidate for the local council, I did not even associate the event with the Castlewellan meeting. When I was quite a bit older I learned that the National League was a new Nationalist organisation and it was this group that my father and a number of other candidates were representing in the council election.

Beyond knowing that my father had been elected, nothing about the election had impacted until the first meeting of the newly elected body. I went to bed as usual with that section of the family (there were about eight of us at the time), who would have been called the early squad. I was the oldest of the early squad and we did not know until the morning that Daddy had not returned home from the meeting at all and that he was still in the Town Hall. The meeting dragged through the second day and when we said the Rosary that night we prayed at my mother's directive that my father would not lose his job by being absent. In her practical approach she felt that if my father could not go to work on account of illness the GNR would be quite understanding, but if they knew that their valued employee was off work for three days in what amounted to a political argument, it could be a different matter.

In the event, the meeting dragged though the second night because they could not agree on a chairman and looked to be going for a third when late on Wednesday one of the councillors took ill and had to leave the council chamber. A vote was called; one side got a majority, my father's side, and elected a chairman, Peter McMahon, a local solicitor.

Whether or not it was our rosaries that did the trick will hardly ever be known, but my father was on the first train as usual on Thursday morning. That one term was his only venture into politics. The National League must have died the death, for I never heard of it again until many years later when I noted it mentioned in a history of the period.

While the council elections might have provided some excitement for the local populace, for me the most notable event of the period was the homecoming of my uncle, John Carr, from America and my introduction to the tar barrel culture. Nowadays bonfires have to be a hundred feet high, necessitating fire brigades standing by to protect towns and villages, but the tar barrel was sufficient to mark notable occasions in those days all by itself. Of course, the tar barrel at the time was part of the furniture of streets and country roads which all seemed to get an annual dressing of tar and stone chippings. The empty barrels were left forever in nooks and corners in town and country. When emptied, the barrels were left with a solid residue of tar and pitch. A drop of petrol and a match ensured a bonfire for the whole night. Homecomings, departures and returns from honeymoons were all occasions that merited the tar barrel at the door.

This was the first time I had seen Uncle John, for he had departed to the USA in my earliest year or two, and it was a brief encounter in a crowded house in Thomas Street. For me, the highlight of his visit came a couple of Sundays later when he came to our house for dinner. Another brother of my father's, Uncle Barney, travelled on the pillion seat of his brother-in-law's motorbike from Carrickmacross, where he was living. This was the first occasion he came into my consciousness even thought he had lived in the Carr family residence until a year or two before.

When the meal was over, everyone with the possible exception of the dishwashers, moved into the parlour and soon the brothers were catching up on years of separation. If there was a lull in the conversation I was not aware of it but I did hear my father asking John, 'Are you still singing any?' I do not know what the reply was, but my father spoke again, 'Come on, let us hear you.' A request which was backed up by Barney.

John stood up and sang a song I would hardly have heard before, but the air stayed with me until some measure of musical appreciation emerged in my life recognising it as *Scenes that are brightest*. Of all the renderings I have heard over a lifetime, his is the one that has stuck. Barney was next, then my father, and I have to say I sat spellbound, for while I heard my father sing regularly for his own enjoyment and ours I had never heard a voice like Uncle Barney's before.

When my father had finished, Uncle Barney said, 'What about mother's song?'

There was general support for the proposal and my father went over to the piano which had sat in silence throughout the concert and struck a note or two, perhaps even a chord. The three brothers stood shoulder to shoulder in front of the fireplace and sang 'mother's song' which was unknown to me at that stage of my young life, *I Dreamt I Dwelt in Marble Halls*. I need hardly state that my musical appreciation was advanced considerably that day as I learned to distinguish between tenor, bass and baritone voices without knowing the terminology.

The day was not finished for me for I accompanied my father and uncles to Thomas Street; there, we were greeted graciously by the proprietor of the Imperial Hotel who was standing at his premises. I cannot be sure whether or not the adults went in for a drink but I am sure that Mr O'Hare, its owner, passed me a Free State threepenny bit before we left. Months later, the Imperial Hotel closed its doors for the last time and the words 'bankruptcy' and 'Stubbs' came into my vocabulary for the first time. That happened in 1929 and that fact tells me that everything I have written about so far happened before my seventh birthday. The Imperial Hotel then occupied the entire site of the present Thomas Street car park.

3—GAELIC FOOTBALL

A family from Burren, the McMahons, had come to live on Summerhill around this time and the three boys, Eddie, James and John, enrolled at St Peter's School. John, the youngest of the three, settled into my class. He was a quiet, ginger-haired boy, quite unlike his brother, James, with whom I had a difference of opinion in the early days of our relationship. While James was slightly bigger than me at the time, I thought I was fit for him. I made a big mistake, but learned an invaluable lesson for life. James got in the first blow and that was the end of the fight. I never attempted to start a fight with anyone again.

John and I must have been kindred spirits for within a couple of weeks we knew each other well enough to go off together after dinner on a Sunday afternoon. I can pinpoint the season as autumn because the first stage of our adventure took place in the branches of a crab apple tree which was laden with fruit. This was on the road from Clonallon Church over to the waterworks at Donaghaguy. We tasted and discarded the bitter apples and headed, as I thought, for the waterworks. At the fork on the road where it was left for Donaghaguy, John proposed, 'We'll go to Burren,' and off we went right, which was for me unknown territory. It was all uphill, of course, and while we might have stopped here and there for a breather or a blackberry, our aesthetic tastes had not developed sufficiently to stop and admire the panorama which the lough presents from that road. If our eyes were not attuned to appreciate the wonders of nature, there was nothing wrong with our ears, for we stopped simultaneously as the sound of distant cheers floated over the hills. Even as I wondered what the cheering could be about, the more knowledgeable John definitely knew, and I suspect knew even before we left The Point.

'I think Burren's playing The Bridge today,' he said, and I have to confess it didn't mean a lot to me, even though I knew The Bridge meant Mayobridge. Regardless, our amble turned into a good brisk walk and, as the cheers got louder and an air of excitement developed, our walk turned into a trot and maybe into a sprint in the last hundred yards. As we went through the gate of a roadside field the whistle sounded for half-time. In no time at all the spectators gathered on the pitch around the teams in two separate groups leaving John and myself the freedom of the field. When I saw the goal posts at both ends I realised this was not a soccer match, and if I had heard of Gaelic football previously I had certainly never seen it being played.

The referee's whistle sounded to end the half-time interval and it sounded a number of times before all the spectators finally returned to their places. When the teams were lined out properly, and the game got going again, I recognised quite a number of Point fellows on the Burren team, so my allegiance was with Burren straight away. I did wonder, though, how fellows like Jack Hanna, Jack Caldwell, Matt Durkin and Hughie O'Hare and a couple of others could be playing for them, but not for too long. Even my immature football mind soon sensed that this was no ordinary game of football. There was an odd skirmish in front of us and throughout the field, and the odd exchange of blows between the contestants. The spectators, men and women, were in a frenzy of excitement at times and the game was stopped on a number occasions for appeals by both the referee and linesmen. 'Back to the line, back to the line,' was the regular chant. About 15 minutes from the end a real fight developed among the players in the middle of the field and at the drop of a hat everybody was part of the action; that is, everybody except John McMahon and me who were left standing by ourselves on the touch line. John and I retreated to the ditch which bordered the road. Whether our move was prompted on safety grounds or to get an elevated view, I do not know, but soon the casualties began to emerge from the mêlée. Matt Durkin was the first man I recognised as he left the battle with his arms round the necks of two others and holding one leg off the ground. Out, too, came Hughie O'Hare with blood streaming from his nose. Even though it was a dry day an occasional umbrella was raised as a weapon. The battle waged for what seemed an eternity before some semblance of order was restored. There was never any hope of the game restarting.

John and I headed for home, though not by the route we had come, but I trusted him completely as we left what later I learned was Sean Byrne's field. We arrived at the bottom of the hill where I got my first view of Carrick School, and headed for home. We had only walked the short distance to Burren Chapel when McAnulty's bus stopped beside us. Out jumped Uncle Tommy Tumilty and, with a trace of scolding in his voice, posed the question, 'How did you get up here?'

I answered meekly, 'John McMahon took me.'

'Come on the pair of ye, get in,' was the order and in we got gladly. As we stood face to face in the bus there was an exchange of comradely smiles which expressed our feelings without a word being spoken: 'This was a powerful day' — and it was.

That game was my introduction to Gaelic football, and of all the ructions I have seen in the intervening 70-odd years nothing compares. It had a long-sounding echo for me in April 2000; the historian, Eamon Phoenix, a man with Point connections, recalled in his 'On This Day' feature in *The Irish News* an item dated 26 April 1930. It was headed *Visiting Football Team Given The Boot*, and the report went on:

> '... *how a visiting team was chased off the playing field, was told at Warrenpoint Petty Sessions on Friday. Three young men from the Mayobridge district, Thomas Gribben, Hugh J. O'Hare and Thomas McGivern were prosecuted for assaulting two men named Caldwell and another named Bracken, on the occasion of a Gaelic football match at Mayobridge on March 19. Two men named Butterfield were summoned for aiding and abetting. Sergeant O'Flaherty said when the police were sent for, they arrived at the ground where they found a certain amount of excitement. Sticks were produced and the visiting team from Burren were chased. Some of them had to take refuge in a bus which was entered by some of the defendants, and members of the visiting team were assaulted. But for the intervention of the police, things would have been much worse, said the Sergeant.*

Caldwell and Bracken gave evidence that when they were leaving the field parties tried 'to give them the boot' and they ran and took shelter in the bus.

Sergeant O'Flaherty said the defendants were all respectable, with nothing against them.

Thomas Gribben said that when they played Burren afterwards, they got far more than they gave Burren (Laughter).

Mr O'Hare, defending, said the conduct of the match was a disgrace to football. Those in charge of affairs would have to take strong measures to stop the disorder. All the defendants were sons of respectable farmers and he thought the case could be met with a caution. Defendants were placed on probation and ordered to pay six shillings each.'

Now the game which John McMahon and I witnessed at Burren was the return game of which the Mayobridge player Gribben said, 'We got more than we gave them,' and I think he was right.

The McMahon family left Summerhill soon afterwards to reside in Carlingford. There my first companion died at an early age of illness. He left me with one small memory of his short life: the smile we exchanged standing in McAnulty's bus on that memorable day in Burren when he introduced me to Gaelic football.

The day after I read *The Irish News* item I cut it out of the paper, put it in an envelope and handed it to Charlie Carr (no relation, but a good friend) coming out of Mass, with the instruction, 'When you go home read that, and tell me if you were playing that day.' Charlie, a Mayobridge man, could be described as the resident Mayobridge ambassador in The Point for nearly 50 years. Twenty minutes later the phone rang. It was an irate Charlie. 'What the hell age do you think I am? I was still at school at the time,' he said as he laughed down the line.

Many have a difficulty getting their lives into chronological order, but from when I commenced school in 1928 every succeeding year seems to have been marked by an occasion of some importance. Many of them have been sport orientated but few as memorable as my introduction to Gaelic football at Burren. By 1930 I was well-grounded in soccer, so I can ask with a degree of knowledge and even of authority, 'How many readers of this memoir will know anything about the occasion Joe Bambrick scored six goals for Ireland in an international soccer match where his double hat-trick still stands as a record in international games?'

Just as I thought, not too many.

I remember the day well. It was solidly in my mind but I had to consult the *Guinness Book of Records* for the date, 1 February 1930. My father was at the game. It didn't matter that it wasn't broadcast for we did not have a wireless nor did most others of The Point populace. We went to the station to meet him, as we did many days during his working week, and as he emerged smiling from the platform into the station hallway he was met with a chorus of voices, 'Who won Da? Who won Da?' He told us without a trace of excitement, 'Ireland won 7- 1.' We simply did not believe it and felt he was having a joke with us. He responded to our expressions of disbelief with an even more outrageous piece of information, 'Joe Bambrick scored six.'

'Tell us the truth, please Daddy,' we implored.

Joe Bambrick score six in one game, never, we thought. I think there were three of us trailing a half step behind him.

He turned, still smiling, and said, 'You know I do not tell lies.' And we knew he didn't.

We were finally convinced and all the way from Newry Street we badgered him on every detail of the miracle he had revealed. 'Six goals in one game,' was repeated almost as a litany in our house that night and while I shouldn't mix the present with the past, while I write, the combination of footballers which officially represents the Northern part of the country is looking for its first goal in several years. John Mortimer has written a fine book, *A voyage round my father,* but without Mortimer's talents, I have to content myself with a page or two about my father, and mainly directed to his sporting interests. A recent edition of the *Warrenpoint Historical Magazine* reproduced a copy of the 1901 census which lists the residents of Thomas Street. His entry in the Carr household is as follows:

Hugh, son   R. C.   Read   Write 15 Stonemason   Single

He left school at 14 and entered the employment of the Great Northern Railway (GNR), joining his father, John, who had opted for a safe job on the railway after his own father's building business went under. My father spent his entire working life with the GNR, though he did some work as clerk of works for a couple of years after he retired. Until the railway strike in the early 1930s, I had never known him to miss a day at work. A working day began for him when he caught the 7.20 A.M. train and ended when he got back to Warrenpoint at 7.20 in the evening. On a Saturday, he worked until noon and this simple fact resulted in many very happy Saturdays for me.

He was a great Belfast Celtic admirer, if not an out-and-out supporter, and the team of that era evoked his great sporting enthusiasm. From my earliest days and even before I ever saw Celtic in action, I was a Newry Town supporter, but there was something about Celtic which made them special. Being a railway employee he, and indeed the family, had access to cheaper and, on occasions, free travel. None of my older brothers were interested in going to watch games even though they were all enthusiastic players. As a result, I was always available for any excursion to Portadown, Lurgan or Belfast. It was one of the early joys of my life to be asked on a Friday night, 'Would you like to go to the match tomorrow?' While he did not go to all the Celtic games, my father rarely missed any that mattered, though much to my disappointment he would never take me to see them playing Linfield.

The Saturday morning drill on days I'd be going to a game invariably produced a sense of excitement and adventure. My father would have left on the 7.20 A.M. train to go to his work, and I, with my wisdom of 10 or 11 years, would have travelled solo on the 11.30 A.M. Whether the match was at Portadown, Lurgan or Belfast, I was well instructed each time where to get off the train.

'If your Daddy is not on the platform, go to the stationmaster's office,' was always my mother's parting advice. Never once had I to go to the stationmaster's office for my da was always there and always met me with the same greeting, 'my soul man'.

The names of the Celtic men of that decade will ring bells for a declining generation, for Tommy Breen, John Feenan, Bertie Fulton, Keillor McCullagh, John 'Scotty' Walker, Harry Walker, Jackie Vernon, Davy 'Boy' Martin, Jack Coulter, Norman Kernaghan and the goalkeeper and manager Elisha Scott were the demi-gods of the day. My father would have had his own heroes like Mickey Hamill and the Mahoods, men before my time, whom he would have put on an even higher plane. He did not confine his support to Celtic, however, for on the occasional Sunday he would have gone to Dundalk, often with me in tow, on McAnulty's bus to see the Free State fellows in action. I'm sure I'm the only man in The Point who ever saw Jimmy Dunne playing football. Jimmy was the top centre forward in the country, playing with Shamrock Rovers. He was transferred to Arsenal but never fulfilled their hopes for him.

One of those football excursions in my father's company stands out as no other, for while the football action was played out in Windsor Park, the drama of the day took place in a railway carriage en route from Belfast to Warrenpoint .

The occasion was an international match between Ireland and Scotland and I should probably explain that the Northern soccer authority, which still operates under the title Irish Football Association, selected players from all over the country, providing of course, they were not playing in the Free State: so we would have had men like Everton players Billy Cook and Alex Stevenson and other 'Free Staters' eligible for selection so long as they played for cross-channel clubs. I mention this in passing, though it has nothing at all to do with the episode I am about to relate.

In the game in question, Ireland were expected to win and ten minutes from the end it looked as if this would be the outcome, but a couple of defensive lapses saw Scotland score two goals to pull the game out of the fire. We were on our way home, with me being much more disappointed than my father. The train conveying us from Great Victoria Street in Belfast had carriages with compartments, each capable of holding about ten passengers, five facing five. I was sitting next to the window with my father beside me. The compartment had its full complement of passengers, only one of whom was a woman, who sat on the same side as me. The man sitting opposite me opened the discussion about the game and when some others disagreed with his views he was not at all pleased. He was laying all the blame for the loss of the game at the feet of Jack Jones, the centre-half who played for Linfield.

The discussion turned into a real argument and went on for some time. Once or twice the man sitting opposite the lady in the compartment angrily intervened, but she motioned him not to get involved. The argument was brought to a close when the train reached Lurgan, where the woman and the man opposite her rose to alight from the door at my side. The man got off first, gave his hand to the lady to assist her to the platform and then, with one hand still resting on the open door, he faced the man who sat opposite me.

He held his clenched fist almost to his face and exclaimed angrily, 'Only for that woman, you would have got that in the gob. Do you know who she is?'

His temper rose and he shouted the answer in the same sentence. 'She's Jack Jones' wife.'

As he withdrew his fist slowly from the face of the man he was addressing I thought he was going to strike, but he didn't. He addressed the rest of the compartment who were stunned to silence, 'I'm sorry about this,' and he quietly closed the door.

There was little conversation between Lurgan and Portadown where all the others left the train, leaving my father and me the sole occupants for the rest of the journey to The Point.

For me, Jack Jones was a great footballer both with Linfield and Hibernians for whom he played in Scotland, when it was said he was past his best. And to show this ten-year old's in-depth knowledge I can give the added information that his brother, Sam Jones, played for Blackpool and his brother-in-law, Billy Mitchell, another Lurgan man, played for Chelsea. They were all Internationals and I believe on one occasion they formed the Irish halfback line.

My father never spoke much about his own sporting prowess though he modestly confessed to me once that he had played for Down; when he was telling me, he held up one finger to suggest that it had only been once. Neither did he speak to me at any length about the John Martins, which was one of the earliest GAA teams in Down. There was no hiding his great sporting love of athletics, for our parlour housed his collection of trophies. Silver cups, silver jugs, clocks and glassware of all descriptions filled the mantelpiece, the top of the piano and any other available space. Not too many of them survived the ravages of ten children, but a few did.

Much more than football, athletics was the great sporting outlet for the first quarter of the last century and long before. The coming of the GAA, which initially had as one of its aims the control and encouragement of athletics, eventually made them a minority pursuit.

The half-mile was my father's speciality. By all accounts, though not from him, he had a great finishing spurt which earned him the nickname 'Darter,' a name which has come into the present generation of Carrs. If he didn't speak about his own feats, he certainly related the abilities of some of his contemporaries over the years. He would always claim that Eugene Murray was the best sprinter in the country and that Ambie Caldwell was the best miler. Murray was a big powerful man with an explosive temper, while Ambie Caldwell was a slightly built figure and the gentlest of men.

I have now to get myself back on track for what was in many ways an even more memorable year, 1931. It marked the founding of St Peter's GAA Club, filling the gap left by the demise of the John Martins midway through the twenties. I had not heard much of the John Martins at that stage, nor indeed for many years after. My uncle, Tommy Tumilty, was on the committee of St Peter's and when the team took the field for the first time he was the goalkeeper, a position he had also filled with the John Martins.

Football pitches were never too easy to come by around The Point, so the new St Peter's had to settle for a field at Moygannon, a mile and a half out of the town. The compact 'garden,' as some visiting teams called it, saw some great football action. It is still known to those who used it as 'Maggie Connolly's field'. The back wall of the Connolly cottage was only a couple of yards from the actual playing pitch and filled in as the field boundary. Beyond the house was a small barn which served as a dressing room for the home team. In those days the visiting teams stripped 'wherever the hell they liked,' but mostly behind the ditch.

The one thing which impressed me most about this new team was the way the playing gear was handled. Tommy Savage was the man responsible and he lived with his wife, Sarah, in Ashgrove Terrace. He was responsible for all the playing gear, jerseys, pants, boots and balls. Everything, other than the balls, was packed into a large wicker skip and on match days was wheeled to Moygannon on a small cart which Tommy made himself for the purpose. For away games McAnulty's bus would have called to the house to collect it.

There were two official skip boys, Jackie Lynch and my cousin, Joey Carr. Their official status earned them the right to travel on the bus for away games. On match days, when they collected the skip at Tommy's house, they were invariably joined by half a dozen jealous boys (I was often one of them) who would volunteer to do a stint between the shafts, with the result that Jackie or Joey would only do the last short stint up Connolly's lane to get the plaudits from Tommy, 'You're two great men.'

When Tommy pulled back the lid of the skip, it was a sight which no laundry could ever produce. Layers of white pants and blue jerseys—and all garments ironed, folded and packed with a precision which bore tribute to Sarah Savage's expertise. There were no numbers on jerseys in those days but Tommy had evolved some coding which ensured that the players had the same strip each game. It was the same story with the boots. He would pick up a pair, hold them out, take a look at them and call out the name, Barney Hanna, Terry O'Neill or whoever. He never made a mistake. I cannot imagine that Tommy or Sarah ever got a penny of expenses, not to mention anything for their time.

Managers were an unheard of commodity in those days. What advice was offered on the game was given by Patsy O'Hanlon, who I think was the first secretary and a real idealist who countenanced only the most sporting of tactics.

If the founding of St Peter's GAA Club was a landmark of the year in 1931, there were a number of other notable events which are worth recalling. I had moved into a higher level of education at the beginning of the school year the previous September, and by January of 1931 I was well rooted in Master Crawford's room. So well, in fact, that one only used the Master Crawford title to the man himself, to one's own parents, the priests and elderly people who would not have been taught by him. Meet a Point man in any part of the world, and if he asked, 'How's Jackie?,' you knew he was not asking about Jackie Ross or Jackie Lynch or about any of the other Jackies we had in the town over the years. There was only one 'Jackie' and there simply couldn't be another like him.

Promotion to Jackie's room brought a change in the routine of going to school, for a tradition had been established that made Auntie Brady's fruit and vegetable shop an assembly point. Auntie's premises is now the florist *Flowers and Buds*. It was here that older boys from that part of the town would assemble. Desmond Brady, who lived with his parents next door, was a pupil at St Peter's. He would direct a work force of willing helpers in the moving of boxes and bags outside, under a permanent canopy. There were so many boys there it was never a big task, so there was always time for a bit of diversion which would cease immediately the bus from Newry came into view at the bottom of the street. It was 9.10 A.M. and the appearance of the bus with Miss McDonald aboard was the signal for moving off.

Jackie, who lived only a few doors below Brady's, would pass on his way to school and would get the reverential 'master' as he smiled his way through his industrious pupils. Auntie Brady was a partly disabled lady who sat on a raised chair convenient to weighing scales and till. Her niece, Leontia, assisted with the items which were out of her reach. Always within her reach was a slab of dates which sat on the bottom of the box in which it was packed. The top and sides of the box would have been discarded and this solid, rectangular, massive block of dates would have been devoured by the pennyworth. When I think of the sweet, juicy succulence of Auntie Brady's dates, and consider the cellophaned and bland product we get today complete with plastic fork, I recall the satisfaction of licking sticky fingers and sticky lips and long for the taste of real dates.

While there were mornings when Jackie passed us quite early in our exertions at Brady's, there were some mornings when we would catch up on him, for he would be delayed regularly by his participation in a two-man cameo played out mainly in Church Street, The Square or Post Office Street, depending on where the other participant happened to be working. The other participant was Laddie

Da, (or La-di-dah), the billiard player of reasonable distinction. Billiards was by no means his most important gift for he was always a man who was in good form, loved a bit of *craic* and never had the hard word for anyone.

He worked for the Council and would have been brushing the streets before school-time in the mornings. If he were to be in Church Street when Jackie was taking that route, the cameo was sure to be enacted. It could begin at either the Bank Corner or at Tommy Cunningham's on the other side. First, it would be the greeting, and then the short conversation as Jackie spun the tale. Then there would be peals of laughter from Laddie as he brushed away at the edge of the footpath. Jackie would follow in his footsteps, another tale, more hearty laughing and a smiling street, for Church Street was tuned into the teacher and the brusher. If Jackie eyed Dessy Brady and his cohorts moving off, he knew it was time to take his farewell from Laddie Da. He was always in school when we arrived.

Most of us who recall our three-year term under the stewardship of Jack Crawford would view the period as one of the more enriching of our lives, for he gently led us on to another landing of life with humour, gentleness and exasperation. He was wounded once on an occasion which should have brought him and us, his pupils, a deal of joy. The experience, however, forged a bond between him and a section of the school for the rest of our lives.

In this year, 1931, a major refurbishment was completed at St Peter's Church just over the road from the school. My only memory of the operation is the Italian nationals who were responsible for the marvellous mosaic work in the sanctuary which has been greatly admired over the years. Some of them stayed in Granny O'Hagan's in St Peter's Street. She was the grandmother of my cousins, the Thomas Street Carrs, and I would have been in her house occasionally.

While I would not have known it at the time, the liturgical requirements meant that there was to be a dedication ceremony before the Consecration ceremony. This was set to take place in September. The dedication ceremony preceded the consecration and was to be carried out by the Bishop of Dromore, Dr Edward Mulhern. Months before, Master Crawford, the organist and choirmaster at the church, had been given the task of preparing a boys' choir for the occasion. Boys from the two senior rooms combined and went back to school in the evening through part of the summer holidays to struggle not only with the music, but for the first time with the Latin language. This was a solemn pontifical occasion so *Kyrie, Gloria, Credo, Sanctus, Agnus Dei* and all the responses to the different parts of the Mass would be sung. In addition, we struggled with and mastered the *Ecce sacerdos magnus*—Behold, the great priest—sung specially for the Bishop's entry.

As the big day came closer and closer, the master had convinced us that we had mastered the music and for the very first time I sensed a note of elation at the accomplishment. We had a couple of practices in the church to familiarise us with the organ and then on the Tuesday evening before the ceremony was due to take place we were to have the final run through in the school.

There was a full turnout of the boys, all of whom were making their debut as choristers and needless to say there would have been some rough diamonds in the collection. Normally a number of the senior boys moved the old harmonium out from the wall but as they moved to their task the master raised an arm and said, 'Leave it there boys. We'll not need it tonight.'

He stood nervously before us and asked, 'Is everybody here?' and there was a unanimous response of, 'Yes, sir,' from the boys. 'I have some bad news for you, boys,' he started, 'the choir will not be singing at the High Mass on Thursday. The boys from the Newry Cathedral Choir will be doing the singing.' He went on to tell us, to our utter amazement and consternation, that Canon Daniel McAllister had called him into the Parochial House that day and broke the news to him.

At eight years of age I was among the youngest of the boys whose ages ranged from 8 to 14. None of us had the capacity to offer our deeply wounded teacher a word of solace, but we shared the hurt with him. We felt for him for he was as close to tears as I had ever seen any man. I returned home and broke the news to my mother. Only one of my older brothers was involved in the choir at that time.

On Thursday the entire school population marched over to the church and joined the girls from the Convent School in St Peter's. All the members of the choir went up to the gallery to see the usurpers from Newry, their conductor Fr Jim Burke and the Belgian organist Josef Delafaille. It was before the Harvey Smith sign had come into being, but our derisory gesture, which entailed putting one's thumb under the point of the nose and moving the four fingers back and forward, was just as good and was widely used to show derision.

The story did not end with the final *Amen* of Thursday's Mass. In fact, it was only beginning, for there was a wide reaction from the townspeople and it became most evident by Sunday that the parishioners were deeply offended by the action of the Canon, who did not have a note of music in his head. It was the nature of Jack Crawford that despite the awful hurt he had sustained he would have been at the organ on the Sunday morning, but events were unfolding quickly and by Friday night the choir, which included my father, had taken the decision to resign *en bloc*. The Newry boys had to return on the Sunday for the major ceremony when Cardinal Joseph MacRory presided over the sacred proceedings. Our wonderful adult choir was never heard again.

Even at this late remove, it would be in order to offer a word of thanks and prayerful remembrance to Lucy McCormack, who led us in the *Benediction* hymns for many months, for I would be surprised if the Canon ever did. To be fair to the Canon though, we never knew whether he was acting under the Bishop's instructions or whether he acted on his own bat, but the choral crisis he brought about was sorted out in time.

It is remarkable how the hurt and pain we inflict on each other may be forgiven but still felt for a lifetime. Not so with the great natural sorrows which we experience in our lives. The clock calendar in my mind tells me that grandmother Tumilty, the only grandparent who touched my life, died that same year in 1931; I thought my world had come to an end. I cried myself to sleep for weeks, but with natural sorrow the spirit heals quickly and in time Granny became a treasured memory. I owe her something in the writing of this book for she preserved a tattered family bible containing a list of the births and, in one instance, the death of her own family of Tumiltys. It also lists her parents, brothers and sisters, thereby widening family horizons which I had never explored before. This backless, tattered Scripture only came into my possession in later years when Aunt Kitty's house was being cleared; it lay in my own home for many a day before I picked it up to learn a little more family history.

My great-grandfather was Zachariah Groome, a Corkman who married Ellen Gunne of Enniskillen. The first of their children, Emily, was born in Dublin in 1849, Thomas in Kinsale in 1851, Kate and Fred in Templemore in 1858 and 1859 respectively. William, my grandmother Mary, and Edward were born in Warrenpoint in 1860, 1864 and 1866. In the Templemore insertion was the word 'Barracks' which led me to believe that great-granddad might have been a member of the RIC, but a check in the Public Records Office revealed that while there were 48 Morans, including my Uncle Jack, there was not a single Groome enrolled in the entire history of the force. Some years before this book was even thought of I searched the Baptismal Records of St Peter's parish seeking a Groome entry, but in vain. My mother had said to one of my sisters at some stage in her life that some of her people were buried in Clonallon Church of Ireland cemetery. Quite recently I consulted with the keeper of the records, Richard Thompson, and he turned up the relevant information.

Zachariah Groome was a registered vestry member of Clonallon parish and the Baptismal Register contains the names of William, Mary and Edward Groome. After each name is the insertion, private baptism. The Groomes had a mixed marriage and a very happy one. Zachariah died in 1875, at 55 years. Ellen died in 1882. They are both buried in Clonallon graveyard.

One other piece of information revealed by Richard Thompson was the Groome address Patent Slip. A few ago I was at a Christmas Fair at Narrow Water Castle where I met Roger Hall, the then incumbent of the Hall Estate whose family set the Warrenpoint wheels in motion some three centuries ago. In the course of the conversation I asked if he had ever heard of 'the patent slip,' and to my surprise he knew all about it. It was a device or construction which allowed a boat to be unloaded at all stages of the tide. It was sited over from Newry Street, confirming a snippet of information from my mother to some of the family that Granny had lived near the dock as a girl. My great-grandfather Zachariah probably worked at docks in Dublin, Sligo and Kinsale before coming to Warrenpoint. I wonder what he was doing at the Barracks in Templemore.

In much more recent times my cousin Sean Carr, who knew of my Groome connection, presented me with an item his wife, Carol, had culled from the internet Warrenpoint Forum. It is taken from *The Irish Times,* October, 1870 and reads:

> *'On Saturday night last, a young lad named Millar, eight years old, fell into the dock at Warrenpoint when the tide was full in.*
>
> *Mr Groome, the Assistant Harbour Master, happened to be near at the time and threw out a rope which the lad caught and held, struggling until a young man named James McGuigan leaped in and brought him to shore.*
>
> *The poor boy was very weak and exhausted when rescued but is now*

doing well and quite recovered. Very much credit is due to Mr Groome and McGuigan for their prompt and energetic assistance on the occasion and it is hoped the authorities will practically reward such meritorious conduct. This is the fourteenth life which Mr Groome has been the means of saving within the last ten years.'

After that I can be forgiven for being intensely proud of my great-granda, but in even more recent times Sean Carr presented me with a complete picture of Zachariah in the form of a copy of his marriage certificate. The date was 11 November 1848 in the Enniskillen parish church according to the Rites and Ceremonies of the United Church of England and Ireland. He was a private in 48th Regiment of Foot and stationed at Leinster House, Dublin. His father, Frederick, was designated a gentleman. Mary Gunne had no rank or profession and resided at Head Street, Enniskillen. Her father, Thomas Gunne, is designated a dealer. Ellen was not an educated girl. She could not write her name. She made her "X" mark and the registrar wrote her name. I am equally proud of my great grandmother and marvel at the quality of her faith and her integrity. Zachariah obviously recognised those great qualities, too. I now know that he was a foot soldier stationed at the military Barracks in Templemore where two of their children were born.

Richard Thompson also provided another bit of family history in noting that Hugh Tumilty of Donaghaguy paid tithes to the Church of Ireland in 1830. This Hugh was probably my great great-grandfather, though I believe the Tumilty line commenced in Annaclone much further back. My grandfather, Ross, married Mary Groome in 1887. My nearest and dearest Tumilty was, of course, my mother, Mary known as Minnie, who was their third child. She had served her time as a dressmaker at The Bank Buildings in Belfast and I well remember how her patience would be sorely tried by some of the commissions she was asked to take on—like making a pair of trousers for 'wee Jimmy or Paddy' out of a well worn adult's coat. Of my mother I will only concur with Fr Denis Faul's *dictum* that 'all mothers of big families are saints.'

My grandmother Carr died three years before I was born but it was not until I read the 1901 census details for Thomas Street, published in the *Warrenpoint Historical Magazine,* that I learned she was born in England as Ellen Sharkey, otherwise Nellie. Her parents returned to The Point where she went to school. As a young girl she developed a remarkable voice and the high point of her singing career came before her 17th birthday, when she was invited to sing at the opening of St Patrick's Cathedral in Armagh. This was in August 1873, when there was a choir of 200 voices and an orchestra of 50 players. The *Armagh Gazette* reported there were ten soloists but did not name them, though the *Newry Reporter* carried a more detailed account of the musical programme and did name the soloists who sang the *Sanctus* No 2 by Hayden. The soprano was Mademoiselle de la Vega Wilson while the contralto had a more mundane title, Miss Campbell.

I was man big when Maggie O'Brien gave me a graphic picture of my grandmother's singing accomplishments. From my earliest days I knew Maggie to be an organiser and participant in concerts in St Peter's Hall. She and her brother, Dermot, lived with their aunt, Kitty McAteer, who had a restaurant in Dock Street. I was sitting beside Maggie at a function when my cousin Delia sang and I commented to Maggie, 'Delia is hard to beat.'

'Well I have to tell you that your grandmother would beat her,' began Maggie and went on to tell me of an occasion when she was a girl and grandmother Carr was rehearsing for a concert with her Aunt Kitty as pianist in the room over the café. There was a knock on the kitchen door and as Maggie moved to it, the door opened to reveal a man who spoke instantly, 'That voice, I have heard that voice before. It must be Nellie Sharkey.' He went on to tell Maggie that he had been in Armagh Cathedral on the great occasion and the only time he had ever heard her sing. Maggie went on to advise him that she had changed her name to Nellie Carr.

Nellie Sharkey married my grandfather, John, nine years after the Armagh experience and continued to delight the country with her voice until a couple of years before she died at the age of 63. Preaching at her funeral and reported in the *Newry Telegraph:*

> Revd Fr Maginn referred to the 'many good qualities of the deceased whose charming voice would henceforth be silent, that voice that was the sweetest in a choir of sweet singers who delighted until recent years not only that congregation, but visitors who came to Warrenpoint and marvelled at the exceedingly high standard of the singing in their church choir. No one who ever had the pleasure of hearing her sing could ever forget the charming voice of Nellie Carr."

I still regard *I Dreamt I Dwelt in Marble Halls* as grandmother's song and rightly or wrongly, when I listen to Joan Sutherland's version, I am imagining, 'This is Grandma,' and I thank God for the accidents of birth which make us what we are.

5—THE MITCHER

No account of this important year in my life would be complete without reference to the one day in that life when I mitched from school, for if it undermined my scholastic advance, it put me a step further in my football career.

I can say with certainty it happened on a Wednesday morning when, for whatever reason, I did not want to go to school. It certainly had nothing to do with not having an exercise done, of that I am sure. With all the others gone, I mooched about the house looking for anything which would delay me, until my mother said with a scold in her voice, 'You'll be late for school.'

I shuffled out the back door still determined that I was not going to school, and even as I took the first few paces there was a plan of action hatching in my mind. Half-way down our garden there was an old toilet which had been replaced a year or two before by one more convenient to the house, though still outside it. A few furtive glances back to make sure that my mother was not at the window, and reassured that she wasn't, I skipped across the garden and sought sanctuary in the derelict toilet. One was still able to sit on the seat and that's where I sat for the best part of an hour. I had heard my mother at the back a couple of times, but then there was a period of silence and I thought that I would investigate if she was in or out. As I moved cautiously up the path past the new toilet, the latch of the back door clicked. I practically dived for cover into the new toilet and hid behind the door. The door, I must explain, only went to four inches off the ground and despite my best efforts at contortion, my sandalled feet projected under it. To my horror my mother came into the toilet and used it without closing the door or observing the two small feet which protruded underneath it.

I was overcome by guilt so I decided to give myself up and in I went. At first sight of me my mother thought I had been sent home from school. 'What has you home?' she asked. She was speechless as I told her that I hadn't gone to school at all, that I had hidden in the garden for the previous hour and a half.

'Where were you hiding in the garden? I was out in the back a couple of times and I didn't see you. Where were you hiding?' and she was quite angry at this stage.

'I hid in the toilet,' I confessed.

'You hid in that dirty old toilet for an hour?' she asked incredulously.

'No,' I explained, 'I was in the new toilet, too.'

'But I'm only after using the toilet,' she continued.

'Yes I know. I was behind the door all the time.' She was flabbergasted and horrified.

There were two very positive outcomes from that morning. I never mitched school again and my mother never went to the toilet again without closing and locking the door behind her.

What had been a really dismal morning for me turned into a much more welcoming day, for by lunchtime, when the others came home for the midday break and realised I hadn't been at school, she fobbed them off with a story about my being sick and would be off for the day. When they went back to school I was sent on a message to the Post Office, and when I was returning my afternoon took off in a most unexpected manner.

People from outside Warrenpoint would not know that King's Lane (called Campbell's Lane by locals), joins Summerhill and Church Street. Half-way up the lane there is an intersection with lanes serving the properties on Church Street and Summerhill on one side and on the other properties on the lower part of Church Street, East Street and part of Duke Street.

The reason I can state that this particular day in my life was a Wednesday is about to be disclosed for as I came up the lane, intent on taking the right turn up to our back, who is emerging from the lane to my left but James (Butcher) Connolly in trap and pony. He would have been well known to me and I to him for I would have been in his shop often and indeed was later to become message boy and chief sausage maker for him.

'Are you coming for a run to Rostrevor?' he called as he brought the pony to a halt.

'I'll have to ask my mammy,' was my reply. I flew up the lane, up the garden, was given permission to travel and was standing on Summerhill long before James reached the summit. When we got on to the Rostrevor Road at the end of Seaview, James gave the reins a shake and as the pony broke into a trot he handed them to me with the injunction, 'Here, you take her.' I was on the then equivalent of cloud nine all the way to Rostrevor.

As we got to the village James gave the order 'up to the left,' and my mind flashed back to that earlier drive to Rostrevor on the jaunting car. My first thought was, 'this is the road to the football field' and minutes later, when I got the command, 'here we are,' we had arrived at the very field where I had witnessed my first ever football encounter. For me at that age, this was an amazing coincidence.

James got out of the trap, opened the gate and in we went to be greeted by another pony which seemed to be very glad to see us. It was only then he told me the object of the run to Rostrevor. Producing a light rope or halter, he said, 'I'm taking this fellow to James McCormack to get him shod.' After he put the rope over the pony's head he handed the end to me, 'Here, you take him.' We both got back into the trap and with the pony in tow I never felt so important.

At first glance James McCormack was a forbidding figure. A well soiled black hat, a heavy black moustache, shirt sleeved and well worn leather apron suggested to me that he was a tougher man than Neill Bowsie, our own blacksmith on the Dromore Road, who wore a cap and also had a moustache, but much neater than James McCormack's. If one met Neil Bowsie going to church on Sunday, he would have passed for the minister.

'Is this a Point man you have with you?' asked James McCormack, to which Butcher replied, 'He is, and the best man in it.' Mr McCormack, as I called him for almost all of my life, set about the task on hand. While I had seen Neil Bowsie at work from time to time, this was the first occasion I was to witness the complete shoeing operation, and from the closest of quarters. From the measuring, the firing, the cutting, the turning, the hoof paring, the fitting, the smell of burning hoof, I watched enthralled as the nailing of the shoes commenced. There I stood transfixed, knees bent, hands on knees timing every strike to perfection. The hammer stopped suddenly in mid-air, and I lifted my head to see what was wrong. It was the smiling face of James McCormack who broke the spell of his own magic. 'I'm looking at you there,' he said 'and you're like the Warrenpoint goalkeeper facing a penalty kick. You are going to be a great goalkeeper,' he prophesied.

The shoeing operation over, we returned the pony to the field from which we got him and headed back to The Point with James on the reins all the way. He might have been thinking of the work he had to do in the shop the following day, but I was thinking of James McCormack's words, 'You'll be a great goalkeeper.' I got to know James very well in later life for his son, Terry, was one of the great Point and Down captains and his only daughter, Bridie, became a Carr when she married my elder brother, Gerry.

For months and months I played in no other position than in goal and my footballing companions must have thought I was out of my mind. No one would ever volunteer to play in goal and here was I performing all sorts of acrobatics convinced that I was sure to take Elisha Scott's place in the Irish goal at some future date. As it turned out, my goalkeeping ambitions were not of lasting duration.

It is worth making an historical note that James Connolly ceased trading in the butchery business some time later. His premises became a small grocery shop belonging to a man from Armagh, John McCart, a family name which was to become well known in succeeding years. I can still see two small notices he displayed in copperplate handwriting. The card in the window advised, *'If it is not in sight, it is inside'*. Sitting on the small wooden till on the counter the other card quite rightly noted, *'Promises will not fill the till'*.

6—A Significant Year

There can be no doubt that after 1916, the year 1932 must rank as one of the defining years of twentieth century Ireland for it brought the name De Valera into the focus of a new generation of which I, at nine years of age, was part. While I was not aware of the distinctions between the Free State parties at the time, I certainly was aware of Éamon De Valera. *The Legion of the Rearguard* was the national hit of that and subsequent years, sounding the bugle in the blood for many. The last line proclaimed, 'De Valera needs you, soldiers of The Legion of the Rearguard.' As far as my father was concerned, it did not seem to make much difference. He was still convinced that, 'Michael Collins was the best of them all.'

Within a week or two I had forgotten De Valera and was on my Saturday morning routine with my Uncle Hugh in the Foresters' Hall. I had a rota of tasks which would keep me busy for an hour. Joe Williams (he was Mr Williams to me all my life), who was in charge of the bar, was doing his chores on the first floor. It was said that Joe had hands for anything and on the occasions I might have been in the bar I was very impressed with the way it was immaculately kept. One of his features was a collection of photographs of the top teams and footballers of the day which he had tastefully displayed around the walls. I had many of these pictures at home myself, for they would have been issued with *Topical Times,* the one and only football weekly of the period which I remember.

When Joe saw me on the landing, he called, 'Are you coming round to listen to the match today?' and in the same breath, 'Come in, you must see this.' As I entered the room he went to a table set apart from the others. 'What do you think of that?' he asked.

I went to the table to view a large piece of cardboard, cut to the precise dimensions of the table and it lined exactly as a football pitch. The centre circle, penalty area, sidelines and, of course, goal posts were all there. Both teams were lined out in their respective positions, man on man, and as I looked at the names of the opposing goalkeepers (remember I fancied myself as a goalkeeper at the time) there was Frank Moss for Arsenal and Albert McInroy, I think, for Newcastle. I did not care much for the name Moss, so I opted for McInroy and gave my allegiance to Newcastle that day and for many years after. What I had just viewed was Joe Williams' enactment of the first English Cup Final which was of any significance to me.

Come the afternoon and with a goodly crowd gathered in the bar—very few homes had wirelesses—Joe Williams sat a few feet away from the table in the centre of the room on which the cardboard pitch rested, and in his hand he held a long pointer stick. I wondered at the significance of the stick until the game got under way and then it soon became obvious. When I viewed the cardboard pitch earlier in the morning I did not pick up the fact that as well as the particular markings, the pitch had been divided into lighter lines, with the eight squares they formed, numbered one to eight. As the commentary progressed, a background voice would advise, 'square one' or whatever square the play was taking place in and Joe brought his pointer stick into action. From goal to goal, and wing to wing, the corner kicks, free kicks and even offsides were stick pointed by Joe with unerring accuracy. A name I associate with the commentary is Howard Marshall, but I do not recall whether he was 'the voice' or the commentator.

Playing for Newcastle was a chap called Sam Weaver, a wing half-back who we were being continually reminded by the commentator was 'the longest thrower of a ball in the game'. Sam had other qualities, like playing for England, and the more the commentator lauded Sam, the more I was convinced I should be a wing halfback, with a long throw-in. My ambitions as a goalkeeper were exorcised by half-time.

Few readers will know that, much to the surprise of the experts, Newcastle beat Arsenal 2–1. The winning goal came when a chap called Jimmy Richardson crossed a ball which was headed into the net. When the pictures of Richardson striking the ball appeared the next day and later on the newsreels, they showed the ball to be clearly out of play. The goal should not have counted. Of course, nobody had any sympathy for Arsenal who were the dominant team at the time. They were managed by the legendary Herbert Chapman who was the central figure in one of the tactical controversies of the day. It related to what was called 'the stopper centre half' and as far as my nine-year old mind could make out, it meant that the centre half did nothing other than police the opposing centre forward. My simple mind used wonder to itself, 'Who else would mark him?'

Whatever about Chapman's tactics, they did not stop fellows like Dixie Dean (well remembered in Sligo) scoring 60 goals in 39 games. Nowadays multimillionaire players playing 50 games a season wouldn't get near that figure. Dixie would hardly have been paid a tenner a week at the time.

The most important outcome of the English Cup Final was that I became a wing half in the Sam Weaver mould, complete with long throw-in. For a couple of years in Gilmore's garden, Dromore Terrace green or McGuffin's field, I performed the feats of Sam despite the fact that I couldn't throw the ball the length of myself. Unlike O'Hare's garden, Gilmore's garden was a comfortable little pitch at the top end of the Gas Works where Vincent Gilmore, although younger than Liam, directed the football operation. He would never have more than five-a-side, for the space was limited. A man short and we might have sent down for Mr Gilmore. Football at Gilmore's had a bonus in that we were likely to get a slice of bread and jam at half-time from Mrs Gilmore.

Team selection in those days did not present the problems which confront modern-day football. When the kick about became crowded, the call would go up, 'We'll pick sides.' Without any objection, two captains would be named and if anyone had a coin it was tossed for first choice. More often than not there was no coin and a flat stone with a bit of spittle on it would suffice. Of course, the call would be changed from 'heads or tails' to 'wet or dry'. Invariably these selections were real judgements of the captains' capabilities, with the most talented called in order. Sometimes, to his disgust and embarrassment, Sam Weaver was the last man to get a call. It is with a fair degree of something more precious than nostalgia with which I recall the names of those who performed at these venues.

Dromore Terrace itself produced two great goalkeepers in Emmett McGivern and Ted McNeill. Emmett earned his spurs with St Peter's and Down while Teddy starred with Newry Town and Sunderland where he became a great favourite. Teddy's brother Francie was the one who always won my admiration both on the green in front of his home and later as a team-mate with St Peter's. He had a lot of illness as a boy and, indeed, throughout his life, but no one I ever knew put such effort into his football. Of course, Vinto Gilmore himself was the mighty man to emerge from his own garden pitch, playing first with Cliftonville and Newry Town before moving to Dundalk, with whom he won a Football Association of Ireland (FAI) cup medal, scoring the only goal in the semi-final and setting up the shock winning goal over Shamrock Rovers in the 1956/57 final.

In case it might be thought that the venues mentioned above were the only places football was played, it should be explained that street football was the greatest crime on streets which wouldn't see a dozen mechanical vehicles in a day. Football was outlawed. Policemen on foot and on bicycles were the bane of our lives. In the winter, on Sunday mornings after the last Mass, Peter Street, where there never was a car, was a regular venue for young, and not so young, fellows who just played what was called 'backs and forwards' and, of course, with a goalkeeper defending the priest's gates. On occasions a policeman would appear at each end of the street in a sort of pincer movement, which appearance led to a mass flight over the wall into the priest's garden, up the steps, through the side door of the church and out the other side. On these occasions genuflections to the Blessed Sacrament were performed in full flight.

June 1932 saw the great hosting of the Eucharistic Congress in Dublin, and my presence at it came about as a result of the demise of the adult choir in St Peter's Church the previous year. Apart from the leadership of Lucy McCormack there was no organised singing in the church, except on one day, the feast of the Immaculate Conception on 8 December when the Children of Mary provided the music. Even by that date, a boys' choir was in the process of preparation for the Christmas festival under the direction of Mrs Maude O'Hare, who was both organist and choir mistress. I was one of the younger angels who sang at the First Mass of Christmas at 7 A.M. and for years afterwards. In addition to the Christmas programme we took the Forty Hours Adoration in our stride in the early days of January and let the presiding Bishop know what a treat he missed by not hearing most of us on the previous occasions he had been down in the church.

Along with the altar boys, we were rewarded with a great party in the crypt of the church at the end of the month. We were even more amply rewarded when it was announced that we were to be taken to the Eucharistic Congress in Dublin on McAnulty's bus on the Saturday of the Congress week. I am not sure what the domestic arrangements were in our house that week of the Congress, for my mother and the three younger siblings in the family had gone to stay for the week in Dublin with her cousin Kitty O'Meara (*née* Groome).

On the Saturday morning we were due to leave at 7.30 A.M. but we got a rude awakening at 5 A.M. when our door was almost knocked off its hinges by one of our neighbours. The O'Hare family of the Imperial Hotel had come to live on Summerhill, at the house John McMahon had lived in, and it was Mr O'Hare himself who startled us. I rushed down the stairs thinking something terrible had happened and there he was standing in his dressing gown.

'It's time to get up,' he said.

'But Mr O'Hare, it's only five o'clock,' I replied.

He answered back to me, 'Your mother's away. You'll need all the time you can get.'

He was right.

Before my mother left for Dublin it was arranged that she would go to the Congress Mass on the Saturday. We sent the details of the section we would be in, hoping she would meet us, but when we experienced the vastness of the place such a meeting proved impossible. It was only when I looked up some of the newspaper reports of the Congress that I learned Saturday had been children's day—and that over 70,000 children made up the bulk of the congregation. For years I had deluded myself that I must have heard John McCormack singing that day, but that pleasure was reserved for the Sunday congregation. Needless to say, we saw very little of Dublin as we had our food with us in several large hampers.

Even after that memorable first experience of Dublin the year had even more to offer as The Point made their first appearance in the final of the Down Junior Football Championship in the autumn. Despite my enthusiasm for soccer, and my affiliation with Newry Town and Newcastle United, The Point was The Point and it could call on my first loyalty.

Their opponents in the final were Saul. I associated St Patrick with Saul and for weeks before the game I had this mental image of a Saul team of fair-headed giants who would be much too good for our local heroes. This in no way dimmed the hopes of a miracle, and the knowledge that the team was training seriously created a sense of excitement, and even a tension, which was a new experience.

Michael Kerr, a local barber, was the trainer who set the pace on the roads around the town with a few dozen lads of my own age and upwards invariably in pursuit. Team and youthful followers would return to St Peter's Hall where the smell of embrocation would become overpowering as Michael and his assistants got the steam rising. Nothing was spared and the final few evenings saw the Baths being opened out of season for the luxury of hot salts. Such was the air of excitement throughout the town that the youngest of us were sick waiting for Sunday to dawn. Alas, before Sunday dawned, came Saturday, and I am down with the measles or chicken pox. There might be some ailments which can be hidden from mothers but not chicken pox or measles.

'You go back to your bed and stay in it,' was her directive when my mother viewed me on Saturday morning.

I was completely submissive, for already in my mind the shocking reality was forming that I might not be able to go to the match the following day. Even at nine years of age, prayer was the key to miracles, and when the Angelus bell tolled at noon no more fervent prayer went heavenwards than my earnest supplication.

My Uncle Tommy, who was playing in goal the next day, called in the house and came up to see me, but he didn't raise my hopes at all.

Sunday morning came and I realised that if I didn't go to Mass there was no hope of me going to a football match. As I descended the stairs my mother was just coming in from the early Mass. She took one look at me and pronounced sentence, 'You go back to your bed. You are not going out today.'

It was the longest day of my life, even though the traffic through our house for two Masses and dinner tended to be frantic. Those of my brothers who were going to the game left as soon as dinner was over and the younger siblings stayed clear of my bed. The reading material available to me would have been comic cuts *Wizard* or *Rover,* but there was a problem. The perceived wisdom of the time accepted that sunlight was not conducive to recovery from measles, so my mother had hung a dark blanket or curtain over the light curtains which were on the window.

After she brought my dinner there were strict instructions, 'Don't you move out of that bed for the rest of the day,' which meant I was barred from the bed beside the window. With two double beds and a space of less than 18 inches between them, it need hardly be said that there was very little else in the line of furniture in the room. Eventually I dozed off, to be wakened hours later by the sound of cheering coming over the roofs of the houses in Church Street. As the reality of victory was set to music with strains of, *'Here, here, the Blues are here,'* the moment was too much for me. I threw the blankets and caution to the wind, jumped across to the other bed, overbalanced in the darkened room, fell towards the window, grabbing the emergency dark curtain, which came away with me, hit a sizable flowerpot without flowers which sat on the window sill and cracked one of the small window panes. I was still in the horizontal position, enmeshed in curtains, when my mother arrived in the room within seconds, 'We won, we won,' I proclaimed.

My mother was the most patient woman I have ever known.

It was quite an achievement for St Peter's to win a Championship within a year of their existence and those in charge of affairs had their eyes to the future, for within a couple of years it was decided that a schoolboys' league should be organised. It might have been called a schoolboys' league but fellows like Stephen Burns and Christy McGuigan had already left school when I was starting, so a fellow of ten or eleven was very small fry. Philip McKernan, who lived on Summerhill and who was committee secretary, told me that I was registered with Cuchullans, whose captain was Jim Fitzsimons. I went to all the games, but when my team played I was always in the reserves and only once was I called into action for a brief period in the second half of a game. Despite this, I was firmly committed to the Cuchullan's cause, until the 'foreign games' rule caught up with me and I was suspended.

In a roundabout sort of way it was Uncle Hugh Tumilty who proved to be my undoing. I have already mentioned that I lived for a full year in the Foresters' Hall with my grandmother when he was caretaker there. One day, I opened a drawer in the bedroom to discover a box of beribboned medals. I brought it in to Granny and asked, 'Who owns these medals?'

'Those belong to your Uncle Hugh, he won them in the War,' she answered and, I have to say, I was impressed for the box was quite full.

I was a much older boy when I heard the full story of his soldiering days. He was fifteen when the War started in 1914 and within a few months he enlisted in the Army. He was under age, of course, and the family were able to get him back. It was only a postponement of his entry into the war game, for when he became sixteen, off he went, joined up and served right through the conflict with the Royal Inniskilling Fusiliers. When he and his wife, Annie, left the Foresters' Hall, they came to live on Summerhill. He outlived Annie and died when he was close to 80. Never once in my life did I ever hear him speak of the War, nor did I ever see him wear one of his medals. I never knew what happened to them. He was a regular visitor to our family home and to mine when I came to reside there after my marriage. He was fond of a bottle or two, which was sufficient to have him singing. His favourites were *God save Ireland, Ireland boys, Hurrah!* and *The Inniskilling Fusilier.* Another brother, Ross, joined the Irish Guards later in the War, and still later joined the newly formed *An Garda Síochána*, serving until retirement.

As well as returning from the War as a very experienced young soldier, Hugh was also a highly accomplished footballer and, with some other talented Point men like Philip O'Neill, Bobby Stanley and Charlie Burns, played with the Dundalk GNR team which became the present Dundalk club. All of them had retired from football but they agreed to play in a charity game against the then Warrenpoint United side. My tenuous roots in the GAA (third sub for Cuchullans) had not engendered a great deal of loyalty, even if I was aware of 'the ban' at the time. I went to see Uncle Hugh play for the first and last time. I was impressed with what I saw, and the fact that the retired brigade beat the younger men was a talking point for days.

A few days after the game in John Thomas Bradley's field (Dalymount Park, it was billed), I met Philip McKernan in Campbell's Lane. He asked me, 'Were you at that soccer match the other night?' I replied in the affirmative. He mentioned the names of four other boys who were to be told, by me, to attend a meeting of the schoolboys' league committee, in Billy Stewart's house in Post Office Street, the following Monday night. I can only think of the names of three of them, Jackie Lynch, Christy Charles and Luke Glancy and all three with A.N. Other, turned up at the appointed time and place. The five of us trooped into Stewart's kitchen behind Mrs Stewart who had received us at the door. Seated at the table were Fr Dargan, our local curate, Phil McKernan and Billy Stewart who was the sexton at St Peter's Church and chauffeur to the Canon. I was completely at home in the Stewart kitchen for my Aunt Kitty had lived in the house before she moved to Summerhill. It was like coming home.

Fr James Dargan, a softly spoken man whose Mass I had served from time to time, opened the proceedings by asking, 'Were all you boys at the soccer match last week?'

'We were, Father,' was the unanimous response.

I was at one end of the line and he turned to me, 'Barney, why did you go to this soccer match?' To which I replied, 'Father, I wanted to see my Uncle Hugh play football, I never saw him play before.'

He went up the line putting the same question to each boy and getting the same answer, 'I wanted to see Barney's Uncle Hugh play, too.'

We were all suspended for three weeks, and it must be said that without their third reserve, Cuchullans failed to win the league.

The light-hearted reality of my suspension has evoked prayerful remembrance of some of the names I have mentioned. I am tempted to relate the sad stories of some of their lives, but time for me is a scarcer commodity by the day. Suffice it is to say that Christy Charles joined the Royal Air Force (RAF) during the War and lost his life in combat. Jackie Lynch died a young man many years ago in Dún Laoghaire. Luke Glancy, son of the school principal, did medicine and died in the mid-nineties in Canada. Philip McKernan, whose father was town clerk of Warrenpoint before I was born, was my neighbour on Summerhill. He farmed the family land which was on the outskirts of the town and each year McKernan's yard housed four stacks of corn which earned us a day off school for the thresher. After the War Philip left, never to return. For me, another sad story.

If my Uncle Hugh was the central figure in my suspension, it was my Uncle Tommy who was the central figure in another incident which had serious repercussions in Summerhill. Tommy was a different personality to Hugh. His was a gentler character and even as a boy I thought he was very like my mother. He had been a member of Frank Aiken's Fourth Northern Division, as it was called in the War of Independence. As well as being a member of the club committee, he was still the regular goalkeeper of the team. On the day in question, Kilkeel were the visitors to Connolly's field and in the second half he was defending what was called 'the top goals' from where I also viewed the game. I have mentioned earlier that the pitch was of the minimum dimensions and the linesmen of the time had the almost impossible task of keeping the spectators back to the line and deciding on one-handed 'throw-ins'. It was simply impossible to keep the spectators on the right side of the line. If there was an incident on the field of play, it was not uncommon for intervention from the sideline, making mountains out of molehills.

In this game with Kilkeel there was such an incident, and it stemmed from the fact that the referee was a Point man, Joe (Blossom) McAnulty, some of whose decisions did not please the home supporters. When he ordered one of The Point team to the line (Jack Caldwell), there was a rowdy reaction from the home supporters, but some minutes later, when he lined another Point player, (Terry O'Neill) there were ructions, and an invasion of the pitch by the enraged home supporters. Among these was my uncle, Jimmy Carr, a very excitable man at a football match. When the *mêlée* started Uncle Tommy ran down from the top goals to the scene of the action; I have no doubt that his one concern would have been the good name of the club and the Association. He was also a very close friend of Joe McAnulty. In attempting to get the crowd back, he clashed with my Uncle Jimmy, who ended up with a bloody nose. The match was abandoned ten minutes from time. This clash between my uncles is not mentioned in a report of the game which is contained in a scrapbook belonging to Tom O'Hare, one of the players, given to me by his wife, Kay, some years ago. The report was written by Patsy O'Hanlon (Ultonian) who was the club secretary. He laid into The Point supporters in no uncertain terms.

There were two other brothers at the match, so when we arrived home my mother heard three different versions of the day's events at Moygannon. My father did not go to many matches because his involvement with the Foresters meant he was attending meetings on a regular basis; on this day he had been at the Foresters' club for most of the afternoon. When he did arrive home it was easy to see he had something on his mind. He had come up the back way, through the kitchen without a word and into the hall where he hung his hat, and returned to the kitchen to address my mother, 'Your fellow, Tommy, hit our Jimmy and had him bleeding,' and before my mother had time to comment, he added, 'By japers, if I had been there he wouldn't have got away with it.'

There was real anger in his voice which surprised me, for he spoke with a conviction which presented a side of him I had not experienced before. My mother replied as coolly as you like, 'You should go down and tell the police. I don't know why they let them play football on a Sunday.' We all exploded, but my father, still hurting a bit, spoke very little through the tea.

Uncle Tommy lived across the road from us and there were very few days he would not have given us a call. True to form, he appeared later in the evening and as he entered the kitchen I feared for what my father might say or do. My father never got a chance to open his mouth for my mother was on to Tommy at once. 'That was a nice carry-on at the football today,' she scolded, 'the Carrs and the Tumiltys will be the talk of the town.' She went on to lecture poor Tommy and, to my amazement, it was my father who came to his rescue.

'For the love of God, Minnie, have a bit of sense, these things happen every day of the week at the football, there'll not be a word about it this day week,' he exclaimed, and there wasn't.

Even though I was a firm supporter of St Peter's, my own football instincts were still firmly rooted in soccer. My literary sporting diet would have been supplied, in the first instance, on the local scene by the *Newry Telegraph,* and as I advanced in age and wisdom, by Ben Madigan, the pen name of *The Irish News* soccer correspondent who would have been very much into Belfast Celtic. Of course, we all had to wait for my father to arrive home in the evening with the paper before the digestive process could begin.

Most of the football action I write about in those early days was with the red rubber ball on the green at Dromore Terrace, though in Gilmore's garden there was invariably a 'tube and cover,' in the terminology of the time. In those days tubes and covers were hard to come by, so when Johnny Magill introduced the possibility of a real football for every boy in the town, he was on a winner. Johnny, grandfather of Micheál Magill, who won an All-Ireland with Down in the nineties, had a sweet shop in what was then Post Office Street, and he came up with a very simple operation. First of all there was a tea chest with a circular section cut out of the lid wide enough to let an arm go through in comfort. It was more than three quarters full of wrapped sweets which were a peppermint variety and pleasant enough to the taste. The wrapper of each sweet had the name of an English League team printed on it. Eight sweets could be bought for one penny and the purchaser put his arm into the chest, took the sweets out one at a time and laid them on the counter in front of Johnny, who supervised the count. Also displayed in the shop was a list of twenty teams and the object of the exercise was to get twenty sweet wrappers to match the teams on the list. If you did, you had a real tube and cover football. On the way to school and again at lunchtime, Magill's shop was a place of pilgrimage. In a matter of weeks every boy in the school had nineteen of the twenty teams on the list, for a system of swapping and bartering had evolved quite naturally. The missing link to a brand new ball turned out to be Lincoln City. No one could get Lincoln City, but we bought on regardless.

Of course, the taste had long gone off the sweets and as they were bought, unwrapped and discarded, both papers and sweets created the first ever winter litter problem for the town. I do not remember just how long the quest for Lincoln City lasted, but eventually it turned up and to the horror of all the football enthusiasts the lucky man was Peter Murphy. He lived across the street from Magills, and had not the slightest interest in football. No one ever saw the ball being kicked, for shortly afterwards the Murphy family returned to Mullaghbawn.

I do not know whether or not the disappointment of the members of the Carr family reflected itself at home, but when Santa called at our house a few weeks later he left a football, a real tube and cover. By this time the sleeping arrangements of the family saw all the boys in the large front room. Santa judiciously left the ball in the middle of the floor so no one could claim it as 'my ball'.

Some might find it difficult to believe that the concept of Inter-County football and hurling did not come into focus in my sporting life until 1934, when Down's Junior footballers got into the All-Ireland Junior Football semi-final for the first time ever. They were playing Louth in the curtain-raiser to the senior final in which the contestants were Dublin and Galway . Point people had a special interest because Tom O'Hare (of the scrapbook), our neighbour on Summerhill, was a team member.

We still had not risen to a wireless, nor had many people on Summerhill, but I found myself with a dozen men and boys outside the Frontier Hotel, the home of Mr Mahon at Havelock Place on the seafront. Mr Mahon was a retired Sergeant of the RIC and had been one of the founding members of St Peter's Club a few years beforehand. He was one of the gatemen at Connolly's field and his three sons, John, Mick and Kevin, played for the club at different times in those early years.

Wirelesses were not as mobile in those days as they are now but he was able to position his set on the windowsill for the listeners below. The Junior game was not part of the broadcast and I would have to say there was not any great interest in the fortunes of Dublin or Galway. Half-time could not come quickly enough and when it did, it brought the disappointing news that Louth had beaten Down in the opening game. There was nothing more for the on-the-street listeners, many of whom drifted away and let Dublin and Galway get on with it.

It would be unjust to forget about Tom O'Hare, just because he was a member of a beaten side. At nineteen he was probably the youngest of the Down team that day. He retired from football as a comparatively young man before I even started to play, but he made a substantial contribution to the social and sporting life of Summerhill for much of his life. Shortly after the O'Hare family came to Summerhill about four years earlier, he started a 'wee club' in his back house. Here, a homemade billiard table was the centre piece. I recall the wee club most fondly for the sessions of ghost stories which so often made the walk down his garden in darkness and up our own garden path a scary experience. I almost shiver still when I recall Jack McCumiskey's account of how the black dog at Narrow Water jumped on the shoulders of Johnny (Shanty) McGuigan and stayed there until he reached The Square. Later in life, Tom turned his back garden into a croquet lawn, and for many years the clash of mallet and ball was a familiar sound at our back. On occasions there were other sounds which must await recall. One could never have imagined that the supposedly staid and sedate game of the hoop and mallet would, over the years, generate so many competitive clashes on Summerhill.

Uncle Ross Tumility, Garda Síochána, second from left with his sons
Brendan, Raymond (Irish Army) and Roy.

7—Our Town

I have engaged myself in a story without having said a word so far about the stage on which it is set. As I paint in the backdrop of the streets and houses of the town in which I have spent all my life, I should mention that just over half of that span has been spent in my present abode, my third home on Summerhill. In his book *Warrenpoint*, (1998) Liam Bradley wrote extensively about the town's origins and developments, missing little or nothing in his survey. Before that, Denis Donoghue produced his version of *Warrenpoint* (1991), an acclaimed book which raised the hackles of many of the natives. His was a view from the Barracks. Mine is a view from Summerhill.

Warrenpoint wakened early in the morning for there were two waking aids which sounded six days a week. The first came before 6.30 A.M. when the early train with the bread and other essentials arrived, initiating a series of sounds, shunts and whistles which could be heard over the town. They sounded louder on the high ground of Summerhill. If that first aid to waking did not succeed, Billy Stewart with the first Angelus bell of the day at 7 A.M. nearly always did. The only insulation was a strong breeze which sometimes favoured one and reduced the other depending on the direction from which it blew.

Along with the two early trains and a bus or two, catering for those who travelled to work or education, morning traffic was dominated by milkmen. Their vehicles were of just one horsepower, until Narrow Water dairy introduced not only a mechanised vehicle but also pasteurised milk in bottles. All the others had two kegs, complete with taps with the milk measured out by the half pint and pint door to door. James Connolly of Duke Street would have been the first man on the road, to be followed at intervals by farmers from the outlying districts. From the Dromore Road came Fred McMahon, James Coulter, Owen Murphy, Mick McGivern and Mick McArdle. These latter three came from Grinan and Aughnamoira. The Burren Road would have had Robert Donnan and Paddy McKay. Clonallon Road had Tom Tate from Thompson's, James Heenan and Hall Savage. From Moygannon came Billy Collins, John Sloan and Jimmy Bradley. Jimmy deliberately in the last place, for some of the early risers would have been going home when he was only on his way in. It was said at the time that Jimmy's pony could have delivered the milk itself. It knew every house on Jimmy's route and a few other houses to which Jimmy would have called for a beverage which wasn't milk.

The delivery of milk in The Point was entirely a male preserve until Mrs Josephine Heaney from Burren entered the market. Her son, Jimmy, succeeded her and her grandson, Paul, is now the only milk deliveryman we have. It might be well to add that the posse of milk horses, with their brothers and sisters on the farms, provided plenty of work for our two saddlers, Barney McAnulty in Duke Street and Johnny McHugh in The Square, both of whom would have carried the appellation 'saddler' in place of their Christian names. Strangely, while the days of 'the saddler' might be over, we still have a man who carries the appellation, but he sells suits and shirts and other items.

If harness bells and the clip clops of horseshoes were early morning sounds, there were other regular and familiar noises from what might have been called the working heart of the town. This was based in the two small car parks which face each other on King's Lane today. In the space on the Summerhill side was the firm of P. Carvill & Sons, builders, which included their office, machine shop, timber store and limekiln. The space opposite housed F.G. O'Hare's builders office and machine shop, John Grandy's (Purdys) paint and glass store, Wilfred Purdy's joinery works, Jack Campbell's forge (bookie's shop) and garage, and the dwelling houses of the McCumiskeys and of Tishy McGuffin. Owen Carvill, the senior partner in the Carvill firm, lived on Summerhill, while the O'Hare families occupied two houses on East Street.

The other building contractor in the town at the time was James Wilson in Post Office Street, now Mary Street. These businesses would have been the main employers and while Wilson's have long departed from the building scene, the firm of F.G. O'Hare is still one of the leaders in the business, though now based in Newry. Carvills became Gilbert-Ash and it, too, is going strong. Another generation of the Carvill family is back in the construction business in recent years though, not based in Warrenpoint.

The docks and Kelly's coal yard were the other notable employers, but their workforce was largely small farmers from the rural area. Wages were small and by and large even those who were working could just about keep their heads above water. I remember a strike at Carvill's which led to a demonstration, which in turn led to Mick Hanna appearing before the Court. The other strike which affected our family directly was the railway strike lasting for what seemed weeks and weeks. It was the operating and platform staff who were actually on strike. My father belonged to a craft union which was not on strike and so qualified for state benefit. On the first day he received the benefit through the post he passed the two postal orders (one for ten shillings, the other for seven shillings and six pence) over to my mother, with the words, 'There you are, Minnie, that will have to keep you going to next Thursday.' As far as I am aware, the men who were on strike did not get a penny from any official source and I am not sure that their situation was greatly improved by the strike action.

No description of King's Lane (or Campbell's Lane as it was called,) would be complete without reference to the two pubs which dominated half its length. In my earliest days, John McLoughlin was both grocer and publican before Quinn's, and later Dunnes, came on the scene. John had the bar for most of my lifetime before it, too, became a Milestone property. On the opposite side of the lane was Tommy Cunningham's, with the entrance on Church Street. On Fair Days and many other days as well, it was the busiest lane in the country.

The bookie's shop which Jack Campbell operated at the other end of the lane was the only betting establishment in the town at the time, and while my father might have had the odd bet with Jack, my mother would only 'have a go' on big race days like the Grand National, the Derby or the Lincoln, a race which put her in the money on one occasion. The Lincoln was always run on a Wednesday. This was the first leg of the Spring Double and it coincided with the weekly appearance of a street singer whom most people in the town would have called 'Skillara', by virtue of the fact that he only knew two songs, one of them being *Me ould skillara hat*.

Skillara was a well-built fellow with a strong Dublin accent, a ruddy complexion and a strong smell of drink. After a verse and chorus he would proceed to knock the doors and take up his fees. On this day he gave added value for money by advising all his regulars to back 'Marmaduke Jinks' in the Lincoln. My mother and scores of others around the town took his advice and invested in Marmaduke who came home at 33/1; it made the day a nightmare for Jack Campbell, who swore he would hang for Skillara if he ever put his foot in the town again. Jack was in real bad form when I collected my mother's winnings late in the evening. As he handed over the small fortune to me he growled, 'You tell Minnie she'll not hear Skillara on Summerhill next week.'

But Skillara was on Summerhill the following Wednesday and was received with the warmth the prophet receives when his prediction becomes truth, and with money to prove it on this occasion. There was no doubt it was the best payday he ever had in his life. However, when it became known that he had tipped a different horse in Rostrevor, the revelation did not in any way affect his status in The Point.

The facilities available to present day bookies and punters in the computer age we live in are a far cry from those existing when Marmaduke romped home. I have already indicated that Jack Campbell was the only bookie in the town, but with the march of time another emporium was opened by Tom Sloan of Rostrevor. He has already been noted as the outstanding local billiards player of the era.

Tom set up shop in a building which had formerly been known as the Pioneer Hall, and latterly as Jack Hogg's Auction Mart. He operated on the upper floor in a spacious room which had a bay window providing a perfect view of Church Street and Tommy Cunningham's Corner, which led into King's Lane and Jack Campbell's forge at the other end. A punter could come out of the forge, send a signal to a man at Cunningham's Corner, who could in a matter of seconds transmit it to another individual who would be on duty at the bay window in Tom Sloan's office.

I present this mental map before advising that Tom had no direct line to the course, as Jack Campbell had, and not only did Tom not get the 'they're off' call, but he got the results a few minutes after Jack. So when Jack announced, 'Number 6 at Ascot,' that was it. There were 'fly-boys' about The Point then, just as there are today and they soon spotted the flaw in Tom Sloan's communications system. It took three individuals to operate the scam, but how often they did that successfully before being 'caught on' will never be known. I do know that Tom Sloan did not last too long in the Pioneer Hall.

If King's Lane was the hub of the industrial and gambling activity of the town, it still wasn't as exciting as the lane which acted as a tributary for most of the houses on Summerhill and Church Street. There was one dwelling house on it called Swallow Lodge, the residence of the Campbells, Jack, Paddy and Kitty, three remarkable characters. Then there was O'Neills' farmyard which featured half a dozen milch cows, a small piggery, a stable for the pony and trap which provided transport for the family butchery business, and, of course, what every farmyard should have, a flock of laying hens and a couple of roosters. All of this in the heart of the town.

The Town Hall had its back entrance on the lane which housed what would be called today the cleansing department, whose personnel consisted of Johnnie Duffy, Terry O'Neill, Tommy 'Stoker' Reay and, of course, the one and only 'La-di-dah' Paddy Burns. The shed which catered for them and their equipment also provided space for the fire brigade, which was another concern of the local council. The four men in the cleansing department doubled up as fire fighters on the odd occasion fires broke out. Their equipment was rather basic; a hand-drawn cart, a couple of hoses and hydrants and a couple of ladders. The biggest fire of the thirties was at the Garden Cinema in Queen Street. It was serious enough to warrant the brigade from Newry being involved also. If any fire lasted more than ten minutes, James Heather was sure to appear. James lived at Seaview and had his pub in Water Street in Newry where he was the top man in the brigade. Not only had he a remarkable propensity for saving people in fires, but also over his lifetime he would have saved a half a dozen people from drowning.

The caretaker of the Town Hall was Bob Kerr, who combined his council duties with a boot and shoe repair service, regularly availed of by the Carr family, which prompts the observation that, 'I had to get my boots mended, sir,' was an often given and accepted response to the master's query, 'Why were you not at school yesterday?'

Bob Kerr's neighbour was Jack McGuffin who also had a boot repair service, in tandem with his retail boot and shoe shop. Jack kept a cow or two in his back garden and grew an enormous amount of plants, seedlings and tomatoes in a comparatively small greenhouse. He was most generous in supplying all his gardening neighbours with his produce and his seedlings.

Tommy Steenson and his sister, Ida, were next door neighbours to McGuffins. The town's telephone exchange was sited in one of their ground floor front rooms. The other served as a studio, where Miss Steenson, as Ida was known in the town, taught the piano to a wide variety of boys and girls. Many of her pupils annually distinguished themselves at the top music *feiseanna*.

Tommy's artistic talents were not of the musical variety. He had been in the Great War and the effects of shellshock had left their mark on him. One bright spring morning, Church Street and the town wakened to find every door and the odd window on the street, his own included, daubed with grey paint. The town smiled understandingly and there were no recriminations, nor even complaints, for Tommy's little idiosyncrasies were understood for what they were. By lunchtime John Purdy had the street looking its normal self. For many years afterwards, Miss Steenson continued to enhance the cultural life of the area with a succession of good and even great pianists and, as far as memory serves, Tommy never shocked us so colourfully again.

McAnultys are the great survivors, both of 'our lane' and of Church Street. Funeral undertaking, horse drawn brakes, buses and taxis have been their stock-in-trade during my entire lifetime and long before, since 1819 to be exact. With their back entrance and garage opening on to the lane, they provided for me and others the most wonderful opportunities for adventure, education, entertainment and, on the occasion of a funeral, spectacle. Nowadays, the horse hearse is a rarity, moved around the country in a container which houses both hearse and horses and most often used by travellers with disposable incomes. Then, every Tom, Dick, Harry and Mary got the full spectacle with at least one hansom cab into the bargain, driven by Tom McGivern or Dick Ward. It was James Connolly, the publican, milkman and farmer in Duke Street, who provided the pair of fine black horses. James never trusted the reins to any hands other than his own, and he would have inspected everything half a dozen times to ensure hearse and horses were perfect before he started down the lane.

But it was the buses which were the main attraction, for the narrow lane and the minimum reversing space demanded expertise which was at times, even to a child's eyes, dazzling. For me, there was another attraction at McAnulty's and it was the fact that it was a short cut to Church Street. Walk through the garage and yard and you were in Church Street, that was, if Agnes Toner was in good form. Agnes would have been officially designated 'the housekeeper' in McAnultys, but she was much more: even the boss himself, Hugh McAnulty, as well as the family and the men who drove the buses and cars, would have been the objects of her strictures from time to time. Men like Frank Burns, Joe McGuigan, Peter Grant or Jimmy Mackrell didn't always take too kindly to what Agnes had to say, but she always would have had the last word. Because I did the odd message for her I was always in her good books and throughout her life she addressed me as 'Bernie'. This memoir will reveal that I did messages for Agnes long past boyhood.

If Agnes was one of the great characters of Church Street, she was by no means the only one, for she had equals in Maisie O'Neill, Tommy Cunningham, Mick and Annie McCarthy on her own side; and on the other, Mick O'Hare, Joe Duffy, Bridget Carvill, Vincey Havern and Isaac Coffey, all of them involved in business of one kind or another. Who else but Vincey in his front room supermarket could have advised customers whose requirements he could not meet to 'try some of the smaller stores,' a sentence which is still used in the town as a verbal memorial to him. The really big shop was Fosters, with entrances both in Church Street and The Square, encircling the Provincial Bank and Jack Mather the grocer. Pedlows, Newells, Manneys and Minnie Kelly's Tuck Shop completed that side of The Square. The Crown Hotel, The Liverpool and O'Hanlon's Victoria Hotel were popular hostelries for townspeople and visitors while Benny Mallocca and James McAteer, a few doors down Dock Street, looked after the ice cream needs of the town.

Come summer, the town would renew itself with the wonderful simplicities of the holiday making of that era, with the church excursions invariably led by pipe, brass or flute bands. The large railway shed at the station and Charlie McCabe's field on Summerhill were the venues for the catering facilities where hundreds were provided with tea and bags of sandwiches and buns.

Then there were the families who would return year after year to stay in the same houses. The Campbells, the Dunnes, the Cunninghams, all from Liverpool were annual summer companions. The 'Scottie' Carvills came and eventually stayed to become part of the fabric of the town, but whatever happened to Bobby McKaisie, another Scot and a wonderful companion, who came with his mother to stay in O'Neill's in Newry Street? A year younger than me, Bobby wore his kilt to Mass on Sundays and, strange for a Scot, he had little interest in football. A serious thinker was Bobby. Our acquaintance ended with the War. The Carvills were so well known they would not have been considered blow-ins, or in-blown wrack in the terminology of the time. The reality is that everyone's family, at one time or the other, was a blow-in. I have the Linenhall Library set of Fisher prints and one of them has a view of Carlingford Lough from the high ground at Narrow Water which shows one solitary house where the town now stands.

The Pierrots in the Park, the dancing on the Promenade, the skating in the Town Hall and a hundred other things filled those days of delight, when summer was really summer. I haven't even mentioned Duffy's Circus or 'the boats' which left the happiest memories of all. They deserve a chapter to themselves.

In the litany of names I have mentioned I wish to expand on the life of one, that of Tommy 'Stoker' Reay whose son, Willie John, also known as 'Stoker,' was one of my classmates in St Peter's. I had always believed that Tommy got his name from being a stoker in the navy during the Great War, but it is only recently that I have read a newspaper report of his funeral in Sean Daly's barbershop which revealed that he had:

> *'… seen service during World War One with the Machine Gun Corp and Cavalry in France, Belgium and the Holy Land. It was there that he was reported missing and presumed dead. His parents, who resided at 66 Meeting Street, were duly notified, and received the condolence of the late King George V and Queen Mary. Fate had ruled otherwise, fortunately, for Tommy was found buried under a pile of dead and wounded cavalry horses. His parents were shocked at his return as they had inserted his name in the Roll of Honour List in the newspapers and a friend composed a special poem to his supposed passing. "You did not see the pain I bore, you did not see me die. You only knew I passed away and never said goodbye." The mourning was quickly changed to rejoicing and after his discharge Tommy married. For a great number of years he was employed by the Warrenpoint Urban District Council and was always found to be cheery and courteous to all with whom he came in contact.'*[2]

Tommy died in the 60s. His sons, Frank and Jim, are well-known members of the Warrenpoint community.

In case it might be thought that all the characters in the town were domiciled in Church Street, I hasten to introduce two of the three flowers who blossomed and adorned the town for most of my life, Lily Connolly and Lily Heatley. Mary McCarthy was the other, but I'll come to her later. Lily Connolly was a young Dublin girl who came to work in The Point before my time, met Danny Connolly, brother of James the butcher and a Rostrevor man, and married him. They lived out their entire married life in Thomas Street. If Danny was a shy and retiring man, Lily had a natural gift for conversation which usually began when she was about twenty yards away from the recipient. While Lily had a reputation as a good talker she was also noted for 'not having the hard word about anybody.'

The Connollys had three children of their own and the town was mildly surprised when Lily returned home from a visit to Dublin with a little adopted boy called Paddy, whom the town came to know as Patch Connolly. Paddy became the delight of all their lives and his accomplishments on the singing, dancing and recitation platforms were a great source of pride to Lily. They paid off for Paddy, too, for after graduating from The Point Pantomime he made his living in the professional theatre across the water. In later years he came back to create a couple of wonderful musicals, *The Fair Day* and *In The Square,* which reflected the Warrenpoint scene of several generations. It seemed to me that 'Patch' was saying 'Thank you'.

Lily Heatley was a Newry girl who came to The Point in my lifetime and settled as our neighbour on Summerhill after marrying Richard Heatley. Richard died a young man and Lily reared their three children single-handed. She was at her best, or worst, in three spheres of the town's activities, whist drives, auctions and wakes. She was a good card player and while her asides in the course of a game of whist might have had the hall smiling, the 'inquests' after each game were often a torture for partner or opponents and sometimes for both. At auctions she was the bane of Jack Hogg's life for her comments, delivered as she thought *sotto voce,* were loud enough to acquaint the assembly of her estimate of the quality of the lot on offer—and Lily knew her furniture. Her house displayed her good taste. It is said with a great degree of truth that 'wakes are not as good as they used be,' and that is because times have changed and there are no characters of the quality of Lily Heatley. Both Lilys invariably got their status enhanced annually by Frank Hanna and Christy McGuigan in the pantomime.

8—HIGHER EDUCATION

September 1934 might well have been a landmark for Down football by virtue of the fact that its Junior team played in Croke Park. A much more important event for me was my enrolment, along with my brother Hugh, in Burren (Carrick) School where Master O'Hagan, our neighbour on Summerhill, was principal. The exact reasons for the transfer were not completely clear at the time, nor do I recall a great deal of consultation between my parents and myself, but I certainly had no objections to the change, even though it entailed a walk in excess of two miles each way every day. The morning stint was all uphill so in a sense it was 'higher education'.

Some of my cousins, the Thomas Street Carrs, were already at the school, so when we all met up, and were joined along the road by the McKays and Trainors at the 'waterworks', by Peter McGrath at the foot of his own lane and the Stoops further along the road, it all made for a sizable proportion of the school population arriving about the same time. Not that everybody was there every day. The Stoops' farmhouse was a watering place in the proper sense of the word. A small river was, and still is, piped through the wall into a small trough and grating and under the road. Hot or cold, wet or dry, we partook of that wonderful water twice a day.

Carrick was a three-teacher school and along with Master O'Hagan was Master McClean who took the middle classes, with Mrs Kelly (a Warrenpoint lady) being responsible for the early years. Each of them cycled from The Point every day, though in time, and after my time, Mrs Kelly was the first to be mechanised. Carrick School was different from St Peter's in that it had dry toilets; and during the last class two boys would be dispatched to the copse above the school to get kindling for the next day's fire. There were other differences too; it had girls and Protestants. Few schools in the country could boast that they turned out priests and parsons as did Carrick. Maurice and Frank Noel, whose family came to live on Summerhill, both became Canons in the Church of Ireland, while the diocese of Dromore, and the wider Church, has prospered with a succession of great priestly vocations over the years from the Burren area.

In that first year we had a wonderful bonus in the shape of two weeks' holidays for the potato harvest, a break which was not enjoyed by the town schools. Of course, when the summer came round again, we had a much shorter holiday. In the town there were two outlets for potato gatherers, both in Duke Street: Houricans and James Connolly. Both had land on the Bridle Loanin and James was the better payer. He paid one shilling and nine pence a day, while Houricans paid a shilling and sixpence—in today's coinage 9p and 7p respectively. It was James Connolly's horses who pulled the funeral hearse and I remember thinking that pulling the potato digger was a bit of a comedown for them, for the digger lacked the nobility of the hearse; James Connolly sitting on it without his top hat and ribbons didn't have the same stature, either.

With all the potatoes out, we resumed the routine of school life, soon becoming well integrated into the classroom community. From day one, the lunchtime procedure had been set. Get the sandwiches eaten and get the ball out as quickly as possible. The school playground presented quite a number of hazards, for on the side next to the road there was a row of very tall trees which had to be dribbled round. The middle was completely grassless with a stony surface merging into the steep hillside. Regardless of all these handicaps, once the ball was kicked there was a burst of frenetic activity which only ceased when Master O'Hagan emerged from the doorway, clapped his hands and called us to order.

We knew it was match time. Not for him the subtleties of selection. He would hold his hand straight out and make a division of human flesh. A slight movement of the finger or a nod of the head was the balancing mechanism he used, to make things equal. Invariably he played himself in the schoolhouse goals, though he would make the odd sortie outfield to demonstrate his dribbling skills. He used a whistle to enforce the rules, such as they were, and no one ever questioned his refereeing.

The memorable football event of my time at Carrick School came on Confirmation Day, the biggest day in our lives after First Communion. Until comparatively recent times, Clonallon Parish comprised of Warrenpoint, Burren and Mayobridge and the system in being at the time, and for many years after, was that all the children of the parish were confirmed in Burren Church on the same Sunday. It is my recollection that the ceremony took place every three years, and also that the same two people, a Mr and Mrs Byrne, acted as sponsors for the entire assembly of boys and girls. One can imagine the crowds of children and parents who descended on Burren for the occasion, but as ever, McAnulty's buses got everyone there and back on the day.

While the 'Confirmation money' of the era was nothing like the jackpots which the children of today needlessly receive, Terry McAnulty and I decided that we would spend some of our bonus in Omeath. The vast majority of travellers heading for Omeath were going mainly for the beer, but, having recited our Confirmation Pledge a couple of hours before, we were more than happy with lemonade and ice cream. We sailed for free on the St George, as most locals did on all the boats, sampled all the delights Omeath had to offer young probationers and eventually landed back at Church Street a few hours later.

One of McAnulty's buses was sitting on the street and I recognised Master O'Hagan, my brother Hugh and some of the Thomas Street cousins on board. The master came to the door of the bus and asked, 'Are you not coming to the match?'

I studied for a brief second, for I wasn't aware there was a match that evening. I must have registered positive for he added, 'Go and tell your mother. We'll wait for you.'

I rushed through McAnulty's yard and garage, and up our own garden to breathlessly exclaim to my mother, 'I'm going to the match,' and was on the road back to Church Street before she could say 'Yes' or 'No,' though I did hear the words of advice, 'Don't get your suit dirtied.' Need I explain that I was still in my Confirmation suit, the first suit I had ever worn in my life. I was a very proud fellow that day.

The bus left Church Street with me on board, in the company of the master, my brother and cousins and it was only then I learned we were going to Hilltown to play the school team there. Boys got on the bus at various points on the road, but the main assembly boarded at the school and off we went to Hilltown. Arriving there with what I thought was a well-filled bus of boys, it turned out, unfortunately, that some of the selected boys had failed to turn up. The master walked down the aisle of the bus taking stock of the material he had available and he pointed a finger at me.

'You will have to play,' he said.

'Sir, I have no boots or anything,' I pleaded, for I wasn't keen on playing.

'I'll get you what you need,' he replied and you didn't argue with Master O'Hagan. In a few minutes he handed me a jersey. I took off my jacket and tie, putting them carefully on the seat. I decided against taking off my shirt and pulled the jersey over it and as far down the trousers as possible. As I took the field in my Confirmation shoes, socks and trousers I could hear my mother's parting words, 'Mind you don't get your suit dirtied.'

The importance of the game did not become apparent to me until half-time, when the scores were level, and we learned that if Burren could beat Hilltown, the League would be won by Mayobridge School. This important piece of information was conveyed to us by Fr Mick McCartan, then curate in Mayobridge. For us, the most important thing he said was this, 'If you beat these Hilltown fellows, I'll give ye sixpence apiece.'

I have to say that over the hour I touched the ball about four times. I doubt if I had it in my hands once, but I will not shoulder responsibility for the defeat which Hilltown inflicted on us. We were well beaten and my dreams of two nights at the pictures with Fr McCartan's sixpence had evaporated long before the final whistle. In any event, I had enough of my Confirmation money left to see me through 'the pictures' for a few weeks. My shoes, socks or trousers showed no signs of my exertions on my first outing on Mussen's meadow and my mother simply didn't believe that I played in a football match that Confirmation evening.

In these days of education, education, education, round the clock and all for free, it is almost impossible to convey the educational environment of the thirties. The school leaving age was 14 and secondary education was almost entirely the preserve of those who could afford to pay for it. There was one very narrow avenue for those who couldn't and that was the Primary Certificate. A very good performance in this exam might get the student a scholarship to a secondary school, but the reality was that there was only a handful of scholarships for the whole county, and one had to be close to genius to succeed. I have to confess, though, that when attending Carrick School, the educational framework was the least of my concerns, though I was aware that boys in St Peter's did not sit this exam.

The reason had much to do with the principal, Mr Glancy, whose serious personal problems with alcohol reflected very much on the school situation. Boys whose families could afford it left St Peter's after leaving Master Crawford's room and completed their primary education with the Christian Brothers in Newry before proceeding to the secondary school. This may well have been the reason I was sent to Burren to finish mine. But when Master O'Hagan informed me that I would be taking the exam, I sat it and passed reasonably well but nowhere near well enough to get a scholarship. I imagine that the master might well have advised my parents that I might be secondary school material.

At thirteen, I was well aware of the financial constraints of the family, for while my father was in continual and safe employment, there was a family of ten children. When I was at St Peter's School, there were Thursdays (payday on the Railway) when my mother would have instructed me as I left for school, 'Collect Daddy's wages when you are coming home for your lunch.' She needed the money before my father got home in the evening. The clerk at the station, Mr Bridges, would invariably have given me the same advice when he handed the unsealed envelope to me, 'Don't you be going into John McLoughlin's on your way home.'

Being the child of a railway employee carried the privilege of free rail transport to school and this could well have been a decisive factor in my enrolment in The Abbey Christian Brothers' (CBS) Secondary School in September 1936. The opening of this particular school year was something of a watershed for a school which had been a dominant force in Ulster schools' hurling for the previous decade. During that period the school team represented the county, and had qualified for the All-Ireland Minor Hurling semi-final against Kilkenny just a few years before. The decision to replace hurling with football made no impact on me, for at this time I was an avid soccer enthusiast totally committed to Newry Town at home and Newcastle United abroad. Our soccer horizons did not stretch beyond England. Soccer magazines, as we know them now, did not exist. The only one on the counter was still *Topical Times* which appeared in Vincey Havern's every Wednesday, priced two pence. Except for one page which dealt with the Northern soccer scene, the content was entirely cross-channel and I would have to say, I lapped it up. From time to time there were photographs of individuals and teams, all of which were of the highest quality and which I had first seen in Joe Williams' bar. In time our attic, which became a bedroom, was lined with pictures of Raich Carter, Stan Cullis, Dixie Dean and the like. Newcastle United, of course, had a place of honour in the team section but when Peter Doherty transferred to Blackpool they were all demoted to second place. Those who believe George Best to have been the greatest Irish soccer player could never have seen Doherty.

The lunchtime kick-in at the near goals of The Abbey pitch was the only football activity in those early weeks; those of us in the first years remained on the fringes of the half-hour melee and were lucky if we managed to get a kick at all. The PE period was entirely physical-exercise under the direction of Mr 'Waggy' Brown, a former British Army instructor whose no-nonsense approach would certainly have put anyone off joining the forces. While the field exercises were enjoyable, those in the gym were, for me, a torture. Climbing the rope to the top was something I never achieved, being continually put to shame by chaps who could go up like monkeys. I was no better on the horizontal bars.

Brother Newell did not teach either of the first-year classes so we only knew of him by repute as Wee Tosh or Tarzan. He was in charge of football and I was in school some weeks before his path and mine crossed on the first landing.

He beckoned, signalling that he wished to speak to me.

'You are a cousin of Johnnie Carr's?' he asked. When I answered in the affirmative, he questioned further, 'You have football boots at home?' and when I again replied positively, he ordered, 'Bring them to school tomorrow for football practice immediately after school.'

I should explain that my cousin Johnnie, who was three or four years ahead of me in school, was already showing that he would be one of the great football talents in Down and Brother Newell obviously thought that some of it might have rubbed off on me. I should explain also that I did not have a pair of football boots which were specifically mine. In our house we played out of a common pool of boots which my mother was continually threatening to put in the bin or the fire.

When I arrived at school the next day, I had boots, socks and pants but not one item of what would now be called 'my gear' could be called my own, nor completely the right size.

In a matter of weeks the good Brother had a team sorted out and to my complete surprise I was selected at what I would have called, in soccer parlance, 'outside right' for the first game, which was against Armagh CBS in Armagh. We won. I scored three points, and on Monday I was the hero of A1, the only first-year boy on the team. Brother Newell had got us off to a great start and he was justly rewarded when the team won the Rannafast Cup at its first attempt.

Despite my involvement with the school team, I was still immersed completely in soccer and would rarely have missed a Newry Town home game. The school bell rang on Saturday mornings, as on the other five mornings of the week so the jaunts with my father came to an end. Happily the Angelus bell at mid-day heralded the end of the school day and the start of a feverish rush to Dublin Bridge Station. Miss the train and there was a two-hour wait for the next one. On days when Newry Town were playing at home it was essential that one caught the train to have the dinner at home and then back to the Showgrounds on the bike.

Travelling to school by train from The Point was an experience enjoyed by generations of young people until the sixties, when the rail link ended; even by today's standards of youthful behaviour, there were occasions when the escapades went way beyond the pale. Some of them, such as moving from compartment to compartment along what could be called the running board when the train was moving at speed, were highly dangerous. There were vandals about 60-odd years ago, just as there are today, and one escapade will bear relating, though I had left school when it occurred. It was widely talked about in the town at the time.

In more recent times I have had a 'blow by blow' account from the central figure, Ted Bradley, a long-time friend and colleague in various endeavours and retired principal of St Peter's Boys School. He was one of a number of boys who boarded the train at Dublin Bridge on a particular day for the homeward journey from school. It was the practice for the carriage doors on the platform side to be locked; a measure against the door openers and the vandals. What should have been a comfortable run to The Point got under way but two of the five boys who shared the compartment were not concerned about their own comfort or that of anyone else. To the shock and amazement of Ted, they proceeded to engage in what would now be called 'an orgy of destruction'. Seats, lights and racks all came under the hammer and as the train pulled into Warrenpoint Station this particular compartment was a scene of utter desolation.

Before the engine came to a halt, the two boys who had created the havoc and two others who had neither hand, act nor part in the activity, exited by the other door into the next compartment, on to the platform and away. They all probably thought that Ted would follow them out, but he didn't. He sat his ground until Johnnie Dowd, the porter, opened the door. When Johnnie looked through the open door and viewed the destruction, he remonstrated with Ted and promptly marched him to the stationmaster's office, despite Ted's protestations that he had nothing to do with it. Naturally enough, the stationmaster had to see the disaster for himself and, with Johnnie and Ted in tow, out he went to the battered compartment. He retreated to the office on the double, lifted the phone, and within a matter of minutes, a police constable was in their company viewing the damage. For those with memories as long as my own, the constable was a famous figure, Pat Slevin, who earned himself the title Minister for Information, in the War years.

To his credit, Ted never got ruffled and to Constable Slevin, as to the stationmaster and Johnny Dowd, he maintained, 'I had nothing to do with it.'

'Right,' says the constable, 'we'll go round to the Barracks and we'll find out who had something to do with it.'

Out of the station and up Newry Street marched the constable with his youthful prisoner and who was unloading his lorry at the Ulster Hotel but Joe McGuigan. Joe, observant as always, noted this lone boy in some distress and asked, 'What's wrong, young Bradley?' It was the policeman who answered, 'There was some damage done on the train and this young man might know something about it.'

'I had nothing to do with it, Mr McGuigan,' was Ted's response to Joe's questioning glance and those who remember Joe would realise that Ted could have had no better barrister than Joe McGuigan

'You can't take a lad like that to the Barracks without his father or mother,' snapped Joe, which observation led to several exchanges between the pair before the constable closed the issue with, 'You mind your own business, Mr McGuigan,' and moved off to the Barracks with Ted in tow. Arriving there he ushered Ted into the day room and called up the stairs, 'Sergeant'. A couple of minutes elapsed before the Sergeant came down into the room and sat at the table. The constable proceeded to go through all the formalities. 'What is your name? Where do you live? What is your age? What is your father's name?' They both would probably have known even before this that his father was the school principal at Clontifleece.

'Was this compartment damaged when you got into it at Dublin Bridge?' he continued. Ted shook his head and replied, 'No.'

'Did any other boys get in with you at Dublin Bridge?' and Ted nodded and answered, 'Yes.'

'Johnnie Dowd said you were in the compartment by yourself, did they get off at Narrow Water? Did they jump off the train?' Another 'No,' from Ted. 'They got off in The Point.'

'But you were all locked in.'

'Only the door on the platform side was locked, the door on the other side wasn't,' explained Ted, and the policeman got the picture.

'How many boys were there?' continued the policeman. 'Four boys went out, but only two of them did any damage.'

When Constable Slevin asked, 'Do you know their names?' Ted knew he was at the end of the road and replied, 'I do.'

With encouraging nods from the constable, Ted began, 'One of them was a boy called Gerry Slevin,'—the constable's youngest son—and as the constable stopped in his tracks lost for words, the Sergeant, who had only been taking notes up to this, gave his constable a withering look and took over Ted's cross-examination.

'You say young Slevin was one of the boys who did the damage. Would you mind telling me who the other one was?'

'The other one was a boy called Denis Donoghue,'—the Sergeant's younger son—replied Ted quietly, and young as he was I'm sure he heard the deafening silence which ensued.

On his release Ted headed out to The Square and towards the station, where his bicycle lay. Joe McGuigan and his lorry were still at the Ulster Hotel, with Joe sitting in the driving seat. On sight of the lone figure of Ted he alighted to hear Ted's version of his experience. When Joe heard the full story the smile which appeared was part of his countenance for many a day. I cannot say whether or not the pair of policemen compensated the railway company for the substantial damage which was done. I can say there is no record of any charges ever being brought. I can also say that from the very next day Denis Donoghue travelled to school by bus.

9—THE NEW CURATE

While I never knew the exact details, there was some division in St Peter's GAA Club in the 1935/36 period and the name was changed to 'Hearts of Down'. I cannot be sure whether or not it impacted on the younger footballers in the town for most of them, including some of my brothers, were playing for a Warrenpoint soccer team in the Newry Summer League. All the games were played at the Showgrounds, Newry Town's pitch. The Point had a hopeless run in the league and when they were drawn in the cup against Newry Celtic, the top team, no one gave them any chance at all. I cycled up to the game with a few companions to lend our support. Included in the team was Mickey Ruddy, my Good Samaritan who had long since returned from his enforced exile in Belfast. Mickey was still the same happy-go-lucky chap he always was. He played on the right wing in this particular game in which The Point surprised all of us and, most of all, the opposition.

At half-time there was no score; unbelievably The Point had withstood everything which Celtic threw at them. In the second half, Pat Finnison, in goal, was the hero of the evening. Occasionally a break-out of the defence brought the forwards into action, but, by and large, there wasn't a single scoring chance created. No chance that is until five minutes from the end when the Newry men were caught napping with almost every man in The Point half of the field. Even their goalkeeper was outside his penalty area and made a mess of a long ball which passed him and was heading for the empty net. We couldn't believe it, a win over Celtic was the thought in every Point mind. But our dream vanished as quickly as it appeared. Out of nowhere came Mickey Ruddy, touched the ball and put it wide of the gaping net.

'Holy God, Mickey,' was the introduction to the litany which was said in his honour as he lay prostrate on the ground holding his head in his hands. Worse was to follow, for on the kick-out Celtic got possession, went straight upfield and scored the goal which put them through to the next round. Nobody from The Point who was at the game that night ever forgot it, and certainly not Mickey Ruddy who introduced me to the word 'pockle'. Of that performance Mickey would always say, 'I was an awful pockler that night.'

Fortunately for St Peter's and the GAA in general, a new curate came to the parish in the closing months of 1935. He obviously saw what was wrong in the club and by the autumn he re-launched it, almost as a new entity and as St Peter's. The only members of the 'old brigade' to survive were Frank (Tex) Thompson, Frank Hanna and Tom O'Hare. Only two years earlier, Tom had played with the Down team in Croke Park and was still in his early twenties while Tex, who was also a skilful soccer player, performed well when he took up the Gaelic football. Frank Hanna had succeeded my Uncle Tommy as goalkeeper while the others were a completely younger set and included most of the fellows who played for The Point in the Newry Summer League a few months before, among them Mickey Ruddy.

The new-look Blues made their first appearance in a challenge game at Rostrevor. My abiding memory of that encounter is of standing behind the goal which was guarded by Jim O'Neill of The Crown, resplendent in cap, sweater and gloves. Jim was not as active as the young chap at the other end, who was also making his debut on this occasion. I refer to Tommy Kane who for many years was a star performer with Rostrevor teams and played at all grades for Down. Jim O'Neill always maintained that no goals went past him for three games. The new St Peter's was launched, but despite the fact that my brothers and cousins were very much involved in the team, of which I was an enthusiastic supporter, my main football interest continued to be orientated to soccer, and particularly to Newry Town.

Those pre-War years witnessed the high point of soccer in Newry, for 'The Town' got together a combination which was a match for anything in the league. At this time they featured a number of cross-channel players, all of whom were full-time professionals living well on £5 a week. In England, the top money was about £8 weekly with bonus for a win or a draw. It was the ambition of all to play in England or Scotland so occasional transfers hit the headlines. Jimmy Twomey, goalkeeper and Newry native, was transferred to Leeds United and part of the deal brought Leeds to play a challenge game at the Showgrounds. I well remember the two big names of the Leeds team at the time, Gordon Hodgson, a South African of massive proportions at centre forward, and Willis Edwards, a halfback with his own distinctive style. They also had Davy Cochrane, a youthful Portadown winger, who was making a great name for himself. Newry had a centre forward, Billy Redfern, who was an exceptional goal scorer and topped the league-scoring list for several years. He later transferred to Luton Town where he continued successfully until the War intervened.

My own hero of that good Newry Town team was Neil McIvor, a Scot, who came as an inside forward in the terminology of the time and developed into a wonderful wing half. Neil was probably past his best when he arrived in Newry but I never saw him have a bad game. He was selected on Irish league teams regularly and once I saw him play against an English league side which featured such names as Stan Cullis and Stanley Matthews. He was never likely to be transferred back to England or Scotland so Neil settled in Newry and had a sad ending in an accident.

I have already mentioned my other hero, Peter Doherty, whom I only saw playing on one occasion, but you only had to see him once to know that he was special. I think Peter commenced his career with Coleraine before moving to Glentoran and then on to Blackpool. On the outbreak of the War he joined the RAF, but when football resumed after the conflict he soon established himself as the top performer in England.

My Gaelic football career at The Abbey was still under way, but my enthusiasm for Newry Town was responsible for getting myself and one other boy on the wrong side of Brother Newell, some time before my academic career ended.

It came about out of a great Newry performance in the semi-final of the Cup. The game against Linfield was played in Belfast at Solitude, the home of Cliftonville, and Newry astounded friend and foe alike by getting a 1–1 draw. It was the shock of the season and the replay was fixed for the following Wednesday afternoon in Newry. For some reason my father, not a regular supporter of Newry, had been at the game in Belfast and his verdict was that Newry should have won.

He expressed his fears though that they had lost their chance at Solitude.

On Monday the school was agog with excitement, certainly among the town boys, all of whom had an interest in soccer. Wednesday could not come quickly enough. The only snag on the horizon was the fact that the game began at 3 o'clock and school did not finish until 3.30. It would take at least 10 minutes to get us down to the Showgrounds. In effect, this meant we were going to miss the first half.

Being the man he was, Brother Newell would have been very much aware of the match and when a number of us approached him individually at lunchtime, asking to be allowed out at 2.45 P.M., he was non-committal. Probably the slow nodding of the head suggested that he would be considering our requests in due course. As things were, we knew we would be having him for the second last class and we resumed studies after lunch, not knowing if we would be there to see the Blues trotting out. Brother Newell came into the room for his class at 2.15 and as he entered there was an exchange of glances among those who were hoping to go to the game. On the dot of 2.45 he stopped the class and addressed us.

'I understand there is a soccer match taking place down the road today and a number of boys are anxious to go to it.' He spoke slowly, deliberately and with a slight suggestion of menace, continuing, 'Would those boys who wish to go to this football match please stand up?'

With each word, one detected a challenge in his voice and whatever about my enthusiasm for Newry Town my courage was ebbing away with each word. In the seconds it took him to speak I had doubts about wanting to go. The dead silence which followed suggested that everyone was in the same predicament as myself.

There was a movement on my left and I knew without turning a glance that it was Mick Murphy, who was to become father of John, the 1968 All-Irelander and brother of T.P., (a future county secretary) who was on his feet. The match was secondary now and the force which impelled me to my feet was one of solidarity with Mick, rather than the desire to go to a football match.

No other boy in the class shared my notions of solidarity and Mick and I stood alone under the withering eye of Brother Newell. He had a manner of pursing his lips and pausing before making pronouncements and we waited for the worst. Pause ended, and in the gravest of tones he delivered the verdict. 'You two boys may go to this football match if you wish, but I tell you, neither of you will play for The Abbey again.'

Mick and I gathered our books into our bags and left the room to the most deafening silence I have ever experienced. Down the stairs, out into Abbey Yard and half-way down Boat Street before we exchanged a glance, never mind a word. The wind had been taken out of both our sails, but it was replaced by a respect for each other which lasted throughout our lives.

By the time we reached the Gas Works the incident was forgotten as we hastened to get down to the Marshes. In sprints and trots we arrived there about ten minutes after the kick-off. Already the Town was a goal down and by half-time the writing was on the wall. Even my own hero, Neil McIvor, was made to look ordinary and at the end it was a defeat for Newry. For whatever reason, Mick

Murphy and I did not view the game together, but when we met at break the next morning we both agreed it was a disappointing result. That it should have brought the wrath of 'the wee man' on our heads was a double blow. We had no way of knowing whether or not the threat to both our futures with The Abbey team was real, for there was no football in the final term in which the exams were coming up. When we returned to school after the summer holidays we were both called to the colours again. That disappointing game with Linfield was never mentioned, though my enthusiasm for Newry Town and the new soccer season which was already under way, was in no sense diminished.

I would have to record that Brother Newell, for all the tempestuous sides of his nature, was a great favourite with all the boys who played football under his direction. He finished his days in retirement in Omagh where he always had a very warm welcome for any of his former students and more so if they had been footballing students. One name he recalled with equal degrees of pride and sadness was that of Johnnie Carr, whom he always regarded as a *protégé* of his own, and with very good reason. My own stay at The Abbey was not a lengthy one, but it was long enough to establish a respect and friendship with him which lasted over the years.

10—THE BOATS

It would be wrong to give the impression that football was the only pastime for boys in the thirties, indeed there was no activity of the time which was not pleasurable and none more so than the boats. Boats were central to the summer season for generations. With the partitioning of the country into two jurisdictions the boats came to play an important part in the local economy. The extra few pounds made in the summer months made a great difference the following winter when the options for many were the not very rewarding dole queue, or the boat to England or Scotland. Of course, it was the same story for families who kept visitors and nearly every family with a spare room or two, did. It was a short season, however. We never kept visitors for we could always fill any available space ourselves, and the attic which had been a dumping ground in my earlier days was transformed into a comfortable bedroom. At this time our family of ten children was complete.

When the boats are mentioned in the Warrenpoint context, it is the motor boat scene which comes to mind. There was another facet of boating activity which enriched the lives of those boys who were attracted to the beach or the Baths, the two areas for rowing boats. This was a gentler scene. The men who rowed for their few shillings were more placid than their mechanised brothers, though in many instances they were from the same families.

Seafaring careers began on summer mornings, when keeping a boat afloat was a chore welcomed by a workforce whose average age might have been eight or nine; I should explain that the exercise was simply rowing around until the owner got a passenger or two, or 'a freight,' as it was called. Rory Duffy, who had two boats, the *May* and the *Alice,* was a discerning mind, and as one advanced in age and wisdom, the realisation that he had a way with words, became very apparent. Depending on the tide, the distance from Parkinson's Corner, now the Boathouse, to the jetty, from where the motor boats jostled for space, was a distance of approximately 60 yards and in the short space of time it took to walk it, Rory had to sell the advantages of his rowing boat over the much faster motor boats. The number of times Rory was successful was a tribute to his genius. To take a trip with him was to experience the best in Irish storytelling. The great bonus for me was when Rory stowed the sail and a return voyage under canvas beckoned. One was rarely disappointed.

Apart from Johnnie Dinsmore's *Shamrock,* and James McCamley's *Alice,* the other rowing boats were mere part timers. The Magees' *Dolly* and Stevie Bradley's *Rosie* seemed to be kept in training for the Regatta season when John (Skin) Magee and Billy Bradley pitted their sailing skills against Billy Irwin and Peter O'Hagan, both from the Louth shore. Mark McAteer's *Edna* was only used at weekends for he worked full-time at the docks.

There was another scene of row boat activity at the Baths where Hughie White, Ned Lynch and occasionally Anthony Gallagher had the franchise to themselves. They catered more for those who just wanted to try their hands at the rowing for half an hour or an hour. Occasionally they would have a freight to Omeath but generally they had enough to do at the Baths. Hughie was called Turk while Ned was known as 'Skipper'. I often wondered how he got the name 'Turk' and it is only since I commenced this book that I have learned he fought at the Dardanelles in the first World War, earning himself the name Turk in The Point. They were the most contrasting pair one could meet. Hughie was most accommodating and would always respond positively to requests to 'keep her afloat'. Ned, who was the father of Jackie, the boy who pushed the football skip to Moygannon, could be very gruff and one needed to be in his good books to get the nod.

Through all my life in the family home there hung a picture of the local drama group of my father's time. The play in question was *The Colleen Bawn* in which my father played Hardress Cregan. Also in the picture is Hughie White, resplendent in the role of a soldier, a Red Coat no doubt. The impulse to record this fact is merely to suggest that some of Hughie's acting talent might have shown up in the genes of his niece who has been entertaining the great British public for the last 40 years under the name of Cilla Black. She was baptised Priscilla White. Had she been born in The Point, Priscilla's star might never have shone so brightly, such was the abundance of talent we had in the town and which has been keeping our Panto going for more than 50 years.

No reference to the rowboat scene would be complete without a mention of the men from the Omeath shore who outnumbered The Point sailors by quite a stretch. The O'Hanlons, the Boyles, the O'Hagans, the McKeowns, the McCarthys and the unforgettable Mick McQuade, all the most decent of men. Mickey McKeown was related to the Tumiltys through marriage. He lived in a small cottage along the shore on the other side and 'the dinner's ready' was signalled across the lough every day by the hoisting of a single white shirt on the line.

It was the motor boat area of activity which was central to the town's summer activities. The earliest roll call of the fleet in my time would have been headed by the *St George,* owned by the Magee family and brought to Warrenpoint in 1920. It was a twin screw, two engines, of very small draught and ideally suited to the lough. It was licensed by the Board of Trade to carry 140 passengers.

I would be one of the few people still alive who would remember the *Ros na Ree,* a steam boat owned by the O'Neill family. It was a long slender craft, slow and cumbersome compared to the *St George* and did not have anything like the same carrying capacity. For all that, it must have been a great payer for the O'Neills in its time. I often heard my mother say, 'They would take the money home in a big bucket.'

Then there were the smaller boats, Dinsmore's *St Patrick,* McGuigan's *Little Flower,* Steven Bradley's *Madonna,* Paddy Duffy's *The Newry* and Danny O'Neill's *Fair Play.* After years of competition the owners of these five boats formed a combine which sailed under the Red Star flag. Their selling point was, 'five boats on the one ticket'. This in time turned to six, seven, eight and nine boats on the one ticket. Tom McGuigan, who had sailed a lone course in his *Santa Maria,* joined the combine when he acquired the *St Anthony* from the Boyle brothers on the other side of the lough. Another addition a year or two later was a second Dinsmore boat, which boasted the name, *Girl Pat,* a significant name at the time, for it was the name of an English coaster which sailed off into the South Atlantic, complete with captain and crew, to the consternation of the owners. It was described at the time as a modern-day peaceful *Mutiny on the Bounty.*

The competitive edge on the motor boat scene was sharpened considerably when a new boat, the *Fairy Queen,* sailed in from the Clyde. I was a very junior member of the boating fraternity which gathered at the pier head the evening before to welcome her. We gathered behind the wall on a damp, miserable evening of poor visibility and a steady drizzle. All were anxious to get the first glimpse of this vessel which had prompted such great reports in the weeks before. In the failing light the wiseacres proclaimed, 'she'll not be here the night' and the welcoming committee dispersed and went home disappointed.

I was down at the dock at the earliest opportunity the next morning, and there she was, being admired by boatmen and townspeople alike. Blue hull, white wheelhouse and saloon, over which was sited a spacious deck area. In the morning sunlight and gentle swell, she looked everything her name implied. No vessel in The Point has ever had such a meticulous inspection and she had no difficulty getting the 'A1 at Lloyds' from the locals. Her port of origin, Glasgow, painted on her stern ensured that her canvassers called her 'the big Glasgow boat.'

The owner of this fine ship was Chris O'Boyle, a Donegal man from Killybegs who, before my time, had married a local girl, Ellen Doran. They had one son, Joe, known to the locals as Chris, born in time to be a civilising influence on my life. For Chris senior, this new boat was a substantial investment and a lot of hard work. To begin with, even though he was from Killybegs, he was neither sailor nor engineer, so he had to employ a skipper, an engineer and two other hands for duties fore and aft.

The big day was Sunday. In the fiercest competition imaginable, row boats, the Red Star Line, the two big boats, a Tinnelly boat from Rostrevor along with Bobby Anderson's *Slieve Foy* from Omeath, all managed a share. During the week, however, the daily run to Carlingford had been a *St George* monopoly, until the appearance of the *Fairy Queen.* In a matter of weeks a price-cutting war developed, often leading to verbal and even physical confrontation, resulting in both parties appearing in court on a number of occasions, each charging the other with assault. Major McCallum, the RM, who lived in Osborne Terrace, invariably took the *via media* by binding both parties to keep the peace, which they did until the next flare up.

The normal fare to Carlingford was one shilling and sixpence, but both parties alternatively cut their fares until the fare on both boats was sixpence, at a time when the fare to Omeath was nine pence. In those days there was no railing around the dock. The only barrier between street and tide was a chain, carried at intervals by iron fixtures in the ground. The chains could be stepped over or dropped to give access to the boats when the tide allowed boarding at the dock. Tickets would have been touted from early morning and sailing time for both boats was 2.30 P.M. I arrived down at the dock on one occasion to find a great sense of excitement; I heard there had been a heated argument and a blow or two between the canvassers a short time before. Both boats were fairly well laden and every potential passenger was being harangued rather than canvassed as soon as they appeared on the horizon. Departure time came and Chris gave a final call before signalling the 'let go'. Astern went the *Fairy Queen* with most of the upper deck passengers waving a 'good bye' which would have done justice to a departure for America. Of course, the bystanders on the quay were equally robust in their response.

It was nearly ten minutes later before the *St George* pulled out with yours truly on board and as we rounded the pier head the Fairy Queen appeared as a big dot beyond what was called 'the Black Rock' off the Omeath shore. With its twin screws the *St George* was a much faster boat so the gap closed, gradually at first, but eventually quite quickly. By this time many of the passengers felt they were in a race and were quite enthusiastic in their shouts of encouragement to Jim (Crab) Magee, who was at the wheel. He stood unsmiling, looking straight ahead, making no response to the clamour. He was an experienced seaman and a regular pilot of ships to Newry, but even this knowledge did not prepare me for what was to happen in the next few minutes. The passengers on both vessels were urging on the respective skippers and as we closed I expected Crab to move well to starboard for the passing, but no, and to my horror, he remained firmly on course. The shouts of encouragement turned to shouts of panic as every head, my own included, turned in his direction. He still stood unblinking and oblivious to the shrieking passengers, one of whom fainted on the *St George*. One could almost have stepped from boat to boat as we passed and for the one and only time in my life I felt in danger on the sea. After what probably took a minute, but seemed like twenty, we finally drew clear to the relief of all. When it was over, I marvelled at Jim Magee's expertise but still felt very shaken.

When the *Fairy Queen* docked behind us in Carlingford, the first man ashore was Philip O'Neill, the skipper, and for a time it looked as if there was going to be one hell of a row. However, wiser counsels prevailed and it didn't come to blows, though I imagine it left bitter feelings.

11—A Twelfth to Remember

It was the Red Star boats, however, which provided many boys with their first opportunity to earn some pocket money, and after serving as an able bodied volunteer for a couple of years I was a fully fledged crew member by 1938, when the Twelfth was held in Warrenpoint. From a few days before, the town was weighed down with bunting and Union Jacks. This was normal procedure when the town hosted the major demonstration and no remarks would be passed. I certainly have no memory of any local friction. On Summerhill at the time, where there were nearly as many Protestants as Catholics, no one took great exception to the flying of flags, though there were only a few houses which would have been flag bearers.

A town hosting the Twelfth in those days would have been wakened early by 'the slashers,' as we called the Lambeg drums, so it was to a chorus of drums, flutes and pipes that I headed down to the boats on this occasion. As I came into The Square, the first sight to greet my eyes was the tricolour flying defiantly on the near perch which was one of the two marking the channel for boats going to Newry. I smiled and wondered who the flag raisers might be. The route of the parade ensured that all the visiting brethren would have to view the rebel flag for a few minutes before turning on to the Promenade at Parkinson's Corner, unless of course they closed eyes, and faced the possibility of marching straight ahead into the sea.

In due course a few boats, including my own craft, the *Madonna,* moved to the boarding pier in the hope of attracting some of the visitors to the delights of Omeath and the Free State, but there were very few takers. Truth to tell, being able to look across the water and see the Louth shore convinced most of them they were looking across at a foreign country, and one they wouldn't touch with a 40 foot pole, let alone buy anything in it.

About half an hour before the parade was due to set off from the Newry Road on this fresh July day, two men called Sam and Tom, both wearing Orange sashes, emerged from among the huts which sold confectionery and fancy goods at the top of the beach. I had no difficulty recognising the two well-known local Orangemen, one of whom later came to be my very good neighbour on Summerhill. Whether or not they approached the owner of the boat beforehand, I do not know, but they pushed one of the punts, complete with oars and rowlocks, into the water and began rowing in the direction of the perches where the tricolour flew. My vantage point for the developing incident was the stern of the *Madonna,* where my task was 'holding her up' or even 'houlin her up' with the help of a lengthy boat hook. This simply meant that you held the boat against the wind. There were many days when this was no easy task.

It soon became apparent that Sam and Tom were not expert oarsmen, but they eventually reached the near perch where the offensive emblem fluttered strongly in the breeze. Sam mounted what must have been slippery steps, wrenched the flagpole from its binding and with a triumphant flourish tossed the offensive rag into the channel.

The tide might have been ebbing at the time, but inside this 15-year-old able-bodied seaman, in the stern of the *Madonna,* there was a rising tide of anger. As Tom and Sam neared the shore I was ready to explode. I looked up to the top of the beach where a number of seasoned boatmen were viewing the episode with what I felt was alarming detachment. Ever after, I thought if Joe McGuigan had been about there would have been an international incident. As the boat beached, I was tempted to run across, armed with my boat hook, to accost the defilers, but then I thought what Stevie Bradley might say if he came down to find the *Madonna* battering herself against the jetty.

Sam and Tom landed, pulled the punt a length out of the water and proceeded up the beach without a disapproving word from anyone. It could well have been that my nautical seniors felt that any interference would be bad for business, but the reality was that hardly two dozen of the marching thousands ventured across to Omeath that day.

My patriotic anger was slowly subsiding, but the hurt was to change in a matter of minutes. Unnoticed, a boat had put out from the far shore and initially it looked as if it was just another Omeath man heading for The Point. Soon it became apparent that he was heading for the perches, to the increasing interest of the growing crowd. The lonesome boatman went first to the perch on the Omeath side, made his boat fast, and went up the steps before producing an even larger tricolour than before. To be sure, he gave it a victorious flourish and proceeded to make it fast, all to a rousing cheer from the crowd. Having completed his task he returned to his boat, pulled across to the other perch and repeated his performance to even louder cheers. Need I say that my patriotic pride was restored and Eddie O'Hanlon, who turned out to be the lonesome boatman, was put on a pedestal.

All of this happened in the last 30 minutes before the parade got under way and when the marchers, bedecked with banners, flags, swords, sashes and musical accompaniment, faced across The Square and along the dock they had to take in the sight of the twin flags on the perches. Some may well have closed their eyes but none of them walked into the dock or off the pier head.

I would have to confess, as far as The Point was concerned, there were no problems about the matter of parades. The big demonstrations were only held in the town every six or seven years. The annual events, when the local lodge marched off to main demonstrations on the twelfth, Scarva on the thirteenth and Black Saturday, the last Saturday in August, were an accepted part of the local scene. For most of my life, if I was about the house, I would always walk to Church Street to witness the departure or return of the local brethren. The only provocative feature which I can recall in those formative years were the reports of the speeches at the various demonstrations, where many speakers seemed to compete in a contest of vituperation directed at Fenians and Catholics, who were regarded as two sides of the same coin. Over 60 years on, I can recall the horror and the hurt I felt on reading a clerical Orangeman claim that, 'One can tell the Catholic area in any town in Northern Ireland by the smell of it.' This was completely at odds with the way we lived in The Point.

If July had 'the Twelfth,' August had 'the Fifteenth' which continues to be the zenith of the summer season. Back in the thirties, when there were comparatively few private cars and not a lot of buses, it is hard to conceive how the thousands of men, women and children got to The Point for what was their only day-out of the year. Admittedly there was the train which served Newry and all points north to Belfast, but it was no benefit to the inhabitants of Mourne, Mayobridge, Hilltown, Castlewellan or all of South Armagh for whom The Point was the mecca on the day.

While the doctrine of the Assumption was not a defined dogma of the Church until the mid-20th century, it has been a Church holiday in Ireland probably from emancipation. At some stage in its development, the green tinge provided by the Hibernian Association led to it being considered something of a green twelfth, when there was much more musical emphasis on *God save Ireland, The Boys of Wexford* and *The Foggy Dew,* than there was on hymns to the Mother of God, though admittedly *Faith of our Fathers* always got due recognition. Whatever the mixture, it made the Fifteenth the day of the year in The Point. The wonder of it all was that nothing was organised.

Bands came with their supporters and marched and played the day long and, of course, a lot of drink was taken. By evening there would be a buzz about the place as the odd argument and even a fight heightened the tension. Old scores would be settled and possibly the embers of a row from the previous year would re-ignite. All of it gave the police their busiest day of the year, with the result that the petty sessions on the Fair Day in September dealt with the fallouts of the Fifteenth.

The big difference between the 12th July and the 15th August celebrations was, and is, that no matter how big the Orange demonstrations might be, by 6 o'clock in the evening one would hardly have known they had been in the town. On the other hand, the visitors on the Fifteenth would still be coming into the town almost to midnight.

12—MY FIRST ALL-IRELAND

While the All-Ireland Football Final has been such a special occasion for most of my life, in 1938 it was just another sporting event. I was aware of the excitement the previous year when Cavan met Kerry in what was a controversial game. I don't think my father was ever at a final in his life, so there would not have been any great talk about it at home. I would have known that Kerry were playing Galway, but the notion of going never entered my head until the morning of the match. I had been to first Mass and was standing outside the church with two or three others, one of them my cousin Johnnie Carr, when Fr Alex McMullan came round from the vestry and out through the gate to speak to us.

He spoke first to Johnnie indicating that he would be ready to leave at 11.30 and then he spoke to the rest of us and asked, 'Would any of you like to go to the match in Dublin?' Neither of the other two boys was interested but I jumped at the invitation, for I had never been back in Dublin since the Eucharistic Congress, nor had I ever seen an Inter-County Gaelic match of any substance before.

'I would like to go, Father,' I told him, and was advised to be back at the parochial house at the appointed time.

When I broke the news to my mother and assured her that I had enough money left from my boat earnings upstairs, she replied, 'I hope you have, for I have very little.' However, when I was leaving the house she pressed a half-crown into my hand. 'That will get you your tea,' she said.

As we went down the Newry Road Fr Alex advised us that he had to come back directly after the match, but that he had arranged for us to come home in one of McAnulty's taxis which was going to the game. He gave us details of the pick-up point and the leaving time, 11 o'clock and not a minute later, at the Rotunda. The wonder of the day ahead was already away beyond my expectations, and to imagine myself in Dublin at 11 o'clock at night was something else. We talked football and we sang most of the way down, but now, 70 years on, as I put myself in the back seat of that small Standard car, it is the goodness of the two people sitting in front of me which comes to mind.

Fr Alex succeeded Fr Dargan in late 1935 and revived a moribund St Peter's Club in his first year. While he did not know it at the time, he was to complete the biggest part of his priesthood in the parish of Clonallon, for as Canon McAllister advanced in age and infirmity, it fell to the curate to take over the running of the parish. In those days the clergy did not retire, they died in harness.

Canon McAllister had few interests beyond the spiritual welfare of his flock and the physical fabric of the churches and schools in the parish. I remember him well for two particular incidents, the first being the decision to dispense with the services of the school choir; the second occurred at the collection in the church one Sunday morning. I did not witness the incident, but it was widely discussed at the time. The collection required a layman with a pencil and notebook to record the names and amounts of the contributions called out by the Canon and the curate. When the plate was put in front of Frank Connolly, known as Yank Connolly and a member of the local council in my father's time, he put a threepenny piece on it. The Canon looked at the plate and looked at Frank before commenting, 'Ah now, Frank, you can do better than that.' But Frank didn't do better and when the plate moved to the next seat he got up and left the church. Thereafter he attended Mass in Rostrevor, walking when the weather was suitable and when it wasn't he travelled in one of McAnulty's taxis. I do believe his funeral took place in Rostrevor, though in those days Mass was not the norm at funerals.

Fr Alex had the job of looking after both the parish and the Canon for over twenty years. He had a great affinity with the place for his grand-uncle had been administrator of Clonallon many years before. He was chairman of St Peter's Club for his entire sojourn in The Point, as well as serving a six-year term as chairman of the Down Board, during which Down appeared in its first two Ulster Senior Finals.

My cousin Johnnie comes even more vividly to mind. About four years older than me, he was one of the emerging stars of Down football. We were both at The Abbey at this time and he would probably have made his debut for the Down team before this. He certainly played a month later, when he fielded for them at Hilltown against Armagh in a National League game. A penalty kick struck by him was the deciding score in one of Down's occasional wins over the neighbours. When he was still at school he was selected for the Ulster Railway Cup team.

Even at nineteen, he had a beautiful tenor voice, and the town 'listened in' to hear him compete in a competition sponsored by John McCormack, on what was then Radio Athlone. *'Erin the Tear and the Smile in Thine Eye'* was what he chose to sing and the town agreed that 'he sang it well, but he was a bit nervous.'

However, the competition was won by a Down man, Hugo Stirling of Portaferry, and there was some compensation in that.

Driving down to Dublin that day no one would have been thinking of War, but before the All-Ireland Final of the next year was played, Europe was again in the throes of conflict. To say that it ended and changed many lives is the most basic statement which can be made about it. It changed Johnnie's life, for he and hundreds of others from the northern counties answered the call for volunteers for the National Army. He thrived on the military life and hoped to make it a career. His football stature was enhanced for he was a leading light in Down's first Ulster Final appearance against Cavan in 1940. Sad to relate, before the War ended, he fell ill and was invalided out of the Army. He died in 1948 at 28 years of age, which fact reminds me that another Point man, Sean Crawford, was also invalided out of the Army and died a comparatively young man.

Now I am in Dublin on my way to Croke Park, for my first time. Fr Alex was fortunate in having a ticket for one of the stands. I followed Johnnie and in no time at all we were entering the ground at the Canal End and viewing the Cusack Stand for the first time—a breathtaking experience. The stand had only been opened earlier that year and even the pictures which had appeared in the newspapers had not prepared me for the massive construction. Compared with this, Windsor Park did not rate. I was most impressed and even open-mouthed, as we wended our way across the Canal End to stand underneath this massive mountain of stepped concrete and steel. The pre-match preliminaries with the Artane Boys' Band, the parade, the rolling cheers and finally *A Soldier's Song* all combined to satisfy my deepest patriotic instincts. The atmosphere generated by those two rows of marching men, all seemingly like giants, with every face signalling determination even unto death, was overwhelming. I couldn't wait for the game to begin.

I have to confess that I went to this game with a completely open mind, aware that I was seeing Gaelic football at this level for the first time. By the end of the first quarter I was committed to Galway, but even more importantly, I had come to the conclusion that Gaelic football was not for me. There was a ruthlessness about the Kerry defence which to my ordered soccer mind was almost savage. I am not sure if this was Joe Keohane's first final, but I am sure that any Galway man who came within hand or foot range of him was in physical danger. In the course of the game I think Keohane injured himself trying to get at one of his opponents and had to retire. He got no sympathy from me. This was a Kerry team which featured such names as Charlie O'Sullivan, Bill Casey, Willie Myers and Paddy Kennedy.

Over the hour Galway were a much more constructive side, playing a type of football I could appreciate. Even though they were much the better side the game was in the balance right to the end, and I was slightly disappointed that Kerry managed a draw. The replay did not bring me back to Croke Park, but it brought some satisfaction to me that Galway won when they met a couple of weeks later.

Disappointing as the game was, it did not in any way cloud my expectations, which increased every step of the way to an O'Connell Street that I was walking for the first time. To begin with, we had a wonderful tea for which my mother's half-crown amply covered my share of the bill. Then it was out into the street and if it was all new to me, it certainly wasn't new to my cousin.

'We'll go to the Palm Grove; they've powerful ice cream there,' he suggested, and that's where we headed, to begin for me a hugely satisfying relationship with the ice cream parlour. When I read of its closure some years ago the memory of that initial visit, on that special day so many years before, evoked the mixture of a smile and a tear.

Mixed grill consumed, *Knickerbocker Glory* experienced for the first time, our thoughts turned to entertainment, for it was still only 7 o'clock and we had four hours left. But first we had to do our shopping, and mine began and ended quickly with that most traditional present of the time, the bar of rock, which being brought to Warrenpoint was like bringing coals to Newcastle. It took a little longer to decide which picture we were going to see, but after a quick tour of the cinemas around O'Connell Street we opted for *Pinocchio,* the wooden puppet who made his debut on the world stage that year, 1938, with a very pertinent story about lying and long noses. Like the Palm Grove, the cinema is now non-existent but *Pinocchio* is alive and well and still entrancing young and not so young.

Our enthralment with the puppet over, it was out into the still throbbing street. The realisation that we still had twenty minutes left before pick-up time prompted one last indulgence. It was back to the Palm Grove for a quick one, a lesser helping than the Knickerbocker Glory, but still a taste to savour. On the dot of 11 we were at the Rotunda where Frank (Jockey) Burns was already showing signs of impatience for we were the first to arrive. The remainder of the load, comprising half the Collins family and Francie Grant, all from Moygannon, arrived *en bloc*. A good sing-song all the way home ended the best day of my 15 years.

Grandmother Carr (Nellie Sharkey) with Bernard and James on chair

The long Meeting 1929
Back row left to right : ?? Mick Fay, James Brown, Tommy Gracey, ????
Front Row left to right : Thomas McGuigan, Hugh Carr, Peter McMahon, Thomas Brown, Frank Fox

An early St Peter's Team
Back row, Left to right : Michael Kerr, Henry O Neill, Tom Sands, Mick Mahon, Tom Tumilty,
Peter Bracken, Hugh O Hare, Jim Caulfield
Middle row, left to right :Barney Hanna, Willie Caulfield, Rostrevor, Hugh Brennan,
Killowen, Terry O Neill, Tom O Hare, Jack Hanna,
Front row left to right: Joe Savage, Terry McCormack, Eddie Cole , Rostrevor, Jim Cassidy, John Flynn

The Polleys approx 1932
Back row left to right: Ita, Maureen, Anne
Front row left to right : Veronica, Sarah Polley, John Polley, Eithne
Monica kneeling at front

Left to right Paddy Burns (Laddie Da), Peter Sheehy, John Magee(Skin)

Fr Alex McMullan

The Madonna

The Fairy Queen and the Saint George.

PART II

13—Matters of Coincidence

When I commenced this memoir I felt the milestones of memory were so clearly marked by each year of the calendar that I could sail through the story without any real difficulty. I have reached 1939, the most momentous year of the twentieth century. I was very unsettled in school, even though I had got my Junior Certificate the year before. It was the practice that a number of boys would do the exam after two years and I was one of them. I was due to sit it again in June, to improve my result, but at the turn of the year I knew that I had lost the concentration of the first two years. It had become evident to me that my parents were stretched to the limit. With five younger siblings and a couple older, who had taken apprenticeships at a few shillings a week, it was hard going for my father and mother. My elder sister, Molly had gone off to London to do nursing, (St James' Hospital, Balham), spending the entire War years there, and having some hair-raising experiences to record.

Brother O'Donnell, the principal at The Abbey, realised I was unsettled and gave me every encouragement, but I did not return to school after Easter. I looked forward to the boating season which was soon to follow. As well as being the owner of the *Madonna*, Stevie Bradley acted as the co-ordinator of the Red Star Line operation. All cash returns were made to him after every run and all the boat owners met in his house in Thomas Street on Sunday and Thursday nights. The Thursday night divide was essential because the first four days of the week had a substantial tourist traffic provided by bus tours operated from Larne and Bangor. These mainly northern English people came on package holidays and each day of the week were taken to different parts of the country. They would have lunch in the local hotels, mainly the Balmoral, and then it would be across to Omeath where they would experience the jaunting car trip to the Calvary at the Charity Fathers, a mile from the village. Thursday was the big day of the week when there might be as many as ten busloads. This provides a backdrop to the boats as well as giving an idea of the tourist trade of the time.

All the motor boats berthed in the dock and on occasions the tidal movements required they be moved out very early in the morning, especially so on Sundays when traffic commenced that bit earlier. On this particular Sunday, I came down knowing that Stevie would have moved the *Madonna* out to anchor, off the beach. That would be his only chore with the boat on a Sunday, for it was his nephew, Harry Peers, who acted as Sunday skipper. A number of other boats were at anchor and in due course other crew men and boys arrived. Someone took a punt and left us at our boats where we made them respectable for the passengers: seats cleaned, decks and floor scrubbed and bilge pump brought into action. If it had rained the night before this was the most demanding task of all.

This was a morning remarkable for its absolute tranquillity. The mountain masses on both sides of the lough cast reflections rather than shadows on an almost departed tide. A church bell sounded from the Omeath shore, a regular

Sunday morning sound from the Protestant Church of St Andrew's. At relatively short intervals it was joined by what we called 'the brother's bell' from the Alexian Community on the Rostrevor road, and then by the Church of Ireland's gentle tone from Church Street. These would have been the regular Sunday morning sounds, but the elements would rarely have been so generous as on this occasion. Years later, when I read Wordsworth's *'Composed upon Westminster bridge'* for the first time, I felt his words did greater justice to Carlingford Lough that day than to the Thames estuary:

> *Earth has not anything to show more fair:*
> *Dull would he be of soul who could pass by*
> *A sight so touching in its majesty.*

I had sounds as well as sights and even as I breathed the serenity of the morning, Billy Stewart, our sexton, added the commanding tones of St Peter's call to prayer and to the last Mass, a couple of hundred yards from me. I stopped whatever activity I was at, blessed myself as much from habit as from prayer, but the words 'Peter speaks' came from my lips, giving expression to the inner certainty of Christ and the church. I sat down to savour the moment and the beauty of my surroundings.

In the blinking of an eye I was in a different existence, no longer a 16-year-old boy but a mature spirit and conscious of being a light, or what I would describe now as a lumined spirit. I was experiencing an unspeakable joy. In another area of the firmament remote from me there was an aura of light which I knew was coming from the light itself. Close to this aura of light was a small number of lights which I knew to be spirits as I was. I was conscious that I would come to experience the light itself. There was no sense of time nor haste nor of personal identity, nor was I conscious of being anything but a spirit.

As suddenly as the experience began, it ended and I was still sitting in the *Madonna* but with one difference, I was now facing the Omeath shore. In the interval the tide had turned, the boat had swung round, but after my experience the beauty of the mountains and the lough seemed trivial by comparison. I stood up in the boat, grasped the narrow gunwale with both hands and addressed the Lord like a youthful Abraham, 'Lord, I will never leave this place.' These were the first words which came to mind for in the months since I had dropped out of school I was already contemplating a future which would have taken me away from The Point for lengthy periods.

By the time Harry Peers came aboard to commence the day's operation I had buried my experience deep in my consciousness where it has remained for almost 70 years. Admittedly, an odd exhumation for wonder and quest to the Lord for meaning, 'What was that about, Lord?' but never any thought of disclosure to anyone. The only man who might have believed me was Harry Peers for he used tell the most amazing stories which I half believed, until some of the senior boatmen alerted me to his limitless imagination. I never remember taking a decision to live out my life in The Point based on that unique experience, though I have to thank the Lord for blessing me with a lack of ambition and a sense of contentment.

The only occasion in my life when I referred to that morning on Carlingford Lough was in the mid-eighties, when I was responsible for a news sheet of St Peter's GAA Club, *The Gaelic Scene,* which came out in alternate weeks for a couple of years. On one occasion I was short of material, and I needed a filler in a hurry. I sat down and tried to describe the beauty of that memorable morning without ever considering the most memorable moment of it. Not in a million years would I tell that, was my thinking. Surprisingly, a number of people complimented me on 'that piece you wrote about the bells.'

For no reason other than to satisfy my vanity I attempted to write much the same descriptive piece into this book but a series of remarkable coincidences has made me tell a fuller story. In telling it now, I am mindful of 'the man in our country' during the War, who reported to the police, the military, and whoever would listen to him, that he had seen a plane fly over the hills above Rostrevor, and that he had seen a parachutist jump out of it before it crashed. A comprehensive search was carried out by both police and military, but there was no trace of plane, nor parachutist. Until the day he died, the man was known as 'Parachute Paddy'. Since I am unlikely to live as long after this telling as he did after his reporting, whatever title I get will not annoy me.

I have to encompass a period of over 60 years which is about the span the Trodden family had been part of the Warrenpoint community. Louis Trodden succeeded Master Glancy as principal of St Peter's School a short time after he married Lilian McArdle of Newry. She was a remarkably gifted singer, having won an international competition in London some time before. He completed his teaching career in St Peter's, while she became a well-known teacher of choirs and soloists. She formed the Dun Eimear singers who not only competed at *feiseanna* round the country but also at festivals across the channel. They had three children, Gráinne, Russell and Bill. Louis Trodden died in 1979. Mrs Trodden lived to an advanced age and ended her days in a local nursing home, surviving her son, Russell, who died in 1999, by a couple of years. Russell was a fine musician and as well as teaching in the school setting he had an array of private pupils. He was a great conversationalist with a sense of humour, mixed with mimicry, which only those close to him experienced. He was a deeply religious fellow who had a problem accepting some of the liturgical changes in the Mass after the Second Vatican Council.

The contents of the family home went to auction in July 2002 and, with many others, I went to view them. I had a personal interest, for not only was I friendly with all the family, but I had been chairman of a small support group of the Dun Eimear Singers, which included William Gordon, the conductor of the Warrenpoint Silver Band, Una Lawless, a talented pianist and teacher and Joe Cooper, who I will just describe as a well-known local character, raconteur, and a great friend of the Troddens.

In his younger days Louis Trodden, a Newtownhamilton native, had been active in the GAA and was largely responsible for the founding of the Glenn, John Martins club. One lot of GAA memorabilia included three or four programmes of All-Ireland Finals. One of these was the Galway-Kerry Final of 1938, my very first final. I thought, 'I'll go for that.' There were also some books in Russell's room which interested me too, but beyond these there was nothing else.

The auction was the following day, a Saturday, and I went round convinced that as far as the GAA memorabilia was concerned there was hardly likely to be anyone but myself interested. One of the first lots was a set of Canon Sheehan's novels, which hardly anyone under my own age would have read. They were ready to go for £8 when, out of respect to the memory of the Canon, I bid a tenner and got them. The GAA item came up and I thought I was generous starting at a fiver. I was surprised to hear 'ten' and lo and behold, I had to chase my 1938 programme to £75 before conceding defeat. I went to the buyer afterwards, a local man, with not the slightest interest in the GAA, and asked what he would take for the 1938 programme, but I was told politely it was not for sale.

When it came to the books in Russell's room, the few which had my interest were in separate three-shelved lots. There was little or no interest in them so I got everything that was on the six shelves for £10.

It was Monday before I went round to Dun Eimear to pay for and collect my purchases. It took quite a few runs up and down the stairs before I had the shelves cleared. In clearing the final shelf I noticed two little booklets which had lain under the books, probably for years and years. I lifted them and immediately recognised them as Catholic Truth Society publications, both written by a name out of the past which was familiar to me, Fr Daniel Considine, S.J. I put both the books into my jacket pocket and off I went with my car boot full of books; they lay in that store for months before I gave them another glance. Not so the little booklets, for while I had completely forgotten about them, they came to hand the first time I had my hand in that pocket more than a week or two later. They were each priced three pence and the front cover of the first one I looked at had the title, *Trust in God,* and underneath that title, '*Notes on retreats given by Rev. Daniel Considine, S.J.*' I opened it and skimmed over the pages, noting the subject headings, and, as my glance dropped to the bottom of a page, I noticed a sentence in Latin and in italics three words, *Secretum meum mihi,* with a footnote above it. I looked to the foot of the page for its meaning, 'My secret to myself'.

I looked at the small paragraph to get the context in which it was set, and I read, 'Those favoured souls to whom God grants consolation in prayer are inclined to guard their secret jealously. "*Secretum meum mihi,*" says Holy Scripture. Such things are too sacred to be talked about.'[3]

This is just a week or two after I had written my draft of the happenings of that Sunday morning, without mentioning the most momentous moments of it. I had to ask myself, is this just an amazing coincidence or is the Lord telling me something? I settled for coincidence when I resumed writing, and moved on to another topic.

On the first Saturday of September there was an item in *The Irish Times* indicating that a conference sponsored by the G. K. Chesterton Institute of Sefton Hall University, New Jersey, would be held in Maynooth on 13–15 September. The conference had been arranged for the previous year, but because of the events

---

3   Rev. D. Considine, S.J., *Trust in God*, London, 1958, p. 14. *Secretum meum mihi*, Isaiah 24;17.

in New York on 11 September 2001 it had been called off. At the time, *The Irish Times* had a religious affairs correspondent named John Cooney, who was to have been one of the contributors at the original 2001 conference. Whether or not he was asked to take part in the conference of September 2002, I'm not sure, but he bad-mouthed the conference, and those who were organising it, on the Saturday before it was due to take place. I think John takes the view that we should sever our links with Rome and found a national church which will cater for everyone, from free thinkers to free Presbyterians. I must confess that, over the years, John had not been my favourite commentator on things religious, especially when he wrote about the Catholic Church, and on this occasion I found him particularly offensive. If Cooney was 'agin it,' I was for it.

On the Monday morning, I picked up the phone and booked a place at Maynooth, even though I had never read Chesterton seriously. I first encountered Chesterton when I was at The Abbey, through his poem *The Donkey*, but it was stories about Chesterton which interested me as much as what he wrote himself, and especially those which dealt with his absent-mindedness.

While it had been my intention to drive down to Maynooth, my daughter Louise insisted that I should go on the train or she would drive me down and collect me on the Sunday. I travelled free on the train to Dublin and had I booked my ticket at Newry though to Maynooth, I would have had free travel all the way. It was simply wonderful to be 79 and able to enjoy the benefits of 'free travel.' As I emerged from the station at Maynooth, a passenger emerged from what I thought was a taxi, and I said to the driver, 'Taxi?'

'Oh no, that's my daughter I'm leaving,' and he added, 'where are you going?'

'I'm going to The College,' to which the kind driver responded, 'Hop in, I'll drop you up,' and that he did, to the door.

About 80 or 90 people enrolled for the seminar, many of them coming all the way from America, and with the Saturday night's entertainment being provided by John Campbell and Len Graham, two names well known to me, it turned out to be a very enjoyable weekend. During an interval on the Saturday afternoon, I was browsing at the bookstand. Beside me was a Jesuit priest, one of the three McGuckian priest brothers, whose acquaintance I had made earlier in the morning. I confided to him that I hadn't read a lot of Chesterton, and wondered where would be the best place to start.

'I haven't read a lot of him myself,' he confessed, 'but I did read *Orthodoxy*, and I think it mightn't be a bad place to start.'

I purchased *Orthodoxy*, with a couple of other titles, and when I had time to relax a couple of weeks later, I lifted the book. I have never been a very serious reader and I have the bad habit of reading the chapter headings of a book and sometimes reading a chapter whose title takes my fancy. When I looked at the chapter headings in *Orthodoxy* the one which caught my eye was *Paradoxes of Christianity*, and true to form, that's where I opened the book to read well down the page, 'The more complicated the coincidence, the less it can be coincidence.'

For several weeks I had been considering, from time to time, the remarkable coincidence presented by my purchase at the Trodden auction—and then here is Chesterton telling me, 'Barney, it's not likely to be a simple coincidence.' But the reality is that it doesn't matter whether there is a coincidence or not. Logic tells me that if I had jumped overboard from the *Madonna* all those years ago, swam ashore, and run up the beach shouting of my experience, no one would have listened to me. The boatmen would not have believed me, even if I had walked on the water from boat to shore, and certainly not Stevie Bradley who would probably have taken his pipe out of his pocket and lit up. What would have happened at our dinner table that day if I had recounted the experience? Most likely my mother would have sent for Dr O'Tierney.

Whether or not it was part of the continuing coincidence, it is a fact that a chap called Richard Dawkins came to Dublin early in February 2003, to create a bit of a stir among the intellectual classes and, in particular, the Humanist Appreciation Society at Trinity College. In case there are a few readers who have not heard of this gentleman I should advise that he has a string of academic credentials to his name, and has been named as being among the ten best intellects in the world. While collecting all those honours, he has had time to write six books since his first one in 1976. His most recent work at that time was *A Devil's Chaplain,* and its promotion probably prompted his visit to Dublin on that occasion.

During his time there he lectured at Trinity College, wrote a feature for *The Irish Times* and was a guest on Marianne Finucane's morning chat show on *RTÉ,* after which he was described as 'pompous' by Professor William Reville, scientific writer for *The Irish Times.* Dr Reville, a believing Christian, went on to state that Dawkins despises religion, particularly the Catholic Church. 'He homes in on miracles, which he labels as devices used by religion, particularly Catholicism, to hook children and unsophisticated adults.'[4]

Now if Dawkins is right, I am a fool and a bigger fool for attempting to take him on in a debate, but then the God in whom I believe has always looked kindly on fools and even used them on occasions. In fairness to Dawkins though, I have to state my own academic credentials gained at St Peter's Primary School, Carrick Primary School where I gained the Primary Certificate, and The Abbey CBS where I left with the Junior Certificate. In order not to put Dawkins at too much of a disadvantage I will not mention a day course (for 30 weeks) at the Rupert Stanley College in Belfast, nor a two weeks residential crash course in Social Studies at Manchester University, nor that outside these academic attainments I had qualified as a bus driver at the second attempt earlier in my life.

It was November 2003 when I thought I would take a look at what Dawkins had to say, so off to Newry I went and purchased the book, which is not an original, but a selection of Dawkins essays edited by Latha Menon; in other words, 'the best of Dawkins.' In her introduction she writes of the title of one of the chapters, *A prayer for my daughter,* as a summary of the themes of the volume.

'It expresses a hope that future generations will strive for an understanding of the natural world through reason and based on evidence. It is a passionate plea

4   The Irish Times, 13 March 2003

against the tyranny of mind numbing belief systems'[5]

The surprising title was my starting point of the book. It was equally surprising to learn it was borrowed from a poem by WB Yeats and it carried a sub-heading *Good and bad reasons for believing*. I went down the chapter headings to find at the very bottom of the list, *A prayer for my daughter*. The girl is ten and he confesses, unhappily, that he has only seen her for very short periods of time, when it was not easy to talk about the important things of life.

In his very first sentence to Juliet, Dawkins writes, 'I want to write to you about something that is very important to me,'[6] and proceeds to ask a series of 'how do we know' questions about the sun, moon and stars. The answer to these questions, he rightly states, is evidence. 'sometimes evidence means seeing or hearing or feeling or smelling that something is true.'[7] No one would disagree with that proposition. Dawkins then proceeds to examine 'tradition' and particularly the tradition that Mary, the mother of Jesus, was lifted into heaven, and he compares the story to Snow White and the Seven Dwarfs. Now clever man that he is, he can disprove the story of Snow White, but he can't disprove that Mary was assumed into heaven, if he does not believe that heaven exists. All he can say is that such an unlikely tale is against the Natural Law, and he doesn't believe it.

In his process of 'indoctrination,' he questions the reality of God, belief in heaven, belief that Mary never died (that's a new one to me), belief that Jesus never had a human father, belief that prayers are answered, belief that wine turns into Blood, and bread into the Body of Christ, and asserts that not one of these beliefs is backed up by any good evidence. He admits that millions of people believe them, as he states, 'Perhaps this is because they were told to believe them, when they were young enough to believe anything.' I suppose that was when they were younger than his daughter of ten, to whom he was writing on one of those rare occasions he had any contact with her.

Evidence is the key word for belief, according to Dawkins in this letter to his daughter of ten. I can only hope that she has not taken his scientific advice on affairs of the heart too seriously. He wrote:

'People sometimes say that you must believe in feelings deep inside otherwise you would never be confident of things like, "My wife loves me."

'But this is a bad argument. There can be plenty of evidence that somebody loves you. All through the day when you are with somebody who loves you, you see and hear lots of little titbits of evidence and they all add up. It isn't a purely inside feeling, like the feeling that priests call revelation. There are outside things to back up the inside feeling: looks in the eye, tender notes in the voice, little favours and kindnesses; this is all real evidence.'[8]

The only comment I would want to make on that very unscientific observation is that the Divorce Courts around the developed world are finding it difficult to keep up, dispensing marriage dissolutions to couples who thought that 'looks in

5   L. Menon (ed), A Devil's Chaplain, London, 2003, *p.* 4

6   *Ibidem, p.* 242

7   *Ibid., p.* 242

8   *Ibid., p.* 246

the eye' and 'tender notes in the voice' were the harbingers of love and happiness.

But the gem of Dawkins letter to his ten-year old daughter comes in the second last paragraph in which he explains how all the children from the various religious groups grow up

> *'... utterly convinced that they are right, and the others are wrong, and that they believe different things for exactly the same kind of reason as you speak English, and Ann Kathrin speaks German. Both languages are, in their own countries, the right language to speak. But it can't be true that different religions are right in their own countries, because different religions claim that opposite things are true. Mary can't be alive in the Catholic Republic, but dead in Protestant Northern Ireland.'[9]*

I trust little Juliet got the point.

Latha Menon is over generous in suggesting that Dawkins' *A prayer for my daughter* sums up the key themes of the volume. There is more to her hero than Mary's ability to be alive and well in the Republic (Catholic or otherwise) and dead in the North.

When my class was preparing for the verbal examination by Bishop Edward Mulhern, prior to Confirmation, Master O'Hagan told us the story of the boy who was known to be a bit of a character in the school (but not Carrick School, I hasten to add), who was asked by the Bishop, 'What do you know about the Blessed Trinity?'

'Nothing, my Lord,' the boy replied.

'Are you telling me that you are presenting yourself for Confirmation, and you know nothing about the Blessed Trinity?' asked the Bishop, almost in horror.

'That's right, my Lord,' came back the boy, 'you see, you're not supposed to know anything about it. It's a bloody mystery.'

Now that bright boy might have had the right philosophy, but according to Richard Dawkins, he had a virus of the mind, as indeed, Dawkins would claim, have all those who would have any time for any of the mysteries expounded by the Church.

As he says:

> *'Take the 'Mystery of Transubstantiation.' It is easy and non-mysterious to believe that in some symbolic sense, the Eucharistic wine turns into the Blood of Christ. The Roman Catholic doctrine of transubstantiation, however, claims far more. The whole substance of the wine is converted into the Blood of Christ; the appearance of wine that remains is 'merely accidental,' 'inhering in no substance.'[10]*

He makes no reference to the bread or the Body of Christ, but goes on to battle about the serious violence to the normal meaning of words like 'substance' and 'literally'; he proclaims 'the "mystery is a virtue" idea' comes to the aid of

---

9   Menon, A Devil's Chaplain, *pp. 247–248*

10   *Ibid., p. 138*

the Catholic, who would otherwise find intolerable the obligation to believe the obvious nonsense of the transubstantiation and the 'three in one.'[11]

Anthony Kenny observed of his own puzzlement as a young seminarian: 'For all I could tell, my own typewriter might be Benjamin Disraeli transubstantiated,'[12] though I doubt if he made the observation to the Bishop who was ordaining him. As a young priest he wrote:

> *'It was touching the Body of Christ, the closeness of the priest to Jesus, which most enthralled me. I would gaze on the host after the words of Consecration, soft eyed like a lover looking into the eyes of his beloved … Those early days as a priest remain in my memory as days of fulfilment and tremendous happiness, something precious, and yet too fragile to last, like a romantic love affair brought up short by the reality of an ill assorted marriage.'[13]*

It would appear Kenny is now a disciple of Dawkins. The latter, needless to say, is pleased with his conquest and he writes:

> *'Happily, viruses don't win every time. Many children emerge unscathed from the worst that nuns and mullahs can throw at them. Anthony Kenny's own story has a happy ending. He eventually renounced his orders because he could no longer tolerate the obvious contradictions within Catholic belief, and he is a highly respected scholar. But one cannot help remarking that it must be a powerful infection indeed that took a man of his wisdom and intelligence—now President of the British Academy, no less—three decades to fight off. Am I unduly alarmist to fear for the soul of my six-year-old innocent daughter?'[14]*

I do not know how long it is since Tony Kenny wrote what Dawkins quotes of him, but Kenny did make one observation which has special relevance for those who have a problem in accepting Church teaching.

> *'If Catholic doctrine is true, every priest validly ordained derives his orders in an unbroken line of laying on of hands, through the Bishop who ordains him, back to one of the twelve Apostles.'[15]*

While Tony goes on to have some fun with the idea of spiritual ancestry, there can be no doubt he has expressed Church teaching on Holy Orders.

I have to admit that my favourite Englishman is the now recently beatified Blessed Cardinal John Henry Newman, and I often have recourse to him if I need to seek a higher opinion on matters spiritual. For those who feel called to receive the sacrament of Holy Orders, he has a solemn warning:

---

11   *Ibid., p.* 139

12   *Ibid., p.* 138

13   *Ibid., p.* 144

14   *Ibid., p.* 145

15   *Ibid., p.* 144

'so again, those who enter Holy Orders promise they know not what, engage themselves they know not how deeply, debar themselves of the world's ways they know not how intimately, find perchance they must cut off the right hand, sacrifice the desire of their eyes and the stirring of their hearts at the foot of the Cross, while they thought, in their simplicity, they were choosing the easy life of quiet, plain men dwelling in tents.'[16]

It is a tall order to ask of any man and the wonder is that so many in the almost two thousand years of the Church gave total allegiance to Christ. In Ireland today hundreds of elderly priests, brothers and nuns who have carried Christ's message to the ends of the earth are being cared for by a declining number of younger priests, brothers and sisters in their communities. Hundreds more lie buried where they laboured, and thankfully hundreds more, clerical and lay, are living out their lives in the newly-created vineyards. All of this is for the modern era when Ireland, and indeed the Western world, is once again mission territory.

Admittedly the latest vaccine conjured up in the last century and becoming widely available in what we call the developed world, is a vaccine called 'affluence,' and it seems to be coping with the milder forms of the Christian malady, especially in Ireland.

I have no doubt that Richard Dawkins would decry some of the side effects of the affluence vaccine, as much as any believing Christian, but however long the world lasts, it ends for each of us at the hour of death. The scientific proposition as espoused by him is that death is the end, as against the Christian view, that death is a new beginning.

Douglas Adams, the author of The *Hitchhiker's Guide to the Galaxy,* is another individual for whom Dawkins had tremendous respect. He delivered the eulogy at his funeral service in 2001. Dawkins refers to his friend as having a Damascus experience even though the original Damascus experience was a fake, if Dawkins is to be believed. It came for Adams after he had made acquaintance with a particular modern book on evolution, and of which he spoke in the following terms:

'It all fell into place. It was a concept of such stunning simplicity, but it gave rise naturally, to all the infinite and baffling complexity of life. The awe it inspired in me made the awe that people talk about in respect of religious experience seem, frankly, silly beside it. I'd take the awe of understanding over the awe of ignorance any day.'[17]

On another occasion, Adams was interviewed impromptu by Dawkins on a television programme, and he is all the more passionate for that:

'The world is a thing of inordinate complexity and richness and strangeness that it is absolutely awesome. I mean the idea that such complexity can arise not only out of such simplicity, but probably absolutely out of nothing, is probably the most fabulous extraordinary idea. And once

---

16   I. Ker, *Newman On being a Christian*, London, 1990, p. 113

17   *Ibid., p.* 170

you get some kind of inkling of how that might have happened—it's just wonderful. And... the opportunity to spend 70 or 80 years of your life in such a universe is time well spent, as far as I am concerned.'[18]

I could be standing shoulder to shoulder with Adams sharing the awe at the simplicity and the complexity of the universe but for one thing, something even more simple and even more complex; the coming of Jesus Christ into our world. What could be simpler than the birth of a child? What could be more complex than that child in manhood leaving us Himself, in the Eucharist, and with the promise, not of 70 or 80 years in his company, but of eternity? Transubstantiation is of greater simplicity in its basic ingredients of bread and wine, and of even greater complexity than the universe itself.

There can be no doubt that this outstanding man Adams deserved any tribute Dawkins could pay him, but to suggest that there is any relevance to what happens to his body, and a conclusion that there is nothing else after death, is not a scientific proposition. Dawkins cannot come to a conclusion on something he believes does not exist. All he can say is that he simply does not believe it. But I have one great advantage over the Dawkinses of this world. I have had a live preview of the beginnings of an after-life. The experience does not give me an automatic right of entry into the Lord's presence, for I was not aware of a judgement. I am aware that I will face one, and that it will be a just one.

Richard Dawkins has asked for evidence. I have given my evidence and he cannot disprove it. All that he can say is that he does not believe my story, or that I am a fool with a vivid imagination.

I cannot be sure that it was part of the same coincidence which drove me to Dawkins, but it is also a fact that when I purchased *A Devil's Chaplain,* a title on another shelf caught my eye: *I was a teenage Catholic.* Its author, Malachi O'Doherty, is a contributor to BBC television and radio programmes as well as the writer of a column in the *Belfast Telegraph.* On the front cover of the book below the author's name was a comment from *The Irish Times,* 'O'Doherty has taken on God, in a frank, compelling and committed dialogue.' A comment on that comment is that it was hardly a dialogue. God hardly got a word in.

I have two reasons for introducing Malachi's book; the first is to note the fact that Fr Oliver Crilly, A well-known priest in the Derry Diocese, had told him 'that all the CTS[19] pamphlets had come under his control when he headed the Catholic Information Service. He had them all buried in a landfill site which is now under the road out to The Point Depot in Dublin.' Obviously Fr Oliver did not do his job very well for he missed the two I found on Russell Trodden's bookshelves. If he had done his job properly this book might never have seen the light of day.

The second is to note that in much the same way as Dawkins, Malachi regards faith and God as an intellectual challenge, overlooking the fact that most of us are not up to intellectual challenge. I have already quoted from Ian Kers'

---

18   *Ibid., p.* 170

19   Catholic Truth Society

Newman on being a Christian, and I am back to its very first page, where Newman's reaction to one of his younger brothers abandoning the Christian faith is dealt with. He wrote:

> *'The rejection of Christianity rises from a fault of the heart, not of the intellect, since a dislike of the contents of Scripture is at the bottom of unbelief. Hence, the most powerful arguments for Christianity do not convince, only silence; for there is at the bottom that secret antipathy for the doctrines of Christianity, which is quite out of the reach of arguments.'*

Long before he became a Catholic, Newman was well conscious of the corruption in the Church and he came to realise that corruption was inseparable from a living Church, 'things that do not admit of abuse have very little life in them.' I leave Newman with one final quotation on the Church:

> *'Christ has so willed it, that we should get at the truth, not by ingenious speculations, reasoning or speculations of our own, but by teaching. The Holy Church has been set up from the beginning as a solemn religious fact... as a picture, a revelation of the next world, as itself the Christian Dispensation.'*

In truth, when I read the reference to the *Catholic Truth Society* booklets in Malachi's book I thought of Chesterton's *dictum,* 'the more complicated the coincidence, the less it can be coincidence.' I return to the quote which set this chapter in motion, namely *secretum meum mihi*. Without telling him my interest, I asked Fr Oliver Treanor, a priest friend, a scriptural scholar and a fine scriptural preacher, if he could place it for me. I showed him the booklet and wondered if he had ever heard of its Jesuit author, Fr Considine. He hadn't. When I met him again in a couple of weeks he said, 'I couldn't find, nor place that quotation. I doubt if it's scriptural.' Then he added with a smile, 'You know, you couldn't be up to those Jesuits.'

So, on the most important question which man has to consider, 'Is there an after-life?' Richard Dawkins says, 'No way, such a notion is a virus of the mind.' Malachi O'Doherty is an 'iffer'. If God exists, is the quandary he poses for himself, while coming up with insights which are as close to the reality of God as one can get.

Barney Carr, the third name in this distinguished trinity, was never a doubting Thomas, and it is not to be wondered at, that on odd occasions over the years he has pondered the significance of the experience of that summer Sunday in 1939. I would have been happy enough taking my secret to the grave, but the thought of the Lord saying to me at our planned meeting, 'Did you not get the message I sent for Dawkins and O'Doherty?' has made me cover that eventuality.

In the course of re-writing this chapter, it occurred to me that the date and time of my experience is etched in time and history, by virtue of the fact that it occurred at low water on a Sunday in the month of June, July or August of 1939, a statistic which should not be too hard to locate, and it had to coincide with the times of the church services on the day. About three days later, I was on my way home from Mass as Jim McCart was emerging with an elderly couple from Ardkeen Court where he lives. He bid me, 'Good morning, Bernard,' and added as an after-thought, 'Today's tide is the highest of the year.'

I may have asked him, 'Is that right?,' but I didn't break my step. Passing the Orange Hall I thought, 'that's a bit of a coincidence,' I am interested in a low-tide of the thirties and Jim tells me about a high-tide of 2003. It dawned on me that Jim, a former long-time member of the Harbour Authority, might have access to a tidal calendar of some kind, so later that day I rang him to ask if he and his visitors had been discussing tides, when I passed them earlier. He assured me they weren't.

'Why did you tell me it's was the highest tide of the year?' I asked.

'I had no reason, I was just after reading it in the paper,' he replied.

Without telling him why, I gave Jim the task of checking where I would get information on the tidal times for the summer of 1939.

Two weeks later, when I had not heard from him, I contacted him again and after his profuse apologies he assured me, 'I'll ring you back in a couple of hours.'

Well inside that limit, he rang back, giving me a phone number which turned out to be that of Bidson Observatory on Merseyside. It was on a Thursday evening when I spoke to two very courteous ladies in that establishment, indicating the information I was after. On Saturday morning, I received the Warrenpoint tidal charts for the entire summer of 1939, on a date-only sequence. The only day and date which I remembered for the summer of 1939 was Sunday 3rd September, the day Neville Chamberlain declared War on Germany, so I was able to put days on dates.

I had to ring back to Bidson on Monday for clarification of a hand-written note indicating the commencement of British Summer Time. I also had to take into consideration that Mass times changed for the summer months. Finally, I came to the conclusion that the experience I have described could only have happened on one of two Sundays, 9 or 23 July 1939. This fact provided me with a problem with which I have struggled for much longer than it is taking to write about. Low water on 9 July was at 11.33 A.M. On 23 July, it was at 11.34 A.M. Now I had always been of the opinion that my 'experience of the spirit' lasted for the length of time it took the Madonna to swing round on the flowing tide. The tidal times tell me now it must have lasted almost 35 minutes if it began seconds after St Peter's bell rang around 11 A.M.

It might interest some 'ancient mariners' in The Point and Rostrevor that, in my search for tidal times, I came on a piece of nautical information which reiterates my point previously made about the healthy boating scene of that pre-War era. I have already indicated that the *St George* motor boat was owned by the Magee family and was licensed to carry 140 passengers. In or before 1939 it was purchased by John Tinnelly of Rostrevor. I quote from the Newry Reporter of 26 August 1939:

> *'John Tinnelly, Rostrevor, was summoned by District Inspector Nelson for carrying 12 excess passengers on his motor boat, the St George on July 16th. In evidence, Sergeant Donoghue gave evidence that he counted 152 passengers on board the boat, 12 more than it was permitted to carry.*

The RM imposed a fine of two shillings and costs, plus one shilling per head for each of the extra passengers.'

In February 2006 Richard Dawkins presented two hour-long programmes on television based on his book, *A Devil's Disciple*. If he does another, I trust he will invite me to take part.

On Sunday, 23 July 2006 I heard Tony Kenny for the first time. He was a guest on the morning radio Sunday Sequence programme. I was a listener sitting at my breakfast on Summerhill. Tony is now Master of Balliol College, Oxford, a source from which one would expect clarity of thought and expression. This ordained priest, now happily married, forsook the priesthood and the Church because, like Dawkins, he could not accept the reality of Christ and an after-life. In the course of the interview he confessed that in times of stress he prayed, but to whom he prayed or to what purpose, he could not speculate. I can only comment that Tony sounded a very confused Master of Balliol.

In October 2006, Richard Dawkins produced another book, *The God Delusion*, related to his two television programmes which were based on his previous book, and the bewildering cycle continues. It was sheer chance that I heard Dawkins being confronted by David Quinn, a journalist and a believing Christian with a sense of mission, on an *RTÉ* morning programme. Dawkins dismisses the hard questions, and particularly the question of free will, by declaring that it is 'a difficult philosophical question and it is not one that has anything to do with religion.' Nor was Dawkins very forthcoming when Quinn asked about the origin of matter. 'We are working on it,' he proclaimed.

On Sunday 3 December I was late tuning into Sunday Sequence but in time to hear that the full programme on 10 December would feature the man himself, Dawkins. I wondered if I would have anything to contribute to the discussion and after giving some thought to the matter I felt that I had. The next day, Monday, I tried to contact the producer but he was out of the country. On Thursday I rang again to be put in touch with a production assistant. When I told him I might have something to contribute to the programme he asked, 'Which side or you on?'

'What do you mean, which side am I on?' I asked back of him.

'Are you a creationist or an evolutionist?'

I replied, 'I suppose basically I'd be a creationist but that doesn't rule evolution out of the picture.'

I went on to tell him that I was more concerned with Dawkins' claim that there was nothing after death. 'I'm more concerned with where I'm going than where I came from,' I said. He was a very personable fellow and the discussion closed with his assurance that he would be back to me after he had a discussion with the producer. In the meantime I spoke to the Lord, 'If You want me on the programme I'll be on it.' When I returned home in the evening there was a polite message on the answering machine indicating that all places had been allocated.

On Sunday morning I listened to the entire programme and marvelled at the eloquence of most of the contributors, including a Warrenpoint man, Fr Feidhlimidh Magennis. The entire discussion centred on where we all came from, not a word about our destination, and that is my main concern. The Lord knew it was no place for me so it is unlikely that I will ever tangle verbally with Richard Dawkins.

On 6 January 2009 an atheistic advertising campaign at a cost of £140,000 was launched on British buses and on the London Underground. The advert stated, 'There's probably no God. Now stop worrying and enjoy your life.' Supporters at the launch included the scientist Richard Dawkins, the philosopher A.C. Grayling and Graham Linehan, a co-writer of the Fr Ted comedy series.

I have a piece of good news for these three very sensible men and for all who would think like them. Even as the printers and the slogan stickers were at their work, I was experiencing a most tender, loving, forgiving and reassuring God. An experience, need I say, too personal to relate in this book.

14—The War Games

Conscious as I am that this was meant to be a 'mainly sporting memoir,' I find after that run through my life, which has knocked the chronological balance of this book awry, it is extremely difficult to get back into a 1939 mode: to recall listening on the radio to the British Prime Minister, Neville Chamberlain, declaring War on Germany on that first Sunday of September. It was also the day of the All-Ireland Hurling Final, a match which I was hardly aware of at the time. One was very conscious of the foreboding expressed by a generation of parents who had vivid memories of the events of the Great War which had got under way 25 years before. For our family it brought almost instant concern for my eldest sister, Molly, who was working in London during the War.

In a roundabout sort of way it was the outbreak of War which brought me into the GAA, in what was a real Damascene conversion.

By the spring of 1940, Britain was girding itself for War with thousands of young Englishmen, Scots and Welsh dispersed in their regiments in towns and villages over the North of Ireland, all training in a massive preparation for battle. For the first year there were no soldiers based in Warrenpoint, but the Welsh Regiment had a couple of battalions in Newry, where they had a team or two in the Newry Summer League. Before my brothers opted for Gaelic football they had played in the summer league for teams organised by a chap called Jimmy Toman; he used to push a three-wheeler bicycle from Newry to The Point, complete with a freezer of ice cream which he sold as penny pokes and sliders. He met me one day and asked if I would play for his team and I agreed.

All the games were on the Newry Town pitch and in my third outing the opposition was provided by the Welsh Regiment. They were a slightly older and much heavier side, though we were more than holding our own coming up to half-time, with no goals having been scored. Like my hero, Peter Doherty, I was playing at inside right and, though I say it myself, I gave a beautiful pass to our left winger. He made headway down the line as I proceeded forward. He then sent a great cross back to me and I threw myself at the ball, connecting with my head in the most spectacular fashion only to see my effort go inches past the upright. There was applause from my teammates and 'even the ranks of Tuscany could scarce forbear a cheer'[20]. One of the Welsh players ran to help me to my feet and as he clapped my back, exclaimed several times, 'Hard luck, Paddy,' 'Well done, Paddy'. Now the chap meant well but little did he realise that he might as well have been hitting me on the head with a hammer, as calling me 'Paddy'. I had not the slightest animosity to the British Army, despite my own national instincts, but to be called 'Paddy' and by a Welshman, was, to my sensitivities, deeply offensive. We changed ends at half-time and in the course of the second half, a number of the opposition addressed me as 'Paddy,' 'Sorry, Paddy,' 'Well done, Paddy' or even 'Watch it, Paddy'. To add to the evening's indignities we lost for the first time in three games. Jimmy Toman gave me a shilling for my bus fare which cost nine pence and off I went home with a slight resentment for all Welshmen other than

---

20   Thomas Babington Macauley (1800–1859), *Horatius*

my Cardiff cousins. I never would have dreamt of calling one of them Taffy.

The next morning I was going down Campbell's Lane when I met Philip McKernan with newspaper open and pipe in mouth. Paper down, pipe in hand, he greeted me. 'I saw you getting on the bus last night with your brown paper parcel under your arm. Were you going up to play soccer?'

Phil was now the secretary of St Peter's Club, and I remind readers that he was one of the three-man inquisition which suspended me for going to see my Uncle Hugh playing all those years before.

'Yes I was,' I replied. 'We were playing the Welsh regiment and they beat us.' 'They didn't beat you half enough,' he replied.

We bandied words for a few seconds and I asked him, 'Philip am I suspended?' 'Not at all; sure you never played for The Point. How could you be suspended?' 'Right then,' I ventured, 'I'll not be playing soccer anymore and if I get my place on The Point team, I'll play.'

In due course I got notification to be at McAnultys on a Sunday for a game at Glenn, where I made my debut in the blue jersey. Most seventeen-year olds would have switched codes with very little concern one way or the other, but I found it a very big decision to give up soccer.

It would not be my intention to dwell too long on individual games, but that very first one at Glenn set me wondering if I had made the right decision. The notion of confronting the O'Hares of Glenn had not come into my thinking, but with Black Paddy, Peter, Colman and Kevin in action that day, I realised I was not quite mature enough for this level of contest, so I kept out of the action as much as possible. My progress was slow, but the team had been knitting together for a few years and was beginning to show some semblance of cohesion. There were no teams in either Burren or Rostrevor, so players from those parts were available to other clubs. The Point was fortunate to have the services of Terry McCormack, the son of James the blacksmith, Eddie Cole, also from Rostrevor, and John McClorey from Burren. All three were established county players, though while Eddie did not have the prominence of the other two, he was one of the great clubmen of my time. Not only did McClorey play for Down, but he was also honoured by Ulster on a number of occasions and this in an era when the Railway Cup was second in status only to the All-Ireland Championship.

If my introduction to Gaelic football did not make the headlines in 1940 there was one thing which did, and it was the occasion of Down's first appearance in an Ulster Senior Final at Breffni Park where they met the reigning Champions, Cavan. My brothers were already figuring in Down teams and I would have been actively supporting them, but it was the thought of playing in an Ulster decider which really set the imagination going. Down had beaten Tyrone, and then Monaghan, to qualify for the final and there was a great surge of enthusiasm in the county. The enthusiasm was especially strong in The Point, which was providing four members of the team, Terry McCormack, John McClorey, my cousin Johnnie and my brother Gerry (Joker). I think my other brother Hugh was a sub. Such was the excitement in our household that both my father and mother were talked into going. I think my mother was seeing her first football match, certainly her first

Gaelic football match. The whole town seemed to be aboard the train that morning as it pulled out of The Point station to a chorus of cheering and corncrake rattles. In reality, it was the greatest football occasion of my life until then, and I was savouring every minute of it.

It's a long road to Cavan by train, and the nearer we got the greater were all our expectations. I did not go to the game in the company of my parents, but joined 'the boys'. We were parading to our seats on the sideline, a raucous bunch, complete with all kinds of homemade colours, corncrakes and bells, when we were accosted by a gentleman who, while known to me, would not have been recognised by any of the others in the assembly. It was John Henry King who had been county chairman for a number of years and a very well-known figure in the GAA at the time.

'What are you fellows doing? Do you think you are at a soccer match?' he asked to an incredulous gang, in a well-polished voice. One equally well-polished voice, that of Louis 'Bunny' O'Hare, answered from the gang, 'I wonder if you would go and take a running jump at yourself, sir,' which riposte brought a thunderous cheer, and sent John Henry off in dismay and disgust.

The story of that first Down versus Cavan meeting is still hurtful to recall; Down simply did not perform on the day and while it was still a noisy train on the way home, there was no concealing the general disappointment.

There was one great moment left to savour, and it came when we were all settled and my grand-aunt Mary, on her way home from her Sunday night *céilí*, called to see how we had enjoyed the match

'Well Minnie, did you enjoy the football?'

My mother stopped in her tracks and with an accusing finger pointing to my father declared slowly and solemnly, 'I am never going out with that man again. He disgraced me today before the whole of Cavan.' Defeated or not, everybody went to bed laughing that night.

If the Ulster Final result was a disappointment, there was some compensation for The Point a few months later when St Peter's won the Down Junior Championship for the second time, and I was the proud and fortunate fellow to be getting a Championship medal in my debut season. I couldn't wait for the new season to come.

At that time the new season really began with the Railway Cup semi-finals, and the announcement of the Ulster selection was an eagerly awaited event. When the team was selected with three Down names included there was a local sense of achievement, for two of them were Point men, John McClorey and Johnnie Carr. The other was Brother Mick Lynch, a De la Salle brother, who played, along with a couple of others from his community, for Downpatrick. Both he and Johnnie Carr had been reserves the year before.

In this second year of the War there was no private transport, and from this part of the world there was no public transport which would get one anywhere near Cavan on a Sunday in February, so the country tuned in to Micheál O'Hehir for the broadcast of the game. Imagine the shock it was for Down listeners, to hear him announce that John McClorey had had an accident on the way to the game and would not be able to play. Johnnie Carr, who had travelled with him in the taxi, was playing, so everyone was puzzled at the turn of events which did not unfold until Johnnie and Terry McCormack arrived back in McAnulty's taxi, driven by James 'Stokes' Mackrell.

After picking up McClorey at his home along the Corrags Road, 'Stokes' headed for Newry. He had hardly gone a mile when engine trouble developed. After examination the defect was traced to the petrol feed to the carburettor. In those days the engine cover was lifted from both sides and some cars had what was called a running board. At the time, John McClorey worked at Jimmy Byrne's garage in Warrenpoint and he would have had a fair knowledge of car mechanics. With one foot on the running board and the other leg on the mudguard he was manipulating the feed pipe as the car moved slowly forward. Suddenly the car shot forward and the unfortunate McClorey was thrown off and in to the ditch of the narrow road. The car stopped, the others all got out to assist as John got to his feet, dusted himself down and declared bravely, 'Oh, I'm all right boys.'

The car proceeded to Cavan and the players were having lunch in the hotel in Cavan town when it was noticed that John was not his normal self and, in fact, was not tuned in to the day's events. It became obvious that he had severe concussion. He was taken to Cavan Hospital and detained for a few days before being allowed home.

My first taste of Inter-County football came when the minor Championship got under way in 1941; I was delighted to get a place in the team which played Armagh in the opening round. Our victory there gained us a semi-final place against Antrim at Corrigan Park in a game we looked to have won, but the home side equalised on the stroke of time to earn a replay with us at Newcastle. Partnering me in the middle of the field, both at Corrigan Park and at Newcastle, was Jack Shortt and opposing us were John Gallagher and Frank McCorry, both of whom went on to do great things for Antrim. They did great things for Antrim minors in that replay, for they put us out of the Championship. Both Jack Shortt and Frank McCorry entered the priesthood and both later shared a passion for golf. Fr Jack, alas, died on a golf course in Wellington, New Zealand, where he had gone to minister. Thankfully, Fr Frank is still going strong in retirement. On at least one occasion he took the Irish amateur title. John Gallagher, who had a distinguished career in the Irish Army, died a number of years ago.

If there was some disappointment in being knocked out of the minor Championship that year it was soon forgotten, for the Point were playing in the Down Senior Championship for the first time in many years and, might I add, playing really well. So well, that we qualified for our first senior final ever and against Bryansford, who were the dominant force in Down football at the time. They had won the two previous years and were out to complete the hat trick. They were one of the great club teams of my lifetime. Physically they were the biggest club team I have ever played against, but they did not depend on their height and strength for they had a very constructive approach to their game. John O'Hare, Paddy Howard, Bill Keating, Paddy Steele, Mickey King, Jim Joyce, Tommy Hannity,

John King, all giants, mixed up with Tommy McCann, Peter Reavey, Jay Steele, Pearse McConvey, and Charlie McConville. Until recently there were two survivors of that great team, Pearse McConvey and Charlie McConville. Sadly Pearse died quite recently to leave Charlie the last man standing.

Our team did well to get to the final for we were weakened the entire season by the absence of three of our best men who had enlisted in the Army, Johnnie Carr, Pat Finnison and my brother, Hugh. While they could get leave for Inter-County games there was no such a thing for club games. It was understandable enough in the circumstances of the time, for it would have been a nice 'how do ye do' if the country was invaded on a Sunday and half the armed forces were all over the place playing football.

A few days before the game we received an unexpected blow when we got word that Terry McCormack, our captain and midfielder, might not be available because of work obligations. Terry had gone to work in the Belfast shipyard where Sunday work on occasions was obligatory and this particular Sunday was one of them. Being the man he was, McCormack had every hope that he would be able to make Newcastle in time for the game. One memory of the day is of The Point team and mentors anxiously watching the gate and their watches for the advent of our captain, but he failed to make it. Even through the first half, in which he was badly missed, there was a hope that he might be there by the interval, but on the resumption we took to the field as we were. We lost the game by two points and we entered the dressing room to be greeted by a very sober faced McCormack; he was almost in tears, and looking more distressed than any of us who had been playing.

Terry's tale of woe was centred in the wartime traffic restriction which ruled out private motoring, restricted taxis to a ten-mile radius from their base and permitted the minimum of public transport, especially on Sundays. The bold McCormack had explored every avenue and had ascertained in the days before that a bus left Belfast at 2 P.M. on Sundays for Ballynahinch. Even though he was not due to finish work until 3 P.M., he was on that bus. From Ballynahinch he thumbed lifts on anything which was moving in the direction of Newcastle, be it car, tractor, pony and trap or bicycle. Of course, he never stopped walking or jogging between lifts and he eventually arrived at St Patrick's park about five minutes from the end of the game, more physically drained than any of us. Terry blamed himself for letting the team down, but everybody else blamed the War.

Earlier I have described being present at a game in Maggie Connolly's field between The Point and Kilkeel which had to be abandoned; now I cannot leave that hallowed spot without recalling another abandoned game in which I was a participant. Annaclone were the visitors and Terry McCormack and I were opposed in the middle of the field by Dan Morgan and John Killian. Killian was small of stature but a real dynamo who would never give up. He was a real 'pocket battleship' and covered an amazing amount of ground in a game. He got into contention with one of our defenders, Jim Collins, a Moygannon man who lived a few fields up the lane from the pitch. Blows were struck and in seconds there was turmoil as his brothers and neighbours got involved. It didn't end until a shout went up, 'Killian's hurt' and it stopped immediately. The bold John was on the floor semi-conscious. There were no water carriers in those days, but Mrs Connolly herself appeared like Florence Nightingale with jug and glass. It took some minutes before John got shakily to his feet. The referee wisely decided not to continue with the game and while most of our team retired to the barn, the arguments continued on the field.

In the course of dressing, someone remarked, 'Thank God we'll not be going to Annaclone again this year.' We had already played them at home. Joe McGuigan, who was the club secretary, silenced us with the information, 'Well, I have to tell you that I wrote to Annaclone on Thursday accepting their invitation to their Sevens next Sunday.' He added, 'The committee will decide on Tuesday night whether you go or not.' Tuesday night came and the committee decided that we would fulfil our obligation to Annaclone, for sports and Sevens were an integral part of the sporting fabric in every parish in those wonderful days.

It was with a little foreboding that we travelled to Annaclone the following Sunday. I am not sure whether we won the tournament or not, but in any event the draw kept The Point and Annaclone apart. I do clearly recall half-time of our first game when John Killian came out to the middle of the field to shake hands with all the members of The Point seven.

In later years, and long after we had both finished with football, I would meet John in The Point every 'Fifteenth,' and always with the same warm handshake which he extended to us the day of the Sevens. I have to confess, though, that I never had any reservations about going to Annaclone, for the first day I ever played there, Pat and Hugh Barney Tumilty, two well-known pig dealers, introduced themselves to me advising that they were the same Tumilty connection as the Warrenpoint Tumiltys. I think most of the Tumilty families in Down must have had their roots in Annaclone, for Joe Tumilty of Downpatrick, a well-known football name before my time, and whom I did not meet until 1960, was the image of my uncle, Hugh Tumilty. Another Annaclone man, Briany Tumilty, who travelled to America with us in 1962, would have passed for one of my Welsh cousins. It did not surprise me to learn, after his death, that Briany was a cousin of Pat and Hugh Barney.

While Gaelic games provided an outlet for sporting battles, the overall picture of life in The Point and elsewhere was dominated by the War. Even though the declaration of the conflict had been in September 1939 the real action did not begin until the spring of 1940 when the Germans overran the Netherlands, Belgium and much of France to make an invasion of Britain and Ireland a distinct possibility. Dunkirk and what was described as the Battle of Britain followed, and the British are right to claim that they stood alone and saved Europe from the tyranny of Hitler.

Our family's immediate concern was the welfare of my sister in London, whose letters often bore the imprint of the censor's blue pencil. This concern extended further to my Welsh cousins whom we had never met. With two or three of them in the Army as they came of age, and one in the merchant navy, they were constantly in our thoughts. Their mother, a Mallon from Rostrevor, and my mother were great correspondents, so we were kept well abreast of their well-being, though like my sister's letters, hers very often had the censor working overtime too. The Rosary was prayed most nights in the Carr household but very often with a reduced congregation, and while the intentions for each decade varied from night to night the fifth mystery had a fixed intention, 'the Tumiltys in the War'. The Carrs in the Irish Army never got a mention.

Then there were the food parcels which my mother used send both to my sister in London and to the cousins in Cardiff. Most foodstuffs with the exception of tea were available in Omeath, though only in the summer when the boats were running. Some items which could be bought in Omeath could not legally be taken out, while on the Warrenpoint side hardly anything could be taken in or out. This did not make any difference to the thousands of day-trippers who flocked to the town, particularly at weekends, and by using a variety of ruses nearly always managed to make their trip worthwhile. Years later, when I finally met my Welsh cousins for the first time and they were all grown men, they were profuse in their thanks for the food parcels my mother had sent over during the War years.

Before 1941 had departed, the town had taken on the appearance of a military Barracks when a battalion of the British Army, the Monmouthshires, came to stay. Every vacant house in the town was commandeered, as was the Foresters' Hall, the Scout Hall, the Orange Hall and, indeed, any facility for which they had a use. The massive shed which had been built by the Great Northern Railway in Newry Street, which served as a feeding centre and shelter for day excursion parties, was a ready-made canteen, and, on occasions, the venue for battalion and inter-battalion boxing contests. There would have been something in excess of a thousand men fed there every day, though with the various companies on different training exercises they would never have been fed together. And then there was our expansive square, almost the equal of Horse Guards' Parade, where those young men were the chewing fodder for the sergeants and sergeants major. Depending on the day and the time, this could happen in front of an audience of locals who accepted the proceedings as a bit of light entertainment.

They came in their turns, the Monmouthshires, known as the Mons, the South Staffordshires, the Cheshires and then the Yanks. They were all infantry regiments, and their preparations were for close quarter combat. We had a platoon as next door neighbours on Summerhill, and we became very much aware of what they suffered during the square bashing, the route marches and the field exercises, in which they would be away for three or four days at a time on the hills and mountains. They returned exhausted, but come next morning they had to respond to the Sergeant's 'rise and shine' as usual at 7.00 A.M.

One thing appealed to me about the Mons. They had a reasonably good band and on occasions it played for inspections by the battalion commander or other high rankers. However, it played every Sunday for church parade and led the ranks to the respective churches in the town. The Church of Ireland, the Methodists and the Presbyterians would have had the vast majority, with a comparatively small number of Catholics 'falling out' at St Peter's where they were always made welcome.

It would be churlish of me not to record one very positive outcome of the placement of the Mons in The Point, which was to be of later benefit to St Peter's Club. There was a private enlisted in the regiment with the very Irish name of Tommy Duffy. Tommy fell for a local girl Eileen Ryan, and when the War was over he came back, married Eileen and settled in Warrenpoint. All of Eileen's four brothers played for the Blues as they came of age and ability, which ensured that Tommy was well disposed to the GAA. Years later, when the club decided to build its own premises, it was Tommy, a plasterer by trade, who spearheaded the voluntary operation. He left a lasting imprint on the front of the building, the crest of the Association, which remains a tribute to his craftsmanship.

For whatever reason, the Staffordshire personnel did not register with me at all, but those from the Cheshires certainly did. No one of my vintage in The Point who ever witnessed the Cheshires perform on The Square could ever forget 'Piggy' Jones, the regimental Sergeant major who threatened and brow beat every unfortunate soldier who was in any way out of line in either appearance or drill precision. Commissioned and non-commissioned officers were not immune from his invective. It surprised me somewhat to find that he was a most amiable and reasonable man when he came in to drink in a local hostelry in which I worked a few evenings a week. There was a small private snug which was reserved for himself and a commissioned officer who happened to be a brother of the commanding officer of the regiment, a Lieutenant Colonel Bromley-Davenport. With a double-barrelled name like that, it was no surprise that after the War he became a member of the British Parliament for the Conservative party.

The Cheshires were very much into sport and that attracted my interest. I got to know a number of them quite well. Bill Hayes was one of those who had played professionally with Oldham Athletic. He was a great all-rounder, a good athlete and he performed well in the boxing ring. There were many like him in the Cheshires. On one occasion he advised me there was to be an inter-battalion or inter-regimental match in which Jack Rowley, a Manchester United star of the time, would be playing for the opposition. I went out to the Plots, as the Brothers' field on the seafront was called, to see the game. However, Rowley was not playing and Hayes was profuse in his apologies the next time I spoke to him. As it turned out, I was to see the English international on a more hallowed soccer shrine some years later. All in all, between the drill performances on The Square, their football, athletics and boxing tournaments, the Cheshires left a definite impression.

While there was no hostility shown to the British forces when they were in the town, it would be true to say that the populace had a much cosier relationship with the Americans when they arrived. Whether this was because, compared to the British, they were bigger spenders, were better dressed and spoke with Hollywood accents, is hard to say. My youngest brother, Paddy, who would have been in primary school at the time, became friendly with a couple of Americans from another part of the town. He shocked my mother one evening by landing home with the pair of them in tow, thereby commencing a relationship which has lasted to the present day.

I did not meet them until a subsequent visit and when I did, it turned out that while I was only 20, they were both younger than me. One was Jack Fair, a gentle giant from Jacksonville, Kentucky, and the other, Bill Stanfield from Reidsville, North Carolina, a slightly built and more reserved chap. Stanfield, an only child, celebrated his 19th birthday at 5 Cloughmore Terrace and a few days later received the news that his father had died suddenly back home in Reidsville. He was allowed eight hours compassionate leave, all of which he spent in Summerhill being consoled by my mother.

In the following months they were regular visitors to our home, before leaving on the expedition which took them to the Normandy beaches. They were not in the early landings but were in the thick of the action shortly afterwards and while Fair made it through the War in good shape, Stanfield was badly injured at Metz in France and was invalided back to England, and then to America. Of course, after they left The Point they were registered in my mother's prayer list.

With the ending of the War, communications were resumed, and in the early sixties my youngest brother emigrated to America, first to Bill Stanfield in North Carolina before moving to Chicago. Stanfield visited us a number of times until 'The Troubles' intervened but he has been back in more recent years.

While the War disrupted sport of all kinds, it was mainly in the matter of transport that the GAA was affected. The Championships, internal and Inter-County, went ahead as usual; Down's second Ulster Final test with Cavan in the space of two years was remarkable for the fact that it was played outside the province, at the Athletic Grounds in Dundalk. The Point had four representatives on the team on this occasion. A very exciting young fellow called Liam O'Hare, better known as 'Toots,' joined John McClorey, Terry McCormack, and my brother, Gerry, in a vain attempt to dethrone the dominant force in the province. There was not a great deal of confidence behind the Down team and the worst fears of the supporters were realised with Cavan running away with the game by a margin of twenty points. Even though I was only playing Gaelic football a couple of years, I was deeply committed to Down and this further humiliation by Cavan was a bitter pill to swallow. As far as Down was concerned, the Cavan stranglehold on the Ulster Championship was to continue for many years after.

The picture as regards St Peter's Club was already taking on a rosier hue. A set of younger fellows emerged to make their mark in developing a style of football which set the standard for a decade or two. Liam O'Hare, Chris O'Boyle, Tim Donoghue, Eugene McKay, Arthur Bradley, Paddy O'Hare, John Hillen and myself, the oldest at twenty, powered through the Senior Championship and eventually, after a replay, got our revenge on the great Bryansford side which had dominated the senior competition for the four previous seasons.

It was understandable that The Point would have a sizable contingent on the Down side when the Inter-County competitions got under way in 1944, so when we won the first ever senior trophy, the McKenna Cup, to rejoicing of almost Championship proportions, there were no less than seven St Peter's men on the team, with two others in the subs. This included my brother Hugh, who was listed as 'Irish Army'. In those days the McKenna Cup was considered a prestigious competition, so when the Championship got under way there was an air of confidence that we might make it to another tussle with Cavan in the Ulster Final. Unfortunately, we lost to Monaghan in the semi-final by a solitary point after looking likely winners for most of the game.

With Down's exit from the Ulster Championship, the spotlight for us in The Point was the defence of our county title. Even though we were to eventually fail in that task, we were a party to one of the greatest Championship sagas which Down football has seen. Four years earlier, in 1940, we had got our feet on the first rung of success when we met Clonduff in the Junior Final and we were able to maintain our supremacy over them for the next few years. A tremendous rivalry had built up between the clubs. In league games and Sevens competitions, a Clonduff-Point encounter was always well worth watching, so when we both qualified for the 1944 final, the county at large was in a heightened state of excitement.

Despite all the travel restrictions which were in place, it was a record crowd which turned up at Newcastle on an October Sunday. It took nearly three months to decide the outcome; it finally came on Christmas Eve after a series of three games, all of which were memorable, both for those who played and those who watched. While we did not have our Army men we still had a remarkably good side. Clonduff were powered by the Browns, all five of them, Andy Murnin, Eddie Grant and Paddy O'Hagan, all of whom made their mark at county level. I have cause to remember some who might not have played for the county, but were outstanding performers.

Sixty years on, I do not wish to write about the games in any detail, but both the October and November meetings ended in draws, the latter after extra time, so one can imagine the level of excitement which was abroad in the county. Even the War had taken a back seat in Down.

I am going to relate a diplomatic incident which occurred between the second and third games and to which I was a party, even the instigator. The other party is long since dead, but I can visualise his smiling face if he had sight of this memoir. The man I am referring to is Fr Patrick Keenan who was Parish Priest in Clonduff through that great era of football success. He was one of the senior priests of the diocese and chairman of Clonduff Club, and I met him often enough over the previous couple of years when The Point-Clonduff rivalry was building up. Being the man he was, it was not surprising that on Sunday mornings, when the church was full, he would have talked a bit about the football situation. Everybody was talking about it.

I worked on the buses at this time and would be meeting Clonduff people every day of the week. It was the Sunday discourse after the second drawn game. I was meeting Hilltown people who were telling me things like, 'Fr Keenan was hard on yez on Sunday,' or, 'Fr Keenan hadn't a great word about The Point on Sunday.' In the course of the week more than half a dozen Clonduff voices relayed much the same tidings to me.

I began to wonder what Fr Keenan was at, for while I could understand the normal arguments and expressions of opinions which go with the sporting scene, the notion that the priest had made disparaging remarks about The Point at Mass on a Sunday was enough to make me get my pen and paper out. With all the gravitas of my 21 years, I sat down and wrote a letter to Fr Keenan expressing my surprise that he would offer critical comment about The Point at Sunday Mass, of all places. Upholding the finest principles of sportsmanship to which our team subscribed, I finished with a poem of which I can only recall the last two lines thus:

'And if we should win, let it be by the right with our heads and our honour held high.

And if we should lose, let us stand on the ditch, and cheer, as the winners go by.'

When Christmas Eve came there was another hosting of football enthusiasts at Newcastle, and as we approached the partitioned Nissen hut which served as a dressing room for both teams, who was leaving the Clonduff side but Fr Keenan. He approached me with hand outstretched and a smile on his face.

'Barney son, I got your letter, but whoever told you about what I said must have been standing in the porch, for I said nothing but good about The Point.' We both laughed and as I moved off he caught me by the sleeve and in lowered voice he asked, 'Who wrote that poem you sent me? It's a good one.'

'I don't know, Father,' I replied and as I headed to join my teammates he called with a chuckle, 'Good luck, but I hope you'll be standing on the ditch when we're going home,' and so I was.

It would be remiss of me not to record that in those three games of the greatest sporting intensity, there was not a man put off, nor do I recall anything which could be called 'a serious incident'. It is most likely that the same referee did all three games.

To finish the events of that day I must refer to the journey home. At that time, it was required by law that taxis could only operate within a ten-mile radius. The first leg of the journey ended in Hilltown where we transferred to our Warrenpoint taxi which was being driven by Hugh McAnulty, the boss himself. We were heading for Reed Hall almost in the twilight, when someone in the back seat remarked, in a tone which dripped of disappointment, 'Ah well, there's the new moon anyway,' as if the sight of the new moon was some compensation for our defeat. The car came to a halt with a sudden jolt which took us all by surprise. Mr McAnulty bowed his head a little and slowly took off his glasses. With great deliberation he spoke to his youthful passengers, 'Let no one tell me where the moon is, until I get out of this car.' Head down, and without glasses, he moved slowly from the car and stood on the narrow verge, scanning the evening sky until he picked up the thin crescent. He blessed himself, put his glasses on, and got back into the car without a word of explanation. The mystery did not unravel for me until later, when I recounted the incident at home, where my mother put us in the picture by indicating that some people believed it was unlucky to get the first sight of the new moon through glass.

That Christmas final is still talked about by a dwindling band of enthusiasts who have survived the generations, and I could not leave it without recalling the celebrations which followed. When the Christmas festivities were well over, Fr Keenan had both teams with their officials to dinner in the parochial house, and there was no prouder man in Ireland that night. Neither the War nor rationing restrictions were in evidence and he set the seal on the occasion with a magnificent speech, some of which Síle Nic an Ultaigh (Sheila McAnulty) made part of her GAA story. 'The earnest spirit of both teams had created a wholesome and enthusiastic rivalry, such as drew forth as brilliant an exhibition of football as has ever been seen in the county.'[21] It was great to be part of it.

There was another aspect of the Clonduff relationship which I valued greatly at that particular time, and it relates to another commodity which was severely rationed: sweets and confectionery. In the back of our ration books there was a page or two of sweet coupons which had to last God knows how long. No shopkeeper would supply sweets or chocolate without coupons, otherwise they would not be able to replenish their meagre stock. That is, no shopkeeper with the exception of Katey McGeough, who had a sweet shop on Hilltown's Main Street; it became a mecca for Point teams, whether playing the local Clonduff side or teams further east. There was always a stop at Katey's for sweets without coupons. Unbelievably, and to the chagrin of the locals, this privilege of 'sweets without coupons' was reserved to 'The Point fellows'. Complaints from the locals were never entertained by Katey, who continued to insist on their coupons. Indeed, there are some Hilltown people who still feel that sense of injustice.

Another Clonduff-Warrenpoint relationship came out of those years when my younger brother, Aidan, married a Hilltown girl, Rosemary Bradley, settled in the village and in due course the Carr name appeared on the team sheets of Clonduff and Down football and camogie teams. Imagine, the first and only Carr (Ross) to win an All-Ireland senior medal with Down is a Clonduff man. By the looks of things this will continue to be the case for some years to come.

Clonduff won three County Championships in four years with that team and into the bargain, they provided the backbone of the side which brought Down's first All-Ireland Championship, the Junior Football title of 1946. Anyone involved in the GAA less than 40 years of age will almost certainly ask, 'What was Junior football?' In the chronicles of Championships, Junior Football has long ceased to exist. Eligibility to compete in the Junior competition at that time depended on a player not having played in the Senior Championship of the previous year. So if the best footballer in the county missed the senior competition, he was eligible for the Junior team next time round. As well as this, a county could be designated 'Junior' and their best team over a period of years could play in the Junior competition.

The oft-told story of Down's fortuitous first round survival in that Junior campaign, after a defeat by Antrim, bears repetition and explanation. Sean Carey, a Down man, and elder brother of Jarlath, who himself was later to win an All-Ireland with Down, was not properly registered as a player for Antrim and the subsequent protest from Down was upheld. Down had a few individuals who had extensive senior experience but who were past their peak. One of them was my brother, Gerry, a seasoned performer who might have been past his best at senior level, but had much to contribute as leader and captain. The only other Point man on the team was 19-year-old Emmett McGivern, who in making a spectacular save injured himself so badly against the upright that he had to be replaced. My brother, Aidan, was among the reserves.

It was 1948 before The Point were back in the Down Senior Final and this time Kilcoo were our opponents. While we won convincingly enough, the memory of that day is not the victory, but the awful injury sustained by one of the Kilcoo men, Stephen O'Hare, in the simplest manner imaginable. Stephen was in possession and was being challenged by my brother, Gerry. As the Kilcoo man threw the ball out to kick it, 'Joker' knocked it away, with the result that Stephen's full-blooded kick hit nothing, only thin air. I'm sure I was 30 yards from the spot, but I heard the crack and the shriek of the unfortunate Stephen as he collapsed in agony. I ran at once to him but I was absolutely shattered by the sight of that knee and had to turn away. I have never seen a worse injury before or since. It took Stephen quite a while to recover, but never well enough to resume playing football.

For the remainder of my playing days a visit to Kilcoo nearly always earned me a bit of hassle from a few of their followers who were under the impression that I had been responsible for Stephen's injury, something which hurt more than a little. I hasten to add that the hassle was never anything other than verbal.

My third and last Championship success came in 1953 when Burren were our opponents in the final. With two teams from the same parish contesting the decider, it was assumed that it would be a game out of the ordinary, but the reality was something different. Wind and rain turned it into one of the poorest finals for years, with The Point winning by a single goal to a single point. Part of The Point's problem that day might have stemmed from the absence of Liam (Toots) O'Hare who was on 'enforced' business on the day. Toots, at the time, was president of the local St Vincent de Paul Conference which was hosting a diocesan meeting in Warrenpoint on that Sunday. He went to Dean Fitzpatrick, the local administrator, a few days before to ask him to make his apology to the meeting, explaining to the Dean that he would be 'playing in the Championship final against Burren on Sunday.'

'Oh, Liam,' the Dean exclaimed, 'you couldn't miss the diocesan meeting for a football match.' Liam did miss the match and it was years later that I heard the real story behind his absence.

Burren Club had been reformed after being out of football for many years. The most notable name on the Burren team on this occasion was John McClorey who had served St Peter's with such distinction for twelve years. It was completely fitting that he should finish his career in a Burren jersey. This infant club, which was to become one of the great forces in Down and national club football, was powered for a generation by the McGoverns, his nephews.

Mention of John McClorey recalls another 'broken-leg' incident, the first part of which occurred when Saul were visitors at the field owned by Johnnie Ward, the butcher. This field, complete with slaughterhouse, was on the Lower Dromore Road. It was a dreadful pitch. One half was reasonably flat and the other half was along the side of a steep hill. The flat half was heavily tufted and in the course of the game a Saul player, Johnny Cusack, was taking a free kick in his own half of the field. He obviously intended getting well under the ball which sat on one of these tufts but it was a clump of earth he kicked. He collapsed in agony, his leg broken and not a man standing within 20 yards of him. The next time, and the only time I played at Saul, the 'broken-leg syndrome' appeared again. As I was walking down the narrow lane which led from the pitch, two chaps came alongside me, one asking, 'Are you as good a man now as you were in The Point when you broke Johnny Cusack's leg?'

I was dumbfounded and angry and yelled, 'In the name of God go and ask Johnny Cusack who broke his leg in The Point!' Both chaps seemed taken aback by my outburst, for they faded from the laneway.

The fact is that a leg had been broken in the match I had just played in, and which I had completely forgotten until Al Connolly from Dundalk recently visited me. Originally a Ballykinlar man, Al is the father of Susan, my daughter-in-law, so we are both grandparents to the same set of rascals. On this occasion we were talking football, and out of the blue he said, 'sure my mother got her leg broken in a game against The Point. It was John McClorey who was responsible.'

'In a match at Saul?' I asked incredulously, the same match I have just referred to. In tones of mock anger I asked, 'What the hell was she doing over at a football match in Saul?' The reason was simply that she was over visiting her sister and they went to the match, on what was a beautiful summer evening.

I should explain immediately that Mrs Connolly, his mother, was not playing in the game, but she was sitting on a rug on the ground with a couple of other women near the touchline. When the action swung close to them, the very solidly built McClorey landed among them with drastic consequence for Mrs Connolly. I was quite close to the scene myself and helped with ministrations to the shocked women. Mrs Connolly made a good recovery, but I don't think she became an ardent football follower.

While I never played competitive soccer following my humiliation by the Welsh Regiment in 1940, I always kept myself abreast of what was happening in the game, which, during the War years, could be described as 'not very much.' The ending of hostilities brought the game back to life. As far as 'the ban' was concerned in relation to watching soccer, it hardly existed, so if one went to see a soccer or rugby game it was inevitable that one would meet members of the GAA fraternity. I was very glad to have the company of one of the clan on an occasion I went to a game in Celtic Park.

The first year after the War ended there was a cross-border competition called The Inter-City Cup and the final between Cork City and Linfield was staged at Celtic Park in Belfast. My interest in the game was stirred by the Cork centre forward, Jimmy Turnbull, who was one of the most prolific goal scorers of the time. An Englishman, Jimmy played with Belfast Celtic, before moving to Cork after the outbreak of War. Most seasons he would have tallied about 60 or more goals, though once he scored 80. With Cork he still kept banging them in, so I thought I should not miss the opportunity of seeing this scoring phenomenon.

I stepped off the trolley bus on the Falls Road and had only taken a few steps in the direction of the ground when I heard someone call, 'Hey big fellow, where do you think you're going?' It was a familiar voice, so I turned to look, and saw the smiling face of Basil McGuckian, a pocket dynamo of the Derry team at the time, and, some years later, of the Banbridge Club in Down.

As we shook hands he continued, 'You're in big trouble Barney for I am the official Derry vigilante here today,' to which I enjoined, 'and I am performing the same task for Down.'

We proceeded to the game together, neither of us being too familiar with the geography of Celtic Park though I had been there in my younger days with my father. We soon realised we were in the middle of the Linfield following, but as it was the normal pre-match banter we thought we would stay where we were. When Cork took the field, the noisy, boisterous crowd turned into a howling mob, spewing out a torrent of epithets, all of which were embroidered with the Nazi tag and accompanied by the Nazi salute. Basil and I spoke to each other with our eyes and slowly inched our way out of the maelstrom to calmer waters. As for the Cork team, one could almost see them wilting in the first blast of their venomous welcome, which was repeated at intervals throughout the entire game. Linfield won by three or four goals, and Jimmy Turnbull, the man I came to see, hardly touched the ball half a dozen times in the game.

Another man I went specifically to see was Charlie Tully who was leaving Belfast Celtic to join Glasgow Celtic at the end of that particular season. Such were the plaudits which Charlie was getting from the pundits that I thought, 'I'll have to see Charlie for myself before he goes.' The occasion was provided by a midweek game against Linfield, an Antrim Shield final I think, which was played at Solitude, Cliftonville's ground. As usual I went off on my own, but made sure I was among the Celtic fraternity inside the ground. If Jimmy Turnbull didn't perform when I went to see him at Celtic Park, there were valid reasons. The same could hardly be said for Charlie who didn't perform either, despite having an adoring crowd, a perfect pitch and against what I would have called ordinary opposition. Possibly he had his mind set on Clydeside already, for his heart did not seem to be in it on the day. When he did move to Glasgow later, he went on to become one of the great names of Scottish football and is still regarded as one of the Celtic all-time greats.

If Charlie did not excite me that day, something else did, for I let out a loud shout of encouragement or censure at something which happened on the pitch and which fell on the ears of a Celtic supporter about ten rows below me. 'Hey Barney, what the hell are you doing here?'

The voice belonged to one Jimmy Morgan, who had played successfully with Antrim for a number of years but at this time had turned to soccer with Glentoran. When we got to speaking distance he greeted me thus, 'I would recognise that voice of yours in a million, especially if you're excited.' I think Jimmy is still going strong.

15 — The Road to Wembley

Warrenpoint, like many places, had prospered somewhat in the War years, and change was in the air everywhere. *"At the age of seventeen, I was 'prenticed to a grocer,"* is a line from the ballad *Courtin' in the kitchen*. At the same age, I was an apprentice grocer in *The Vitamin Stores* in Church Street owned by Patsy Fitzsimons and Frank Savage. Frank and Patsy were men of contrasting personalities but I had long left when the partnership was dissolved and Patsy opened his own shop in Mary Street.

By the end of the War, I was an established Down footballer and an experienced bus conductor thanks to Norman McKinley, a friend and companion from school days. He had commenced work with the Northern Ireland Road Transport Board (NIRTB) and a couple of weeks later invited me to join him. He was never into sport but had a very active and exciting life which should have inspired a book. The NIRTB was the controlling body which came into being in 1935 and which replaced all private bus companies, including McAnulty's Yellow Line. I was reasonably content, but a couple of small clouds appeared on the sporting and personal horizon.

The first one was occasioned by the retirement of Sergeant Donoghue from the Royal Ulster Constabulary (RUC) and the move of the family to Tullow in Co. Carlow, which was Mrs Donoghue's home place. While there might not have been many tears at the departure of 'Old Steve,' there was genuine regret, particularly in the GAA fraternity, that 'Young Steve,' Tim, was breaking the links with the team and the town.

The second was the departure of Joe (Chris) O'Boyle to London. He had sought to gain a place at the teacher training College in Belfast, but despite having very good senior leaving results he failed. He did his teacher training at one of the local authority training colleges in London and obtained the religious teaching certificate which qualified him to teach in the Catholic education system in England. He had hoped it might be acceptable at home, but it wasn't.

It was many years later that I learned that entry to the training college needed something else besides good results. The outcome was that The Point lost a great footballer and a great teacher. By this time his father had died and his mother was on her own attempting to run a declining business. With all, he had no option but to make his career in London.

While Chris was a top ranking Gaelic footballer, almost in the Sean O'Neill mould, he was equally adept on the soccer field, and he wasn't too long in London before he was showing his paces with one of the top amateur sides. He was on Derby County's books during Peter Doherty's spell with that club, and he confirmed to me that Doherty, my boyhood hero, was as wonderful a fellow off the field as he was on it. He had the good advice from Doherty to concentrate on his teaching career, for at that time, soccer players were being paid buttons, and by today's standards, were slaves.

By the spring of 1948, Chris was well settled in London, when Manchester United and Blackpool qualified for the final of the FA Cup. I had a letter from him inviting me over for the game, but I took it with a grain of salt for tickets in that pre-television age were even harder to come by than they are today. An exchange of letters took place and he insisted there was no need to worry about the tickets, assuring me that 'Ben will get them.' Although I had never met 'Ben' I knew him to be a Dublin chap who had become very friendly with this small group of Warrenpoint exiles who lived reasonably close to each other. Accepting O'Boyle's assurances, I arranged to take a week of my holidays and juggle a few extra days into the bargain.

Except for one trip to the Isle of Man on Warrenpoint general holiday, I had never been out of the country, so it was with a sense of adventure that I sailed out of Belfast heading for Liverpool on the last Thursday of April, aboard the good ship, *Duke of Lancaster*. Of course, I was an old 'sea dog,' having served my time on the Omeath and Carlingford routes under sail, on the oars, and under Stevie Bradley on the *Madonna*. Noting every action of the crew members when I sailed up the Mersey the following morning, I felt myself to be a qualified seaman and I'm sure the thought struck me that if I ever got tired of the buses I could return to the boats.

Even 60 years ago, the Mersey mud flats were not the most welcoming approach to England's green and pleasant land, but the early morning sun and sky indicated another fine day was in store. The train journey from Liverpool's Lime Street to Euston revealed the ravages of the War in many of the urban areas, but the air of optimism was clearly evident among the passengers who shared my compartment.

Euston at last, and the welcoming grasp of my dear friend who had managed to get the afternoon off, 'To meet the brother from Ireland.'

Greetings over, my first question was, 'Did Ben get the tickets?'

'Don't you worry about the tickets, let Ben worry about them,' and then he added, 'he didn't have any last night.'

Chris stayed with a couple called Walter and Liz Smith in the Wealdstone—Harrow area, almost in the shadow of the famous school, which became a familiar landmark throughout the following week as I travelled in and out to Central London. They were an elderly West Country couple who had lived in the London area for most of their adult lives, but had retained their beautiful accents. My only exposure to such accents was on the radio or the odd individual voice over the years. To live with it at close quarters for a week was an added pleasure. Walter was the caretaker at one of the local primary schools which kept him out of the way of his wife for most of the day, five days a week. He wore two things continually, a cap on his head and a smile on his face which was never distorted even when his wife was complaining about one thing or another, as she often did. Both Chris and Walter were away early in the morning, so Mrs Smith and I did quite a bit of talking about herself, her husband and my friend O'Boyle.

The Smiths had no children of their own, so when Chris came to stay with them he really became an adopted son. He was a lucky fellow, for they acted 'in loco parentis,' ensuring his diligence in his studies at the training college and his strict adherence to his religious duties—not that Chris would have been any way slack in his practice of the faith. The fact that the Smiths were not Catholics, or indeed great churchgoers themselves, had no bearing on Mrs Smith's responsibilities, as she saw them. Every other week she wrote to Mrs O'Boyle, so no mother in the country was as well informed about her son, and he hundreds of miles away.

My first evening in London saw me on a tour of Warrenpoint *émigrés*, beginning with Joe Williams, the man who had introduced me to my first Cup Final broadcast in 1932. He and his wife were most welcoming. Here I was sixteen years later, standing on Wembley's doorstep hoping and praying that Ben Courtney would come up trumps the following day. In due course, Mickey Kelly, Tommy Trainor, Pat Finnison and a number of familiar Rostrevor faces arrived at their 'local'. Everyone, that is, except Ben Courtney. No one had heard from Ben for days but my friend O'Boyle's faith in Ben never wavered. When a barman, who was on first name terms with most of my companions, advised that, 'Ben wants to speak to some of ye,' it was Pat Finnison who went to the phone.

He returned after a short interval and I thought I read bad news on his countenance. He addressed O'Boyle and myself. 'Ben won't be in, we're to meet him at such and such a pub tomorrow at twelve o'clock.'

In desperation I asked if he had got the tickets and got the rejoinder from Pat, 'He never mentioned tickets,' and an aside from O'Boyle, 'Didn't I tell you not to worry; leave it to Ben.' I didn't really worry, but I didn't rule out the possibility of listening to the radio broadcast of the game in the company of Joe Williams and his family.

The morrow dawned, and we were in the appointed pub at least fifteen minutes before the due time. On the dot of twelve I was more than relieved to hear O'Boyle announce, 'Here comes Ben.' My eyes went to the door to view a well-suited, stocky, bespectacled figure with a large Manchester United rosette pinned to his lapel and across his shoulder and chest the strap of a binocular case. The smiling face exuded complete confidence. If he had been wearing a top hat, he would have been equally at ease at Royal Ascot.

Ben was a Dubliner who had been working in London when the War broke out. He had been in the RAF during the War and had returned to take up his position in the Guinness operation. Nothing was a problem to Ben, and when in later life I got to know the television show 'Bilko,' where the character of Ernie Bilko was played by Phil Silvers, there was much to remind me of Ben Courtney. When O'Boyle gave voice to some of my concerns of the previous evening Ben expressed mock hurt that his ability to deliver would be in question. Armed with the tickets and all bedecked with Man United rosettes, we headed for Wembley.

While it might be thought that I was one of the band of Man United's original fan club, I have to confess that any loyalty I had to them was engendered by the fact that Tommy Breen, who had commenced his career at Newry Town, had played for them before the War. More importantly, Jack Carey, one of the great Irish defenders of all time, was captaining the side that day. Carey had been transferred before the War from some of the Dublin Junior clubs for the sum of £250. He resumed his career with United when football got into its stride in earnest after the ending of hostilities, and captained the Rest of Europe side which played a British selection to celebrate the end of the War.

Another great name on the Manchester side was Jimmy Delaney, who had starred with Glasgow Celtic in his younger days, and ended up in his twilight years with Shamrock Rovers. Also included in the side were Jack Rowley, whom I didn't see and Charlie Mitten, whom I had seen in their Army days in The Point. Blackpool, who were United's opponents on the day, had their share of star names including Stanley Matthews and Stan Mortenson. At this stage in his life, Matthews was a national institution and had been capped umpteen times for England. He had played most of his career with Stoke City, but had never won a cup or Championship medal, with the result that everyone outside of Manchester was hoping he would achieve the medal which had eluded him so far in his career. It was not to be. United were the better team and won deservedly 4–2.

By 1948, I was tuned into the atmosphere of GAA finals of all varieties and while I was appreciative of the tactical milieu and the precision passing of professional soccer, the passion and the fervour which are part of Gaelic sport were missing. Even though 'my' team won, I could not be enraptured. Still, it was a wonderful occasion and a great start to my week in London.

Before leaving the Wembley scene, I would mention that Stanley Matthews went on to win his Cup medal five years later when Blackpool beat Bolton Wanderers in the final. He was 40 at the time, and, unbelievably, he continued to play first division football into his fifties with his first love, Stoke City. He was the first footballer to receive a knighthood.

Sightseeing began as soon as we had eaten, and in due course I found myself in Hyde Park, at Speakers' Corner where anyone with a cause to espouse or condemn is assured of an audience. Three years after the War, the immigration from the West Indies and other parts of the British Empire was well under way, and many immigrants seemed to be in Hyde Park that Saturday evening. What struck me most about them, whether they were on the soapbox or making their individual voices heard in support or protest, was their intense sense of injustice. As I lay in my bed in Wealdstone that night contemplating the events of the day it was those angry black voices which suggested problems down the line.

There was no Sunday morning lie-in to be enjoyed for O'Boyle had already indicated, 'We're for Mass in Westminster Cathedral in the morning,' and what a wonderful start to the day that was. The Latin Mass was the norm, of course, but the sung pontifical High Mass, as intoned at the centre of English Catholicism, was something else. The solemnity of the ritual, the quality of the music and, indeed, the fragrance of the incense, all combined to delight the senses and stir the receptive heart to the reality which was at the centre of it all.

It would not be my intention to give a running commentary on this, my first visit to London, but a couple of events of that Sunday are worth recalling. My wish was O'Boyle's command and when I suggested to him an hour or two later that I would like to pay another visit to Speakers' Corner he had me there in no time at all. It was much more crowded than on the evening before, with some of the speakers having very sizable crowds. I do not remember that there was amplification so speakers needed to have very good diction to be heard at the fringes of their audiences. Needless to say, there were several Irish voices, each with its own brand of nationalism. Moving through the groups, I came on a voice and a face which I recognised instantly, that of Rev. Donald Soper, a Methodist who was a hugely popular radio personality and very much in the printed media of the time. He became even better known later with the advent of television. Soper was well known for the humorous manner in which he dealt with hecklers, but he was also well known for his capacity and willingness to engage with what might be called sensible interventions by actually debating a point with a member of his audience.

When he had finished, he would engage with individuals in a most open and sincere manner. In the brief conversation I had with him I alluded to the great sense of injustice I had picked up from the members of the coloured community, and I added, 'They seem to have more chips on their shoulders than the Irish have.'

'That's right,' he commented, 'and I will tell you that we will pay a heavy price for the Empire in the next hundred years.' That was in 1948.

My first Sunday night in London did not see me hitting any of the bright spots for by nine o'clock we were back in the quiet avenues of Wealdstone, preparing to go to a dance in the Wealdstone Parish Church Hall. I was to find out that the local Catholic parish was administered by the Society of the Divine Saviour, popularly known as the Salvatorians Fathers, an order of which I had never heard before this time.

To begin with, there was a very friendly atmosphere, the music was good and the girls were quite gracious and mannered. It didn't surprise me at all that my friend O'Boyle seemed to be known to most of them. A few of those I danced with, sensing my 'shyness', would immediately open the conversation with, 'Oh, you're Joe's friend from Ireland.'

The night flew and on the stroke of twelve the band finished the last dance. With the final chord sounded, a priest appeared on the platform and everyone in the hall dropped to their knees to leave me the only man standing for a confused second or two before realising what was happening. The priest led us in our night prayer, gave us some good advice on our behaviour on our way home and blessed us. Good Christian lad that I was, I was deeply impressed and wondered what would have happened if the priests at home had attempted the same exercise.

Sometime before the last dance my friend and I had two lovely girls lined up to be left home. He knew both of them, of course, though they were not together at the dance. He had sort of hand-picked Madge for me and I had danced with her a few times during the night. She was a good dancer who showed remarkable tolerance to a rather ungainly chap who hadn't full control of his feet. Not only was she a good dancer, but she was a very nice girl. O'Boyle's partner, whose name was Edel Jackson, was another lovely girl and by the time we strolled to the place where our paths had to separate we had agreed to make a foursome for a cinema or a show a couple of nights later.

That agreed, and after I had got strict instructions as to how I would get back to the meeting point with O'Boyle, we went off in our different directions.

Edel must have lived a considerable distance away, for when I returned to what I thought was our meeting point, there was no sign of O'Boyle. After fifteen minutes, which seemed like an hour, I began to panic and wondered if I had taken the right route, for there was a great similarity in the avenues of Wealdstone. I turned to retrace my steps and met a policeman walking on the footpath pushing his bicycle. To my 'good night,' he replied, 'good morning,' and I detected an emphasis on the 'morning'. By this time I was getting concerned and it occurred to me that back in The Point, during the wartime blackout, our coterie of friends used a whistle signal to make one another aware of our presence. It was something we picked up from a film and it consisted of a seven-note phrase which brought a recognition phrase: so if, in the War, I went down to Tommy Cunningham's Corner and chirped out my seven-note signal, more often than not I would get the recognition signal from the darkness of the Bank Corner. But now this was almost a midsummer's night in Wealdstone and as I turned and retraced my steps back up the avenue, chirping my call signal at intervals, I spied the figure of the same policeman, this time riding his bicycle. He had obviously doubled round another avenue to come back to check me out. He dismounted a few yards from me at the edge of the footpath, and polite as you like, he spoke first.

'Good morning, sir. Do you live in the area?' he asked.

I started to explain that I was waiting for a friend and I had hardly half a dozen words out of my mouth before the early morning silence was broken, not by a whistle, but by a voice, 'di-de-di-de di-de-di-di.' It was O'Boyle, who was the worst whistler in the world and would never have attempted the art. I was too embarrassed to give him the recognition whistle, so I said to the policeman, 'That's him coming now.' When Joe got our length and greeted the policeman with a humorous denial of any knowledge of my identity, the constable was satisfied that we were *bona fide* travellers and off he went.

As we continued en route to home I asked O'Boyle if he had heard me whistling, for I doubted if he could have got my signal. He didn't, but we had both used it and we marvelled that the old call signal which had served us so well in The Point should have been renewed in Wealdstone. Later, in our room, I expressed my pleasure on the enjoyable night, and passed some remark about the reception the priests at home would get if they asked the dancers to kneel down and say their prayers at the end of the night.

O'Boyle looked at me with a smile on his face. 'But half the people there to night were not Catholic. Edel is not a Catholic, Madge is not a Catholic,' he said.

'But they all knelt down and blessed themselves and I'm sure they all joined in the prayers,' I replied.

We talked religion for a while and after a short silence he said to me, 'You know, I have visited Edel's home on a few occasions. Her parents are a very nice couple; you'll have to meet them before you go. I have a feeling her mother is Irish, though she has a very English accent.'

Monday morning saw me well refreshed after a good night's sleep. A leisured breakfast, accompanied by an informative briefing on the attractions and pit falls of London from Mrs Smith, prepared me for the day ahead. I gathered from her that she and Walter rarely went into the city and only on a very big occasion. The last time she had been there was to celebrate Victory in Europe (VE) Day which marked the end of the War in Europe. She had vivid memories of seeing the King and the other members of the Royal family on the balcony of Buckingham Palace. Both she and Walter seemed to be committed to the monarchy, as indeed everybody else appeared to be at the time.

Off I set again from Wealdstone, to explore the streets of London confident in the experience I had gained in two days' usage of the underground, which was a model of simplicity even for me. My first port of call was the Keith Prowse ticket agency; there, to my surprise, I was able to get what turned out to be exceptionally good seats for both *Oklahoma* and *Annie get your gun,* the two great Broadway musicals which were on their first London runs. In the next four days I fitted in as much as was possible of what London had to offer. Where I started or finished has long since gone out of focus, but one afternoon my visit to the science museum, on the advice of my friend O'Boyle, proved to be quite historic. It was being patronised by a comparatively small number of visitors and as I was proceeding along an upper balcony, which had a wide view of the ground floor and the entrance below, I became aware of what might be termed 'frenzied activity' from officials and attendants. I sensed an emergency of some kind. After a couple of officials had passed me almost on the trot, I stopped one who was approaching at such a speed he would have qualified for a place in an Olympic walking final.

When he was about three yards from me I put up a halting hand and asked quickly, 'Is there an emergency on?'

'Yes, yes,' he replied even more quickly, 'His Majesty the King will be here in fifteen minutes.' This, in the most courteous tones imaginable, and without breaking his hurried step. In fact the last few words were delivered over his shoulder to me.

I smiled and thought, 'This is indeed a rare honour that the King should come to see me.'

For the next ten minutes I leaned over the balcony rail surveying the hurried preparations which the occasion demanded. In very little time and with all the museum staff in place, the King came in with the officials who had welcomed him outside. There were introductions all round, but everything was low-key, a very informal visit indeed. From my vantage point, I missed nothing at all and as the King and his escorts moved off I thought the excitement was over. Lo and behold, they moved to the stairs leading to the very balcony where I was. It became obvious that he had to come in my direction. There were two or three other viewers on the balcony and I expected the King would shake hands with each of us as he approached and this gave me intense satisfaction. The thought of telling Johnnie Craig how I came to shake hands with the King of England flashed into my mind.

Johnnie was a bus driver from Dromore, Co. Down who made no secret of the fact that he was a loyal Orangeman, and a committed Unionist. Dromore crews operated into Newry on a daily schedule and when Johnnie was the driver, after parking his bus on the Mall, he would proceed to the rest room complete with lunch bag. If Mickey Bannon, a Newry driver and brother of the depot manager was among the group which sat on our seat in the sun, the following cameo would be enacted. Once Johnnie put his foot on our side of the street Mick would rise, put an imaginary flute to his lips and proceed to whistle *The Sash*. Without breaking his step, Johnnie invariably declared among other things, 'You can smell the Fenian air once you get to Damolly.' However, when Johnnie had his bite taken he would be out to sit on the seat to join in the banter without a word of rancour.

So I am back in Kensington museum with Johnnie Craig in my thoughts and the King on the top step and on the balcony. I am prepared to meet the monarch, but to my intense disappointment, he merely acknowledged the other people on the balcony with a respectful nod of the head. The officials who accompanied him certainly did not encourage any intimacy or warmth, so when he got my length he gave what I considered was a shy sort of nod which I returned with genuine respect. He remained in the building for under an hour and took his departure without me having the opportunity to bid him farewell.

I took my own departure shortly after for I had to be back in Wealdstone to prepare for our outing to the West End.

My friend O'Boyle had acquainted the girls of the outing the previous evening and the arrangement was that we would all meet at the Railway Station, but as we had time to spare he thought we should call for Edel at her home where I could meet her parents. This we did, and as a friend of Joe's I was very well received, and the drinks were on the table immediately. Mr Jackson took O'Boyle to the garden to show him something he had planted, leaving Mrs Jackson and myself chatting together. Despite the accent which many years of life in England had moulded I was picking up some traces of Mourne in her speech.

'What part of Ireland are you from?' she queried and when I replied 'Warrenpoint', she paused a second. I detected the semblance of a sigh as she spoke softly in clear Mournese, 'Many's a good Fifteenth I had in The Point.'

Then it was off to the station where Madge, looking even lovelier than she did on Sunday, was beginning to think we had forgotten about her. Within the hour, we were in excellent seats in the splendour of the London Coliseum awaiting the arrival of Annie Oakley on stage. There was an air of excitement as the house filled, the lights dimmed and the orchestra struck up the opening notes of the overture which featured the airs which had already become popular.

My heart warmed to Madge when she leaned over and whispered in my ear, 'In case you might think otherwise, Barney, this is the first time I have ever been in a theatre in the West End. I am absolutely thrilled, thank you so much.'

My reply into her ear was to ask, 'Will you be free to come again on Thursday for *Oklahoma?*'

With a smile which included a look of disbelief, she gasped, 'My mother will never believe this.'

Annie get your gun was an excellent show even though I felt the leading man, a chap called Bill Jonson, was a bit wooden, but with a fine voice. Annie was played by a really dynamic personality whose name escapes me but whose performance could hardly have been bettered by the great Ethel Merman who opened the show on Broadway, where it was still running. Altogether it had been a wonderful day and a wonderful night.

When my friend O'Boyle and I met back at the ranch house in Wealdstone, after we had deposited the girls at their respective homes, we had a lot to talk about as we got ready for bed. He arrived home some time after me, saying that Mrs Jackson had waited up for Edel had and himself to come home and that she wanted him to wait for supper, but he declined.

'Yes,' I said, 'that's what I would expect from a kind hearted Mourne woman.'

'A Mourne woman?' he queried incredulously.

'Yes indeed, and a Catholic in her younger days,' I added.

In a scolding voice he exclaimed, 'You weren't discussing religion with her I hope.'

'The subject was never mentioned.'

'And how do you know she was a Catholic?' he almost snapped.

'Well,' I replied 'when she told me that she spent "manys a good Fifteenth in The Point," I thought to myself that not many Protestants from Mourne came to the Point for the Fifteenth.' We both fell back on our beds and chuckled ourselves to sleep.

In the next two days I packed everything London had to offer into a memory box of great London experiences, which I have renewed and added to over the years. If the opening show at Wembley was just a little disappointing, the Grand Finale at the Drury Lane Theatre on Thursday night left me singing all the way back to The Point.

I had spent the full day in London, and was meeting O'Boyle and the girls at the theatre. Everything went as arranged, and their arrival in the foyer brought an admiring and welcoming greeting from me, for both girls wore different frocks from our previous outing and while I was never very much into glamour at this time in my life, I recognised it when I saw it. Glamour apart, there was no denying they were both lovely, no-nonsense girls who were a joy to be with.

Now *Oklahoma* was a different genre of musical to *Annie,* even though both were set in the American West. The sharp shooting *Annie* realised, *'You can't get a man with a gun,'* and was at a distinct disadvantage to the lovely Laurie, who had the much more romantic music to sing and a much more romantic Curly, in the person of Howard Keel, who looked made for the part. Over the years, I have seen *Oklahoma* a number of times but the magic of that Drury Lane performance is never to be forgotten.

All the way home Madge and I sang the showstopper, *People will say we're in love,* and with feeling, may I add:

> *Don't praise my charm too much.*
> *Don't look so vain with me.*
> *Don't stand in the rain with me.*
> *People will say we're in love.*

And that's the way it was all the way to Wealdstone where Madge's mother had stayed up to welcome us with a lovely supper. Mrs George was a charming woman who looked more like an elder sister. She joined us for a while but then judiciously took her leave. This was my third and final meeting with Madge and needless to say it took longer to say goodbye. I ambled down the Wealdstone Way in the direction of home, still singing *People will say*. Of course, at that hour of the morning, I had the road all to myself and anyway, it hardly mattered what the people would say, for I was heading for home later in the day.

O'Boyle and Walter, the man of the house, took their leave of me while I was still in bed, for both left early for their respective stations. Later I took leave of the good lady herself, Mrs Smith. She was genuinely sorry that my week was up and I left with an equally genuine invitation to 'come over any time you wish.' In fact, I was back inside three years when I went over to act as best man at the wedding of my friend O'Boyle and in case anyone might be wondering if he married the girl who accompanied him to the Drury Lane, I have to indicate that he didn't. But that's another story. When I left Euston Station in the early afternoon I was heading homewards but not home, for I was taking advantage of my first visit to England to visit a number of friends resident in the environs of Liverpool. My arrival there that Friday evening coincided with the first rain I had seen since leaving home. They had given me precise instructions how to get to their homes so I took the number eleven green bus which would be sitting outside the station. I asked the conductor to let me out at such a corner. I took the first avenue on my left and theirs was the fourth bungalow on the right. I was in time for tea at Freshfield, with the Nevin family, whose friendship took root in Forkhill some years before in the home of Mick and Nancy Rafferty on the Longfield Road.

I had one other family to call on and this I did on the Sunday afternoon, after getting instructions from my hosts on the whereabouts of the address I had been given. I was calling to see two girls, one a daughter of the house, Frances Cunningham, whom I had met when she was on holiday in Ireland with the other, her cousin Marie McEvoy from Meigh, whose father was principal at the local school. Frances was a student teacher, Marie a student nurse. After I met the family they took me to see the sights of Liverpool on a Sunday, and eventually across the Mersey to New Brighton to experience the fun fair, many of whose attractions scared the life out of me.

Often over the years I have thought of that happy, happy day, mercifully not knowing what life held for any of us. My story is still unfolding 60 years on from that day. The stories of Marie McEvoy and Frances Cunningham ended only a few years after that New Brighton experience. Marie died at home in Ireland in her twenty-second year and three years later, Frances joined her in eternity.

The leaving of Liverpool took place on Monday night and on Tuesday evening I was on the late run to Belfast, a tired but happy man.

For those who might wonder what happened to Madge, I have to confess that we exchanged a couple of letters. One of hers contained a very nice picture of herself, with a request that I send her a likeness of myself. As I had no picture that did me justice I was unable to oblige, so she was left with nothing but the memory. Like most holiday romances the relationship petered out, but I have never heard *People will say we're in love* without thinking of that charming girl from Wealdstone.

In any event, the prospect of a weekly run from Warrenpoint to Wealdstone on a bike put me off, and I, too, sufficed with a memory for a month or two.

16 — The Road to Rome

Castlewellan and The Point qualified for the final of the Down Senior Championship in 1950, much to the delight of our supporters, but when the September date of the game was announced it presented a serious problem for two members of the team, Liam O'Hare and myself.

As most Catholics will know, the Church declares a Holy Year every 25 years, when it calls on the faithful, and those not so faithful, to participate in a unique way in its divine mission. One of those ways is to visit the great churches of Rome on pilgrimage. This particular year, coming just five years after the greatest carnage in human history, was regarded as a great year of thanksgiving for peace.

Long before the Down finalists were known or before the date was set, Toots and I had our arrangements made to travel to Rome to celebrate the jubilee with the Pope. If we had been out of the country for only one Sunday the game could probably have been switched to suit us, but we were going to be away for three Sundays, so the game had to go ahead on the second Sunday of September as arranged.

I should explain the circumstances of how our trip to Rome evolved. As part of our religious upbringing my mother ensured that *The Standard* or *The Universe* was in the house every week. It was in the latter publication, about Easter time, that I noticed an advert which offered a two weeks trip to Rome for £41 ten shillings and for another £8 the pilgrimage could be extended to take in the passion play at Oberammergau. The fact that it said 'hostel accommodation in Rome,' did not make it any the less attractive. When I showed it to my long-time friend and companion, Toots, he was enthusiastic and we agreed to write off for details. By the time the details came back Toots had enlisted the interest of a colleague and friend of my own in the Newry depot, Cyril Connor. We decided 'this is for us,' for even with the added expense of getting to London it was still value for money. All the arrangements were left to me and consequently there were a few hiccups between our initial booking and our departure from Belfast en route to London on the first Friday evening of September.

Coming down in the train from Heysham we had scanned the papers to see what football games were on in London in the afternoon. Charlton Athletic and Tottenham Hotspur were providing the only first division game on that day, and even though we realised it was unlikely to be 'the match of the day' it would have to suffice. On arrival at Euston we were greeted by O'Boyle and my younger brother, Brendan, who had arrived in London some months before.

Brendan had been an apprentice bricklayer 'serving his time' with James Wilson & Son before he decided there was more to life than building bricks. He joined a nursing order of priests and brothers known as the Order of St Camillus, where in religion he was known as 'Br John'. He trained as a nurse at one of the London hospitals and spent over 50 years of his life at Camillian foundations in England, Australia and Ireland, where he died at Killucan, Co. Westmeath in 2004. He had a wonderful sense of humour and could tell a good story. He loved The Point and its people and he probably influenced one priestly vocation.

Sunday morning Mass in nearby Westminster Cathedral started our day early. There was no breakfast before Mass in those days. Within a few hours we were heading for Dover and Ostend from where our continental journey was to begin. The route to Rome for us was to Innsbruck in Austria by train and from there by coach to Rome. I was really looking forward to the trip.

Even though I was aware that conditions on the European mainland were far from normal, it was still a bit of a shock to find the train we were boarding at Ostend had only wooden seats and did not have a dining car. My first thought was that this was a pilgrimage as challenging as Lough Derg and thereafter I was prepared for anything. Still, when we settled, there was a really happy atmosphere, for all the people in the carriage belonged to our group. The carriage had the corridor along one side with compartments seating eight passengers on the wooden seating. Across Belgium and Holland it was like a geography lesson as the familiar names of the towns passed by. Here and there the ravages of the War became evident but it was not until we were into Germany, and the Cologne area in particular, that the massive scale of damage hit us. The devastation in the city itself was made more dramatic by the sight of its famous cathedral standing stark and untouched, like a lighthouse in a sea of ruins. Evening was dropping down then and there followed what I would still describe as the longest night of my life. At intervals of a few hours we stopped at stations where a very limited amount of food could be bought, before we finally pulled into Innsbruck at 3 o'clock on Monday afternoon.

The soft seats of the coaches which carried us up the spiralling mountain route to the Brenner Pass might have suggested an ascent to heaven; such was the comfort after a very uncomfortable night on hard wood. The name of the Brenner Pass was as familiar as any townland at home, for it was here that Hitler and Mussolini met in the glare of the world media before turning Europe into a graveyard for so many millions. It took some little time for the border formalities between Austria and Italy to be completed, so quite a number of the party got out and stretched their legs by walking across the line, to the consternation of the customs officials on both sides. The Brenner is about 5,000 feet above sea level and even in September it was quite cold.

Bolzano, on the Italian side down the mountain, was our resting place that night, and from there on the penitential side of the journey was over, even though the continental breakfast and the packed lunch which was to see us down to the Mediterranean coast was hardly adequate fare for strapping young Irishmen. Such was the scenic quality of Northern Italy and down past Lake Garda that food was not the uppermost thought of the day.

We were heading for the coastal resort of Viarreggio, which proved to be everything a Mediterranean resort should be. Our sea-front hotel, with direct access to the beach, allowed us both a midnight and a pre-breakfast dip. Might I state that while I have lived by the sea I had never been in the water before breakfast, nor have I ever been since.

We were early on the road to Pisa and its leaning tower. Back those 50-odd years ago, it hardly seemed that it would have stood for another half a century, for even then there was concern for its future. But I trust that someday my grandchildren will follow in my footsteps completely confident in the tower's security.

The road to Rome ended for us that evening, Wednesday, and I had enjoyed the trip so much I felt that I had already got my money's worth. Admittedly the train journey had been more than exhausting, but the run down to Rome had dispelled the memory of the discomfort. Into the bargain, the normal bonding process had begun. Ours was one of three coaches which set out from Innsbruck on the Monday. By the time we reached Rome all its occupants were on first name terms.

Before we had even booked the trip, my two friends and I had wondered how comfortable the 'hostel accommodation' might be but the consensus view was 'what the hell as long as we get a bed, what more do we need?' Our arrival in the city that evening introduced us to that accommodation. We had driven past some of the familiar sights with our friendly driver, who by then had become a great favourite since we first met in Innsbruck three days before. He provided us with an interesting and humorous commentary. Eventually, we passed through a pair of pillars, up a curving avenue and parked along with many other buses on what looked like a barrack square, which indeed is what it was. On its perimeters were huts, mainly of uniform shape but here and there much larger buildings stood between them. In the next half hour our 'hostel accommodation' was revealed to us. It was, in fact, a wartime military camp, in which the minimum requirements of civilised living were available.

To begin with, we were allocated our wooden huts which had accommodation for eight, though we had only six, which left things a little more spacious for us. Along with my companions from home there were Liam and Eamon from Dublin and an English chap from London, who was very polite and mannerly but did not seem to be completely at ease with five Irishmen. The camp staff showed us the washing and showering facilities which were in the open air. This was a type of zinc trough, which would have been familiar to us who had experience of the facilities 'enjoyed' by the British Army in The Point during the War. This camp, however, had flush toilets, a facility which was not available in all the Army billets at home.

We also had our instructions about the dining arrangements, which were simply breakfast in the morning and dinner in the evening. We headed at the appointed time to the biggest building on the site, and when all were seated there must have been over four hundred people, the greatest mixing of the races I had ever experienced. One felt proud and humble at the same time at being part of the Universal Church—and not only a worshipping Church, but an eating and sleeping and cleansing Church. We ate morning and evening at the camp and we ate everything we got.

The first morning at breakfast we were joined by a Scottish couple, who picked up our Irish accents as quickly as we picked up theirs.

'What part of Ireland are you from?' asked the husband.

Pointing to my companions in turn, I gave the necessary information. 'Those two fellows are from Dublin, this is a Newryman and Liam and I are from a place you would hardly have heard of, Warrenpoint.'

The Scot smiled; 'I know it well. When I was a bairn I used go with mother and father on my holidays to Warrenpoint every year. I remember we always stayed in the same house.'

As he put his cup to his lips I could nearly see his recall process in operation as he plucked the images out of the past. 'The house was outside the town,' he continued, 'we walked to it from the railway station. It had a name,' and I could see him digging away for the name which eluded him.

I was digging in the memory garden myself for the names of those houses outside the town which kept visitors, and I volunteered 'Pleasure Step,' 'Mountain View,' 'Riverside,' 'Rose Cottage'.

'None of those,' he said, 'I remember you went up the hill to it. It sat on the top of the hill.'

With this final piece of information, the penny dropped and I exclaimed in triumph, 'Ardallan!'

'That's it, Ardallan, and the woman's name was Mrs O'Hare,' was his equally triumphant response, 'a lovely lady.'

'Meet her, son, Liam,' I laughed, as I motioned to Toots who was sitting beside him in utter disbelief. That was indeed a very happy breakfast.

If our camp had a name it eludes me, but it was situated close to one of Rome's notable churches *Santa Croce*—the Church of the Holy Cross—where relics of the True Cross are honoured. It was here we went to Mass each morning and invariably those of us who had experience 'on the Altar' were pressed into service, so many were the priests of all nationalities who were offering Mass.

The Latin Mass made for no language barriers, though there were occasions when the Latin of the celebrant would have been out of tune with the Canon's pronunciation back home. By the same token the celebrant might have given us a look of disbelief or exasperation with the version of the *Confiteor* we said in unison.

Mass, of course, came before breakfast in those days of fasting from midnight, so we were always early on the ball, and after the meal the day was our own. For us it was eight glorious days and nights. Any reservations we might have had about our accommodation vanished on the second night, for we were so tired we could have slept on the floor. Amazingly, to us who were experiencing the Mediterranean climate for the first time, four or five hours sleep was sufficient to charge the batteries for the next day's endeavours.

Cardinal Eugene Pacelli, as Pope Pius XII, had come to lead the Church just months before the War broke out, and through those awful years the clarity of his thought dispersed in his letters and addresses covered an amazing variety of insights into the life of the Church, and the world in general. It was no wonder, then, that our audience with him was a very special occasion. We were in his presence twice, the first in St Peter's and the second, four days later, at his summer residence at Castel Gondolfo. With many thousands of others we had packed into the Mother Church in the cool of the evening to await the arrival of the Pontiff, who in those days was always carried into the basilica on the *Sedia gestitoria,* an essential piece of Vatican furniture at the time. As he was borne up the aisle there was always an amazing atmosphere for we were well used to seeing it on the newsreels at home. No All-Ireland welcome home could ever be as frantic as the Pope's entry and procession up the aisle on his elevated chair.

My companions and I were at the front row at the barrier, even though we had neither badge nor ticket between us. As he was carried past, he bowed in acknowledgement and raised his hand blessing each side alternately, but it was with his eyes that he spoke and everyone in the applauding thousands experienced that eye-to-eye contact with the slim, almost gaunt figure in white.

It was in an entirely different context that we met the Pope the following Sunday afternoon at Castel Gondolfo, on a hill above Lake Albano. Some of us had been rowing on the lake and when we got back to the shore there was word that the Pope had been at the residence for the weekend, and that he might be meeting people later. Our bus took us up most of the way, but we finished the distance on foot, eventually walking into a courtyard where a couple of hundred people were already gathered. We were just in time, for within a couple of minutes the Pope emerged on to a small balcony overlooking the people, and not at a very elevated position. There was polite applause, unlike the rapturous welcome in St Peter's, and when it ended the Pope said something which sent ripples of laughter through the Italian-speaking people in the crowd. This set the tone for the next twenty minutes in which the most informal exchanges were conducted in a number of languages, including English, and the ever-smiling Papa invariably had the last word in whatever tongue was spoken. Of course, we '*Irlandesi*' always made our nationality clear to the Holy Father.

In recent years, that most humble and saintly Pope has been the target of a number of vicious attacks in print, mainly from Jewish authors who were critical of his wartime role and who felt he had not done enough to protect members of the Jewish community. There are still many of us around who remember Golda Meir who had been Israeli foreign minister before she became prime minister. This is what she said in her message of sympathy when the Pope died in 1958:

> '*We share in the grief of humanity at the passing away of His Holiness Pope Pius XII. In a generation marred by wars and discord, he upheld the highest ideals of peace and compassion. When fearful martyrdom came to our people in the decade of Nazi terror, the voice of the Pope was raised for the victims.*
>
> '*The life of our times was enriched by a voice speaking out on the great moral truths, above the tumult of daily conflict. We mourn a great servant of peace.*'

While John Paul II proclaimed saints at an all-time record rate, I was rather disappointed that he never got round to Eugene Pacelli, in whose eyes I saw something which I saw in the eyes of no other man.

Having fulfilled our penitential obligations and sampled almost everything which Rome had to offer in those eight days, we headed North, through Perugia to

Florence, where we only had a six hour stop to view some of the masterpieces of that city. Finally, on Friday evening, and after a short train journey from Innsbruck to Munich, we arrived in the coolness of the mountain village of Oberammergau.

The world knows that Oberammergau is a beautiful mountain village in Bavaria and that every ten years the villagers produce the Passion play which is a compelling experience for believing Christians, and indeed for many others besides. The world would not know that on this particular Saturday afternoon, Oberammergau and a neighbouring village, Unterammergau were playing in a soccer match. The Down equivalent would be a game between Upper Mourne and Lower Mourne.

Now the game itself did not attract too many spectators, nor was there anything like the passion we would have in a local derby game at home. It did, however, produce a high degree of skilful passing and remarkable goalkeeping which gave me my first insights into Continental football, and this was at its lowest level. I was highly impressed, though I do not remember who won the day.

I do remember that the next day my tummy, which had troubled me the day before, had settled sufficiently to give me confidence to take my seat at the depiction of The Passion of The Christ, which the villagers have been presenting for centuries, always with a sincerity and simplicity which touches the soul. It was a wonderful follow-up to Rome.

Monday morning, it was downhill all the way to Munich to catch a train with soft seats heading for Ostend.

It was Wednesday morning before we arrived back in The Point and the little sleep which I had on the boat from Heysham had to do me, for I was back on the late Belfast duty commencing at 3.30 P.M.

This chapter began with the announcement that Castlewellan and The Point were playing in the final of the Down Senior Championship without their two pilgrims, Toots and myself. The outcome of that game was like the sword of Damocles hanging over our heads all the time we were away, for if The Point lost, the finger of blame could be pointed at the pilgrims, who put the faith before the football. Happily, The Point didn't lose and were almost certain winners four minutes from the end when they led by four points. Those last few minutes, however, did not happen for the ball went over the wall at the town end of St Patrick's park, where Castlewellan were defending. It took some little time for it to be retrieved and when it was it was found to be punctured. Unfortunately for The Point, there was no other ball available as they had overlooked taking a spare, and so the game could not be finished. Many a boxer was 'saved by the bell' but very few football teams have been saved 'by the pin' as Castlewellan undoubtedly were that day.

The legend grew in The Point that John O'Hare, the Castlewellan goalkeeper, and my former captain and colleague on the Down team, was the culprit who thwarted our ambitions, but many years later he revealed the name of the guilty party to me. The man is long since gone to his eternal reward. I trust the Lord gave him a good judgement despite the prayers which were prayed on him in The Point.

We had another bite at the cherry and, with the two pilgrims back in harness, there was a reasonable degree of confidence that we could take the title at the second time of asking. Alas, such was not the case, for when the teams met again a few weeks later, Castlewellan were the victors by a single point—I have ghastly memories of my own display in that encounter.

Losing the Championship that year was not the biggest loss the club suffered for one of our great clubmen, Paddy O'Hare, died after a lingering illness. Paddy, a year younger than me, was one of our group who mixed football and friendship. With his own business, and engaged to be married to Kathleen O'Neill, he looked set to make a great contribution to the town. Both he and Kathleen, who died some years ago, are well remembered by those who knew them.

17 — The Oval Ball

In case it might be thought I only infringed the 'foreign games' rule' in going to watch soccer games, I also experienced the atmosphere of the oval ball on quite a few occasions. It was hard to work up an appetite for rugby when one had had no experience of playing or even seeing the game being played, except in newsreel shots of important games in the cinema. My only attempt at playing the game occurred when I was a comparatively young fellow. We were playing on the green in front of Dromore Terrace when, for a bit of diversion, someone suggested we play rugby. This we did with a round ball and our own version of the game as we might have seen it in the movies. My active participation in that game, and indeed in the rugby code, came to an end quite abruptly when Emmett McGivern's head was coming up out of the scrum as mine was only going down. The impact which followed left me with a broken tooth and Emmett with a nasty gash on his forehead. Forever after I confined my interest in rugby to the sideline.

My earliest view of organised rugby was at Inter-Provincial level, though only on a few occasions, but nothing I saw made me any more enthusiastic about the game. Success however, in whatever sport, inevitably attracts, and when Ireland won the Triple Crown in 1948, for the first time in I don't how many years, there was great delight throughout the country. The following year they repeated the achievement on Welsh soil and were set for three in a row in 1950, when after defeating England and Scotland, they had Wales at home to complete the task.

The game was at Ravenhill and I turned up expecting to be part of the historic occasion. In a sense I was fortunate to be there, for I had fractured a collarbone the previous Sunday and was off work. No better way to go to a rugby match than with your arm in a sling.

I was hardly into the ground when I heard the familiar, 'What are you doing here, Barney?' from a youthful Christian Brother Skehan who had taught in Newry before moving to Belfast. We had hardly settled our elbows on the rail which surrounded the pitch when there was another, 'What are you doing here boy?' This time from one of my colleagues on the Down team, Willie McKibben. I introduced him to Brother Skehan only for the good Brother to retort, 'When I get back to the house, the first thing I am going to do is ring Paddy O'Keefe.' Paddy was the General Secretary of the GAA at the time and would hardly have been worried about the transgressions of the ban.

This was the era of Jack Kyle, Carl Mullan, Jim McCarthy and Tom Clifford who were the powerhouse of this talented team, so it was with good reason that Irish hopes were high on this occasion on home soil. As the game developed, it became obvious that Ireland was in for a hard, dour struggle and overall it was a very frustrating first half, with the home crowd welcoming the half-time whistle.

In any brand of football the winding down of tension at the interval is always a blessed relief for the convinced supporters of both sides, as the misses and mistakes of the sides are brought back into focus. On this occasion, however, we never got to talking about the happenings of the previous 40 minutes for the tensions turned quickly to unbelief, amazement and even shock, when out of the crowd in the far corner a figure appeared carrying a sizable tricolour. There was a mighty cheer as he paraded down past the stand. Immediately every policeman in the ground rushed to bring the intruder to book. The standard-bearer of the national colours had obviously played a bit of rugby for he broke into a sprint and evaded the first few tackles with all the delicacy of a Kyle, and to roars of encouragement from the crowd. Eventually, force of numbers told, and he was hauled to earth in front of the stand and hustled out to the nearest Barracks.

No doubt there were many in the crowd who applauded his capture and who were appalled by the display of the 'foreign emblem', but for the nationally minded Ulstermen present it was an occasion for a chuckle.

The offending Irish supporter was a Dubliner, a student at University College Dublin (UCD), whose name, I think, was Joe Hughes, who later qualified as a solicitor. He died a comparatively young man and his obituary contained reference to his escapade at Ravenhill. I have never been back to Ravenhill since that day. With a view to refreshing my memory of the occasion I sought out newspaper reports of the game; the *Irish Independent* had no reference to the incident in its report of the match, but the *Belfast News Letter* felt strongly about it and commented:

> 'The antics of enthusiasts who went on to the pitch before the start were for the most part good humoured until one individual in a dark green shirt and apparently wearing a false black beard, produced an Eire tricolour and flaunted it before the spectators on the unreserved side... The band of the Royal Ulster Constabulary played God Save The King, which was taken up and sung by most of the large crowd, Irish and Welsh alike, though an ill-mannered youth in front of the reserved stand shouted 'up the rebels,' while others apparently tried to start up A Soldier's song.'[22]

In reading the papers of that weekend 50-odd years later, I was shocked to realise what I remembered and what I had not. I had forgotten the catastrophe which the *Irish Independent* headlined, *Welsh Victory Ends in Tragedy.* It went on to tell the story of how 80 people perished when their charter flight plane crashed on the return journey that Sunday as it was about to land at Llandow Airport, in Glamorganshire. In a separate piece it highlighted *Irish Victim's Tragic change of plans,* and went on:

> 'Radio Officer on the plane was Tony O'Carroll aged 26, a native of Omeath. He was due to go on a flight to Bermuda, but when he learned that the Tudor plane was to carry Welsh supporters to Dublin he was transferred by request so that he could visit friends in Dublin. In his school days he was a keen Gaelic footballer, playing for Co. Down minors.'[23]

In his school days he was a year or two behind me at The Abbey CBS and well known to me.

I read the *Newry Reporter* account of his funeral which took place in

Carrickcruppin, where his parents, Bernard and Alice, lived at Camlough. His sister, Mary Lewis, was well known to me, too, for she had married Gwyn Lewis, a Welshman, and bus driver at the Newry depot. Four of his former schoolmates were the pall bearers, Harry Collins, Seamus Blaney, Tom Small, and Tom Murray, all familiar Newry names to my generation. All have gone to their eternal destiny. Present at the funeral was Fr Mick Hardy, an Omeath man and an outstanding Louth footballer.

I could not leave that game, and the reports I read of it, without reference to Jack Kyle who created an aura of greatness in which his artistry, achievement and modesty were the ingredients. I heard him interviewed on the 50th Anniversary of the 1948 Triple Crown win. He was asked about 'squad training' and he indicated that there was no such thing in his day. The players came together the day before the game. They talked about the game for a few hours in the evening and they went out the next day and performed. Those were the days with no managers who could be blamed for defeats. Kyle was a medical doctor and with the rugby world at his feet he could have risen to the heights of his profession in Ireland or Britain, if he had wished. Instead, he went off to Africa and spent his working life there as a medical missionary. I sought him out in *The Encyclopaedia of Ireland,* expecting to get some details of his professional life, but not a word. Every detail of his rugby career in the Irish jersey is listed, but not a word of his life's work in Africa. That may well have been his own wish, but I feel Christian people should know of their heroes. I have met Jack Kyle once in very recent times and I am glad to know that he is living in retirement in Co. Down.

I have already introduced Liam Robbins as one of the two Dublin chaps who had teamed up with us on our Roman experience. He and I kept in touch with each other and when the South Africans came to play Ireland in Dublin, he invited me down for the weekend. I gladly accepted, for I had never seen the Springboks, the All Blacks or the Australians in action. Games against these teams were always prestige events that were fiercely competitive. While the game itself was exciting and enjoyable, it ended with a victory for South Africa. I recall, though, remarking at tea in the Robbins' household afterwards, that it was the first game of rugby or soccer I had attended without meeting someone from the Gaelic fraternity who recognised me.

On the following Friday, I was walking from Edward Street Railway Station in Newry to the bus depot at Hill Street, and as I turned left on to Monaghan Street I spied Seán McAteer coming in my direction on his carrier bike.

Any reader who had any involvement or interest in the GAA in Down from the 1940s to the 1990s may well smile at the mention of Seán's name. He was a GAA purist. I doubt if, in his lifetime, he would have played or watched any games other than Gaelic football, hurling, handball or camogie. It would surprise me, too, if he had ever danced anything but *céilí* dancing, of which he was a good exponent. He would have considered himself qualified to judge the expertise or otherwise of those who took part in the games and particularly of those who refereed them. He had a sense of humour and a caustic wit, which made sitting within earshot of him at a game an entertaining experience, unless, of course, you were the butt of some of his witticisms or criticisms, as I often was. His brother, Frank, was Treasurer of the Down County Board in my early playing days and his son Seán Óg McAteer is now the Secretary of the GAA in Down.

So here I am with my thoughts far from football, and Seán on his bike about 30 yards away. With one hand guiding the bicycle and the other gesticulating with pointed finger towards me, he asked loudly, 'Where were you on Saturday?' And as he passed without stopping, added, 'You go to the Savoy and you'll see where you were.'

I laughed to myself all the way over Monaghan Street and past the Savoy, where the Movietone or Pathe Newsreel featured in the programme for the latter part of the week. To satisfy my own curiosity, I went to the early showing that evening and sure enough, Ireland versus the Springboks was one of the items on the newsreel. When it came on screen, I scanned the crowd shots intently, for I had been standing behind the goals and thought I knew where to look. It was only in the last fleeting second that I saw my image. I never would have noticed it if I had not been forewarned. Even forewarned, I nearly missed it and I could only marvel at the remarkable powers of observation which Seán possessed.

Seán died a comparatively young man, years before his older brother, Frank, but he was in his heyday in the sixties when Down ruled the world.

Liam Robbins, whose guest I had been that previous weekend, did not even live to see the sixties, for he died in his early thirties from a brain haemorrhage. He was the healthiest looking fellow one could meet, my own height and better built. He worked as an engineer with the Dublin Port Authority but, best of all, he was a wonderful companion. Our comparatively short friendship introduced me to his father who, by any standards, was a remarkable man and like most remarkable men, a modest personality.

In one of my early visits to the Robbins home in Fairview, I noticed the picture of a young fellow in military uniform whom I thought bore a striking resemblance to another brother of Liam's, and I volunteered the obvious, 'Well that's a Robbins for sure.'

'Indeed it is,' responded Liam, 'it is my father in 1916.'

I lifted the picture and looked at it intently. 'He was only a boy,' I said to myself.

Frank Robbins was 19 when he enrolled in the Irish Citizen Army in 1914. Among the three men who interviewed him was Sean O'Casey. Two years later he was attempting to hoist the tricolour over the Royal College of Surgeons, but he had to give up the task because he was too heavy for the flagpole he was attempting to climb.

It was 60 years later that he was finally persuaded to write an account of his involvement in the national struggle in that historic period. His book, *Under the Starry Plough,* which was published in 1977, is a remarkable document of which Dr Donal McCartney wrote in his foreword:

> *'Close ups of people and events taken as it were with the box camera of the amateur, have a quality for the historian which is never captured in the skilful arranged portraits of the professionals. Here then is a valuable and*

largely unconscious contribution to our understanding of the revolutionary period in our history, in the form of a memoir written by a man whose only University was the Irish trade union movement, but who found himself participating in events that shaped the destiny of the nation.'[24]

My own response on reading *Under the Starry Plough* was to applaud the integrity and even the humility of its author. Not recorded in the book is the fact that Frank Robbins was later delegated to travel to America, to receive the personal records and papers of John Devoy, 'the last of the Fenians'.

---

24   Frank Robbins *Under the Starry Plough*, Dublin 1977, *p. 9*

18—The Crossroads of the Town

In the course of my life I wrote a song, in which one of the verses began with the line, 'McAnulty's kitchen is the crossroads of the town'.

I now write in prose that the seat which sat outside their front window had all the ambience of *'the stone that stood outside Dan Murphy's door.'* When the day's work was over we'd meet there, not so much in the winter but certainly in the spring and summer, sometimes before football, but always after. Terry was the only boy in the family and in our younger days would have enjoyed his football on the street, or down in O'Rahilly Park. That would probably have been the limit of his participation. In regard to Point and Down teams, he was a fanatic, even in the lean years. But there were many things up for discussion on McAnulty's seat besides football. Nellie and Billy McCabe, who lived next door, had their own seat, but when the *craic* was good would often use the neighbour's. Very often both seats had a full complement and the same *craic*.

I described Agnes Toner earlier as the controlling influence in the McAnulty household of my childhood. She had often put the fear of God into young boys like me, on our way through the McAnulty property to Church Street, but never did I imagine that she would be a major catalyst in my life.

This is now 1951, a long time from my first scolding from Agnes in the late 1920s. By this time, she had mellowed and I had matured sufficiently to know that when Agnes came to the front door to look up and down the street she was really noting who was on the seat, or on Billy McCabe's step, which invariably seated the overflow. She would retire and then after an interval of a minute or two would reappear and beckon the one she felt best suited to do her message.

This particular evening in early May, in the closing hours of what had been a beautiful day, Agnes appeared at the door. She took her customary look down the street shading her eyes from the descending sun. Then with a quick glance up the street she took in the information she needed without ever passing a word. In she went and after the allotted time span she reappeared. She beckoned me with her index finger, 'Bernie, a wee minute please.'

I followed her back into the kitchen expecting to be going down to Malocca's for two sixpenny sliders which was a regular run. But no, this was something more important and I sensed a degree of confidentiality in her tone.

'You know where Nurse Brogan lives?'

'I do surely.'

'Well there's another nurse lives with her, Nurse Polley, and I want you to give that parcel to her. It's a coat I'm sending back to Newell's,' and with a shake of her head added, 'I don't like it, and she's leaving it back for me.'

As she passed the parcel she warned, 'Don't tell any of those ones outside your business.'

Now I knew the Nurse Polley, to whom I was taking the parcel, by name for she travelled daily to Newry on a monthly ticket on which the holder's name was written. There was no linkage between us on the occasions she travelled on my bus, beyond the normal pleasantries extended to all passengers. Once, when I returned a fountain pen she had dropped on the bus, she was most gracious. She had thought it was a gonner.

On delivery of the coat, the doorstep conversation which followed initiated the first steps on the circuitous route which ended at the Altar rails in Leitrim Church just over two years later. Few men would make public the intimacies of a courtship but what I am about to reveal is much more personal than any of the 'kiss and tell' stories which make up so much of today's popular literature.

I was one of three men who married Polleys from Dundrum, and we all came to realise that the Polleys 'were something else'. I cannot document the experiences of the other two, but certainly a short time after Anne and I were informally engaged, I was seated in Seaview when she picked up a piece of material and an assortment of threads she had been working with before I arrived.

'Have you started something?' I asked.

'Yes' she answered, 'a fire screen,' and when she saw the query on my countenance she added, 'it will also be a coffee table.' It took me some time to cotton on to the mechanics of this combination of fire screen-coffee table, but I figured she knew what she was doing.

As the winter closed in and we spent more nights sitting in, she said to me one night, 'You are coming round here to sit there twiddling your thumbs when I'm working. You could be making a rug while you're sitting there.'

'Me make a rug?' I asked incredulously.

'Of course you could, it's so simple even you could do it.'

'Right you are then, you get the materials and I'll have a go at it,' was my grudging assent.

In due course, I got into the intricacies of rug making, which for most people is a comparatively simple operation. I, however, managed to make regular messes of the system which had to be sorted out by my instructor. 'such an unhandy man to be marrying,' is an observation which came into our relationship even before we married, and became a permanent part of the union with the simple change of tense.

Whatever about the rug, as the spring evenings turned into high summer, the fabric end of the fire screen turned into a work of art. By this time I had acquired an appreciation of Jacobean design in the expertise of my intended, and a couple of sore thumbs through my exertions and mistakes on my 'readicut' operation.

When Anne brought her finished product to show her colleague Nurse Hendron (they were the first health visitors in Newry), the latter was very impressed, and with her benediction, offered the advice, 'I know the very man who will make a beautiful coffee table with that, Alex Hanna. You take that to Alex Hanna.'

As it transpired, Alex Hanna had his business in a street just off the Shankill Road in Belfast, so the following week we each took a day off and headed down to Belfast on the bus and to North Street Depot, which was quite close to the Shankill Road. A single inquiry and we were directed to Tennant Street, a street which became a very common name throughout 'The Troubles' because of its police Barracks. We found the shop with the name A Hanna painted above the window, which could hardly have been said to have been arranged to attract customers.

We entered and stood looking around for a little while, before a movement at the rear indicated a smallish man emerging from what might have been an office. In the friendliest of tones he asked, 'How are ye doing?' rather than the more usual, 'Are you looking for something?' I warmed to Alex at once. He had a cap on the back of his head, glasses well down on his nose and wore a sleeved waistcoat. Before she even unrolled the small parcel, Anne was telling him what she wanted and that Miss Hendron from Newry had recommended him as someone who would do a good job.

'I haven't seen any of the Hendrons for years,' said Alex, and asked, 'did Cissie ever marry?'

When Anne explained that Cissie hadn't married and that she was the Miss Hendron she worked with, Alex ended that part of the conversation with the verdict of many a man: 'A brave girl she was.' He went on to take and examine the fabric which Anne had produced and listened to what she wanted done with it. He studied for a while before making the comment, 'That's as nice a piece of Jacobean[25] as I've seen in a good while,' and it was obvious he was impressed. 'It will take something very well done to do it justice,' and then after a long pause he added, 'I'm a bit past that kind of fine work, but I know the man who could do the job for you.'

'Did you come in a car?' he asked,

'No, we're on the bus,' I replied.

'Well, I'll tell you what you'll do,' he began, 'go back to Lisburn on the bus. Get off down at The Square,' and he followed with a stream of directions which ended, 'when you get to McCarter's furniture factory, ask for Willie. You tell Willie that I sent you, and he'll do the job you want.'

As we took our leave, thanking him profusely, he called after us, 'Don't forget to tell Cissie I was asking for her.'

We had a cup of tea, got the next bus to Lisburn, followed Alex's directions to the letter, and landed at McCarter's furniture factory.

'Would it be possible to see Mr Willie McCarter?' I asked at reception.

'He's out on the factory floor at the minute, but I'll see if he's free to come up, what's the name please?' the girl inquired.

'Our names would mean nothing at all to him, but if you tell him Alex Hanna sent us, it might mean something,' was my advice.

Much quicker than I expected, a tall, smiling man entered the office and as I rose to greet him, the most welcoming voice said, 'Ach, you're friends of Alex. I haven't seen him in a long time. How is he keeping?'

I hastened to explain that we had only met Alex for the first time a couple of hours before, and I was apologising for taking him from his work. He put up his hand in a silencing motion to put us at our ease with the pronouncement, 'Alex Hanna only sends special people up to me. What can I do for you?'

We were hardly over the introductions before there was a knock on the

---

25   Originally a type of English embroidery with a strong oriental influence, of the type first done during the Restoration period. Jacobean designs are nowadays found most frequently as upholstery fabrics.

door, and the receptionist entered with a teapot and a selection of food on a tray which was fit to set before the Queen of England.

Over tea, Anne explained how she wanted her fire screen/coffee table and Mr McCarter knew exactly what she was talking about. When he saw the fabric he, too, was most impressed and agreed it would make a fine piece of furniture.

'Yes, we'll do a very nice job for you,' he promised.

As Anne and I both expressed our satisfaction with nods of approval, he asked, 'What kind of wood would you like it in? We can do it in oak or walnut or mahogany or whatever.'

A brief consultation and Anne advised, 'I think we'd like it in mahogany, Mr McCarter.'

Mr McCarter leaned back in his chair and I could see the smile forming on his lips and in his eyes, 'I hope you won't mind me asking you, but would you be Roman Catholics?'

'As a matter of fact we are,' I answered, 'but why would you ask?'

'Well, I have always found that the Roman Catholics are very partial to the mahogany.'

The three of us collapsed in laughter. On regaining my composure I had to confess that I had heard of 'rice Christians,' and many kinds of Catholics, but never 'mahogany Catholics'.

I only met Willie McCarter once again in my life and that was a few weeks later when I called to collect the finished article; after 50 years of service it is as good, and as much admired, as the day I brought it home. Willie McCarter was an older man than me, as indeed was Alex Hanna, and I'm sure both have gone to their eternal reward. Sharing eternity with them in whatever mansion will make heaven all the more wonderful.

Now I can hear readers already asking, 'Whatever happened to your rug, Barney, did you ever finish it?' Well indeed I did, and it has given great service, too. For the early years of its life it was a much-admired hearthrug. Then for a lengthy period it was demoted to the bedroom where I stepped on its welcoming warmth first thing in the morning and last thing at night for many years. For a time it lay untrodden and unused in the backhouse, but latterly it has come back into service, as a doormat—a backdoor mat. I will be instructing Cathal McAnulty not to be too concerned about my coffin comforts. He can lay me gently on my bed of 'readicut' and send me off to the Lord with every confidence that I will arrive in His kingdom well rested.

Having introduced my grandchildren to a grandmother they will never know, and recalling my early ignorance of my own family tree, I feel compelled to broaden their knowledge of the remarkable family to which she belonged. Her father, John Polley, was a native of the Strangford area, who spent his early working life with the Belfast and County Down Railway, before moving to work for one of the Belfast fruit importers. He married a Belfast girl called Molly Walsh. The first born of the Polley family was a boy who survived for twelve days. There were six other children, all girls, and Molly died a week after the youngest was born.

Johnnie Polley was left to bring up six girls. He had the good sense to marry again, to a teacher, Sarah Dummigan, one of the gentlest women I have met in my life. To the Polley girls she might not always have seemed 'the gentle lady' for there was a firmness in her character which one would have expected in a teacher of the time. Her humour was gentle, too, and very often the school-based incidents she related were against herself.

She was a very tall lady, over six feet. On one occasion she visited St Mary's Hall in Belfast to view an exhibition centred round the life of Patrick Murphy, the Killowen giant who was over eight feet tall. He is buried in Kilbroney Cemetery at Rostrevor and it is said that the huge high cross over his grave was exactly his height. As she was coming down the stairs after viewing the exhibits, two young Belfast lads were going up. As they passed her, one said to the other, 'Holy God, Mickey, that must be the giant's sister.'

Whether it was her influence or not, three of the girls opted for the teaching profession. The eldest, Eithne, set the example, though the next in line Vera, chose the religious life with the Daughters of Charity, otherwise known as the Butterfly Nuns. She was something of a trailblazer in that she was one of six nuns who introduced the order to Australia in the mid-thirties. Next in line, Eileen, spent a couple of years in primary teaching before following her sister into the order. Maureen also went into teaching, Anne into nursing and Monica into the civil service, for which choices Niall Brannigan, Willie McKibben and I were very grateful.

Johnnie Polley and Molly Walsh did not live long enough to experience the joy and wonder of their six girls whose lives, with the nurturing of Sarah Dummigan, reflected the values they inherited. These girls and their families have carried those values across the globe. I have never heard the parable of the mustard seed related that I do not think of that small, happy household in Moneylane.

One strand in the Polley story began in Kircubbin where Daniel Walsh, a Cork man and a Sergeant in the RIC, along with his wife, Eliza, reared a family of six boys and two girls. Three of the boys, James, John and Arthur, entered the priesthood and a fourth, Cornelius, was intent in following them but died from tuberculosis at an advanced stage in his studies. Fr James taught in St Malachy's College. He, too, suffered from tuberculosis and went to a sanatorium in the Black Forest, accompanied by his sister, Ellie, where he died and was buried. Fr Arthur, also a TB victim, died while a curate at Ballykinlar. Fr John served in various parishes in the Down and Connor Diocese and again I have recourse to Eamon Phoenix and his *On This Day* feature in *The Irish News*, to complete his story.

'Dateline December 24 1935. Headline 'Belfast priest dies in New York fire.'

> News has been received in Belfast of the death under distressing circumstances of the Rev. John Walsh, who for some years was attached to the diocese of Down and Connor, before he left for the mission on the far continent.
>
> In a letter to the deceased's sister, Mrs E. McGlade, 87 The Mount, Mountpottinger, Mr James Walsh, a brother, who resides at Utica, relates

how Fr Walsh met his death.

A fire broke out in the presbytery of the church of St Anthony of Padua, Chadwick, New York of which he was pastor, and in a heroic attempt to extinguish the flames he received fatal burns. The late Fr Walsh was ordained at Maynooth College in 1902 and his first curacy was on Rathlin Island. He was appointed ecclesiastical inspector for the diocese of Down and Connor, after which he became curate of St Mary's, Belfast. Some years later he was appointed curate of Lisburn, and after a period in the parish, was changed to a curacy in St Malachy's, Belfast.

In 1923 he went on the missions to America and was appointed assistant pastor in St Mary's, Binghampton, New York. He then took charge of St Anthony's, Chadwick.'[26]

To complete the Walsh saga and the parable of the mustard seed it should be recorded that Ellie, Molly Walsh's sister to whom the letter was written, was the wife of Patrick McGlade. They reared a family of ten children, among them a priest and two nuns. Fr Joe McGlade, a Columban father, was rector at Dalgan Park, Navan in 1975 when he went to the Columban house at Boston on holiday, where he died suddenly, and is buried there. He was aged 57.

Nora and Mairead McGlade both joined the Dominican Order of nuns. Mairead, the youngest of the McGlade family and the only survivor, is still active in South Africa. Nora, known as Sister Casimir, died in Belfast at an advanced age in October 2008. She was one remarkable woman even in her years of retirement.

There is one last segment of the Walsh saga and it concerns Eliza, who, with her policeman husband Daniel, later lived in Derramore Avenue on Belfast's Ormeau Road. She died from gas poisoning in 1910. She was asleep in her bedroom when the gas fire went out because the metered money was used up. Someone in the family came into the house and put money in the meter not realising the fire in her room was extinguished. She was dead when discovered some time later.

The Polley saga began as far back as 1844 when an earlier Anne Polley was born to William and Isabella Polley of Churchvale, Ballee, Co. Down, and I now introduce her 20 years later via the annals of the Sisters of Mercy, Ardee:

'On September 29th 1864 a fifth postulant entered in Ardee. She was Anne Polley, daughter of William and Isabella Polley of Co Down. She was received on July 27th 1865 and made her religious profession on November 21st 1867. The most Rev. Michael Kieran, Primate of All Ireland, officiated at the profession.

A large number of friends and many of the leading gentry in the Catholic families of Louth, Meath and Co. Down were present. Archdeacon Tierney, P.P. Drogheda, delivered an appropriate discourse, which was listened to with marked attention by all who had the privilege of being present. The sermon was eloquent and impressive, and beautifully illustrated the obligations and advantage of the religious life and the means by which perseverance is obtained. After the ceremony the clergy and other visitors

26   *Irish News*, 24 December 2004

were entertained hospitably by the good Sisters of the Convent

Sr M. Joseph's sister, Mary, —Sr M. Brigid Polley entered in 1872. While still a novice, a big trial awaited her. Sr M. Joseph became seriously ill. Sr M. Brigid nursed her dying sister and did all she could to alleviate the suffering of the poor patient, but to no avail, and it was with a sorrowful heart that she followed the coffin of her sister to the Convent Cemetery just one month before she herself was to make her holy profession. These were the first two sisters to enter the Community and their time together as religious was indeed short.'

In contrast to her sister, Sr Mary Brigid had a long life and died in her 88th year in July, 1937. These sisters were the great-aunts of the Anne Polley I married.

19—The Goal That Never Was

My Inter-County football career came to a veritable end in 1952. When a centre forward or midfielder is selected to play in the corner, he knows his days are numbered, so after ten years of senior county football, I called it a day. In those days there was none of the concentrated training which has enabled players of the modern era to go well into their thirties and the odd one even beyond. The game then required pace just as much as it does today, so a decade at county level was a reasonable spell. But already my interest in all GAA activities was broadening. I had begun representing the club at divisional and county conventions, and the county at Ulster and National Congress. I had also taken up refereeing, as many county players did at the time. The Ulster College competitions provided an outlet for chaps like myself who were still active playing football at club level. While 1953 brought the most important match of my life in my marriage to Anne Polley, within weeks of that event I was involved in a match which has come back to life in a series of 'replays' on many occasions since.

At this time Fr Hugh Connolly was in charge of football at St Colman's College, Newry, and he would call on my services on occasion. On a particular Saturday I had agreed to referee a MacRory Cup game between St Colman's and St Patrick's, Armagh. It was a working day for me and I was squeezing the game into an interval of two and a half hours which I had created. He had me picked up by one of the teachers and I was getting togged out when Fr Hugh entered the room.

'Barney,' he began, 'would you have any objections to us playing with one umpire at each goal today. I have already discussed it with Armagh and they are in agreement.' Apparently there had been a game in which the umpires had differing views which led to a needless arguing match; it was the desire to avoid a repeat of the incident which engendered the proposal.

I considered his words and while I was aware that the proposal was against the rule which distinctly required two umpires at each goal, I could not see any complications.

I said, 'Father, you realise when umpires differ, the referee makes the decision. Are you saying to me that the decision of the one umpire will be final in this game?' He indicated that he had discussed this with Father So-and-so from Armagh, and they were in complete agreement.

'Right,' I concluded 'if you are both happy enough, I'll go along with it.'

Let me state that Colman's had a very good team that year and had high hopes of another MacRory Cup. Within ten minutes, they had a ten-point lead without a single score from the Armagh boys. I describe the game a few minutes later when Armagh were on one of their rare attacks and I am well placed just outside the 14 yard line. An Armagh forward comes in solo from the right, fires in a real screamer of a shot, which went across the face of the goal and to my mind, was a yard wide.

Now the single umpire behind the goal was Fr 'Loughy' McAleavey, a former student and talented footballer at St Colman's (and with Clonduff), who immediately went for the green flag and signalled a goal. There were no goal nets, and I was in a quandary.

I ran into the goal area, 'Father, are you sure that was in? I thought it was well wide.'

'Oh, definitely a goal, Barney! Definitely a goal!' he answered.

Flummoxed, I turned, pointed to the 21 yard line indicating 'the goal' stood and observing the chap who put the shot over jumping the height of himself in exuberance at this gift from the gods. While there were protests from some of the St Colman's defenders, they were not over demonstrative, for this was Armagh's first score. At half-time, with Colman's leading by 12 points, the 'goal' wasn't mentioned.

When play resumed after the interval, St Colman's still exerted dominance in the early minutes without adding to their lead but Armagh's persistence gradually brought a few points, resulting in the Newry boys beginning to lose their way. They missed quite a number of good chances to add to their confusion. By contrast, the Armagh lads were scoring with half chances and five minutes from the end they were back in the game with a chance. St Colman's were absolutely shattered as Armagh kept up the pressure and came with a goal almost on the stroke of full time, which I felt was enough to see them in front.

The moment I sounded the final whistle there was an invasion of boys from the line, some shouting, 'Was it a draw ref?' Others, 'It was a draw ref!' I knew Armagh had got home by a point, but to give reassurance to this jostling crowd of boys I did a formal count of my score sheet before announcing, 'Armagh have won by a point.'

Then the cry went up, 'What about that goal in the first half, ref? That was no goal.'

It wasn't, but it sealed St Colman's fate that day.

When he came into the room where I was dressing, Fr Hugh was as grim as I had ever seen him. I could only make a gesture with my open hands and shrugged shoulders.

'No blame to you,' he assured me, 'I'm the culprit.' Then he turned to me and in a different tone of voice asked, 'Do you know what I am going to do on Monday morning?' and before I could even hazard a guess, he added, 'I'm going to order a new set of nets, even if it should put the College into bankruptcy.'

Fortunately or otherwise I had to hurry to get back to work, missing the inquest and the cup of tea.

The following Monday evening I was finishing work to get the 6.20 P.M. bus home when the inspector on duty told me there was an urgent message in the office for me. In I went, to be handed a piece of paper with the injunction, 'You're to ring that number before you go home.' This I did, to find myself speaking to Fr Christy Murray in Banbridge.

'Barney, I need to see you tonight,' and this with an urgency in his voice which suggested something serious.

'Well, Father,' I complained, 'I was catching this 6.20 bus home.'

'What time is the next one?' he asked and I retorted, 'In one hour's time,

7.20.'

He continued, 'Barney, this is urgent, I really need to see you. If you wait until I get to Newry I will run you home to Warrenpoint.'

'If it is that urgent, Father, I'll certainly wait,' I volunteered, and I sensed his relief as he brought the exchange to an end with, 'I'll leave this minute.'

It was a miserable night and I went into the adjacent snack bar for a cup of tea. While drinking, I was contemplating what could be so important. Not once in our phone conversation did Fr Murray allude to the matter which was so urgent, and I awaited his arrival almost with a sense of foreboding. Inside twenty minutes his car drew up at the Belfast Bank where we had arranged to meet, in sight of the snack bar. He opened the passenger door and as I got in he thanked me for waiting, and before I could even ask, 'What is the problem?' he shattered me with a question.

'What are you going to do about this match, Barney?'

I had been sitting in the snack bar, considering possible issues for discussion but the thought of football, and certainly not 'this match,' never entered my mind. Indeed it was a great relief to me to learn that the urgency of our meeting was nothing more than a game of football.

'What do you mean, Father, what am I going to do about this match?'

'Well, you'll be making a report on it.'

'I'll be making the normal report.'

'But you'll have to mention that goal, that wasn't a goal at all.'

'Look, Father,' I said with more than a little exasperation, 'Fr Loughy gave it as a goal and that has to stand, there's nothing I can do to change that.'

Fr Murray went on to sermonise about Fr Loughy's eyesight, but finally admitted that he had been clutching at straws. Our exchange of views finished just in time for me to catch the next bus home.

For some little time after, the game provided no end of discussion between a couple of St Colman's old boys and myself. They held the view that the game should have been declared null and void because there was not the required number of officials.

I have to advance the fast forward button over 30 years to continue the tale, when, as a servant of the Southern Education and Library Board, I was approaching the entrance to the Beleek Primary School in Co. Armagh; the door there had already been opened for me by the principal, Mrs Duffy. I was aware that she was taking the farewell of another visitor, whom I was to discover later was also from the Board and who was standing back a step or two with a bemused smile on his face.

'This man thinks he knows you, Mr Carr,' said the welcoming Mrs Duffy.

I looked at the well-made figure complete with moustache, receding hairline and a broadening smile.

'Did you play a bit of football?' I probed, and he nodded, 'Yes.'

'You certainly didn't play in my time,' I continued, as I tried to picture the face without a moustache and a more lavish covering of hair.

'Oh, indeed I was a long time after you, but you did a bit of refereeing, too, and once you were short of umpires,' he countered with another broadening smile.

The penny dropped for me, and I gasped, 'You are not Patsy Kerrins, are you?' He nodded in assent and laughter, as I observed to Mrs Duffy, 'The man who scored the goal that never was.'

I push the fast forward button another decade and I am in the Cusack Stand with my daughter, Louise, for the 1995 hurling final, occupying our ten-year seats for the first time. On our left was a friendly man and wife with whom we soon established conversation. The fact that this chap had spent all his working life 'in the South' did not disguise his northern accent. We soon sorted out our identities and it transpired that he was Seamus O'Hanlon, a very capable footballer both with Armagh Harps and the Armagh county team. He was, and is, living in retirement in Carrickmacross after a career in *An Garda Siochána*. He asked after Des Slevin, another Harps man, who has lived in contented exile in The Point for most of his life, rearing a couple of good Down footballers in the process.

The annual Croke Park get-togethers with the O'Hanlons were going for some years before Seamus said to me one day, 'Every time I come here I leave home with the intention of asking you about a particular game of football, and invariably I have forgotten, so before the excitement starts today I want to ask it.'

I looked at him intently expecting to be asked about some game in which Down had been involved, as he continued, 'Do you remember refereeing a MacRory Cup game between St Pat's, Armagh and St Colman's?'

'Do you mean the game of Patsy Kerrins' goal that should never have been?' I laughed back at him.

'The very one. I was playing in that game and you should remember me for at the end of the game I had an argument with you, for I thought we were beaten.'

I had no memory of an argument, but I had a very clear memory of a tall, dark lad jumping sky-high when I told him Armagh had won by a point. No tall, dark lad now, I can tell you. A year later, Seamus told me I was right, there was no argument, he was recalling a different game and a different referee.

I have been a member of the Dromore Diocesan Historical Society since its inception and on 8 September 2004 I went to Lurgan for a lecture, to find the building we regularly used locked. 'It must be at the room which is part of the church building,' I thought, and retraced my steps and up the narrow stairs where, on hearing voices, I knocked on the door and entered. There wasn't a big crowd of people in the room, but every face turned to the door at the intrusion. To my dismay, there was not one familiar face in view. I knew this was not the Historical Society and was withdrawing with profuse apologies when the chap who appeared to be chairing the meeting stood up and exclaimed, 'Hold on a minute, Barney,' and addressing those in the room, most of whom were females, he declared, 'This is my favourite referee whom I haven't seen in a long time.'

He left the room with me to search for the Historical Society, but we soon discovered that I was a week early for my lecture. He had introduced himself to me as Brendan McStravick, a name which was quite familiar to me on a couple of counts.

When I asked where he had experienced my refereeing skills, he began, 'Well, I went to St Colman's.'

Before he got another word out I was finishing the sentence for him, 'And you were playing in the game when St Pat's got the goal that never was.'

'No,' he laughed. 'I was only a sub and was only on for a few minutes at the end, but we were disappointed that day.'

I have no doubt that when Brendan went back to his meeting, the story of 'the goal that never was,' got another airing.

In August 2008, I was at Daisy Hill Hospital visiting Charlie McConville of Kilkeel, the only survivor of the first Down team to play in an Ulster Championship final in 1940. As I made my way through the foyer to the Exit door I was greeted by Val Murphy of Rostrevor and his son, along with a familiar smiling face I struggled to put a name on.

'Do you know this man?' asked Val and as he saw me struggling, added, 'he's a Derryman.'

'Holy God, it's Phil (Stuart),' I exclaimed.

Phil, who had his good wife by his side, proceeded to regale Val, his brother-in-law, with an account of a match in which he had played and for which I had been the referee, and how badly I had treated him. I soon realised the game he was talking about was the very game I have been writing about.

'Are you telling us about the game with the goal that never was?' I asked, for I never would have associated Phil with St Patrick's, Armagh.

'Yes,' said Phil, 'I was playing in the middle of the field for St Pat's and Patsy Kerrins was the man who never scored the goal.' And then followed a rehash of that match of 55 years ago. I promise I will never write another word about that game.

20—Tragedy on the Lough

It was still 1953 when I created a sensation by collapsing at Mass on the first Sunday of December. Of course, I didn't become aware of this until I 'came round,' sitting on a chair outside the church with my wife of three months holding a glass of water to my lips. I did not feel ill at all and had no problem walking the short distance to Church Street where we lived at the time. I was puzzled, though, for we had been out the previous night at a Newry Musical Society offering of *The Desert Song* and I had never felt better.

I had breakfast, felt completely normal, and declared my intention of going back to the High Mass to commence the three days of prayer known as the *Triduum,* in preparation for the Marian Year, which was to open on the feast of the Immaculate Conception, 8 December, two days later. I was a member of the choir at the time and probably felt they would have a job coping without me. Despite the protestations of my wife and her sister, Eithne, who had been with us for the weekend, off I went, opened the Marian Year, came home and almost collapsed into bed. A severe attack of pneumonia ensured that I didn't get out of it again until New Year's Day. It was the middle of January before I was back at work. Never again did I disobey my wife in matters of medicine or health care. I mention the Marian Year, because we had decided we would go to Lourdes during the year. We opted for a date in June and while there were plenty of organised pilgrimages going out, we decided we would go under our own steam, for there were a couple of calls we were making on the way. There could have been an economic argument, too, because as an Ulster Transport Authority (UTA) employee, I had a travel concession right to the coast of France for myself and my wife. As well as that, we had free accommodation in London with my friend O'Boyle, who had married three years earlier. I had been back in London then to be his best man.

We stayed just one night with the O'Boyles, intending to stay longer on the way back. I remember the most important item on the 6 o'clock news that Saturday evening was a raid on Gough Army Barracks, Armagh, by the IRA who made off with a couple of lorry loads of arms and ammunition.

I had booked rail tickets and hotels and everything went according to plan. On the way back we spent three days in Paris and, as the Polley family had shares in the organisation known at the Daughters of Charity, we had strict instructions to visit the *Rue de Bac* where the motherhouse is located. As it turned out, a few Irish nuns had already been advised we would be calling, and we were given a royal reception. The *Rue de Bac* is not among the most fashionable streets of Paris, nor is the entrance to the convent the most impressive, but once behind the massive gate, heaven on earth begins. It was peopled by dozens of the Butterfly Nuns among whom were some very good cooks, and we experienced French *cuisine* at its height.

Eventually, we were back in London, intending to have a few days at the same pace we experienced in Paris. After a good first night's rest with the O'Boyles, Anne and I set off to see the sights of London. This was her first visit to the city. We went for an early lunch to one of the Lyons Corner Houses which were then very popular in London, and were shown to a table immediately. We didn't have time to lift the menu before a newspaper was thrust in front of me and a familiar voice saying, 'That was a shocking tragedy at home yesterday, Barney.' I glanced up to recognise the distressed face of Kevin Duffy, whose family had their shop across the street from us.

I read the front page of *The Irish Press* which he had put in front of me: *'Carlingford Lough Disaster, seven lost in boating accident.'*

Those lines have been imprinted in my consciousness to this day. I could scarcely read the paper as I announced the names to my wife—Hugh O'Hare, Maisie, his wife, Brian, their seven-year-old son; Bernadette Ogle, a sister of Maisie whom the locals would have known as Pip, Frank O'Hare and Ernie McManus. The other name, Josephine Keegan, I did not recognise. There was only one survivor, Charles McDonald of Newry, who had a gents' tailoring and dress shop. He was a brother of my first teacher, Miss Eithne McDonald.

Kevin, Anne and I were all close to tears as we turned the tragedy over and over. We hardly felt like ordering food. Indeed, London had lost its attraction for us. We returned to the O'Boyle household early to tell them of the dreadful news. Like myself, Chris knew all of them with the exception of Josephine Keegan. Cynthia, his wife, even though she would only have spent a few holidays in The Point, knew the O'Hare and Ogle families quite well.

We headed for home the next day, earlier than we had intended and arrived back to a devastated town in time for the last of the funerals.

While one never can get the full picture of such an event, it would seem that a combination of circumstances came together quite innocently. It was only 8 o'clock on a June evening when the boat left Carlingford. A strong ebb tide and a breeze off the land probably created a problem which called for more experienced seamanship. It's a treacherous bar and always has been.

Despite a slight disability, Hugh O'Hare was a strong swimmer and he obviously made a tremendous effort to save his little boy, Brian, who was found in the clasp of his father on the northern shore of the lough. They are buried beside the graves of my parents and brother. The bodies of his wife, Maisie, and his sister-in-law, Bernadette (Pip), were never recovered.

Ernie McManus had been a Dubliner who came to The Point as a youth sometime after his elder brother, Jack, the professional at the Warrenpoint Golf Club, married Theresa Devlin, a Warrenpoint girl. For us, Ernie was 'the original Dub'; a strong accent and a great sense of humour made him a well-liked figure. He would have been regarded as a true Point man with a Dublin accent.

Frank O'Hare, who was a few years ahead of me in primary school, was a very good student. He was one of a number of Warrenpoint fellows who served in the Irish Army during the War and was very highly thought of in the town.

Fifty years later, on 22 June 2004, the tragedy was commemorated in Carlingford and Warrenpoint. After services in the respective churches, wreaths were cast on the waters which were much angrier than they had been on the fateful night. Before the Mass in Carlingford, two members of the Carlingford

Heritage Trust read an account of the happenings of 50 years before, with a stark simplicity which completed the picture for me. The full story of Josephine Keegan, which I had not known previously, was included. I record it in full:

'The party had been on a picnic in Carlingford, and were returning to Warrenpoint.

They left Carlingford about 8 o'clock, and it appears, that when some distance out from the shore, the engine of the motor boat stalled and the vessel began to take water. There were heavy seas and squally winds, and quickly the boat foundered. While people on both shores watched helplessly, most of those in the water disappeared, but wild shouts for help could still be heard by watchers on the Carlingford shore.

When the first alarm was given, by Miss Eunice Boyle, of North Street Commons, who phoned the Guards that persons were struggling in the water, many Carlingford residents rushed to the waterside. Unfortunately the tide was at low ebb, and the bigger boats, which would have got quickly to the scene, were high and dry and could not be floated. Only a few rowing boats could be launched—the first by our own,, Tommy O'Hare and Joe McGuinness and a second with Guard Rice and Mr Dave Murray, on holiday from Dublin where he is a radio operator with Aer Lingus. They set out for the foundered vessel, and had great difficulty in making headway against the heavy seas. It was around nine o'clock before they reached the boat. On it they found the lone survivor in an exhausted condition, and with great difficulty he was taken on board and returned to Carlingford.

Meanwhile other boats had come on the scene, from both sides of the lough, including some RUC boats, equipped with searchlights. For a considerable time the area was searched, but no sign of bodies could be found.

The survivor, Mr McDonald, was taken ashore at Carlingford, and after attention, was brought to Louth Infirmary in Dundalk, suffering from shock and exposure. Mr McDonald told his rescuers that the engine had stalled, and hit by heavy seas, the boat heeled over. The occupants all jumped and he saw Mr O'Hare making a grab for his little son.

Then he saw no more.

News of the disaster cast a gloom over the entire Carlingford Lough area, where the victims were all well known. Mr O'Hare was a well-known Newry Commission Agent, and had three other children, in addition to the little drowned boy. Mr McDonald and Miss Keegan (a native of Co Mayo) had announced their engagement recently. The party, with the exception of Miss Keegan, had come to Carlingford on a picnic, and had met many local people during the evening. They persuaded Miss Keegan, who was a teacher in Bush Post Primary School, and who lived in Carlingford, to return with them to Warrenpoint. She left in the boat after acquainting Mr Vincent Kieran, Headmaster of the school that she would travel to the school, by bus

via Newry the next morning.
Josephine Keegan was never to stand in the classroom again.
Let us again remember those who died 50 years ago today.'

Seven candles were carried to the Altar in memory of the seven victims as their names were called in turn. A teacher at Bush Post Primary School carried the candle in memory of Josephine Keegan. The celebrant of the Mass was Fr Jim Carroll, CC.

In Warrenpoint, the occasion was commemorated an hour later at an Ecumenical Service of Remembrance in St Peter's Church, conducted by Canon John Kearney and Fr Peter McNeill, for all who had lost their lives in Carlingford Lough in living memory. On the altar steps glowed 121 candles in red glass holders, each denoting one of those lives. In the course of the service a name was called for each one of them. Being one of 'the elders' in the congregation, the mention of some of those distant names evoked sad memories of many occasions. One of those names was John Tumility from Newry, a cousin of my mother's, who was a fireman on the *Retriever*, the coaster which collided with the *Connemara* at the entrance to the lough in 1921. For some reason he was late getting down to the Albert Basin and the boat left without him. He borrowed a bicycle and cycled down the Omeath Road passing the boat on the way. He boarded the *Retriever* at the Victoria Locks and sailed to his death on the return trip to Newry. John was the grandfather of John McArdle, a member of Newry and Mourne District Council.

One other name was Colm Garvey, an eighteen-year old clerical student in his first year at Maynooth and on holiday with his relatives, the McCart family, in Duke Street. He was walking along the Promenade at Osborne Terrace when a girl got into difficulties in the water. Her screams for help prompted him to jump from the sea wall at its highest point. He managed to get to the girl and she was saved but he himself drowned. In the jump from the wall he had hurt himself and could not manage to get back to the shore. When all this was happening in 1937, I was at the stern of the *Madonna* with my boathook in the water wondering what the commotion was up at Osborne Promenade.

After the ceremony in St Peter's Church, the congregation moved to the breakwater at Osborne Terrace where, in driving wind and rain, the commemorative wreath was cast upon the angry sea by Canon Kearney. I left the ceremony in the company of Bill Quinn, a Mourne man I have known for most of my life. In the course of the conversation I observed to him, 'I never liked that bloody boat. She was a stubby tub if ever there was one.'

He said, 'I never liked her either and I built her.' He went on to explain that Hugh O'Hare had got the design plan from a boat builder in England and he, Bill, was given the task of building her.

Not many months after that June evening in 1954, there was another death in the town in the person of my uncle, Tommy Tumilty, a veteran of the War of Independence. He had lived with Aunt Kitty and her husband, Jack Moran, who had been a Sergeant in the RIC until that force was disbanded.

Tommy was taken ill on the last Sunday of October and became a patient in Daisy Hill Hospital that evening. The following evening, I called to see him and found him in reasonably good form. He indicated that he was due to have a series of tests in the next week. In our conversation I told him that Anne and I were going to Dublin at the weekend to see my sister, who was in hospital in Co. Wicklow.

On Wednesday, when some of my family were visiting him, he sent word that he wished to see me. Up I went that evening and I found little or no change in him. After the regular opening exchanges of a hospital visit he pulled himself up in the bed and I knew by his demeanour that he was about to indicate the purpose of the visit.

He shocked me when he said in the coolest possible manner, 'Barney, son, I am not going to come through this operation.' With a slight movement of the hand, he brushed aside my reassurances that he would take it in his stride, and continued, 'I want you to do something for me, for if I die "the boys" will want to give me a military funeral. I would be honoured to have one, but I would not want anything which would embarrass Jack. He has been like a brother to me over the years and I would not want to cause him the slightest embarrassment.'

Eventually, I took my leave of him with the reassurance that he would be back home in a week or two and I really thought he would be. Anne and I went to Dublin on Saturday morning, spent the day and night there and on Sunday morning took the bus to Newcastle, Co. Wicklow, where my sister was a patient in hospital. We arrived at the hospital about noon to learn the news from my sister that Uncle Tommy had died a few hours before. We had intended staying in Dublin that night but we were out on the road within half an hour, and back to Dublin for the first train home.

As Tommy predicted, 'the boys' were anxious to honour him with a draped coffin and body guard. Two of them called with me the next day, Barney Murphy and Arthur McLoughlin, to acquaint the family of their wish, but they were most understanding when I indicated, without ever telling them why, the family's wishes were for the normal funeral. Tommy had always been my favourite uncle. His concern for Jack in those closing days of his life canonised him in my eyes.

21—The Birth of *Linesman*

The GAA is credited with being the most democratic institution in the country. When one considers the structures as they existed in my day, from the club at the bottom, through divisional, county, provincial and national levels of authority, it probably was. As my playing role was gradually drawing to a close I was gently getting immersed in the administrative culture of the organisation. I was the exception rather than the rule so far as county footballers were concerned.

At the Ulster Convention held in January 1955, I was one of the six delegates elected previously at the Down Convention to represent the county. The Ulster Convention was to be held in Rostrevor to mark the completion of the presidential term of Fr Joe Pettit, a curate in that parish, and a quiet but tremendous force in the Down GAA of the time. The election of his successor was to be among the day's business which was carried out in St Bronagh's Hall. The morning business of the Convention was always tedious, for it involved all the reports of the year's workings—invariably a slow moving operation. This made the prospect of lunch in the Great Northern Hotel a desirable break.

Gerry Arthurs, the long-time Secretary of the Council, was a stickler for time. While reports had to be read and commented on, there were always delegates who would be making mountains out of molehills. Even though we had not progressed nearly as far as Gerry had hoped, we broke for lunch at 1 P.M. with resumption due at 2.30 P.M. About 70 delegates piled into their cars and headed for the hotel, about half a mile away. I was not in the vanguard but when I did arrive down five or ten minutes after the others, the hotel foyer was a seething mass of hungry Gaels who were getting a message from the reception desk that they were not expecting us. Gerry Arthurs himself eventually arrived and a way was made for him to the desk. The horrible truth emerged that they were not expecting us. There was no party of 70 in the book for that day. Gerry being Gerry, went out to his car and came in with confirmation of his booking from the hotel. The unpalatable fact was that someone had made a grievous mistake and there was no lunch for us, at least there was none ready. The staff who were on duty that day made a tremendous effort to rustle up something for us. Between tinned soup and sandwiches we survived. I would have been on first name terms with most of the staff in the hotel and some of them were apologising to me for the rest of their lives for the meal we had that day.

Gerry Arthurs was most magnanimous in thanking the staff for the efforts they made in circumstances which were not of their making. I learned from one of them afterwards that there never was a word of complaint from the Association.

We were well behind time getting back to Convention business, but before we did, George Tinnelly, the Down: Chairman said to me, 'Barney, I'll run you home at the finish,' but I indicated that there were plenty going home through The Point with whom I could get a lift.

'No,' he retorted, 'I'll take you in, I want to have a yarn with you.'

'Fair enough,' I concluded, 'I have all evening.' I didn't even consider what he might want 'to yarn' about.

At the finish, and with most of the delegates already departed, I got into George's car and headed for home. There was no more entertaining travelling companion than George, though I did not expect him to be in normal mode on this occasion. He was, and we were outside my home in Church Street without me being aware of anything which he wanted to yarn about. My wife was entering the house as we arrived and after he switched off the engine we must have talked about nothing for close to twenty minutes.

I was on the point of asking him what he wanted to discuss with me, when he said, 'I'll tell you what I want to ask you. Will you take charge of the county team this year?'

I was taken completely by surprise. I took a few seconds considering, before answering, 'George, I doubt if I would be the right man for the job.'

'Well the County Committee think you are the right man for the job and so do I,' was his rejoinder.

The phrase 'mature reflection' did not have its modern Irish political equivalent at that time but, after some reflection, I said, 'George, if the County Committee think I am the man for the job, I'll take it on.'

George took his leave of me and I went upstairs pondering what Anne's response would be when I told her of the job I had just accepted. It must have been 25 minutes since she had seen me arrive at the door.

'What do you mean keeping George talking down on the street? Why didn't you take him up for a cup of tea?' she scolded and I laughed at the idea that I might be keeping George talking.

When I told her the matter of our discussion and my acceptance, she asked, 'Does this mean you'll not be playing any more football yourself?' The reality was that I had received a couple of minor injuries in the previous year and she was anxious for me to retire completely. I understood her concerns.

A week passed; a second week went by and I had heard nothing from George or the County Board. In fact, I never heard another word from anyone, but I did read in *The Irish News* that Gerry Brown had been appointed to take the team.

I was not particularly disappointed but I was rather concerned where the power centred in the County Committee. I never raised the matter with George for I thought too much of him to cause him any embarrassment.

It had been my practice since ending my playing connection with the senior team to go to the dressing room before a game as a sign of solidarity and support. I did so again when the first match came round and wished Gerry every success. I had played with him at school and on the county team for many years. He was a man who induced both respect and confidence. His approach to football was not very different from my own and he had a wealth of experience in the PE field, at The Abbey and before that in the Irish Army. It was a major surprise that he only stayed in the Down camp for a single season before moving to Tyrone and guiding them to their first two Ulster titles.

One of the major defects on the local GAA scene at the time was the scarcity of informed comment in the local press. *The Frontier Sentinel,* which was regarded as the nationalist voice, gave a degree of coverage to both South Armagh and

Down games, but it was sporadic and hardly inspirational. In 1949 a new paper had come into being, *The Mourne Observer*, which would have been described as Unionist, but the following year it introduced a columnist, 'Midfield,' who provided regular and informed comment in what was a comparatively small column. It did not surprise me when I discovered that 'Midfield' was none other than Paddy O'Donoghue, a much-respected figure in the county and son of former chairman Gerry O'Donoghue, who played an important role in the development of the GAA in Down.

Around this time the *Armagh Observer* was extending into South Down in a big way, with Bertie Leckey as correspondent. Bertie was secretary of the South Down Board and later a member of the County Board who had his finger on the club pulse as few others had. I always used McAnulty's phone to contact him and when Bertie and I got on the phone, the McAnulty phone business came to a standstill for lengthy periods.

Towards the end of 1956 I approached Mick Keogh of *The Frontier Sentinel*, which was owned by the Ulster Herald Group, and printed in Omagh. I offered to provide a regular weekly coverage of Down GAA affairs and he readily accepted. Even though Joe Connellan, a former member of Down County Committee, and then sitting as a Nationalist MP at Stormont, was the editor, it was Mick who was mainly responsible for the day-to-day running of the paper. I was not going into sports journalism as a complete novice as I had gained a little experience a few years before when the *Warrenpoint Weekly* hit the local news-stands. Patsy Carvill, who worked with *The Frontier Sentinel* for a time, was the man behind the venture. It was published from his mother's front room in Slieve Foy Place and printed by *The Irish News*. It had a fleeting life, lasting from March to November, 1953.

Patsy invited me to do a weekly piece on sport which I did under the name of *Linesman*, and I volunteered a localised column under the name, *Rambler*. Patsy himself moved on to greater things with *The Irish News* and later became the first editor of the *Sunday News*.

My interest was not solely focussed on Inter-County affairs but more on the internal club scene and the Association in general, so the second incarnation of *Linesman* appeared after the Down County Convention of 1957. For months I wondered if anybody at all read what I was writing but slowly there was some reaction. I set out my programme of visiting a club game each week and commenting not only on the game but also on the quality of the referee, the pitch, the markings and, indeed, the conduct of the spectators.

Even before the rebirth of *Linesman* in *The Frontier Sentinel* in 1957 tournaments were at the height of their popularity, producing the most enjoyable competitive club scene which could be imagined. It was greatly enhanced by the injection of an Armagh–Down rivalry with the inclusion of Killeavey, Carrickcruppin, Mullaghbawn and occasionally Crossmaglen. I am revisiting that wonderful competitive and sporting era to write about some of those games, one of which I did not witness, and others in which I was a participant.

The game I did not witness was one which had this Armagh-Down tag attached, for it featured Clonduff and Carrickcruppin in the semi-final of the

Saval Tournament. It was played on a beautiful Monday evening in May, 1957. I was living in Church Street at the time and answered the doorbell shortly before 11 P.M. to find Terry McAnulty on the doorstep. He had received a phone call from someone in Hilltown saying that Brian McGreevy had died in the game at Saval and asked Terry to convey the message to me. No item of news from a football field has ever caused me such distress since that night. What follows is largely the tribute I paid to Brian in *The Frontier Sentinel* a few days after his death, for much of what I wrote then is even more relevant today, when fitness levels are becoming much more important than football skills, and injuries are occurring at a rate unheard of in my playing days.

'Tragedy is a much-used word in football language, for how often do we hear of a tragic mistake, a tragic goal, to describe some minor incident in the course of a game. This week we have experienced tragedy in its deepest physical and emotional sense. A young man has died on one of our sports fields, as a result of what was to all intents and purposes, an awkward fall, and anyone who has ever togged out on a football field must instantly feel, but for the grace of God, there go I.

Our games have been singularly free from serious accidents over the years. It is only on an occasion such as this that the possibility of risk enters our heads. Many players and the parents of up-and-coming players may well ponder on the wisdom of taking part in games — but there should be no need for any anxiety.

Thanks be to God, serious injuries are few. Monday's tragedy is the only one of its kind in most of our experiences in Down. Thanks be to God, too, that none of the players taking part in the game was in any way responsible. All of them were playing the game as it should be played, keen, hard fought, no temper, no anger, no bitterness. That was the pattern of the exchanges.

How different it could have been. How many times have we seen games riddled with rough and even dirty play, with anger and with bitterness, and all of it encouraged by spectators, whose only desire is victory, or even revenge. Again I say, thanks be to God, that none of these base elements were present in the making of this tragedy. Once again this is a case of the innocent suffering, that the rest of us must have a lesson.

Yes in this tragedy there is a lesson for all of us, players and spectators. How dreadful it would be if any intentional action of mine as a player should result in injury to an opponent. How dreadful it would be if, as a spectator, I incited or encouraged players in tactics which might result in injury to someone else, or even to themselves. That is the lesson in the death of Brian McGreevy. The risks on a football field are many, even under sporting circumstances: never make them greater by any other tactics. I have referred to Brian McGreevy as a young man but to me he was a boy whom I got to know very well when he was travelling to or from school in Newry. Himself and his Clonduff companion, Brendan Doyle, made it their business particularly on a Monday morning, to have a rendezvous with me to go over the previous day's football in the county.

Their keenness and enthusiasm for football ensured that they would have as much news for me as I had for them but I was human enough to detect the enthusiasm of a two-boy 'Barney Carr fan club' for I was well known on the county scene at the time. They were both ardent Clonduff disciples but able to appreciate the quality of other teams. Brendan went to The Abbey CBS, while Brian went to St Colman's. Being a day boy, he was at a disadvantage and did not figure in any of the school teams. Of my own club, he had a very high opinion and he would never venture a prediction on our clashes with Clonduff.

When I first saw him play as a minor, he had a very middling game and I think he was disappointed that I had not seen him on a better day.

The next time I saw him playing was with the Clonduff senior team and I still remember how proud he was that I should see him play with some of those stalwarts who, a few years previously, had been his heroes. I think in wearing Clonduff's colours, his lifetime's ambition was achieved. He was not a football genius, but he had those qualities which genius often lacks, loyalty, enthusiasm and above all, a tremendous pride in his club.

The Clonduff club obviously recognised these qualities, for they had made him team captain at the beginning of the season. There can be no doubt he appreciated the honour and the responsibility. I was at Moygannon on Sunday and saw him lead his team to a victory in which he played a captain's part. His point from a sideline kick in that deciding game with Warrenpoint was the vital score of the day.

The Sevens over, he travelled back to Belfast and on Monday evening he again made the journey home to take part in what was to be his last game.

On Wednesday in the spring sunshine we walked in front of his remains. There was not a club in Down which was not represented in this final tribute to this boy, who lived and died for football. He was laid in the graveyard not too far from one of his boyhood heroes, Thomas Brown, himself not much older than Brian when he died the year after he had helped Down win the All-Ireland Junior Championship. Below their resting place is the broad Mussen's meadow, where Clonduff teams have performed their notable deeds down through the years, and where he himself spent so many happy hours.'[27]

Brian's soul-mate of the time was Brendan Doyle, a cousin of the O'Neills and the McCartans, (their mothers were sisters); Brendan himself had played with some distinction for The Abbey CBS and Clonduff. He spent his working life in Dublin where he is now enjoying a healthy retirement. I met him a couple of years ago at a function where he recalled 'the piece you wrote in *The Frontier Sentinel* when Brian died.' It was this reminisce, and a copy of the piece from his collection which he sent to me, that prompted the notion that Brian McGreevy should be

---

27   Frontier Sentinel

remembered here; he was the embodiment of what a Gaelic sportsman should be. In the last year or two, I met his elder brother, Gerard, at Andy Murnin's funeral and I intimated to him that I would be remembering Brian in this book. He said, 'Brian would be very pleased for he thought something of you.' So when we recall great names of the past in recounting the Down GAA story remember the name of Brian McGreevy who, for me, was 'the sportsman of the century'.

Some weeks after the Saval tournament, it was the turn of my own club, St Peter's, to introduce its tournament. The opening round and the semi-finals produced a remarkable series of games and the two finalists were Rostrevor and The Point. At any time, a game between us is a serious business but the final of a tournament, especially The Point Tournament, added a completely new dimension to the meeting. I had retired from football at the end of the previous year after dislocating a shoulder in a tournament game up in Killeavey, where we had been playing Carrickcruppin. My medical adviser, the good wife, put her foot down and there was little I could do.

In the few days between the second semi-final and the decider, a fever of an All-Ireland dimension broke within a three-mile radius of Moygannon. It also affected our committee of which I was a member, for somebody suggested that I consider coming out of retirement for the occasion. I rubbished the notion out of hand but as the ifs and buts were being considered I realised the more responsible members were being drawn to the notion too.

'This is not an ordinary match. This is not an ordinary final. This is Rostrevor. Imagine Rostrevor beating us in our own tournament final.' These were the arguments I had to contend with and they finally broke my resistance. I had not played competitive football that season. I was half-way through my 35th year and I hadn't trained seriously for football in my life. My wife's only comment when I broke the news to her was, 'If you end up in hospital again I will not be visiting you,'—and she said this with our first born of four months, Hugh, in her arms.

On the night, the biggest crowd of people assembled at Moygannon since Armagh played Down a few weeks after their defeat by Kerry in the All-Ireland final of 1953. The stories coming over from Rostrevor in the days before the game all told of complete confidence. They were even bringing the band over to lead them home in victory. Some said later that the instruments were stowed under Moygannon Bridge. Others said that they were packed in Tinnelly's lorry further up the road. As the game went, Rostrevor looked the better team and led narrowly for most of the way but about five minutes from the end we were awarded a free from around the 50 yards mark. Micheal O'Hagan took it and I made what I think was my only contribution to the game, getting a hand to and guiding the ball to the net. I will never know how I got my tired body off the ground for that vital touch which won the game for The Point.

'Square ball, square ball, square ball,' was the cry on every Rostrevor tongue but Malachy McEvoy, the Armagh midfielder who was refereeing the game, wasn't listening. It would have been impossible to decide whether I was in or out of the square, for the reality was that I was airborne for a few yards and even though I say it myself—it was a great goal.

Rostrevor were shocked but took their defeat well without ever conceding that it was anything but 'a square ball'.

Afterwards, whenever I was driving the Rostrevor school bus, all I got was the chant, 'Square ball, Barney,' and ever since there hasn't been a Rostrevor man of that era who hasn't queried the legality of that goal.

Even now, Seán Tinnelly who comes into The Point a couple of days a week to work, invariably greets me with a pointed finger and the declaration, 'It was no goal. You were in the square.' No other game with which I have had an involvement has stood the test of time as a talking point.

In August 2002 I was walking down Church Street in the company of Anita Morgan, a Warrenpoint girl who is married and domiciled in Spain. I had not seen her for some time. We were both coming from Mass. Half-way down the street I spied a familiar face and I said to her, 'I see Seán Rice coming up the street and I'll have to stop to talk to him. I haven't seen him in years.'

Anita said, 'I'll stop and talk to him too. I haven't seen him for years either, and he's a cousin of mine.'

When we got Seán's length, I introduced Anita, whom he did not recognise, until he heard her father's name, Owen. Seán had settled back in Rostrevor a year or two before, after spending most of his working life in Dublin. In his playing days, he had been a towering figure on Rostrevor teams and had certainly played on Down Junior teams. He had played at centre half for Rostrevor in the Tournament Final I have just described. We talked football at some length and as we were about to take leave of each other he said, on a very confidential note, 'Barney, there's one thing I've often meant to ask you, but I never really got you on your own. Do you remember the night you beat us in the final of The Tournament? Were you in the square or were you not?'

Of course, I knew that would be the question, and I replied, 'Seán, I am writing a book about that match and I'll tell the full story.' I don't think he believed me.

In an early chapter of this memoir I introduced a youthful American soldier, Bill Stanfield, who became a friend of the Carr family in 1943. After the War, he visited us a number of times with his wife and son, and stayed at the family home on Summerhill. In 1968, he bought a Volkswagen beetle in England for his touring holiday and brought it back to Reidsville where he sold it at a profit in the year 2000. He had never visited throughout the years of The Troubles.

He had arranged to come in 2000 but the North Belfast trouble erupted and it caused him to change his plans. Ireland was not part of his European trip. He came in July 2003 and I picked up him and his wife, Vera, at the Europa Hotel in Belfast. On the drive home to Warrenpoint he was reminiscing about his first visit to Ireland as a young soldier. He was billeted at 5 Cloughmore Terrace, and he wondered if he might get a chance to view that house again. I told him there was no problem. I knew Larry Lynch well. He also recalled 'a little guy' who used stand in a doorway in Church Street when he was going up and down to the canteen. He often gave him candy and other goodies.

'I'd love to see that little guy if he's still around,' he mused.

On Sunday Bill (known to his wife as Alvis), went for a walk on his own and as he was passing Cloughmore Terrace, Larry Lynch and his wife were emerging from No. 5. He introduced himself to the Lynchs and they invited him to 'come down any time.'

By Monday he and I had visited Cloughmore Terrace where we were warmly received and were taken on a tour of the house, something he appreciated very much. His own room on the top, which he had shared with three others, had to be photographed. Before leaving the Lynchs, it was arranged that we would meet Larry in the Victoria Hotel later that evening.

When Bill, Vera, and I arrived in the Victoria, I noted that Oliver Havern, son of the unforgettable Vincey and a retired Irish Army veteran, was among the clientele. We were not there five minutes until it was discovered that Oliver was 'the little guy' to whom Bill Stanfield had provided the candy on a regular basis. Earlier that day, the proprietor of the Victoria had told Oliver about this Yank who had been billeted in Church Street 60 years before, so Oliver returned in the evening to give the 'Yank' the once over.

We were in a small room off the bar and had been joined by a couple of others, including a youthful American, who was delighted to meet this Yank who had been billeted in Church Street 60 years before. In the course of the night one chap, Gerry Hosier, who had been standing in the small area, chirped, 'Barney, you made your name with the Down team in 1960.' At which observation, Oliver Havern jumped to his feet, thumped the table and declared in deliberate tones, 'Barney made his name the night he scored the goal in the Tournament Final against Rostrevor.'

Bill Stanfield had known of my association with the Down team, but this was the first occasion he had heard about the Tournament Final with Rostrevor.

Jimmy Morgan was a Rostrevor man who married a Warrenpoint girl and settled in The Point. He had spent his working life in the grocery trade, first with Quinns, The Milestone, and later with Dunnes Stores. He was manager of their Warrenpoint branch when he retired some five years before. He had been prominent in St Peter's Club and had managed a number of teams at various times. As well as football he liked a game of poker and when the croquet club on Summerhill was going in Tom O'Hare's garden, he was a regular member. In more recent times he was an indoor and outdoor bowler. He was well known for his repartee and his quick tongue.

He took ill and after many months and a series of tests and procedures the prognosis was not good. He did not disguise this from those of us who would have been in his circle of friends. He was having good days and bad days and I thought I should go down to see him.

Kathleen, his wife, greeted me warmly. 'He's in great form today. He'll be glad to see you,' and she added, 'Seán Fearon's there.' Seán, a Rostrevor man and a fine footballer with Rostrevor and Down, had been chairman of the Down County Board for a couple of terms. He had been a key man in the Dunnes Stores operation in the North before he retired so there was plenty to chat about.

The *craic* turned to having arguments with people and Jimmy confessed, 'The worst argument I ever had in my life was with Andy Tohill. I was the president of the bowling club and he was the vice president.' He went on to tell us the bones of the argument but assured us that he and Andy had made it up and they were firm friends. I'm sure Andy will not mind me observing that Jimmy was not the only man in the town with whom he had an argument.

'Jimmy,' I said, 'that's nothing to the argument you had with Jack Campbell at the croquet.' Jack was then the elderly retired bookie. Croquet normally is a sedate game played by gentle, if not genteel, people, though this would not always have been the case in the Summerhill club. The high point of the argument between Jack and Jimmy was reached when Jack declared, with the mallet above his shoulder, 'You put your hand near that ball, Morgan, and you are a dead man.'

As Jimmy described his part in the action to Seán and myself, it was so hilarious that Kathleen came from the kitchen to see what the commotion was. Normality was restored and Jimmy said quietly to me, 'The biggest argument I ever had in my life was with you.'

I looked at him incredulously, 'You never had an argument with me.'

'By God, I had. The night you got the goal when you were in the square, you bugger ye, I was the bloody umpire. I still say you were in the square,' and he spoke with conviction.

I turned to Seán Fearon who was one of the dominant figures in the game, as we both exploded in laughter with Jimmy joining in.

'Jimmy, I did not stop to argue with you or anyone else once I touched that ball.'

'I know bloody well you didn't, but we argued for an hour after the match in the hut and on the Moygannon Road after that.'

Again we were all in hysterics and Kathleen appeared at the door, smiling and thankful that Jimmy was in such good form. When Seán and I left some time later, we could only marvel at the tenacity and courage of this man who had touched our lives to such effect.

Jimmy died a couple of weeks later but he will always be associated with the legend of the Square Ball. So much did that game add to Warrenpoint-Rostrevor folklore that I feel all who took part in it deserve honourable mention, so I include the teams as follows:

Rostrevor: Martin Parr, Jimmy Russell, Pete Ryan, Jim Magennis, Seán Cooper, Seán Rice, Paddy Joe Kielty, Seán Fearon, Brian Murphy, Tommy Kane, Frank Farrell, Willie Kielty, Paul Tinnelly, Seamus Daly, Val Murphy and Patsy Cunningham, who came on as a sub.

Warrenpoint: Ian McGarrity, Des O'Hagan, John O'Hagan, Seamus Ryan, Killian Higgins, Micheal O'Hagan, Brian Grant, Ted Bradley, Liam Bradley, Paddy Carr, Tony Campbell, Pat Ryan, Des Lavery, Barney Carr and J.J. Henry.

Many from both teams have gone to their eternal reward but I wish to tell a fuller story of one Rostrevor man, Paddy Joe Kielty, known to everyone as 'Rinty'. Rinty was as good a free-taker as there was in the country. Anything from 50 yards in was a score, right or left. Rinty would show no emotion or reaction to the plaudits of his admirers. He just did the business.

The story I wish to tell of Rinty begins at a Benedictine monastery at Bec, Normandy where a young Belfast monk Dom Mark Ephram Nolan had his prayers answered when his superiors decided that a Benedictine presence might have a reconciling influence on the northern troubles. It was in 1987 that a small group of Benedictines settled in the Diocese of Down and Connor near Downpatrick. After a couple of years and unable to get a long-term base they returned to Bec. In 1997 they returned to Ireland and put down tentative roots at the Convent of Our Lady of the Apostles in Rostrevor in the Dromore Diocese and in a very short time became an important part of the Christian community. The years were passing and they were still without a home of their own when an angel appeared on the scene in the person of Paddy Joe Kielty. Paddy had married a Newry girl Philomena McDonald who taught in the local school. They did not have any children so when Paddy inherited a small farm on the Kilbroney Road he donated most of it to the monks who proceeded with much effort to build what is now known as Holy Cross Monastery of Kilbroney which will be a remarkable reconciling process in the country. In its cemetery there is just one grave that of Paddy Joe. So if you go to pray at the Holy Cross Monastery, or maybe just driving past to Hilltown or Rostrevor, remember Rinty who lies below in his own ground.

The Sunday after the Tournament Final The Point had Kilcoo as visitors at Moygannon in a league game, and the hero of Thursday night was induced to turn out again. It was not a game of any importance and there was only a handful of spectators, in contrast to the 'full house' of Thursday. Through the first half it was as placid a game as could be imagined but shortly after half-time a Kilcoo defender and our youngest player, J.J. Henry, got entangled and a blow or two was struck. I was full forward and I ran to cool things and got the pair separated, but lo and behold, when I turned round there was a series of individual fistfights all over the pitch. When order was restored there were a few bloody noses and, I have to say, mostly Kilcoo noses. Sean Collins of Ballymartin was the referee and he eventually managed to get order restored. The game resumed and was played to the finish as if the fracas had never occurred.

On the following Wednesday evening, Kilcoo and The Point met in the semi-final of the Kilkeel Tournament and needless to say there was a fair crowd present. Some might have expected fireworks, but the game went through without a single incident and resulted in a victory for Kilcoo. The events of the previous Sunday were never referred to, and in my experience this is the way it has always been in the GAA.

That first year of my journalistic life in *The Frontier Sentinel* saw a remarkable pairing in the Down Senior Final between Clonduff and their parish rivals, Cabra. From the day the pairing was known there was a chorus of speculation never before heard prior to a Down Final. 'It will be a dogfight'; 'It will never be finished'; 'They'll murder each other,' and there was even a letter in some of the papers calling on the County Board not to go ahead with the final. I expressed my own view on the nonsense which was going the rounds and on so many tongues. In the event, the game was played with all the ferocity of Championship final fervour but it never got out of control at any stage, and I had reason to commend my brother, Hugh, the referee, for his capable handling on the day.

22—The County Board

The year 1957 was another disappointing year for Down at Inter-County level, with failure against Donegal in Ballyshannon in the first round. Down travelled in high hope for they had a team which seemed capable of giving them their first Championship win in years. Alas, it was the same old story. It is always easy for commentators to come up with hindsight suggestions as to how things might have been done better; I was no exception. I always like to think that I had a gentler touch than most. In the succeeding weeks and months I was putting forward ideas which might be worth considering.

The structure of the Down GAA at the time gave divisional boards two representatives on the County Committee. A number of clubs had nominated me for one of the positions. Fr Barney Treanor had indicated he was retiring and he suggested to me that I should let my name go forward; this I did, and I was selected in his place at the 1958 Convention.

At the first meeting of the Board the various structures were being put in place for the year. For some members the most important part of the meeting would concern the various selection committees of the county teams. In my own playing days the entire County Board picked the teams, but for a few years prior to 1958 it was a three-man selection committee for the senior football team. I think I was the only newcomer to the County Committee, and I was most interested in seeing how the Board worked. Paddy O'Donoghue had asked me before the proceedings commenced if I would stand for the selection committee. I declined, recalling my experience of 1955 without mentioning it to Paddy. I believed, though, that in the overall picture I would be contributing more by continuing to write about the games and the Association.

It was decided that we would stick with a three-man selection committee. In the previous couple of years Maurice Hayes, Brian Denvir and Paddy O'Hagan had been in charge, the latter two both former playing colleagues on the county team. Maurice and Brian were re-elected but surprisingly there was a deadlock over the third position. Paddy O'Donoghue proposed a couple of names, but some reservations were expressed about them, mainly by Maurice. Paddy, sitting across the table from me gave me an eye signal and a nod of the head which I interpreted, 'Will you stand?' I gave him back an assenting nod.

He proposed my name, got a seconder and no reservations were expressed.

At the end of the meeting I spoke to Paddy asking if he would take over my *Linesman* role in *The Frontier Sentinel* but he dismissed the suggestion out of hand. 'You'll have no problem doing both and anyway I look forward to reading you on a Saturday,' he laughed. So *Linesman* was installed as a Down selector on his first night at the County Board.

In case anyone might be thinking that I was making my fortune writing in *The Frontier Sentinel,* I should explain that I wasn't being paid at all, until I realised that it was costing me a little money by way of phone calls and postage, not to speak of getting myself to matches. Before Christmas, I mentioned this to Mick Keogh and he said to me, 'Would ten shillings a week cover you?,' and I replied, 'That would be ample.' The *Frontier Sentinel* then paid me back to the day I started.

Within a couple of weeks we had a panel of players, a trainer Danny Flynn, and a medical adviser, Dr Martin Walsh who had been a good athlete and a talented footballer. He and I were colleagues on a few Down teams. I was on my way out when he was coming in. It was agreed that I would take charge of the team as tactical coach and the training operation got under way shortly after at Downpatrick.

The panel of players with which we started had a fair blend of youth and experience. Kevin Mussen and Kieran Denvir had been regulars on the Ulster team. Jarlath Carey, George Lavery, Seán Fearon, Paddy Doherty and Brian Morgan all served Down for some years and when names like James McCartan, Pat Rice, Leo Murphy, Pat O'Hagan and Eamon McKay are added it can be seen that this was a talented bunch of footballers.

I was conscious of my own lack of experience. I had never played in an Ulster Final, never played in Croke Park and never even captained my own club team. I had captained Down on one occasion when John O'Hare was injured. However, I was confident that I knew football and how it should be played. We trained two nights a week and we had a series of challenge games, all of which showed continuing improvement in the side. An earlier defeat by Armagh in the McKenna Cup did nothing to lessen our confidence when we came to play Donegal in the first round of the Championship at Newry in June. When we won with a margin of six points the victory was received with the elation of an All-Ireland success. It was the first Senior Championship game Down had won for many years.

Tyrone, who were the reigning Ulster Champions, provided the next hurdle at Lurgan where we went in as underdogs and emerged as a gathering force with a comprehensive victory. Gerry Brown, who had taken them to their title successes the previous two years, was fulsome in his congratulations but there was something he said to me afterwards which indicated that his short spell with Down was not a happy experience. I put what he said in the back of my mind where already there was a mild concern about a key aspect of our operation.

Nothing, however, could dim the exultation of either team or supporters at being in an Ulster Final for the first time in sixteen years. Our preparation had been well near perfect from the very beginning. Maurice Hayes, a highly influential figure at Central Council, was able to arrange a key challenge game at Knockbridge with Louth, the reigning All-Ireland Champions.

We were a quietly confident group as we set out for Clones on Final Day to meet our opponents, Derry. We had arranged lunch at Castleblaney where team member George Lavery was to join us. We were not over-concerned when he failed to do so before departure, for the feeling was that he would have gone direct to Clones. Thirty minutes before the throw-in, we were now seriously worried when there was still no sign of him, nor any inkling of what might have happened. We were forced to recast the team with the least possible upset. The pattern of our progress so far was that the tactical approach to a game would be covered on a Thursday night and the pre-match buzz would be about getting the confidence mode right. The absence of our most experienced defender was a real body blow, and getting my own confidence mode right, not to speak of that of the players, was a new experience.

Down needed to have their best team playing their best-ever football on that day, for Derry were no mean side. Jim McKeever, the Gribbens and Sean O'Connell were all top-class performers and a match for any side in the country. Not only did they beat Down, but they went on to beat Kerry in the All-Ireland semi-final before failing to Dublin in the All-Ireland decider.

Poor George had hung on at the crossroads with the ducks in Magherlin, waiting to be lifted, but his car failed to arrive. Eventually he went home to listen to the game on the radio. What an experience that must have been for him! In hindsight, we all knew things that George might have done, but we were not waiting in Magherlin where the only moving things on a Sunday morning were the aforesaid ducks.

The Down supporters were bitterly disappointed by the turn of events and the result, but most were consoled by the fact that we had got to the final after such a long sequence of annual disappointments. There was one redeeming feature of that disappointing day, and that was the success of the minor team which included some individuals who were to be the vital cogs in the future Down machine.

Of course, the whole episode of George's absence would not have occurred if we had taken cognizance of a Castlewellan motion at the County Convention earlier in January. It read, 'that Down County Committee make adequate arrangements for transporting selected players to games.' To be fair to Castlewellan, at the 1959 Convention I don't think they even mentioned how we singularly failed to follow their directive on players' transport. Indeed, both divisional and county conventions were very buoyant occasions that year and even *Linesman* got favourable mention.

Even before the 1958 Ulster Final I was having some concerns about the team selection; there were times when for one reason or another Brian Denvir was not available on team selection nights. The first night it happened Maurice advised me Brian was not available and added, 'I have asked George to sit in.' I would have had no problem selecting a team with Maurice on his own, but I was concerned that he would invite anyone in on team selection without first consulting me. George Tinnelly, a popular County Chairman, was one of the most respected figures in the Association, but, while I enjoyed a deep respect and friendship with him, he would never have been on my panel of selectors. We were still far from the time when the team nearly picked itself, and I felt we needed a selection system which was not a hostage to fortune.

The opportunity to remedy the situation did not come around until the first meeting of the County Committee after the 1959 Convention when everything was up for review. I had some very definite ideas in my head going into that assembly.

When it became time to consider the senior operation, George McKeown, by right of custom as he was the longest serving member of the Board, was first to voice his opinion. He lauded the team and the team management for the great work they had done in reaching the Ulster Final for the first time in sixteen years. He was very sincere and he felt the selectors should be given a vote of confidence to continue with the good work. Two or three others spoke in the same vein and while I could understand their intentions I had to get my spoke in before the wave of popular support swamped my intended purpose.

'Mr Chairman, could I have a word?'

George gave me the floor and after thanking all the members for their generous words I brought the room to silence when I continued, 'I am not happy with the way we have selected our teams and I propose that we extend the selection committee to five members.'

Before anyone could say yea or nay, Maurice interjected, 'It would be impossible to get five people without one of them being a crank.'

I spoke directly down the table to the secretary: 'Maurice, I have always had a problem in deciding who is a crank and who is not, because there are many people in The Point who would regard me as a crank in some aspects of my life and they are right. I have no doubt there are some people in Downpatrick who would regard you as a bit of a crank in some aspects of your life.'

If I had created a silence with my proposal, I created a deafening silence with my riposte to Maurice. I broke it myself.

'Mr Chairman, would you put my proposal to the meeting to see if it has a seconder?'

He did, and a number of hands went up in support. The proposal was put and carried with only one dissenting voice.

It took very little time to appoint the two additional selectors, Martin Walsh and TP Murphy. I have already indicated Martin's abilities as a player. If TP did not make the senior Inter-County stage, he was one of the great club footballers of his era. They were both very sensible men and definitely not cranks.

When we got the selection committee sorted out, I was back in to complete the work I had come to do. 'Mr Chairman, I have another proposal to make in relation to the selection committee.'

George gave me the nod to proceed. 'I propose that one of the selection committee be appointed team manager.' I added, 'I want to stress, that it does not have to be me.' I would have been disappointed if it hadn't been, though. I thought that as manager I would be aware of everything which was happening concerning the team. Innocent me! The proposal was put and carried, and the chairman asked for nominations. I was proposed and seconded. I thought it was going to be a unanimous approval but to my surprise Maurice proposed Brian Denvir. My surprise was not occasioned by any concerns about Brian's ability to do the job, but in the climate of the meeting it was obvious that I was the favoured choice and by proposing Brian, Maurice was merely showing his disapproval. In the event, he did not get a seconder, so the only voice of dissent to my appointment was the one with whom I had worked closest in the previous year.

The meeting ended and as the members drifted out I spent some time discussing immediate matters with George, Maurice and TP in a slightly frosted atmosphere. Eventually I left the room to find Paddy O'Donoghue waiting on the landing for me. 'That's a great night's work you did,' he said with enthusiasm, as we descended the stairs together.

There were a couple of County Board members who never let me forget that meeting, and one of them, Arthur Doran, for ever after commenced every meeting I had with him with the query, 'How are all the cranks in The Point?'

We moved our training base to Banbridge for the 1959 campaign and soon there was a warm, congenial atmosphere established in the active club. The addition of the best of the minor team to the panel made an enormous difference. In normal circumstances one would have to wait for minor talent, however promising, to mature, but Sean O'Neill, with a couple of senior outings in the National League, was a seasoned performer at nineteen years of age, and there were others who enhanced the overall strength of the panel.

One of the factors which had boosted our confidence still further was our appearance in the Wembley Tournament against Galway. We qualified for this by beating Derry in a test game a few weeks before. It had been just over ten years since I had stood behind the goals encouraging Man United—and here I was, directing a Down team at this most famous of English sporting venues.

Quite apart from the game and the famous victory over Galway, it was a joyful weekend involving reunions with my circle of friends in London as well as a huge coming together of Down exiles from most of southern England. Thirty thousand was a massive crowd for a game in London. One would have thought the limitations of the Wembley pitch might have cramped the styles of the contestants, but in fact the game was a classic, and by their victory Down served notice of 'the new force' emerging in Ulster football.

Within a couple of months the Everest of the province, Cavan, was conquered for the first ever time. Since that day I have regretted that there was no film or television evidence of what I always considered was the complete football performance. In due course there were greater victories, but with a video of that game one could stand before any class or group and say, 'This is how football should be played.' I will wax lyrical about that performance until the end of my days.

On the Tuesday before our semi-final meeting with Galway, I was coming off the Mall towards the bus depot in Newry. I was finishing my work and carrying the box which was the bus conductor's office at that time. I turned the corner at the Imperial cinema which gave me a full view of the bus office set back from Hill Street between Woolworths and the Breffni Arms Hotel. I hadn't taken five paces towards it when 'the Big Man' emerged from the door. 'The Big Man' was Jack Bannon, the depot manager, and a very big man he was. Whatever way he came out of the door at least 80 yards away, I knew instantly, 'this bloody man wants to see me.' Big Jack did not have much to do with the day-to-day operations but I thought there might be an emergency of some kind which would necessitate me working later. I made up my mind instantly, 'I'm going home.'

While we were still 40 yards apart he shouted something and waved his hands. The only words I picked up were, 'Fr Esler.'

When we finally got to speaking distance he repeated a message I wouldn't forget in a hurry, 'Fr Esler has been on that phone three or four times. He's like a weasel. You're not to go home without seeing him. Here, gimme that box and I'll leave it up for you.' As he took the box from me he added, 'By Christ, I wouldn't like to be going to confession to that man this evening.'

Now I was catching the 5.15 bus home, and it was already 5.00 o'clock, but the parochial house is only yards away. I think there are four steps up to the entrance porch and I had just put my foot on the top one when the inside door opened and the tall, lean figure of Fr Hugh Esler appeared like a tiger ready to pounce.

'What the hell are you doing with this team? Do you think you're going for a holiday to Croke Park? Barney Carr, are you out of your mind?'

I got angry with him for such a barrage. 'What the hell are you talking about?' I snapped back.

He wasn't even listening to me. 'You're in an All-Ireland semi-final for the first time and you're taking the team to Butlins. Good God man, are you mad?'

'Have a bit of sense Father, there's no way this team is going to Butlins,' I assured him. This sent him into a further frenzy; we were now in the hallway.

'Listen to me, for God's sake, listen to me, whether you know it or not, your team is booked into Butlins for the weekend.'

I knew then that what he said was true, for he had the ear of George Tinnelly and would know what was happening.

'Father,' I said, 'I find this hard to believe. There is no way this team is going to Butlins and I'll make that very clear to George.'

'Barney, you know George will not decide. You know that better than I do.' He finished and he was really distressed.

'We'll see,' was my final comment as I left. The 5.15 bus had long gone and I had to wait to 5.45. I had plenty to think about on that short journey to The Point.

A little over an hour later I heard the 'toot toot' from George who was picking me up for the training in Banbridge. I knew he would have a couple of the players in the car so when I went out I invited him back into the house under some pretext which gave no indication of the business in hand.

'George,' I began, 'I have heard in the past hour that we are booked into Butlins for the weekend. Is this true?

Yes. Maurice had arranged it and he had gone along with it.

George was such a likable and civil man that one could not be angry with him, but I laid it on the line that there was no way the team would spend Saturday night in Butlins. He agreed that it would be changed.

When the training session at Banbridge concluded, I came back into the clubhouse. George was engrossed in conversation with Maurice and he beckoned me over. 'Maurice says it would not be possible to get alternative accommodation in Dublin at this late stage,' he said quietly. I said nothing and turned from them in disgust and frustration.

I'll say no more about the decision to go to Butlins. I will say, however, that when we arrived as 'happy campers' on the sultry Saturday evening the place was alive and bubbling with the excitement of hundreds of others who were getting their bearings for the week which lay ahead of them.

As we walked from the bus to our chalets, George Lavery, aware of the excitement of the masses, said to me, 'Do you think we were wise coming to

Butlins?'

'I think we were mad,' I replied.

Danny Flynn and I shared a chalet; he had also shared my feelings about the whole operation when I first broke the news to him at the Tuesday training session.

Later on in the night, when things were really buzzing, Danny and I took a walk around the place for we had a curfew set. As we appeared in the various areas of activity, some of our charges were disappearing out through another door. We had no real fear that any of them would overstep the mark and they didn't. They were an outstanding bunch of fellows and I doubt if any of them would have been taking a drink at the time. Danny and I retired to our chalet, said the Rosary and left everything in God's hands.

Strangely, I never heard the full extent of James McCartan's experience of Butlins until I read Jack Mahon's book, *The Game of My Life*, in which he published a wide-ranging and somewhat exaggerated interview with James, part of which reads:

> 'staying in Butlins was a major mistake. I'll give you my own experience of it. Usually before a big game we always had a steak breakfast after Mass. We left to go to Butlins on Saturday evening at 3 o'clock and reached it at six. Our tea was beans on toast. No supper. They told us next morning, if we went to second Mass we'd get breakfast. Breakfast was over when we returned. I went on to play in Croke Park weak from the hunger, not having eaten since 12 noon the previous day. It was also one of the warmest nights I ever remember and the chalets were like ovens.'[28]

Leaving Butlins the next morning we were a happy, confident group and I would never claim that being there played a significant part in our defeat by Galway later that day. Still, it was no place for Down to be that weekend. We had the beating of Galway when we had them on the ropes in the first quarter of the game, but the sledgehammer blows which we normally delivered in periods of ascendancy did not come. Galway had learned something from their experience with us at Wembley. On this occasion, we learned quite a bit, too.

Few teams have gone through to an All-Ireland Final after winning their first provincial crown, and though Down didn't do it either, there was quiet resolution that we would make 1960 our year of destiny.

We had qualified for the National League semi-final against Kerry, who were the reigning All-Ireland Champions, after beating our conquerors, Galway, the previous September. The game took place in April in a gale of wind which was fiercer than anything March ever produced. I went up with a group of the players into the Cusack Stand to view the pitch even as the crowd was coming in. The intensity of the breeze was even more obvious from that vantage point, and it occurred to me that Kerry would be expecting us to play with the breeze if we won the toss. I spoke my thoughts to the players and added, 'I think we'll surprise them and give them the breeze if we do win the toss.' That was exactly as

---

28   Jack Mahon, *The Game of my Life*, p. 263

it happened, and in our victory I felt that we had landed the first blow in the test for the Championship.

It was Cavan who provided the opposition in the League Final a couple of weeks later; after their experience in the Ulster Final of the previous year it was understandable that they were out not only for a measure of revenge but also to give notice of their Championship intentions a few months down the line. A record fifty thousand people gathered for the occasion, and they were treated to a robust encounter which showed Down not only a talented bunch of players but also a tough bunch, too!

With the National League captured for the first time, and another facile win over Galway at Wembley, we set out to defend our status as Ulster Champions. The final in which we again met Cavan saw us confirm our supremacy and well on track for the greatest prize of all. A provincial title invariably brings an outbreak of All-Ireland fever and, while we had experienced it the previous year, this second dose was even more overwhelming.

Offaly had won through in Leinster for the first time ever. They were managed by Peter O'Reilly who, as a wing half back, had been an outstanding performer on Dublin and Leinster teams in the fifties. He was a player for whom I had great respect. Offaly had come 'out of the blue' through Leinster in much the same manner as Down had done in Ulster the year before.

As 'Linesman,' this is part of my report on the game in *The Frontier Sentinel:*

> *'While it is always considered somewhat unsporting to blame a referee, it would be impossible for any honest Down point of view to be expressed, without a reference to his performance. It has been reported, that this was his first ever experience refereeing in Croke Park, but there were times on Sunday, when one could be forgiven for thinking, that this was the first time he had refereed anywhere.'*

Understandably, Mick Dunne in *The Irish Press* was not as extreme as that but this is what he did write:

> *'It was the low point in an unhappy refereeing debut by Tom Cunningham. Surprisingly, for one who is still a player in the top grades, he was rarely up with the play, and often so far away, that many infringements escaped him.'*[29]

Both Mick and *Linesman* were in full agreement that one of his greatest mistakes was awarding the penalty kick to Down from which Paddy Doherty evened the scores. Had a foul been given against James McCartan for over holding we could not have complained. The intuitive mind of McCartan smelt a penalty and he got away with it. Only a team of Down's stature could have withstood the physical squalls they had to contend with right through, but particularly in the first half. We had run into squalls before, but the deadly accuracy of Doherty and Sean O'Neill from frees made it too costly for most teams to persevere. On this occasion we seemed to be without protection, though for once the impeccable

---

29   The Irish Press

Sean O'Neill was having a poor day.

Paddy McGuigan, our masseur who had been attached to Belfast Celtic in Elisha Scott's time, caught up with me as we left the pitch at half- time, and in a sort of confidential tone said, 'Barney, son, I'm not going to tell you your business, but I saw Celtic being done down like that a couple of times and do you know what Scott told them when he got them in at half-time? "When you go out again, boys, kick everything above the level of the grass except the goalposts".'

I took Paddy's advice with a smile, but while I would not have settled for a draw at half-time I would gladly have done so ten minutes from the end. As we were trooping in after the final whistle, with almost audible sighs of relief, I asked Maurice to ensure the same chap was not in charge for the replay.

A County Committee meeting had been arranged for the Tuesday evening after the game, for in the event of winning a place in the All-Ireland Final quite a few decisions would have to be taken. It can be imagined that it was a relieved and concerned County Committee who met in the Donard Hotel in Newcastle on this occasion. In keeping with tradition, George McKeown led off in matters of moment and he gave what I would have called a reasonable assessment of Sunday's events. One or two others contributed their concerns before Maurice dropped a bombshell by intimating that the players had held a meeting after the game, and it was the consensus view that they had not been properly prepared for the game with Offaly. Maurice couched the message, though, in more diplomatic language.

To say that there was a silence is putting it mildly. My own sense of shock was heightened when the reality of the situation struck home. I had not the slightest doubt that if the players had had a meeting Maurice was aware of it, and was most likely a participant. Why else would he not advise me and the other selectors of such a serious outcome? This surely was a matter for the manager and all the selectors.

I looked across the table at Paddy O'Donoghue whose gaze was already on me and his distinctive double nod indicated that we were on the same wavelength. We were both remembering some advice he had given me on the night I was appointed manager. He spoke before I did, expressing the view that the manager and selectors should have been advised of this meeting on Sunday before they left Dublin, that was, if it had taken place in Dublin.

When I did eventually speak, I was surprised that I remained as calm as I did. This was the first time I realised that anger and revulsion were separate emotions. Revulsion can produce a clarity of thought that anger expels; I said I found it difficult to believe that our failure to beat Offaly could be put down to a preparation which had seen us undefeated in competition since the semi-final against Galway the previous year, and which included wins over Kerry, twice over Cavan and again over Galway at Wembley.

'No one is going to tell me that there was anything wrong with the preparation for Offaly,' I concluded.

After some further discussion, it was agreed that the matter be left to the manager and the selectors to consider on Thursday evening when training was to resume.

Paddy O'Donoghue was the only man I spoke to after the meeting and that very briefly. His parting words were, 'I wouldn't attempt to advise you. I know you will do the right thing.'

I drove home with George Tinnelly, who had the good sense to know that I was deeply wounded, and for most of the road we drove in silence.

County Board meetings were always late-night affairs but this was much later than usual and Anne was quite anxious when I eventually arrived home. I don't think the term 'body language' was invented at the time, but she realised almost at once that I had a load on my mind. Before I did finally drop off, I had my mind made up on my reaction to what I considered was an act of gross irresponsibility—not by the players, but by Maurice, in not acquainting me or the other selectors of the meeting. Had I not been a member of the County Committee, Down would have been looking for a new manager and, no doubt, a new trainer, the very next day.

Sleepless night or not, I was on the floor at 7 A.M. and my first concern was for our trainer, Danny Flynn. I did not want him to be hearing about the events of the previous night's meeting before I had spoken to him. It was near mid-morning when my bus duties allowed me to ring him from a kiosk adjacent to the bus depot in Newry. This was the first occasion I had ever phoned him at work, and the first time I had spoken to him from the Sunday when it had been agreed that we would resume training on Thursday evening. Danny was principal of a school with an enrolment in excess of 800 pupils and would have been used to surprises and even shocks, but as he told me afterwards, nothing had prepared him for the story I had to tell him.

When I had completed it, there was a second or two of silence, before he spoke in very measured tones, 'Barney, I think we should both resign.' In the course of our discussion I was able to reassure him that the fitness of the team was not in question, but that the aim was to undermine me. Danny accepted this, for he was well aware of the problem Maurice had with my managership. We left it that things would be as they were until the selectors met the following night.

When I arrived home that evening Anne told me Danny had been on the phone and wanted me to contact him as soon as possible. I rang immediately.

'Barney' he opened, 'I have thought of nothing all day but what you told me this morning, and the more I consider it the more I am convinced we should both resign.' He said a few other things, too, in the course of the discussion. Finally, I asked him to forget any thoughts of resignation and we would have another exchange of views before the selectors' meeting. By this time, I had a very clear idea of what my options were, and they were not many. There was no lack of confidence in my own mind that this team would take Offaly in the replay, but I realised that I was over a barrel, for there are no certainties in sport. If the worst happened, and we were beaten in the replay, there would be no doubt where the blame would be laid. Thursday evening came and I had a short talk with Danny and then with the players, but not about the events of the previous few days.

At the selectors' meeting there was no indication from Maurice of the how, when or where of the players' meeting, nor did any of us ask him, for the situation had moved on by this stage. We were quickly into the heart of the matter. Should we now seek outside advice? I knew what Maurice wanted and so did the others, but the decision was left to me. It did not take me too long to indicate that in the position I had been placed, I had no option. It was agreed that we would approach Peter McDermott, who had a long-time association with Down.

On Saturday, Maurice Hayes, TP Murphy, Martin Walsh and I went down to Navan to meet Peter and he readily agreed to come up to Newcastle the following Tuesday evening. He came up again on the following Sunday and Tuesday to give us the benefit of his experience. In due course, we met Offaly the following Sunday, 11 September, with Mick McArdle of Louth as referee. Down won a dour game by two points, for this was a good Offaly team, as they demonstrated in the years which followed. Our dream of dreams had been fulfilled and we were in an All-Ireland Final with Kerry.

At this remove it is almost impossible to convey the mood which was abroad in Down in the interval between the defeat of Offaly and the meeting with Kerry. There were two emotions shared by the populace, unbelief and expectation. Working on the buses I was a very public face, so I was meeting scores of people every day whose only topic of conversation was the final. One of those meetings has stood the test of time more than any other. It occurred on the Friday morning before the game when I dropped into Newry Cathedral to catch the end of the 9 A.M. Mass. I stayed for a few minutes after most of the congregation had left, and as I emerged from the side door towards Hill Street I recognised the elderly man who stood at the street gate. To me, he was Mr Lambe, father of Joe and Barney, who would both have been well known on the local hurling and football scene with Clann Uladh and Shamrocks. He was probably well into his seventies at this time and I had the feeling he wanted to speak to me.

'Mr Carr,' he began 'when I saw you in the cathedral I thought how wonderful it was for Down to be in an All-Ireland Final with Kerry. I never thought I would live to see such a thing happening.' He paused for a second before continuing, 'Mr Carr, do you really believe that Down could beat Kerry?' He said this with the simplicity and sincerity of the saintly man he was.

While I might have been smiling inside, I replied in a tone which matched his. 'Mr Lambe, I really think we can beat Kerry, but we'll need a bit of luck and a lot of prayer.' Again he began, with a twinkle in his eye this time, 'Mr Carr, I will not be at the match on Sunday. I can't provide the luck but I'll provide the prayer.' The rest is history.

In contrast to their experience of the previous year in Butlins, the players stayed at St Colman's College or in their own homes and travelled down to Croke Park on Sunday morning. What a day it turned out to be for Down men and women. We have feasted on it for 50 years and as the years pass it gets better with the telling. I could not recount the details of the game at this time in my life but I do recall an exhausted *Linesman* writing into the early hours of Thursday morning to meet a noon deadline later that day. This is some of what he wrote:

'In years to come when any of the thousands of Downmen and women who thronged Croke Park on Sunday are asked what has been the greatest thrill of their lives they are sure to reply 'seeing Down beat Kerry in the All-Ireland final.' Without a doubt this was the greatest sporting spectacle ever witnessed in Ireland, for not only was it thrilling to Downmen, but pleasing to every county in the land including the defeated Kerry who took their defeat like true Champions. But not alone was it thrilling for Downmen, it was also uplifting, joyful, tearful and memorable. All the best of human emotions were given full expression in that surge of feeling that swept the vast arena when the final whistle sounded.

What a sight the historic stadium presented as the Down fans bathed in the pure ecstasy of this memorable achievement! From the playing pitch those great waves of emotion swept upwards to the top-most heights of the Hogan and Cusack stands, to Hill 16 and the vastness of the Canal embankment. From these peaks they rolled back to where they began only to be redirected upwards and downwards, backwards and forward until the complete picture was painted. And what a canvas the finished article was.

Laughter, tears, pride, humility, exuberance, sense of achievement, admiration; they were all laid on at the same time against a colour scheme of red and black. Could anyone be critical of those followers who put on such a show?

It has been said that Down beat Kerry at their own game and to an extent that is true but Kerry have no complaints on that score. The tradition that Kerry have built up over the years was made up mainly of determination and courage. No northern county other than Cavan could match them in this respect. Down won this great victory because all fifteen men went out prepared to die for victory. Never have Downmen displayed such courage and never have they been so effective in countering all that a team of Kerry's reputation had to offer. This was the stuff that had won Kerry so many titles but as there is no copyright in Gaelic football the Munster men have no redress.'

There are two other notable events of that day which deserve to be included in the Warrenpoint Annals. The first is that the local Irish National Foresters Band travelled in support of the team. From Amiens Street, they marched almost to Croke Park followed by the entire passenger load of the train and gathered hundreds more en route. They had arranged to leave their instruments in a hall close to the ground. When they picked them up again a few hours later the world had changed. Down were the All-Ireland Champions. To this day, memories of the return march led by Teddy McNeill down and up O'Connell Street and thence to Amiens Street station, are vividly recalled, and not only by Point people. People from all over Down have told me over the years how they would gladly have marched home behind the band that night. When the band did arrive home they paraded the town before finishing up at McAnultys with the national anthem. Terry McAnulty was a member of the band and despite his exertions he was back in Dublin the following morning to join the Down party.

The other notable event came as the thousands of Down fans were celebrating on the Croke Park pitch after the game. One of them, Hugh Campbell, whom I have already written about as the boy who led the school rebellion on the day the seaplane landed on the lough, spotted the Down flag flying high above the arena with the Kerry colours and the tricolour. He thought this would be a nice souvenir of the great occasion so he located the ropes at the back of the stand and in no time the red and black was sliding down the flagpole. Before it got to ground level he was accosted by a couple of members of *An Garda Siochána*. He spun a yarn about being authorised by the Down Chairman, George Tinnelly to get the flag and bring it to the celebration banquet.

Needless to say, the officers were not impressed with his story and brought him to an office in the stadium. GAA officialdom was not impressed either, but unbelievably Hugh emerged smiling and with the flag draped round him. The flag stayed in the family home in Whitecross and later in Warrenpoint until he died. His wife, Annie, later presented it to the St Peter's Club who were pleased to receive the red and black which flew in Croke Park on that day of days.

We celebrated for months and the county has never been the same since. It is the official celebration which took place in Newry Town Hall to which I wish to refer at this stage. It was attended by the president of the Association, Dr Jim Stuart and the secretary, Pádraig O'Keefe. Such was the moment of the occasion that it took some little time to get round to the presentation of the medals. It was done with deserved acclaim for every man. Then it was the turn of the team management. Maurice had been given the task of getting suitable mementos for the rest of us who were involved and when I was called I was delighted to receive the small plaque handed over to me by Dr Stuart. As I walked down the hall I glanced at the silver shield which was its centrepiece, expecting to see the word *bainisteoir* but instead was a word I had never seen before, *roghnóir*. I knew instinctively that it meant selector. I could only smile at the Machiavellian impulse which prompted my designation, 'selector'.

The half smile on my face as I reached our table did not escape my wife's notice. 'Was there something amusing up there?' she asked.

'Yes,' I replied, 'I got a message from Maurice and if I ever write a book I will write about this night.'

When we did eventually land home, the first thing I did was to get out my Irish dictionary to confirm that at least I was a *roghnóir*. Anne was standing looking at me, thinking I was out of my mind looking through a dictionary in the early hours of the morning.

'Did you know that I am a *roghnóir*?'[30] I asked, and went on to explain the significance of the wording. She was not amused.

The plaque had a chequered history in its comparatively short life. When my son, Hugh, got a fluency in Irish early in his school career he said to me one day, 'Daddy, weren't you the manager in 1960? That says 'selector'.' He was at the match as a three year old. 'Yes,' I replied, 'but I was a selector, too,' and left it at

---

30   Irish for a 'selector'

that.

The year 1960 was important to me for another reason. I returned to live on Summerhill. The year before, we had tried to buy a house on Great George's Street which was up for auction and I went to the sale after agreeing with my wife that fifteen hundred pounds was as far as we could go. When that price was reached there was only one other bidder and I stayed with him until sixteen hundred and fifty, my last bid. When I went home to Church Street and told Anne, she exclaimed, 'Thank God you didn't get it, where would we get sixteen hundred and fifty pounds?'

In early spring of 1960, I came home one evening and at our meal Anne said, 'I have seen a house I would like to live in and it's for sale.'

'Where is that now?' I asked, and when she replied, 'Summerhill,' I nearly choked on my food as I exclaimed, 'My family is on Summerhill. My Aunt Kitty is on Summerhill. My uncle Hugh is on Summerhill, and you want to go and live among them all.'

As calmly as you like she answered, 'Well, if they don't bother me, I'll not bother them.' In due course, we moved in between Grants and Mooreheads, both long-established residents on the hill, and we lived happily ever after.

It was good that our most important visitor that year was Sam Maguire himself.

With one All-Ireland title to our credit, we demonstrated we were a good team. To demonstrate that we were an outstanding team we set out with confidence towards that goal in the New Year of 1961. We strode through the preliminary games of the National League, known then as the Lagan Cup, with all our opponents going out of their way to recognise our status as Champions. Tributes and after-match receptions were the order of the day until we met Derry in the final at Casement Park in late March. They showed scant respect for our status as Champions. Joe Lennon was the only man missing from the team which had beaten Kerry, though he came on as a sub in the course of the game. Derry were still a strong side and they beat us decisively by six points.

That game brought tragedy to the Carr family circle, for shortly after half-time my uncle, Jimmy, a fanatical Down supporter, suffered a heart attack and died a short time later. I had been called from the sideline and missed the remainder of the game.

Derry went on to meet Kerry in the National League semi-final with a fair degree of confidence but Kerry ran them into the ground and went on to win the National League in an impressive manner. Such was the quality of 'The Kingdom's' performance that one headline had them as 'team of the century'. Commentators were suggesting they were on track to do the League and Championship double which Down had completed the year before.

The London County Board had already ordained that their Wembley Whitsun offering would be a repeat of the previous year's All-Ireland Final, a game which was to bring the biggest GAA crowd ever to the English national stadium. The defeat by Derry at Casement Park was our first competitive set back since we had gone under to Galway in 1959 and was probably the best thing that ever happened to us. It showed us that we were not invincible.

Our third successive trip to Wembley was much more important to us than either of the previous outings, for the All-Ireland semi-final pairings were set to bring the Ulster and Munster Champions into contention. A win for us at Wembley would stamp our superiority over Kerry yet again so when Down trotted out they were in effect playing for a place in the All-Ireland Final later in September. I imagined as newly crowned League Champions, Kerry would have been equally aware of the long-term implications of a win over Down. We prepared as for an All-Ireland Final.

The game was a classic and Down's achievement in winning was their third-best performance ever. When the teams did meet in the Championship in August, one felt that Kerry were taking the field as underdogs. Amazingly, Kerry's Championship subservience to Down has lasted to the present day.

If there had been a hiccup in Down's Championship run that year it was in the Ulster Final at Casement Park, where Armagh ran us to three points. Some Armagh people would still claim that they should have been awarded a goal late in the game but 40-odd years on, hand on heart, I can assure them that the ball never crossed the line for I was standing tensed behind that goal.

Having stated that the Wembley success was the third-best performance by that Down team, slightly behind the first championship success against Cavan in 1959I now come to the best. The victory over Offaly in the 1961 final was, for me, the greatest football feat I have witnessed in over 60 years. With memories still fresh from the previous year's semi-final proceedings between the counties, a crowd of over 90,000, the biggest ever to gather for a sporting event in the country, thronged Croke Park.

Teams are prepared in the hope that every conceivable eventuality is covered, but invariably a set of circumstances will develop out of nothing and the best-laid plans are set at naught. Who could have conceived that Down would have conceded two goals to Offaly in the first five minutes of the game? *Linesman* could have died that day of a heart attack but this is how he described the second goal:

> *'A fleeting second of indecision and Peter Daly was in between them to force the ball seemingly, through McKay's legs. It was then Down appeared for what they are—a set of men apart from any other ever to grace Croke Park. With such strokes of adversity most teams would have died, but they only served to bring out the best in the Champions. No final has ever produced goals of such vintage, as the three they went on to score in that first half.'*[31]

No final has ever produced a second half of such intensity as was experienced by that record crowd. Though a goal behind at half-time, Offaly were far from being a beaten side and while Down missed chances, it was the frenzied pace of the exchanges which spurred energies of both the flesh and the spirit, leaving every man involved a hero. As *Linesman*, I wrote, 'when these All-Ireland

---

31   Frontier Sentinel

medals are presented to the Down men they should be inscribed with the words "*for valour*", for no sporting decorations have been so hard earned.'

23—Off to the USA

With two All-Ireland titles back-to-back, and playing a brand of football which had not been seen before, Down were in great demand. It was almost inevitable that there would be a trip to America. Fortunately for us, the GAA in New York, controlled by John 'Kerry' O'Donnell, was at loggerheads with the Central Council. O'Donnell had controlled the American GAA operation for years and his stranglehold was being contested by the North American Board, which had been organising Gaelic games in the major cities outside New York. It was this organisation which invited Down to undertake the most extensive tour by any county going out to the States. The North American Board, under the chairmanship of a very affable Mayo man, Mickey Cavanagh, set the itinerary to encompass games in Boston, Chicago, Cleveland, Philadelphia and San Francisco; everything on the American side had been settled before Christmas of 1961.

When we resumed training after the turn of the year, we were all in an expectant and buoyant mood. The mood, however, in the County Board was not so buoyant because as the weeks passed it was proving impossible to get a plane to take us across the Atlantic. One would have thought it was a simple operation, given the notice which we had, of going down to Dublin and chartering an Aer Lingus plane, but nothing is ever simple. Crisis point was reached when we were coming into April and still without a plane. It was decided at a County Board meeting that the general Secretary of the Association, Pádraig O'Keefe, be consulted and George Tinnelly and Maurice Hayes were dispatched to Dublin the next day. It was a wise move, for Pádraig was an influential figure with good contacts in Government circles in Dublin. Within a few days we were advised that a Pakistani Airline plane would be available to us, but that our departure point would have to be Shannon Airport.

While all this was happening inside the County Board, the team and most of the hundred plus supporters who had booked their seats were blissfully unaware of the uncertainty that hung over the trip. The team's one and only concern was their preparation for the National League Final which was down for decision on the Sunday before we were due to leave for America. Needless to say, we were more than anxious to leave Ireland as League Champions.

On the day of the game, when we arrived at the dressing rooms under the Cusack Stand, I was surprised to see Paddy Downey, *The Irish Times* games reporter and commentator sitting there. It was most unusual to see any press people in the dressing room before a game but when he asked if he could speak to me privately, I wondered what was on his mind. There is not that kind of privacy in a dressing room before a game so I ushered him outside.

We all had a fairly close relationship with the sports writers but I was still taken aback when he began, 'Barney, *The Irish Times* is not sending anyone to America and I would deem it a great favour if you would report the tour for us.'

It had already been announced that Mick Dunne of *The Irish Press* and John Hickey of the *Irish Independent* were to accompany us on the tour and it was a surprise and a disappointment to learn that Paddy would not be with them, for he was a greatly respected figure.

'Paddy,' I said, 'it is out of the question.'

I was committed to *The Frontier Sentinel* and I had promised Paddy O'Donoghue I would supply him with something for *The Mourne Observer*. I regretted refusing Paddy for he was a gentleman.

Paddy persisted, 'Look, Barney—I am not suggesting that you do a full report on the games. You just wire the main features of the game and I'll fill out the story.'

'Paddy,' I persisted, 'I have no experience at all in the wiring business and there's the whole time factor, it would be impossible for me.'

Paddy was back at me. 'The time factor is irrelevant. You'll be six hours behind us and all you have to do is go into any Western Union Office, write out your stuff and hand it over the counter. Nothing could be simpler. We don't want full reports. Just give us the essentials and we'll build on it.'

An intake of breath, a sigh and acceptance, 'Paddy you are the only man in Ireland I would do this for.'

We left Newry in three of Jacksons' buses from Cavan, after being blessed by the Bishop of Dromore, Dr Eugene O'Doherty, a Donegal man, and boarded our Pakistani Air Line plane for my first Atlantic crossing.

When I registered in my hotel in New York, I was handed an envelope which contained, among other things, a sizable notebook and an authorisation card from RCA Communications, Inc. bearing my identity thus: Barney Carr, *The Irish Times,* Dublin, *Evening Mail,* Dublin, *Sunday Review,* Dublin. To be billed to *The Irish Times Ltd.,* Dublin, Ireland.' I still have the card and no doubt my grandchildren will be suitably impressed when they are older.

Forty-odd years on, the memories of that trip are undimmed and it would be true to say that it was a glorious holiday. The five games we played were exhibition games, but in all the cities they were immensely enjoyed. The Gaelic fraternity was well conscious of the star quality of the team and the names of the players were widely familiar. If the games were not memorable there were certainly other aspects of the tour which were.

It was in Boston that we had our first game, and in the evening we had a reception sponsored by the local Association at which most Down families living in the area were represented. Here, I met some Warrenpoint natives, among them two McCaughey sisters who had been at school with my mother. Another sister, Mrs McKinley, was alive and well in The Point. I was invited to the home of one of them, Mrs McClorey, to spend what was a most enjoyable afternoon during which I had my tea poured from a shamrock-decorated teapot bearing the legend, 'a present from Warrenpoint'.

In the course of the conversation one of my hosts said to me, 'There's a man from The Point, Jimmy Watters, who lives half an hour from here and he's not very well. I'm sure he would love to see someone from home.'

The name, Jimmy Watters, rang a bell with me immediately as I had often heard my father claim, in speaking of footballers, 'He wouldn't hold a candle to Jimmy Watters,' and it was soccer footballers he was talking about. As well as this, there was and still is a big Watters connection in The Point. Bob, known as Dodds, and Mick were nephews and their sister, Mrs Gibbons, was my neighbour on Summerhill. The Heaton family, too, were Jimmy's connections. I acquainted my hosts of the sporting connection to Jimmy and indicated I would be delighted to visit him. We left their home shortly afterwards and arrived at the Watters' abode.

We were greeted by Mrs Watters who intimated that Jimmy was not well enough to be up; as we moved into his bedroom, Mrs McClorey announced, 'Here's a man from The Point to see you, Jimmy.' I followed her into the room to observe this grey-haired, obviously unwell man. I stood and gave him a few seconds to get a good look at me. He knew I was testing him and I could visualise The Point family names tumbling in his head. In a surprisingly firm voice, he announced, 'You are a Carr,' and as I confirmed with a nod of my head he asked, 'Are you a son of Hugh's?' The two women left us and we started into litanies of names and places and events. He had been back to The Point once in his life time. That was in 1932 when he returned for the Eucharistic Congress in Dublin. He found it so hard leaving the second time that he never returned. He paused for a second or two and I thought he was unwell. I looked at him intently, then I realised he was in deep, deep thought, if not in meditation.

He started again slowly and I noted that he spoke in the present tense. 'There is one man in The Point that I have prayed for every day of my life and this morning he was very much on my mind; Master Pettit. The good that man has done could never be measured. When I was saying my prayers this morning, I was thinking it will not be too long till I meet him.'

Already I was marvelling at the wonder of the Lord's ways, which we are inclined to call coincidences. As the frail figure in the bed wiped his eyes I said, 'Jimmy, I am going to give you a pleasant surprise. We have a son of Master Pettit with us on the trip, Fr Joe, and I will have him out to see you tomorrow.' Jimmy was overwhelmed but was most anxious that Fr Joe be put to no inconvenience.

The visit ended and I returned to our hotel. Later that night, I recounted my visit to the Watters home to Fr Pettit, who was more than a little surprised to learn of this link to his father, now dead nearly 40 years. He was delighted to have the opportunity to speak to one of his father's former pupils. Next day, he was collected at the hotel and spent much of the afternoon with Jimmy.

There never was a more modest man than Fr Joe Pettit; it might have been my imagination that suggested he was walking 'ten feet tall' when I saw him later that evening. When I asked him how he found Jimmy, he replied, 'Meeting that man today has made my visit to America worthwhile. I know more about myself and my father than I ever could have imagined.'

A couple of weeks after we arrived home, the niece of Jimmy Watters called to tell me that he had died. I conveyed the news to Fr Pettit a few days later. He said with a smile, 'You know, Barney, I did not expect to be able to go on that trip to America, but I did and I don't think God was concerned about me seeing the Down team. He wanted me to meet Jimmy Watters.'

The story of how I got to Johnstown, Pennsylvania, began in the early summer of 1959 as I emerged from the Post Office on Newry's Hill Street. I heard the familiar voice of Jack Bannon, the depot manager.

'Barney,' he boomed twice across the street. I looked towards the gable of the Breffni Arms Hotel where, along with two women, he occupied the seat normally used by the busmen. He hailed me over with his waving arm.

'Barney, these two ladies are from America. They are cousins of Canon Toner.' The Canon was parish priest of Killeavey in Co. Armagh, close to Newry. He continued, 'They have been staying with him for a few days and would like to spend a few days in Warrenpoint. Where would you recommend them to stay?'

I suggested that they go to the Crown Hotel and as I noted that one of the women was quite elderly I said to Big Jack, 'You tell the conductor to drop them off at the Crown on his way to the station.' Their bus was due in a few minutes and off I went with their grateful thanks. This could well have been the end of the story, as far as these ladies were concerned, but for the fact that the next day I was walking on Church Street with my wife and two children when we met the two American ladies. There was mutual recognition and we stopped. I introduced my wife and sons, Hugh and John, who was then only three months old and in his pram. In the course of a friendly chat they said they loved the hotel, they loved what they had seen of the town and were looking forward to a restful few days. Before we left them, Anne said, 'Why don't you come up for a bit of a chat tomorrow evening. We just live over the road there,' pointing to the dental surgery over which we lived. They were delighted to accept.

The next evening was somewhat cooler weather-wise so we lit a fire in the sitting room which overlooked the street to the front and the church green to the side. They were absolutely delighted to see an open fire for the first time in many, many years. In the acquaintance so far, they would have known us as Barney and Anne, and we would only have known them as Canon Toner's cousins, so we had more formal introductions at the outset. The elder of the women was Mary Griffith, a cousin of Canon Toner. The younger, also Mary Griffith, was her daughter, a retired schoolteacher and her only child.

When she had explained the connection with Canon Toner, I asked, 'What part of America are you from?'

'Have you ever heard of a place called Johnstown in Pennsylvania?' she asked in a voice which in no way betrayed her age, and when I indicated that I hadn't, she continued, 'I thought most people would have heard of Johnstown, but it's so long ago now, I guess most people outside America would never have heard of our disaster.'

She proceeded to tell Anne and me what was essentially the story of her life. A Hughes by birth, of Tyrone stock, she grew up in the Johnstown area of Pennsylvania. She married Michael Griffith before she was eighteen and Mary, her daughter, was born before she was nineteen. They lived in the hill country above Johnstown, which at that time was a bustling township. In 1889 Johnstown became a city with a growing number of prosperous industries. Higher on the hills above the Griffiths' homestead stood the South Fork Reservoir which collected and held the water supply for the city below. Some months after city status had been achieved there was a prolonged spell of heavy rain which resulted in the collapse of a retaining wall of the reservoir. The cascading wall of water swept down the hills to the city below. Her husband, Michael, had been outdoors at the time and he was swept downhill. His body was never recovered. He was one of over two thousand people who lost their lives in the disaster. Mrs Griffith described how she grabbed her baby of some months, and how the pair of them miraculously survived. It was no wonder there was such a bond between these two women.

With that link to Johnstown established, a correspondence began when the Griffiths returned to America. A couple of years later we were still communicating via letter and Anne advised them of my trip with the Down team. The details of the trip were not finalised but the Griffiths were insisting that I visit them in Johnstown.

When those details did come eventually, and were transmitted to Mary and her mother, they insisted it was a very simple operation for me to spend a few days with them, as indeed it turned out to be. Our itinerary indicated that we would be travelling from Cleveland to Philadelphia by coach, and from one point on the Expressway, Johnstown was only 60 miles. I had my final briefing from the Griffiths by phone, shortly before we left our hotel, and when I left the coach at Exit 36 they were sitting waiting to greet me and drive me to Johnstown, in a valley in the Allegheny Mountains. We took in the area where the South Fork Reservoir had been located, all those years before, and it wasn't too hard to visualise the trail of disaster of that fateful day.

I was in Johnstown from Wednesday afternoon until Saturday morning and it was evident from Thursday morning that the Griffith mother and daughter were very highly regarded in the community. We went to the parish church for Mass and as we parked the parish priest was just arriving. I was introduced to him as 'a friend from Ireland who is touring with the Down football team.' Minutes later, before he commenced Mass, he said, 'I want to welcome Mary Griffith's friend from Ireland. I know his name is Barney and he's a ball player.' There would have been about 50 people at Mass that morning and I was introduced to most of them at the end. In the café after Mass and next day, when I did some shopping in specific stores, I could see the deference and respect which was accorded to these two survivors of the dam disaster which had claimed and changed so many lives. On Saturday morning I was driven back to the Expressway where I got the bus which brought me to Philadelphia.

Mary Griffith, the older, died in 1969. We had a correspondence with Mary the younger for some years but it ended, we assumed, with her death.

I left Johnstown with a well-produced book on the disaster, which I had for years, and planned to use as an *aide-mémoire*. Alas, it could not be found. Quite recently I phoned 'the brother' in Chicago a few days before he was due to come home for a family wedding, asking if he could get me something on the Johnstown disaster. This he did and presented me with *The Johnstown Flood* by David McCullough, a remarkable piece of documentary writing. In it is reproduced 'A List of Victims' printed in the *Johnstown Tribune* on 31 July 1890, 14 months exactly after the date of the disaster, 31 May 1889. The total number lost as 2,209, and the list is set out in categories. In the category 'not known to have been found' there are over 800 names. One of them is simply, 'Griffith, Mr'. Also included in the same category were:

> 'Carr, Mrs Mary, 42 Woodvale: Carr, William, 7 Woodvale: Carr Patrick, 22 Cambria: Carr, Mrs Sara, 20 Cambria.'

I pray and trust they are all experiencing the joy of the Lord.

From Philadelphia, we took the mighty hop by plane across America to San Francisco, where we were to have our last game of the tour. This stop allowed me to renew acquaintance with a surprising number of Down people who had settled in that idyllic location. There were the Spiers from Hilltown, the McGoverns from Grinan, the Downeys from Rathfriland and the Heatleys from The Point, but it is the referee of the game I wish to write about.

Liam Friel was a Belfast man who in my playing days would have been regarded by most Ulster observers as one of the top referees in the country. In spite of that, he was never considered for any of the plum appointments such as an All-Ireland Final or even a semi-final. But that was the culture of the period, when northern referees and particularly those on the northern side of the border, were not too highly regarded. Meeting Liam heightened the enjoyment of the San Francisco experience.

The second chapter of this three-part tale comes about 20 years later when my long-time friend and colleague, Ted Bradley, asked me if I had heard that Liam Friel had died some weeks before in America. This was very sad news to me and the fact that it had come from Ted, who had played with Friel's club, O'Donnell's, in his early days in Belfast, ensured total acceptance. I prayed fervently for his eternal rest and I advised Anne to put the name of Liam Friel on our Mass list.

Over the next ten or twelve years on odd occasions I would have mentioned to people who would have known him that Liam had died, and I'm sure that they in turn would have spread the sad news.

The third and final chapter took place in the mid-nineties when I received an invitation to a surprise 70th birthday party for Billy Feeney. Billy was one of the stalwarts of both the Antrim football and hurling teams of the '40s. He also served in the Irish Army with my brother Hugh. I would have met some of those present occasionally over the years and some I had hardly seen in 50 years. In due course we were all seated at our meal and as I glanced round the room I got one of the great shocks of my life. I saw either Liam Friel's twin brother or Liam Friel's ghost. I dropped my eyes instantly. It was a second or two before I had regained sufficient composure to take another glance. This time the eyes of the spectre across the room were trained on me. We both rose simultaneously and advanced to meet each other in the middle of the room. It was indeed Liam Friel in the flesh.

I felt the resurrection man needed to be shown to a wider fraternity, so I organised a little get together with some of his older contemporaries in Down. They were all delighted to renew their links with this doyen of referees. A happy day that was. Sadly, three of them, Jimmy McLoughlin, John O'Hare and Gerry Brown, have passed to their own rewards. Both Liam Friel and Billy Feeney died within days of each other in the month of February 2006.

That game in San Francisco brought the tour to an end, but it brought the beginning of an unforgettable trip home. First hop, San Francisco to New York, a four-hour wait before the second hop to Shannon. Finally, it was a comparative crawl from Shannon to Newry. I had one day to recover before I was back at work.

24—Going for three-in-a-row

On the day before the National League final with Dublin part of *Linesman's* piece in *The Frontier Sentinel* read:

> *'Over the years it has been repeated often, that a trip to America finishes a team, and be sure it will be said again, if Down go under, in the coming Championship campaign. But Down have shattered many a football myth already, and I am confident that they will make short work of this longstanding one also. In many instances in the past, teams going to America have shown signs of decline even before they left these shores. Unless they show similar signs, by going under to Dublin tomorrow, I cannot imagine that the same will be said of this Down team, fielding at full strength for the first time this year.'*

Admittedly, we won that National League on the scoreboard with a decisive penalty kick, so, in truth, we had been fortunate to go to America as League Champions, and I was concerned that Dublin had exposed our deficiencies to such a degree. Still, when we met the week after we arrived home to prepare for our first Championship outing against Fermanagh there was an air of confidence. The full squad would not have been present but Down's performance at Irvinestown suggested the cutting edge was as sharp as ever and it inspired media predictions that Down were set for the treble. While we beat Tyrone by six clear points in the semi-final, the score line was slightly generous to us. The pundits still thought we were on track for the treble.

We were due back in Casement Park two weeks later. This gave us four training sessions and while there was not a full attendance at any of them it was only on the last night, with only eight or nine of the selected team present, that the alarm bells began to ring for me. I was a bit concerned that any of the team might imagine that we would have no problems with Cavan. This was a situation we had not met before and possibly we had not the experience to deal with it.

The next morning I was at home after my early stint at work when George Tinnelly breezed into the house in the best of form.

'All set for Sunday,' he beamed confidently as he came down the hall.

I spoke quietly, slowly, and very deliberately, 'George, we are in trouble on Sunday.'

'Ah for God's sake have a bit of sense man,' was his retort.

'Look George, I am telling you that our team is not tuned for an Ulster Final. They still might win but I know this team is not tuned for a final.'

I proceeded to tell him about the turnout the previous evening and I said a little heatedly, 'You were not there yourself last night,'— he never would have missed a session before a final—'you think we are home and dried.'

'You're right,' he said, 'I could have been there,' and he added, 'don't be too worried, they'll be all right.' But I did worry, and it wasn't all right.

The game with Cavan at Casement Park was not too long in progress before I knew we were in trouble; we went in at half-time six points in arrears. As we went up the steps into the dressing rooms, I was joined by an ashen faced county chairman. 'By God you were right,' George said, 'we are in trouble.'

Great play is often made of the miracles which are worked in dressing rooms at half-time but this was not going to be one of those occasions. The other selectors and I went into a huddle with Peter McDermott who, unknown to us beforehand, was at the game. He came to the dressing room in an attempt to draft a recovery campaign. Both Peter and I spoke to the team but it was to no avail.

On the day, Cavan looked a good team but never had Down performed so poorly. To think that our forwards could only manage four points in an hour was unimaginable and I could have cried to see this magnificent team humbled in such a manner. A few weeks later, we saw the real quality of the Cavan team when they lost to Roscommon in the All-Ireland semi-final, which turned out to be one of the poorest on record. The question on all journalistic lips was, 'How did that Cavan team ever beat Down?'

Roscommon went on to meet Kerry in a final which was as colourless as could be imagined, resulting in Kerry taking their 20th All-Ireland crown. It would be true to say they never got one so handy, before or since.

It had been my intention to step down from the managership of the team after the third of what I had hoped would have been a 'three in a row' run, but I realised that it would be the wrong time to quit after a defeat. We went through the National League campaign in 1963 to be beaten by a single point by Kerry in the final. We had beaten Galway by a single point in the semi-final but in doing so we were dealt a cruel blow in losing James McCartan, who had been sent off before half-time. Had James been available for the final I have no doubt we would have taken the League. As the game went, it was a hard, dour struggle in which Kerry did all their scoring in the first half and with Down missing a series of chances in the second period which should have seen them safely home.

In the 1963 Ulster Championship, Down sailed through in Ulster to come up against Dublin in the All-Ireland semi-final. This was their first meeting since the League Final of the previous year and Dublin made it clear early on that they had scant respect for Down's record. In a hard hitting and at times ill-tempered game there was no doubting the superiority of the Leinster Champions, who were always on the top of their form when playing Down.

I had indicated to Danny Flynn and a couple of members of the County Committee earlier in the year that 1963 was my last campaign as manager, so when January came round in 1964, I bowed out with as little fuss as possible. I was extremely glad that Danny elected to continue training the team. If both of us had gone together, something might have been read into a double departure. I did, however, remain on the County Committee as South Down representative for I was very much involved in the general run of GAA affairs.

I wasn't completely out of the football scene though. With the emergence of Down as Ulster Champions I was invited to join the selection committee of the Railway Cup team; with Cavan's Mick Higgins, I was responsible for its direction through most of the decade. I was really happy to be part of the management for the team was powered largely by Down men through the 60's, which proved to be the province's most prolific period in the competition. The advent of television put the skids under the popularity of the St Patrick's Day showpiece. It is long past the time when it should have been laid to rest. Happily the Club Championship is a winner and says much more about the Association than the Railway Cup ever did. It is unfortunate that in the scheme of things it has to be a winter competition, and is likely to remain so for the foreseeable future.

Over the years, I have often been often asked how the Down style evolved in such a short space of time, so I would like to expand slightly on the football revolution which occurred in the space of 30 months, resulting in Down coming from oblivion to taking Gaelic football's premier award. Already I have put on record how the selection committee was reorganised and a manager put in place after the 1958 campaign.

My own formative football years were soccer based and while I never considered myself a natural Gaelic footballer, I believe The Point teams of the forties brought a new dimension to Down football. The village 'Derby game' I had seen in Oberammergau was the first occasion I had seen continental football. The first time I saw a continental national side perform was when Austria played Ireland at Dalymount Park in Dublin in 1951; I watched it in the company of my bosom pal, 'Toots'. I think Ireland won the game, even though Austria had two thirds of the possession. Austria were hopeless when they got near the goals. What impressed me was their passing skills, their pace and their use of space.

A couple of years later, when Hungary became the first team to beat England at Wembley, the soccer world looked on in amazement at the exploits of Ferenc Puskás and his colleagues; they brought a new dimension to the game. The European Cup came into existence in 1956 and for the first time the name of Real Madrid came into focus. I made it my business to see Real any time they were on television. I think they won the European Cup six times in a row.

Even though I was not involved in any kind of team management at the time, I thought it might be possible to translate some dynamic qualities of Real Madrid into Gaelic football. When we did beat Cavan so convincingly in 1959 I felt particularly fulfilled to read the next day in the *Belfast Telegraph* that, 'Down has brought a continental dimension to Gaelic football.' I doubt if any of the Down squad realised that I was trying to get them to play like Real, as I was a rather laidback manager compared with some of the chaps who star in the role today. In the 1960 campaign, when James McCartan came into the half-forward line between Paddy Doherty and Sean O'Neill, the forward line was complete. James had his own natural football instincts; there was nothing more exhilarating than to see him emerge from deep in his own half in possession, knowing intuitively where to plant the ball for any of his forward colleagues, but particularly for O'Neill or Doherty, who with him formed what I called, 'a football trinity'—one mind in three bodies. Add the front line of Tony Hadden, Pat O'Hagan and Morgan and we have probably the best set of forwards ever to grace Croke Park.

In his biography by Owen McCrohan, the master himself Mick O'Dwyer (who faced Down as a player), said of the traditional style, 'Very little thought went into combined play or adopting a more scientific approach.' He went on to say, 'then in the early 1960s Down's revolutionary approach made that style redundant.'[32] In that book, Owen describes me standing on a table in the Kerry dressing room expressing sentiments 'on behalf of the Down team, on behalf of all Down and on behalf of all Ulster...'[33] but I never stood in any of our opponents' dressing rooms in Croke Park or anywhere else.

Some considered that Down had a midfield problem and Terry McCormack's regular advice to me was, 'You'll do nothing with that team until you get a couple of midfielders.' I would invariably reply, 'You get me any better in Down and we'll play them.' On one occasion we felt it necessary to move Joe Lennon into the right corner and bring Tony Hadden back to the middle of the field. I knew Joe, who was based at Loughborough at the time, was not too happy but I was taken by surprise later in the week, when I received a nineteen-page letter from him presenting a closely argued case as to why he should not have been moved.

On another occasion when the Ulster Council had a trial game before selecting the Railway Cup team, Joe was not asked to come over for it as Gerry Arthurs was not into spending money unless it was absolutely necessary. I was not a great believer in trial games myself and we felt there was nothing to be gained by taking Joe over, as his place was assured. Again, I had a ten-page rocket from Joe, who was the most meticulous man I have met in my football life. There were some wonderful occasions when the pre-match banter between himself and James McCartan created an atmosphere which didn't allow for tension. The greatest riposte of all from Joe, however, came on an occasion when we were playing a challenge game in Mayo. The team was stripping out and Joe, with one foot on a bench tying his lace, asked, 'Barney, what time will I be back in Dublin? I have to be at my work in the morning.'

Now I didn't know what arrangement there was to get Joe to the airport, but before I had a chance to open my mouth, James piped up, 'Joe, you wouldn't know what a day's work is.' We all laughed.

Joe took his foot off the bench, drew himself to his full height and with an air of disdain delivered the riposte of all time, 'James, I would like you to know that I do not get paid for what I do, I get paid for what I know.' Such was the cheer which greeted the delivery, the roof was in danger of being lifted.

To be associated with such a wonderful bunch of fellows was much more than a sporting experience. Their place in the history of Gaelic sport is secure.

Having said all that, I recall an occasion in the autumn of 2000 organised by The Abbey CBS past pupils' sports association; when I was getting ready to leave I acknowledged a wave from Joe McAnulty. Joe is the father of the twins Enda and Justin, both of whom had played on the Armagh team beaten by Kerry in the All Ireland semi-final a few weeks before. I hadn't seen him or his wife Mary since that disappointing day, so I thought I should commiserate. It took a longer time than I had anticipated. When we had examined most aspects of Armagh's second successive failure—and there were many areas of disagreement—Joe said to me,

32   Owen McCrohan, *Mick O'Dwyer, Manager of the Millennium*, p. 4

33   *Ibid., p. 199*

'Tell me, what do you consider the most important single factor in Down's success in the sixties?.'

I had only to think for a second, for the question had been posed to me before, and I astonished him with my reply. 'The most important single factor, Joe, was my membership of the Down County Board.'

He put his glass on the table slowly, paused, and with deliberation asked, 'Are you saying to me that anyone could have managed that team?'

'No, I am not saying that. I am sure there were others but there would have been no manager if I had not been a member of the Board.'

I could see that Joe was somewhat perplexed, so I said, 'It is a long story, Joe, and it is too late to start telling it tonight, but it is in the telling.'

It has been stated very often that, 'Even God cannot change the past, only historians can.' It is for that reason I recount Raymond Smith's version of the involvement of Peter McDermott in the Down preparation for the replay and the final of the 1960 Championship.

In his *The Football Immortals,* he writes:

> 'Now I can reveal the story of how he came to coach the Down team.
>
> Peter watched the drawn 1960 semi-final from Hill 16.
>
> I had a hunch that Down were going to effect the big break-through. They had faults, but they had the look of a Championship side.
>
> Peter wrote a letter to his old friend, Alfie Matthews of Newry, pointing out where he thought Down had gone wrong against Offaly.
>
> The result? He was invited to coach Down for the replay. Peter never expected this. After long deliberation he accepted—on condition that it was kept a closely guarded secret.
>
> Many knew that there was a mystery man in the Down camp, but only those close to the team, were aware of his real identity.
>
> In Peter's view teams from over the border were inclined to be too theoretical and he advised Down to forget the blackboard and concentrate on continuous movement and swift interchanging of positions in attack. 'Mobility was to be the keynote,' he said, 'and no man was to be rigidly tied to his position.'[34]

Raymond Smith has gone to his eternal reward and I would not want to be too unkind to him, but I would be surprised if that was the story as told to him by Peter McDermott. Indeed, I would be surprised if Peter was the source of his story.

The notion of the 'closely guarded secret' humoured me when I first read it, for 'Linesman,' in his report of that momentous game, paid tribute to Peter for the assistance he gave in the team's preparation. Even though we trained in schools for quite a part of the time, I can never recall having recourse to the blackboards nor could I imagine that Peter McDermott was unaware of the Down approach to football long before we met Offaly.

I first met Peter when Down and Meath played in a challenge game at The Abbey in Newry in 1944, when we both wore the No 11 shirt for our respective

---

34   Raymond Smith, *The Football Immortals*, Dublin, 1971, p. 215

counties. Meath had such names as Kevin Smyth, Mick O'Toole, Tony Donnelly, Paddy and Micheal O'Brien, Frankie Byrne, Peter Meegan, Seamus Ludlow, Christo Hand and Peter himself. At that time, they had never won a Senior All-Ireland, and it wasn't until five years later that they achieved that goal. Peter had come up to help out with the Down Junior team in the Junior All-Ireland campaign of 1946. He became a regular trader to the South Down area for he had an egg business which ensured a weekly visit and it was always a delight to meet him.

Alfie Matthews, who was a Louth man, was married to Nora, a relative of Peter. They lived in what is now Dominic Street, Newry, where they enjoyed a unique relationship. Alfie collected insurance and he had a few clients among the transport staff. As well as that, his insurance office was just over the road from the bus depot so I would meet him quite often. Besides selling insurance, Alfie kept pigs at a yard close to where he lived in Dominic Street. One would see Alfie, smartly dressed and meticulous about his insurance business one minute, and a couple of hours later he might be seen wheeling his little handcart collecting the swill at the side door of the Imperial or Breffni Arms Hotels, in his work-a-day clothes.

Outside of his work, he had three abiding interests. As well as pigs, he kept bees and he talked football. Alfie didn't talk about a game to you, he played a game for you. If there was a free kick, Alfie put the ball down and either kicked a point or missed a point. If a goalkeeper made a good save, Alfie gave a playback. The imaginary whistle was never out of his mouth. When there were real serious issues under discussion he had an introductory line which I always relished, 'Barney Carr, if I could put it to you this way,' and this with rolling r's.

Regularly he would announce, 'I had a letter from McDermott the other day,' and proceed to take it out of his pocket and read snippets of the games or incidents which Peter was describing. A letter from McDermott was as well crafted as any of Alastair Cooke's *Letters from America*. I used to marvel that Peter could take time to sit down and write such detailed letters of the games in which he had played.

Alfie and Nora were supporters of Newry Shamrocks and great friends of Fr Esler, and regularly they were to be seen walking down to the Marshes to what is now Páirc Esler, but never quite together. Invariably Nora walked about three paces behind Alfie, who was one of Fr Esler's earliest lieutenants. Paddy Gribben and Tommy McKay were others in the early days of that pitch at which Fr Esler's donkey was a source of great hilarity.

It strikes me, though, that I could not write about Newry Gaeldom of that era without reference to Bobby Langan, who personalised the spirit of the GAA in a unique fashion. People still say to me, 'I remember the night when you came home with the first Sam Maguire and you and Bobby Langan led the singing of *The dear little town in the old County Down.'*

Alfie's greatest attraction for me was the manner in which he used to regale me with descriptions of games which he and his brother, Tommy, had taken part in as members of the Louth county team. A name he frequently mentioned was that of Nobby Garland, who as I learned later, was one of Louth's outstanding performers of an earlier era. Sometime after Down's All-Ireland success, I was in a hostelry in Dundalk where I was introduced to Nobby Garland, and in the course of the conversation I mentioned to Nobby that I had often heard Alfie Mathews speak of their exploits on the Louth team. In all innocence I asked, 'What sort of a player was Alfie?'

Nobby looked at me in bewilderment. 'I don't ever remember Alfie playing football, but his brother Tommy was a topper.'

After hearing that, I enjoyed Alfie's exploits on the field even more.

24—The Wind of Change

After the run of success we had enjoyed it was always going to be difficult for my successor. When I retired in 1964, Kevin Mussen took over the managerial reins but he felt he had enough after one year in the post. He was succeeded by Brian Denvir, who was joined by Antrim's Paddy O'Hara as trainer on the retirement of Danny Flynn. Between them they restored Down's confidence to a remarkable degree and took the Ulster title after a most impressive campaign, beating Cavan in the final. This was accomplished without the services of James McCartan who had withdrawn from the Down panel earlier in the year. Galway, who were the reigning champions, provided the opposition. In the third quarter it looked as if nothing would stop Down qualifying for another final joust with Kerry but they squandered a succession of great chances, giving Galway a victory they hardly deserved—a victory which provided the third success in their 'four in a row'.

In her *Down GAA Story*, Síle Nic an Ultaigh (Sheila McAnulty) bemoaned the fact that James McCartan viewed the match from the stand. She commented, 'Had he been on the field he might well have swung the decision in the county's favour,' a view shared by most Down supporters that day. It was the feeling in the Down County Board that James' decision to withdraw earlier in the year was a show of solidarity with Maurice Hayes, who had severed his links with the Association after the controversial 1965 Convention.[35] James made his return to the colours in the Ground's Tournament a couple of weeks later, with Down first beating Kerry narrowly, and then Galway decisively in the final. Down were still the dominant force in Ulster in 1966 but went under to Meath in the All-Ireland semi-final.

The wind of change really got under way after the 1965 Convention which was notable for a number of reasons. After it, Paddy O'Donoghue confided in me that he would be seeking to succeed George Tinnelly when the latter decided to retire from the chairmanship. I believe that George had advised him of the timing of his retirement, for he would have seen Paddy as a likely successor. Paddy asked me if I would take on his role as GAA correspondent in *The Mourne Observer* and keep the column 'ticking over' for him in the event of him taking over the top role. After being elected for the nineteenth time in 1966, George gave notice that it would be his final term.

I had doubts about my ability to do a journalistic 'double act', but Paddy hadn't. A discussion with James Hawthorne, proprietor and editor of the paper, bolstered my confidence, and *Right Corner* was born with proprietary rights to that section of the back page not too long after George made his announcement. When the 1967 Convention came round there was much speculation as to whom his successor might be. Few could have anticipated the close run nature of the vote between Paddy O'Donoghue and Tom Mulholland, a Belfast man who had come to teach in Down and who was chairman of the East Down Board. Both men had an equal number of votes and it was the outgoing chairman's casting vote which swung it for Paddy.

---

35   *Cf.* Chapter 34

Paddy had been the GAA correspondent of *The Mourne Observer* almost from the first year of that paper's existence, but long before that he had been a solid and stubborn full back for Castlewellan. He was very much in the tradition of his father, one of the early pioneers of the Association in Down, and it was entirely fitting that he should follow in his footsteps to lead Down through a term which brought the third All-Ireland title.

While much of the happenings of 1968 have long since been forgotten, it is interesting to recall a few of the events which marked the campaign. Probably one of the more important was the appointment of Gerry Brown as manager after Brian Denvir retired. The other was the return to the fold of Paddy Doherty. He had quit the GAA scene after a dispute with the County Committee arising from a club game in which Paddy and his younger brother, Francie Doherty, took umbrage at some of the referee's decisions. Paddy went to play soccer with Ballyclare Comrades, thereby breaking the 'foreign games' rule' which led to automatic suspension; but on moving to London he returned to the GAA with one of the clubs in that metropolis.

The question of whether he was legally playing did not arise until he was back in Ireland and playing with his own club, Ballykinlar. Then the doubts were raised. There was little doubt that Paddy had played in London when under suspension, but a body which was dubbed 'the mercy committee' truly dispensed mercy on this occasion. The Ulster selectors, of whom I was still one, were delighted, as we had already named him on the Railway Cup team. The entire Down GAA body would have forgiven Paddy anything.

With Doherty in place there was a degree of optimism in Down for the opening games of the National League, even before the winter break revealed evidence of a number of youthful maturing players. Tom O'Hare was already on the team and the emergence of the magnificent Colm McAlarney[36], Brendan Sloan, Ray McConville, Peter Rooney, Mickey Cole, John Murphy and others suggested another break-through. With Gerry Brown in charge, everything seemed to be falling into place until Glenn went to play Annaclone in a league or tournament game on an early summer evening. At the time a visit to Annaclone could be a bit of an adventure and so it turned out on this occasion for James and Dan McCartan.

The most serious outcome of the game was the application by James and Dan for a transfer from Glenn, whom they had served for so long, to Tullylish, their home club. Naturally enough, Glenn objected and the County Committee agreed with them, denying the transfers. Dan accepted the committee's decision with good grace, but James went into another spell of retirement which included retirement from the Inter-County scene. Down had won the National League in splendid style and went on to take their seventh Ulster title at the expense of Cavan.

When a county gets to an All-Ireland semi-final, no stones are left unturned in the effort to get the best possible team on the field, so, having qualified, it was understandable that the mass of Down Gaeldom was praying that James would have a change of heart. Even with that, I was surprised some days later when

36 Colm McAlarney is the only player to have won Railway Cup winners' medals in each of three decades.

I was approached by the county chairman, Paddy O'Donoghue, who asked if I would approach James to see if he would reconsider his decision. I confessed to Paddy my own view that James was unlikely to change his mind, and even more unlikely to do it at my behest. I indicated to him, also, that the one man who might have some influence with James was Maurice Hayes, but by this time Maurice had fallen out with Down and the Association. Having expressed my views I said that if the team management felt I should approach James, I was happy to do so.

A couple of days later, Anne and I set out for Donacloney and the McCartan home where we were received most hospitably by Mrs McCartan; she was as deeply involved in the football scene as any of the male members of the family. She knew instinctively what my errand was, as did Mickey Tumilty, an Annaclone man, who was general *factotum* at the McCartan homestead. Mrs McCartan expressed her own doubts about the possibility of a change of mind by James, while Mickey went searching for him. When he did arrive, he had the friendliest of welcomes for us and the women diplomatically left us together.

Our discussion on the central issue did not last too long for I knew James well enough to know that he was not going to change his mind on my pleading, and I did not persist. When we met the ladies again and I caught the half-hopeful gleam in Mrs McCartan's eye, I had to respond with the shake of the head. Football was not mentioned as we took our tea before leaving.

It is history that Down went on to beat Galway and Kerry, winning their third All-Ireland crown, with one of their all-time greats watching from a seat in the stand—all because of an incident in a game at Annaclone. It was disappointing, however, that this exceptional Down team did not do justice to itself by taking another All-Ireland. Not for the first time, Cavan put an end to our gallop when they were our opponents in the Ulster Final the following year at Casement Park.

If James McCartan kicked his last ball for Down and Glenn in the early days of 1968, it was certainly not the end of James' contribution to Down football for he had a 'second coming' ten years later as Down manager; this was after a decade in which All-Ireland success had eluded us. For a county which had come from oblivion to provide a new dimension to Gaelic football in the sixties, this was a most depressing period, though those of us who had known the earlier lean years tended to be a bit more philosophical.

In 1977, Jack Fitzsimmons, a notable performer himself, was team manager, but for a reason which never became known to me, he resigned. This presented the County Committee with a headache just weeks before the Championship was due to commence. The Board must have breathed a collective sigh of relief when James McCartan agreed to shoulder the responsibility of management.

The county at large awaited the campaign with bated breath. There were a couple of initial hiccups but the ship got on to an even keel quickly enough. The Championship ended at the semi-final stage against Derry, but the early stages of the National League some months later revealed a definite sense of purpose; this was still apparent when activities got under way in 1978. The league run ended when they were beaten in the semi-final by Mayo, but, undaunted, Down went on to qualify for an Ulster Final meeting with Cavan by beating Derry in the semi-final.

Down followers had only hours to bask in the satisfaction of another meeting with Breffni when something of a sporting earthquake hit the county. James and his management team tendered their resignations because they claimed the County Board had not called off internal league games on a particular Sunday. Into the bargain, the players indicated they would not play under any other management.

This really put it up to the County Board, who were continually under pressure from the clubs for as few closed dates as possible. Officialdom conceded, training resumed, and Down went on to beat Cavan but failed to Dublin in the All-Ireland semi-final.

It was not to be wondered that the County Convention in January 1979 was a boisterous affair, in which the clubs made known their dissatisfaction at the continued interruption of the leagues. I was not present at the county assembly, but the Board chairman was Rostrevor's Seán Fearon who was elected for the second successive year. Seán was a principled administrator and one who had given great playing service to both county and club. He had been on the 1958 panel and played in the Ulster Final against Derry. By all accounts Seán did a remarkable job in striking the right balance, and once again Down set off the year in a confident frame of mind. However, the season had hardly got under way before there was another thunderbolt from on high, another management walkout, and again it was the issue of closed dates.

In the previous year, the date in dispute was something like three weeks before the Ulster Final and the body of opinion was that the stance of the County Board was not unreasonable, but to seek closed dates in early March—for only a challenge game—was out of the question. The Board decided there would be no closed date for a challenge game.

Now the walkout problem in 1978 had been settled in a reasonable time but on this occasion the Committee was determined to take a stand. The saga was running a couple of weeks when to my surprise I had a visit from the board chairman and secretary, Seán Fearon and TP Murphy respectively, to ask if I would consider stepping into the breach as manager. It was a long meeting and the fact that the playing panel had indicated they would not play under any other management meant that an alternative panel had to be considered.

After intimating that I was prepared to take on the task, we considered and settled on an alternative panel of 25 players; I was given a free hand when the question of possible refusal was raised. Some of the 25 would have played at county level, some would have been potential county panellists and others would have been good club players without any county experience. Some of them I didn't even know.

I did not speak to a single player but I spoke to individuals around the county whose integrity and commitment to the Association was beyond question. I gave them the names of the players I wished them to contact, and within 48 hours I had assurances that the men whom they had approached would be at Burren for training the following Tuesday night. The night before the County Board meeting I advised the secretary, TP, that I had a panel in place for the following week.

While all this was going on the national press was having a field day, every day, including Sunday. Full-page headlines were the order of the day. 'We refuse to play; Down players threat' was the offering of *The Irish Press* on 15 March. On the same date the *Evening Herald* bettered it with, 'Down are up in arms—players take on officials.' These were largely reactions from some of the players to my appointment as manager. 'We are livid with this latest development by the County Board... in fact the situation is worse now,' was part of a lengthy quote from the *Irish Independent*.

A piece by Denis O'Hara went on, 'It would appear that the players have dug their heels even deeper and will not play under Barney Carr—and there is a hint no other players in the county are prepared to fill the county jerseys if required.'

The reality was that 24 players were prepared to fill the county jerseys. I now realised the players had no real animus against me, and I appreciated the visit of Peter Rooney to assure me that this was the case. Peter, a member of my own club, was the first Point man to win an All-Ireland senior medal with the 1968 team.

Having advised the county secretary that we had a panel, I awaited the outcome of the County Board meeting on the Thursday night. It was Friday before I learned that there was to be another meeting between all the parties involved, in Newcastle on the following Tuesday, at which the President of the Association, Con Murphy, would be present.

Having been active in GAA politics for many years, I knew this was a change of direction by the County Committee and I guessed instinctively that the chairman had been undermined from within. I immediately contacted TP Murphy, the county secretary, and advised that I was withdrawing from the morass, though I attended the meeting as a representative of my club. Very few clubs were represented, I might add, for there was a general abhorrence with what most thought was a squalid impasse.

My withdrawal had left the situation less complicated and in a week or two the *status quo* was reinstated. The real victim of the whole episode was the county chairman, Seán Fearon, who resigned from the position a month or two later when the dust settled. A number of other officials resigned with him, but were induced to return, and I would hazard a guess that Fearon, being the man he is, would have persuaded them to change their minds.

The Association in Down suffered quite a bit from that period of internecine strife and for many life-long enthusiasts the GAA became less of a priority. Player power and the idealism which made the Association what it is are not happy bedfellows.

Tragically, Francie Doherty, about whom I have written earlier in this chapter, died on 12 April 2008 after being attacked in his home in Ballykinlar a few weeks previously.

26—The Field of Education

While Gaelic sport and the GAA played a very central role in my life throughout the 60s, by far the biggest change was brought about through my departure in 1966 from the Ulster Transport Authority to the position of Education Welfare Officer (formerly designated School Attendance Officer) with the Down County Education Committee.

Jimmy Caulfield, who was the local Education Welfare Officer, was one of the small group who comprised the Nationalist Party in the town. He and I were on our way to a meeting in Belfast to get a really focussed and reorganised Nationalist Party off the ground. In the course of the journey he asked me if I had heard he was retiring. When I indicated that I had, he went on to ask if I would be interested in the post. To that I replied, 'Jimmy, the source that told me you were retiring, also told me that Fr Esler has a man for it,' and I named the man. Jimmy expressed some surprise at this.

He surprised me even more when he said, 'If you are interested in the job, Fr Esler will take my advice.' I had always known Fr Esler to be a man who would have found it difficult taking advice from anyone, including the Bishop, but by the firm way Jimmy spoke, I sensed he had some influence with the reverend.

I would initially be taking a cut in income for a year or two but the long-term prospects were attractive. There was the added attraction of a car allowance and a five-day working week, so by the time we arrived in Belfast we agreed I should be a possible candidate. In due course, Jimmy had a word with Canon Esler and advised me to apply when the post was advertised. At that time, education was administered on a county structure, with each county and the city of Belfast having their own education committees. The make-up of the committees would have been largely drawn from representatives of the county and urban district councils, representatives of the various churches and selected nominees.

I was called for interview, with fourteen others, to the panel which consisted of the entire committee. I felt I had created a reasonable impression, and on Fr Esler's proposal I was eventually appointed to succeed Jimmy Caulfield, who had been over 40 years in the post.

Despite the seemingly compelling advantages of education, some children and more disastrously even some parents do not see it as a priority. Even in this enlightened age, non-attendance at school is a problem of immense proportion. In Britain parents are being sent to jail for the failure of their children to attend school.

The public attitude to missing school was reflected in the make-up of my colleagues in the Education Welfare Service. Six were former members of the RUC who had taken early retirement, and two were former soldiers. We had a head constable, two sergeants, and three former constables. I never became aware of the rankings of the former military personnel. Only one of the education welfare officers was a woman. It should be said that they all were excellent colleagues and a few of them became close friends. One of these latter was a Sergeant who had served under the head constable; he summed up his former superior to me one day in a single sentence, 'He knows nothing about anything other than the law and the Bible,' which, when you come to think of it, is a fair bit of knowledge. My Sergeant friend answered to the name 'Clem,' for R.H. Clements, and he was the most unconscious humorist I have ever met. It was 'the way he told them' which made him such a likable fellow.

Few readers may have heard of 'Buck Alick's lion,' not to speak of Buck Alick. In my youth the bold Buck was a well-known wrestler in Belfast who kept a lion in his backyard; from time to time there were news items which made Buck and his lion a very well known couple. Clem told the story of how on one late and fearsome wet night he was on a foot patrol in Belfast with a young raw recruit just out of the depot. To Clem's mind this was the young constable's first time in Belfast. They were sheltering from a downpour in the doorway of a shop when a fellow went down the far side of the street pushing a ladies bicycle; balanced on the frame was a bag of some proportions. The fellow turned round the corner and Clem said to his junior colleague, 'Go after that fellow and see what he has in that bag,' which the constable did, returning in a few minutes out of breath.

'Well, what had he?' asked Clem.

'It was only a bag of dead cats for Buck Alick's lion,' replied the innocent abroad, at which answer Clem pulled his man by the arm and the pair of them set off in hot pursuit. They eventually caught up with the fellow with the bicycle and the bag of dead cats, which turned out to be stolen cigarettes.

Clem died after a very short illness and was buried in Knockbreda Cemetery on the outskirts of Belfast. May 1974 brought the Ulster Workers' Council strike and on the day Clem was being buried, Brian Faulkner (former Northern Ireland Prime Minister and at this time Chief Executive of a short-lived power-sharing executive), was struggling with his conscience over at Stormont. There was a sizable crowd of mourners in the cemetery, for Clem was in both the Orange and Masonic Institutions. In the middle of the ceremony I sensed a buzz going through the mourners who were spread in a fairly large rectangle around Clem's burial plot. Heads turned to hear and then to pass on what they heard. The man next to me got the historic message, passed it to me and I in turn passed it to the man on my left. 'Faulkner has caved in.'

The Education Welfare Service was an improvement on what might be called the legalistic enforcement of school attendance. However, the continuing advances in social legislation relating to uniform grants, free school meals, transport and special education all made the range of its involvement even wider. For all that, the core remained attendance at school and I approached the task with the sound advice of Jimmy Caulfield in the back of my head, 'Use the Court as little as possible.'

I was only a few months in the post and was attending our monthly meeting at Windsor Avenue, Belfast. We were having a cup of tea and after it the education officer, who was in charge of our service, asked me how I was settling into the job. I told him that I was quite satisfied with the way things were going though I had a family of three boys whose father had been prosecuted on a number of occasions in the previous few years. I added that I was getting a very poor response from them since I started.

'When you have time, Mr Carr,' he responded, 'do me a report on the family.' The parents were never very forthcoming and on occasions were hostile when I visited. It would always be a doorstep conversation when I went to the home. The boys themselves were all likable lads and it was obvious that all they needed was a firm line from the parents. It was routine for me to visit their school every week and on one visit only one of the brothers was present. When he came into the room where I interviewed the boys, I was most anxious to put him at his ease and we were having a quite relaxed conversation. In the course of our chat he made some reference to his sister. This rang an alarm bell for me, as I was not aware of the existence of a girl in the family, nor had I come across her name in any of the schools I visited. I thought this strange.

'Has your sister left school?' I asked in a very matter of fact tone and I felt he was just the slightest bit flustered when he answered, 'Oh, no, she's still at school.'

I was not fully convinced, so I continued, 'What school does she attend?' and I realised he was in trouble.

'She goes to the nuns,' he volunteered and when I went over the names of the various convent schools in the area he just was not sure about any of them. The lad left with an air of relief and I sat for a few minutes with an air of concern.

Within a week I was round every girls' school in the area but nowhere was there a record of the girl I sought. There were plenty of the same family name, all registered and happy in school. My wife had been a health visitor and I was aware that health visitors were required to see a child regularly for a considerable time after birth, so I had her advice on birth records and how they might be accessed.

It did not surprise me to find the name of the girl I sought, but it shocked me to find the date of her birth. She was ten years old and all the indications were that she had never been to school. Before I commenced my report I sought the advice of my predecessor; he was even more shocked, for he had been at the home on many occasions over the years.

My report very quickly reached Windsor Avenue and almost on receipt of it I was summoned to attend, a day later, for an in-depth discussion. My predecessor could not have been blamed in any way for the situation for the records indicated that he had visited the home regularly and had taken court proceedings in relation to the boys on a number of occasions. How the girl could have escaped notice for so much of her ten years remained a mystery, but it was certainly obvious that the parents carried out a long-time deception which was almost criminal.

Because the girl would be the age for secondary education in a little over a year, it was proposed to the parents that she should attend a special school, a residential establishment, from which she would return home at weekends. Of course, the parents wouldn't agree to this under any circumstances and the education committee had to resort to court action. In the ordinary run of cases, the welfare officer presented cases in court, but in the more serious instances, where a fit person order or a training school order was sought, the committee's solicitor made the application. As this was my first appearance in court, I was more than relieved.

The case was heard before a Mr J. R. Wilson, Resident Magistrate (RM), whom I was to discover did not relish dealing with juveniles. We had our specialist education psychologist in support but even with that he was reluctant to make the order and when he finally did, he addressed the parents advising them that they could appeal his decision to the County Court. They did as advised.

The appeal was heard before a Judge Brown who, in rejecting it, delivered the most comprehensive and compassionate insight into parenting, education and officialdom I have ever heard. I believe it served me well in the years to follow.

The girl was duly delivered by the police to the school where the normal school environment reigned for residential and day pupils. Within a few days the mother travelled the 50 miles to it by public transport and took the girl home. It was the police who had the task of transporting her back and forward after that. With less than a year's formal education she moved to a local secondary school. She did not have a distinguished attendance record there, either, and left to face the world at the earliest opportunity.

The mother of this child was not an unintelligent woman, nor was the child an unintelligent girl. She probably has grandchildren attending school at present. I trust they are all good attenders.

Not all school cases ended in tears, indeed some produced 'laughter in court'. In my time in Newry, a sizable 'traveller community' built up in the town. Several families had been housed by the Housing Trust but the vast majority were catered for on a site known as the Middle Bank, which later became St Christopher Park. It lay between the Clanrye River and the canal and had been upgraded by the local council. Most of the girls who attended school went to St Joseph's Convent Primary School. The much smaller number of boys who attended—at least regularly—would have gone to the nearby Abbey Primary School where the Christian Brothers were based. The nuns put quite an effort into encouraging the girls to attend. They transported them in their own cars, provided and kept their uniforms in school and ensured personal cleanliness and hygiene. In class, one could never have picked out the traveller children.

It has to be said there were some excellent families but for some others school attendance was very low on their list of priorities. There was a small committee formed to look after the general welfare of all the traveller children and there were representatives from that community on it. Apparently, it was a traveller voice which came up with the suggestion that it might help to improve school attendance if court proceedings were taken against some of the poorly attending families. When the school principal put the suggestion to me I did not give it any real credence, and expressed the view that no purpose would be served by court action.

However, the committee persisted in its view and much against my better judgement I set the legal machinery in motion. The two 'guinea pig' families with whom I was on reasonably good terms received their summons in due course; I visited them a couple of times to make it clear that it was the fathers, whose names were on the summons, who needed to be in court, but to no avail. It was going to be the mothers or nobody, so I arranged that I would call down for them and transport them to the Courthouse.

At that time, the Juvenile Court was held in an upstairs room at the Courthouse, accessed by a narrow staircase and landing which served as waiting space for those who had an involvement. Normally, the education cases were taken first but when I arrived with my two well-proportioned women, one wearing the traditional shawl, I was advised that another case would be heard first. There was no room for my clients on the stairs or landing so I sorted out a couple of chairs and sat them in the court entrance hall, advising them to sit there until their cases were called.

The Juvenile Court is composed of a resident magistrate and two lay members. Decisions are made by majority after the lay members have been advised on points of law by the RM. On this occasion the presiding magistrate was Mr Aidan Cullen who, unlike Mr J.R. Wilson, was very much at home in the Juvenile Court. In private practice he would have done much work with the social service agencies. He was meticulous with every single case that came before him. For him, school attendance was a serious matter.

When we eventually got to the education cases, I explained to the court the fathers in each case would not be present but their wives were downstairs. It was agreed to hear the cases and the call procedure was carried out by a policeman who sat at the back of the room. He opened the door calling to the landing and stairs, 'Call Martin whatever.'

I realised at once that my clients sitting in the entrance hall might not hear the call, so I excused myself and moved quickly to the door, pushing my way downstairs through a larger than usual crowd. When I got to the entrance hall where I had seated my two ladies there were two empty chairs. I moved to the door expecting the worst but found them sitting on the entrance step each enjoying a cigarette.

'Quickly, your case has been called,' I said with a sense of urgency which they did not share. By the time they put their cigarettes out, got themselves gathered and pushed their way up the crowded stairs, a full five minutes had elapsed. As I passed the policeman on the door he grinned and said, 'I thought you were away to the Middle Bank.'

I thought Mr Cullen might be a bit touchy with the delay but not a bit of it. If the Queen Mother and her daughter had entered the room they would not have been more graciously received. When the ladies were seated and settled, and even before the clerk read the charges, the RM addressed them, 'Why are your husbands not here? It is they who have been summoned to attend the Court.'

'Sir, I haven't seen Martin in a week. He went to a funeral in Ballinasloe and God knows when I'll see him.' Now I had seen Martin two days before but I couldn't bring myself to interrupt. Neither husband's whereabouts were questioned after that.

The charges were read and I indicated the various visits I made to the family and probably gave an idea of the overall position of travellers and school attendance.

'What have you got to say about your children's school attendance? It is shocking,' Mr Cullen observed to the first defendant.

There was an interval while she gathered her thoughts and he spoke to her again.

'Would you like legal aid?' he asked.

She looked over at me with a questioning glance and then, turning to her companion, asked, 'Bridget, did you ever taste eagleade?' The Court erupted.

When things settled and Mr Cullen dried his eyes, he and I eventually settled for an adjournment.

Brother McQuillan was principal of The Abbey Primary, a school with an enrolment of 900 pupils at the time, and he kept his finger very sensitively on the attendance pulse. I hardly needed to check the registers for he invariably had a mental list of names who needed to be seen or visited.

I once called with him on some matter when he said to me, 'Your man is not in school today. He'll be in the mart as usual.'

'Your man,' to whom he referred, was a pupil in the 11 plus class. He rarely attended on a Wednesday as that was his day for Camlough mart. Brother McQuillan had drawn my attention to him a couple of weeks previously and although I had paid a visit to the home it did not seem to have had any effect.

'What does he do at the mart?' I asked and the Brother said he did nothing that he knew of. He lived in one of the local estates and had no connection with animals whatsoever. The Brother added that he was capable of getting the 11 plus exam if he worked for it. It was not normal practice to 'hunt down truants' but I decided I would take a run up to Camlough mart and see if I could lay my eyes on him from the description I had from Brother McQuillan.

It had been a damp drizzling morning and I arrived at the mart close to 1 P.M. It was deserted, neither man nor beast about the place. I made a slow survey of the village, drew a blank and headed back to Newry. A hundred yards down the road I saw a lad walking and I thought to myself, 'this could be my man.' I pulled up about ten yards ahead of him and as he drew abreast I asked, 'Are you for the town?' He gladly accepted my offer of a lift and got in beside me.

When we got under way, I asked, 'Are you a Camlough man?'

'No, I live in Newry,' was the answer.

When I asked him, after an interval, what part of Newry he lived in, he declared, 'Barcroft Park,' not the address of the man I'm looking for.

Then an innocent, 'What school do you go to?' brought the response, 'The Meadow'. Again, not the school of the man I'm looking for.

'Tell me, who is the principal over there now?' I queried and got the right answer on the top of his tongue, 'Vincey Cranny.'

'You didn't go to school today,' I continued after an interval.

'No, I was out seeing my grandfather in Camlough. He's sick.'

'What's your grandfather's name, I probably know him?' He was Stephen Haughey and I didn't know him.

'Are you a Haughey, too?' He was and that wasn't the name of the man I am looking for.

By this time, we were at the foot of the Camlough Road and as we approached the roundabout I went left and said, 'I have to go over to see Vincent Cranney and then I'll run you up to Barcroft Park,' at which news he didn't bat an eyelid.

It was coming near the end of the lunch break when I drove slowly into the lively playground in front of the school. A few boys were already at the car when I pulled the window down and asked one of them to go in and ask if Mr Cranney would come out to me. Without much delay Mr Cranney emerged and I motioned to the passenger door. When he opened it I asked, 'Do you know this boy? He tells me he attends this school.'

Vincent asked him his name and he repeated the name he had given me. The principal looked at me saying he had a family of that name in the school, but he could not place the boy, adding, 'Come in, I'll look up the register.'

Off we went through an avenue of bemused schoolboys, up the corridor to the principal's office where the master register was hauled down for inspection. He came to the family name as claimed by the boy. 'You are not the College Gardens Haughey. We have two of them here. We have no Barcroft Park Haugheys.'

Again, the principal spoke to the boy, 'And you say you attend this school?'

'Yes, sir,' the boy replied.

'When were you here last?' asked the principal.

'Yesterday, sir,' came the answer.

'Who is your teacher?' asked the principal.

'Paddy Ahearne, sir,' from the boy.

'Right,' said Vincent, showing signs of exasperation, 'take me to his room.'

Again, the boy, without blinking an eyelid, left the room, followed by Vincent and myself, went down the corridor we had earlier come up, and stopped at a closed door. By this time, all the children were back in class. 'That's it,' he said.

The principal knocked at the door and opened it, revealing a teacher who was not Paddy Ahearne. 'Is that Mr Ahearne?' he asked.

'No, sir,' from the boy.

'Were you in this school yesterday?' in a menacing tone of voice which the boy picked up.

'No, sir,' he responded.

'What school do you go to?' the next question and in the same tone.

'The Brothers, sir,' came the reply.

'What is your name, boy?' was the final demand from the principal.

The boy gave the name of the lad I suspected he was from the outset. With a rueful smile, Vincent said to me as I took leave of him, 'I'm glad he's Brother McQuillan's problem and not mine.'

Back into the car and over to Brother McQuillan who was surprised and delighted to see the wanderer return. The boy did not get the 11 plus, but it would not surprise me if he owns his own mart in some part of the country.

I have no doubt the Education Welfare Service still performs its essential role in a very different environment to that in which I operated all those years ago. I understand a pupil may not be interviewed now without the parents' consent.

The great advance which had begun even before I retired was the integration of special care education facilities into mainstream education. It is a far cry from the Church Hall at William Street in Newry to the new Rathore School which has opened at Carnagat above Newry.

I cannot leave the field of education without mentioning a remarkable book which came into my possession years before I had ever contemplated this memoir. Michael (Mickey) Kelly, who was living in retirement in Warrenpoint after spending many years in Detroit, USA, called to me one evening. He had a white plastic bag in his hand and I thought he had been doing a bit of shopping, but when we had settled in our front room he took a large brown envelope from it and handed it to me saying, 'I think you are the right man to take care of that.' He went on to explain that his grandfather, John Kelly, had been School Attendance Officer a few generations before and this was his only surviving record book.

Opening the envelope I found an ordinary stiff-backed black exercise book containing names, addresses and dates of birth, nearly all of which were in copperplate handwriting, but I did not examine the book in detail until some years later. I never thought of writing about it until now. A couple of pages are held together with sellotape and the first page is missing, but it is in remarkable condition. The first section contains the entire school population of the town listed in streets, with dates of birth and parents' names and address. The benchmark is July 1894 and the age is given in two columns (years-months). George Robert Toombs of Church Street was born on 8 June, 1894. He is included at one month. My mother's elder sister, Ellen Tumilty, was born on 22 June, 1891. She is listed as 3–1. An insertion at the end of the line records, 'died Feb.17th 1895.' She never made it to school. There were some others who did not make it to school either.

The second section of the book is dated 3 August 1896 and deals with the attendance records of children at each of the three schools in the town, Dromore Road National School, Peter Street Male National School and the Convent National School. These are all tabulated, with the final two columns listing explanation of absence and observations. The 'explanations' have not changed much over the years; there are chaps who were 'sent to school' but failed to arrive, as in my own time. I think the Carrs of the time were good attenders for they lived in Thomas Street, almost opposite the school which became 'the old Tech,' and is now a small block of apartments. There were three Carrs listed, my father Hugh, John and George who was unlikely to have finished school, for he died when he was eleven. I cannot remember either of my parents ever speaking about their siblings who died, though we did have a photograph of George.

The final section of the book records the names of the pupils at Dromore Road and Peter Street schools by class and is dated August 1894. There are two pages dated 3 August 1900 which give details of home visits, but the names they relate to are missing.

It is with some regret that I recall a day in my life in the last ten or fifteen years when I was leaving St Peter's Church and was approached by a chap in his late twenties or early thirties. He asked, in an identifiable American accent, if I was a native of Warrenpoint. When I indicated that I was, he introduced himself by name, explaining that his paternal grandfather was of German nationality.

'My maternal grandfather was Tommy Burns who was born in Charlotte Street and worked as a butcher in Ward's shop before emigrating to America.'

Now, I could cast my mind back to the 1920s and while I had clear recall of two Burns families in Newry Street I could not place a Burns family in Charlotte Street. I drove him in my car to the homes of Jim O'Neill and Sheila McAnulty, both of whom were senior to me, but neither was at home. He was pushed for time and had to get back to Dublin but I took his name and address in my diary and assured him if I got any information about his grandfather Burns I would be in touch with him. Neither Jim nor Sheila had any recall of a Charlotte Street Burns. It was many months later before I decided to write to my American acquaintance but could I find my diary?

It may well be that some time in the future an American with Irish and German grandfathers will pick up this book and learn that a Thomas Burns was born on 4 February 1890 in Charlotte Street. He had two younger sisters, Elizabeth and Catherine, and his father was John Burns.

Finally, a word on John Kelly himself, whom I thought was a Warrenpoint native until his granddaughter, Maureen Yorke and his great grand-daughter, Deirdre McManus, enlightened me about this remarkable man. He was a Monaghan man serving as a Sergeant in the Liverpool Police Force when he met a Warrenpoint girl, Rose Magill. They married there and their first born, Bernard (the town knew him as Barney), was born. One of the girls in the family was Rose, who was to be the mother of Bishop John Crawford, O.P. It may well be that John Kelly took early retirement from the police force to take up the post of attendance officer, as so many policemen did in my own time. He certainly left us a legacy of Warrenpoint family names which I hope to make available to a wider readership.

27—The Club

While successful county teams tend to be the shop window of GAA activities—more so today than ever before—it would be a massive mistake to overlook the basic club roots which give sustenance and meaning to it all. I have referred to the John Martins earlier in this memoir, but it is only now that they are being given their deserved status as the men who sowed the GAA seed in Warrenpoint. That was in January, 1888, less than four years after the Association was formed in Thurles. The first chairman was Robert McLoughlin, the secretary Richard Edgar and the treasurer, John Keenan. The only descendants of that trio around today are those of Richard Edgar, one of whom, Seamus Murphy, nationally known as 'Homer,' has recently been chairman for a couple of terms. His cousins, the McGuigans, are also grandchildren of Dick Edgar. Among the committee elected back at the beginning were Thomas Caulfield, William Campbell, (great-grandfather of John on the Burren Road), Ambrose Bettridge and John Carr, my grandfather. The first three lived into my boyhood. My grandfather died the year I was born.

As well as being a member of the committee, Ambie Bettridge was also team captain. At the inaugural meeting of the club he proposed, and John McAteer seconded, that the club be called 'Red Hand'. John Carr proposed, and Thomas Caulfield seconded, that the club be named 'John Martins' which was carried by a large majority.

That year they competed in the Parnell Indemnity Fund Tournament. In 1889 they competed in the first GAA tournament organised in Down 'for a set of silver crosses.' They played and beat Edenmore (Mayobridge) in the final, after which they were led in triumph through Mayobridge by the Warrenpoint flute band. I don't know if Ambie Bettridge lost his place, but the winning team comprised of J. O'Neill (Capt.), T. O'Neill, J. Carr; L. Carr (no relation), A. Millar, C. Millar, O'Brien, Caulfield, E. Groome (my grand-uncle), Murphy, E. Gallagher, A. Gallagher, J. Hillen, M. Hillen, J. McAteer, McKevitt, McCumiskey, Doyle, Burns, McGuigan and McGivern.

From that successful beginning one would have thought it would have been all upwards, but the club seems to have had a chequered history, going through some periods of inactivity. Many years ago someone gave me an old copy of a *Frontier Sentinel*. It was folded into a tiny handful and I never really had time to dismantle it. Recently I took on that task, to discover that the paper had the date 11 April 1908. In one of the pieces on the front page I read the report of a game between Newry Faughs and John Martins (Warrenpoint). The names of both teams were listed (seventeen-a-side) and, as this memoir might be helpful to a history of the GAA in Warrenpoint, I'll take the responsibility of naming the John Martins, beginning with my uncle J. Tumilty in goal, J. Burns, D. Murray, C. Hourican, M. Hourican, M. Ruddy, H. Carr (my father) J. Carr (my uncle), E. Delahunt, Peter Sheehy, N. Screenan, T. Mullan, D. O'Neill, H. Smyth, H. Watters, J. Hoey, E. Murray. Happily most of the family names are still surviving and long may they continue to do so.

The John Martins were alive and well in the early twenties when the famed Shanaghan Cup competition was the prize to be won. A famous game with Clonduff has been part of the local folklore ever since. Possibly it was the departure of one man from the town which led to the demise of the club, for Patrick McGivern appears to have been a key figure on the local GAA scene of the time. He was chairman of the Down Board in 1925 and 1926 before moving to Athlone, where he lived for the remainder of his life. Paddy, as he was called, was the uncle of Emmett McGivern and the McAnultys. There are no records of the John Martins engaged in any activity after 1926 and that explains why I saw my first Gaelic football match in Burren four years later.

If the GAA ceased to exist in Warrenpoint after 1926 there certainly was a well-organised group which had its finger on the national pulse. This was a body called the Irish Dancing Class Committee which organised not only the dancing class and regular *céilí* but also a dramatic society. My first view of Knocknagow, with Leo Tinnelly as Matt the thresher, is firmly imprinted; it probably contributed to my early education. I well remember, too, sneaking into the town hall with some companions to watch the dancing class in action, with the music being supplied solely by Joe Curran from Rostrevor on his melodeon. It was the order of things that local groups like the football club, the camogie club, the Irish National Foresters or even the parish would write in and ask the dancing committee to run a *céilí* for them. Not only was it a very well-organised committee but a lot of its records have survived, much more indeed than those of the GAA clubs, hurling and football, which came into being in the early thirties. A group described as the Young Men's Hurley Club wrote to the Irish Dancing Class Committee asking for assistance in the purchase of hurley sticks. The Committee agreed to purchase eighteen sticks and drew up an agreement in copper plate handwriting with the Young Men's Hurley Club which read:

> *An Agreement made and entered into between the Irish Dancing Class Committee (herein after called "the class") of the first part and the Young Men's Hurley Club (herein after called "the Club") of the second part:-.*
>
> *That the eighteen hurley sticks purchased by the Class and each stamped with the letters W.H.C. be handed over to the club.*
>
> *The said sticks are to be the property of the Club and are to be left in charge of some trustworthy person (herein after called the custodian) the said custodian to be selected by the club.*
>
> *In the event of the club being dissolved or should it later cease to function, then the said eighteen sticks are to be handed back to the Class.*
>
> *Should any sticks become broken during play or practice the part of stick bearing the stamp W.H.C. shall be retained by the custodian and will count in the event of the sticks being returned to the Class.*
>
> *The said Custodian will be held responsible to the Club and likewise the Club to the Class.*
>
> *Should the sticks be returned to the Class then the Class shall be at liberty to put them to any use they may think proper without any further*

question.

In witness to this agreement we the undersigned put our hand this 14th day of April 1932.

Signed on behalf of the Young Men's Hurley Club

Brian Gribben
Dermot O'Brien
Brian Ua hAnnaidh
Peter Grant, Jun
Peadar Ó hÍr

Signed on behalf of the Irish Dancing Class Committee
Jas. F. Caulfield President
H O'Prey
Ml. Fay

The agreement was witnessed by James Edgar, Secretary of the Irish Dancing class.

There can be no doubt that this agreement would have been upheld by any Court in the land such was the legal expertise which inspired its drafting. I remember well the dapper Jimmy Edgar, who was the son of Dick Edgar, the first secretary of the John Martins Club. I have no doubt that he and the president, Jimmy Caulfield, who was the School Attendance Officer at the time, would have been the legal advisers. Mick Fay was later to be prominent in the trade union movement, representing the Labour Party on the local council for many years, while Harry O'Prey, a former member of the Old IRA, was always supportive of things national. The players were equally well known to me with Brian Gribben, brother of Maureen (Fitzpatrick), being a neighbour on Summerhill.

I do not have a memory of Dermot O'Brien being involved in sport but he, like his sister Maggie, was much into the dramatic societies all their lives. Brian Ua hAnnaidh (Barney Hanna) was into both hurling and football in those early thirties. I do not have a sporting memory of either Peter Grant or Peadar Ó hÍr (Peter O'Hare) but the first named was the son of Peter of taxi fame, who had his business and shop in Church Street. Peter O'Hare was a younger brother of Felix, the building contractor, and lived below me in East Street. He signed the agreement on the 14 April 1932 and he died in September of the same year at the age of 21, a victim of cancer. My memory of him is of his involvement in a serious motor cycle accident some time before that.

In due course, the Irish Dancing Class Committee came to be the *Céilí* Committee which in turn became the *Scór* Committee and an integral part of the club. Recently I was shown a minute book of the *Céilí* Committee of the forties and a proposal that Liam O'Hare and Barney Carr be suspended from the committee for their failure to attend meetings. It was passed unanimously. It also revealed that McCusker's *Céilí* Band of nine brothers was paid fourteen pounds for providing the music at one of the regular *céilí*.

The early story of St Peter's Club has already been recounted and I resume it in the late fifties when I was appointed treasurer, in succession to my younger brother, Aidan. In my first year I handled the enormous sum of £447. Looking back, it is amazing what one could do with that amount of money in those days. For much of Fr Alex McMullan's lengthy tenure as curate in Warrenpoint, committee meetings were held in his sitting room in the parochial house. During Joe McGuigan's spell as secretary, meetings were held in the McGuigan kitchen or sitting room, whichever was available. While we enjoyed the hospitality of the parochial house, a few of us were giving thought to getting some sort of a meeting room of our own. We got a spur on when Fr Alex was moved to Ballinahinch as parish priest; while we elected his successor, Fr John McAuley, as chairman, we did not relish the idea of our Tuesday night sitting room meetings being part of his inheritance.

I had my eye on a near derelict property in Mary Street which belonged to Tom Caulfield, who had a tailoring business in Church Street and was, along with me, one of the few members of the Nationalist Party. I raised the matter at the committee meeting and was authorised to approach Tom. I did this in a few days time. I was always 'young Carr' or 'young fellow' to him, so when I entered the shop it was, 'Well, young fellow, what can I do for you?' and he hoping that it was a suit I was after.

'Tom, you have an old derelict house round there in Mary Street and at the club meeting the other night we were wondering if you would consider selling it?'

He expressed some surprise initially but when I expanded on the club's thinking he warmed to the concept.

'I don't think you could make much of that place,' he said, 'but take a look at it anyway, Josie has the key. Tell her I said to give it to you,' were his encouraging words.

Now Josie Mackin was his niece who lived next door to the property and when Liam O'Hare, Ted Bradley and I called with her a few evenings later she seemed very surprised to see us. I explained our mission and advised that her Uncle Tom had intimated that she would provide us with the key, but I sensed she wasn't very pleased. Initially I thought that the notion of having the club as neighbours just wasn't what she would have desired. She did not comment, but went in and returned with the key.

The house was in as poor shape inside as it was out and we realised it would really take a bit of work to put it in order.

About a week later, and even before we had discussed the visit at the committee, I was passing Tom's shop and I heard the voice, 'Young Carr, come here a minute.' It was Tom. 'What house did you look at the other night in Mary Street?' he asked.

'The one beside Josie. Sure, you told me to get the key from her,' I said.

'I know I told you to get the key off her but that wasn't the house I thought you wanted to look at. Holy God, man, that's Josie's house you looked at. I gave it to her a few years ago. She was round here the other day in a bad state. She thought

I was selling it to you,' he concluded.

When I realised the mistake we had made, I was simply mortified at the anguish we must have caused poor Josie that evening. I thought I'd call round with her at once to apologise but I turned immediately to Tom, 'What house did you think we were going to look at?' I asked.

'I thought you were going to look at Brady's Court. Josie has the keys of it, also,' he replied.

The moment Tom mentioned that property, the implications struck me at once. Even though the frontage was worse looking than the house next to Josie, and an eyesore in the street, the site as a whole was quite spacious and was way beyond anything we could have hoped for. Tom did not demur when I said we'd take a look at it and if we thought we could do anything with it we'd be back to him.

So it was back to Josie with our humblest apologies for the unease we had caused her after our previous visit, and it was with her blessing that we proceeded down the street to Brady's Court. As we went through those derelict rooms on either side of Wheelbarrow Lane memories of Granny Ruddy, Christy Charles and Mrs Hornsby came to mind. Out the back were the brick remains of the little row of houses formerly occupied by Hughie McKevitt, Lizzie Rainey and other wonderful people. One could have knocked them over with a good push.

It didn't take us long to make up the collective mind and I was deputed to see Tom Caulfield at his earliest convenience.

He was most welcoming with his greeting.

'Well, young fellow, can you do anything with it?' I indicated we were more than pleased with the site and even though we had not the proverbial shilling we would be keen to take it on. Then I asked the key question, 'What are you looking for it?'

'You know, young fellow, my father was a founding member of the John Martins and my brother Jim was secretary before he went to America, so I would want to support the club on their account.' Jim had been in the War of Independence and went to America after the Treaty. He came home on holiday often and I got to know him quite well.

He paused, and then said, 'Give me 50 pounds and you look after the legal costs.' It was a very informal sale and when I called with him a few weeks later to give him the cheque, he said, 'Young fellow, I'm keeping this cheque but if you ever need 50 pounds come back for it.' In truth we never needed to go back and he never cashed the cheque. I recount the tale of the buying of Brady's Court to ensure that Tom Caulfield is remembered in St Peter's Club.

The new clubrooms were built by voluntary labour spearheaded by Tommy Duffy of the Monmouthshires. There were two rooms, one up and one down, though at this time the one down was not operational until Frank Hanna tiled it some months later. Even so we thought we'd have 'a bit of a night' upstairs for all those who helped in the work. We thought if we had a few singers, a few musicians and a wee supper, it would be a good start.

Musicians were not as plentiful in those days as they are now and when we were discussing the make-up of the night at committee I suggested that it might be nice to ask Joe Curran from Rostrevor to play the accordion. As Joe had played for the Irish Dancing class I thought his presence would be a suitable historic link with that earlier era.

Joe was a Warrenpoint man and lived in Thomas Street where the Carr home was. He went into exile in Rostrevor when he married a girl from that village, but he was always quick to remind Point people that he was a Point man, adding, 'The Rostrevor ones would never let you forget it.' I was very friendly with him and met him frequently when I operated out of Rostrevor on the buses. He had a flourishing fruit and vegetable business and delivered regularly to the Great Northern Hotel where the buses parked. If he spied you he would invariably be over for a chat. At this time, he was in his 80s and before I approached him to come down to play at the opening of our clubrooms I talked it over with some of his family who were pleased that we had remembered him.

If I had handed him a thousand pounds, he would not have been more pleased than with my invitation. On the night, I called out for him myself. He was well received and his contribution to the evening was much appreciated. With over a hundred people filling the upstairs room there was no space for dancing and little enough for the hand-round supper. I had been acting as *fear a tí* but I got a chance to have a word with him during the supper and he was profuse in his thanks at being invited to The Point for the occasion.

'This is the best night I have had for years,' he declared. 'You know I'd be out at things like this every week only our ones keep me down. They keep telling me I'm too old to do this and that. I feel as good a man now as I did 30 years ago.'

At the time, I was inclined to smile a bit at Joe but now that I am of his vintage I am experiencing just how he felt. 'Our ones' are getting a bit like 'Joe's ones'. If I propose to go to Belfast or Dublin or even closer to home I'm met with a barrage of counter proposals: 'Leave it to Saturday and I'll drive you.' John is the only member of my family who has implicit confidence in my ability to look after myself.

Earlier I noted that a young fellow called Jim Curran had succeeded Michael Murphy on the Rostrevor billiards team. That young fellow was a son of the aforementioned Joe Curran and within striking distance of making another century break, when in May 2011 he died in his ninety-ninth year.

Having opened our modest 'upstairs-downstairs' clubrooms, we made remarkable progress and within a few years we embarked on a sizeable extension, carried out by Richard McGuigan's firm. Even that was not sufficient to cater for the expanding activities; a redundant mobile classroom was purchased from St Colman's College and served as a boys' club for many years under the direction of Emmett McGivern and his two right-hand men, Billy Howlett and Jack McManus. For the first time since the Foy cinema closed, Emmett introduced films to the town. He could also take some credit for the establishment of a drama section in the club for he introduced me to John McMahon, a Limerick man, who retired to Warrenpoint after a career in the acting profession.

Emmett had a remarkable knack of getting to know people. He had been telling me about this John McMahon, who had been a member of the *Radio Éireann* repertory company and who had played small parts in some films, including *Ryan's Daughter,* so I suggested we should meet John with a view to forming a drama group. With John as producer, we launched into *The Country Boy, Sive, Anne Frank* and *Our Town* by which time Pat Mooney was the producer. I played two parts in it—the town policeman, Constable Warren, who spoke a few short sentences and the undertaker who had not a word to say. Pat created a wonderful funeral and cemetery scene: he had a section of the club band leading the cortege. Each night we performed, the undertaker shed a genuine tear. In more recent times, Pat has resumed his role of producer in the club with a more youthful band of actors and actresses, while the stage manager of *Our Town,* Pius Tierney of Mullaghbawn, was still treading the boards the last time I was speaking to him.

Having introduced the band, I feel it incumbent on me to explain how a GAA club got involved in the promotion of what might be termed a luxury in any community. The Irish National Foresters' (INF) branch in Warrenpoint had always provided the music for the Warrenpoint community but with the end of the swinging sixties came the decline and demise of the musical combination. Their crowning glory had been their involvement in that historic day in Dublin when they led the Down supporters from Croke Park in triumph.

Two band members, Michael Savage and my cousin Philly Carr, were on the club committee in 1971 when we were discussing a particular promotion which needed the attendance of a band. One of them mentioned the great pity that the INF band instruments were 'going to rot' round in the Foresters club; in no time at all there was a decision to approach the Foresters with a view to buying the instruments. The INF met us more than half-way and the instruments were bought for £600, paid in four instalments of £150. The Foresters had bought the instruments second-hand more than ten years previously from an English police band, so they had seen a fair bit of usage. They had lain in the Foresters club for over three years and some were in very poor shape. To bring them to concert pitch cost much more than the Foresters received for them.

Getting a conductor for the band was the next hurdle and it was felt that Andrew Tohill was the best man to approach. Andy was enthusiastic about the idea of reforming the band but suggested that Auguste Torremans be invited to act as conductor. He was a Belgian national, a true gentleman and organist at Newry Cathedral. This was done. Gus, as we called him, accepted and with Andy as bandmaster, practices commenced in January 1972. The band made its first public appearance at a concert in the Town Hall the following St Patrick's Night when John McMahon took the house down with his rendering of *The Trimmins of the Rosary.*

In the second year of its existence the band competed at the National Band Championships, and substituted for the Artane Boys' Band at Croke Park on the occasion of an All-Ireland football semi-final between Cork and Tyrone. In 1975 it won the Intermediate Bank Championship with Auguste Torremans as conductor. Andrew Tohill was the conductor when the band won again in 1981 and Peter Grant did the honours three years later in 1984. This latter success had a bonus in that the band was invited to play at a prize-winners' concert in the National

Concert Hall.

Even though the competitive element is now confined to the local *feiseanna* the band continues to be a great community asset, and it is a tribute to the new generation of enthusiasts that young people are still being attracted to play in it.

If the provision of our own premises facilitated activities like music and drama for the wider community, it also gave a permanent base to those cultural activities which are part of the GAA's remit, the language and the dancing. Irish classes had been held at various venues over the years. The enthusiasm of men like Jimmy Devlin and Joe Lambe was to be amply rewarded as they inspired both youthful linguists and teachers in the new surroundings. The Céilí Committee came to full flowering in the promotion of dancing and the *Scór* activities which were later to bring great success and honour to the club. The enthusiasm of the club chairman, Liam O'Hare, and his handmaid, Moya McCormack, both of whose lives revolved round their activities in the club, were central to much of that success.

While the clubrooms provided a home for the various activities it also very importantly provided a facility for bringing in finance. Even when it was a single upstairs room the weekly whist drive and the weekly bingo showed that there was money to be made. The whist was organised by Jimmy Morgan and Peter Rice while the bingo was organised on a rota basis of the membership. The long-term aim of the committee was the provision of its own playing field. It was obvious that the Moygannon pitch, owned by the Alexian Brothers and with the electricity supply lines running across it, was not suitable. Even in the late sixties there was a dearth of suitable land in the locality and while occasional inquiries were made about 'Tommy Cunningham's big field' we were always advised it would not be for sale.

I wrote of James Connolly of Duke Street, whose potatoes I picked on the Bridle Loanin. He also had land on Small's Road with access from Jenny Black's Hill. James, who had been a founding committee member of the first St Peter's Club in 1931, was always a supporter. He died quite suddenly in 1944 after returning from a match in Newcastle. In due course, the family sold the Duke Street premises and moved to Great George's Street. In the late 60s the club was advised that the land might be bought, so we had a look at it. It comprised of two fields and while the site was restricted, we thought that with a bit of work we could get a pitch out of it. Mrs Connolly was approached and, to our surprise, advised that not only was there a tenanted house attached to the land but also that she would be happy to sell the whole lot to the club. After the committee considered the situation, it was agreed to negotiate a price with Mrs Connolly, who was most accommodating, for she was in her own way a supporter of the club.

Four years later, we still had not got round to developing the ground because we had concentrated on extending the clubrooms. We were advised that Tommy Cunningham's big field could be bought for a substantial sum of money. In Tommy's field you could put up posts and play football, so we opted for Tommy's field. While this was a few years before land prices soared we still made a profit on the sale of the Connolly land and house. I think James Connolly would have been pleased that the club benefitted from his endeavours. It has taken a new generation to make Tommy Cunningham's big field into the top-class pitch it is now.

If sporting honours have eluded the club in recent years there can be no denying the massive effort which is being constantly made in promoting the games. There have been some green shoots of success in 2009 when the hurlers took their first ever Junior Championship and the minor footballers contested the minor final for the first time in years. The Association is about competing and striving for success.

Until very recent times there existed a tangible link with the first John Martins team in the shape of one of the silver crosses won in that first tournament at Edenmore. It belonged to Johnnie O'Neill, who captained the side that day. I knew Johnnie very well in the early part of my life but I never knew of his association with the John Martins until after his death. Before he died, Johnnie passed the medal to his youngest brother, Danny, who passed it to his son, Patsy. Patsy was a formidable footballer and was on our Championship winning side of 1943. He died a comparatively young man but before he did he had passed the medal to his sister, Kathleen. The O'Neill family had always informed the club who held the medal and when Kathleen died we were duly advised that Donal, the youngest of Danny's family, now possessed the medal.

Donal and his wife Mary live in Charlotte Street, and on a Sunday evening in October 2003 they went to Newry to visit Mary's sister. They left their home at 5 o'clock for what was to be a short visit, for they were going to the evening devotions in St Peter's Church at 7 o'clock. When they arrived back in the house after devotions they found their home had been broken into. Whatever money they had in the house was taken as well as Mary's jewellery and a number of personal items. Among these was uncle Johnnie's medal which had been in the family for over one hundred years. Such a sordid end for the last surviving memento of the John Martins.

Rannafast Cup Team 1937-38
Back row left to right: Vincent Crawford(Warrenpoint),Dan McDonald(Newry),MickMurphy (Newry),
Turlough Murray (Newry), Pat Hanna (Newry), Colman McGeogh (Hilltown), James Walls (Hilltown),
Joe Morgan (Newry)
Middle row left to right: Hugh Hollywood (Newry), Sam McClelland (Newry), Gerry Brown (Newry),
Johnny Carr (Warrenpoint), Jarlath Gibbons (Newry), Arthur Bradley (Warrenpoint), Des Murphy
(Newry)
Front Row left to right: Barney Carr (Warrenpoint), Jack Short (Newry)

First Championship team 1943
Back row left to right : Fr Barney Treanor, John Hillen, Gerry Carr, Barney Carr, Paddy O Hare,
John O'Hare, Eddie Cole, Fr Alex McMullan
Front row left to right: Patsy O Neill, John McClorey, Chris O Boyle, Terry McCormack,
Tim Donoghue, Liam O Hare, Jim Colllins
Missing Arthur Bradley, Willie Peers, Hugh Campbell

Private Bill Alvis Stanfield

On the road to Wembly
Pat Finnison, Ben Courtney, Barney Carr

1953 Wedding in Leitrim
Barney and Anne with Aidan Carr and Monica McKIbben
Grand Aunt Mary to the right

Carr Brothers
Aidan, John, Barney, Gerry, Hugh, Paddy, Brendan

Brian McGreevy, Clonduff

1959 Eve of All Ireland Semi Final
Nurse Carr wheels baby Flynn

At a training session
Maurice Hayes, George Tinnelly, Danny Flynn, Barney Carr

The History Makers 1960

Back row left to right : James McCartan, Joe Lennon, Jarleth Carey, Leo Murphy, Dan McCartan, Seán O Neill, Kevin O Neill, Pat Rice

Front row left to right : Eamon McKay, Pat O Hagan, Paddy Doherty, Kevin Mussen, George Lavery, Tony Hadden, Brian Morgan

Anne, Barney and Hugh after All Ireland Final 1960

Morning after first All-Ireland win
Left to right: Frank Cassidy, (formerly Meeting St) Barney Carr, Síle McAnulty, Edna & Eddie McKay

Sam at home in 1960
Anne, Barney with John in arms and Hugh

Brian Morgan tries the baseball in Cleveland.

Old Crocks Mid 60s
Back row left to right : Barney Carr, Aidan Carr, Des Slevin, Arthur Bradley, Emmett McGivern,
Gerry Carr, Barney Treanor, Peter Bracken
Front row left to right : Pete Ryan, John McClorey, Peter Grant, Jimmy Devlin, Jimmy Heaney,
Philly Carr, Liam O Hare

Good Neighbours
Mary McCarthy and Charlie McGreevy

Opening of Club
Back row left to right : Barney Carr, Dickie McGuigan, Ted Bradley, Canon Esler
Front row left to right: Tom Caulfield, Mick Feeney, Liam O Hare, Seamas O Riain, Uachtarán CLCG,
Paddy McFlynn. Paddy O Donoghue

County Convention
Left to right : Barney Carr, Paddy O Donoghue, Jerry Sheehan, Bertie Leckey, TP Murphy,
George Tinnelly, George McKeown

Point Characters
Lily Heatley, Maisie O Neill, Hughie O Neill, Frank Hourican

PART III

28 — A Remarkable Fellow

The most remarkable of my three children is my second son, John, born on 9 March 1959. It had been a difficult pregnancy for Anne and when I got the telephone message of his birth just before going to work, I was pleased and relieved that it was over. Naturally I was delighted, and as soon as I had completed the early part of my duty, I headed for Daisy Hill Hospital to see mother and baby. Mother showed no signs of anything but happiness and I was taken to the nursery where I viewed the new baby with joy and wonder; I was really walking on air as I went back to the ward where my wife lay. More congratulations and delight before I headed for home. The afternoon part of my duty did not commence until 3 P.M., so I was back at the hospital for the normal visiting hour at 2 P.M. As I settled myself by the bedside, Anne said to me, 'Barney, I have some bad news for you. You were so excited and overjoyed this morning I could not bring myself to tell you.' I was incredulous, 'What could be bad news?'

'The baby is a mongoloid,' Anne said quietly. That term was used even by the professionals in those days. She went on to tell me how she recognised the condition even as the nurse delivered the baby into her arms. The nurse herself, at the time, remained to be convinced and when the baby was brought to the ward for me to see he looked as normal as any baby I had ever seen. Anne pointed out a few minute distinguishing features. To me, though, he still looked completely normal.

Like any couple, we were disappointed; I pondered very much on the fate of this little fellow as I finished my work that March afternoon, in a somewhat despondent state of mind. On my arrival home that evening I dropped on my knees before the Lord. 'Lord, I am tempted to ask, why me, but it strikes me to ask, why not me?' I assured Him that this boy would be dearly loved, but I have to confess that I felt I was doing the Lord a favour in accepting 'this cross.'

We named the boy John, and I am sure that no one other than my wife, Anne, could have seen him through those first three years in which a respiratory condition ensured almost regular crises. We had moved to Summerhill when he was a year old and had established something of a rota for being up at night with him. His doctor, Derek Flood, would have called with him on a regular basis almost from his arrival home from hospital, though Anne would never call the doctor out at night. There came a night, though, when her own ministrations were not bringing the desired responses and she realised she had a major crisis on her hands. It was midnight when the doctor was summoned and he arrived from Newry in double quick time. It was not Dr Flood but his partner and cousin, Dr Blaney, who was seeing John for the first time.

Anne quickly put him in the picture and for the next hour or two he went through a series of procedures with John, none of which seemed to be having the desired effect. I had gone into the room and I could read the concern on his countenance as he straightened up after another sounding with the stethoscope.

He turned to me and asked, 'Do you have a drop of whiskey in the house?' For a split second I thought it was for himself but he soon disabused me of that notion when he added, 'put a spoonful in a glass with a small taste of hot water.' This I quickly did and he slowly fed him 'the drop of punch' off a spoon. Just as slowly the child responded; he was over the worst.

In the passage of 30 months, I had come to realise the nature and reality of the precious gift the Lord had bestowed on me in the form of a mongoloid child. The thought that he might have slipped away from me really hit me. I could almost feel God smiling benignly on me. If he used the wisdom of Dr Blaney and the produce of John Power, that's just the way He works.

Before he left in the early hours, Dr Blaney suggested that we might give John a little whiskey every night when he went to bed and from the next night onwards he always got his little tot, usually in bed.

I move the clock forward until he is in his teens and still lapping up his tot every night and enjoying it. He would rap the floor and we knew it was whiskey time. On a particular night we had a visitor staying which required John to share a room with his sister, who was a couple of years younger. She had been out at something and was going to bed later than usual. He was half awake when she came into the room but his demeanour was such that she asked him, 'Are you all right?' and received a mumble that suggested he was. Even so, his loud mumbling and restlessness kept her awake for some time before sleep eventually overtook her.

Next morning, she indicated her concern about his mumbling the previous night and Anne asked me, 'Did you not give him his whiskey last night?'

'No, I thought you gave it to him,' so we both thought he had not got his whiskey the night before. In due course, John appeared and the first question directed at him was, 'Did you not get any whiskey last night?' He looked somewhat surprised by the question as he answered, 'I did.'

'Who made it for you?' Anne and I chorused together and got the shocking reply, 'I made it myself.'

Now the recipe for John's whiskey was a simple one—a dessert spoonful of whiskey and a teaspoon of sugar in a half cup of hot water served in a glass cup reserved for the purpose. We had no means of telling how much water he had used in the making but certainly the whiskey bottle on examination showed that he had taken enough whiskey to do him for a week of his normal allocation. That was the first and only time he made his own whiskey.

The mentally handicapped had not a lot going for them in the early 60s by way of education or training. It took quite a time before the great reforming legislation of the first post war Labour Government addressed the issue of the handicapped. Eventually it did, but only after a tremendous amount of voluntary effort and pressurising from parents' groups. The range of facilities now available for 'children with special needs' is a far cry from those early days when all sorts of venues, mostly church halls, accommodated small groups of mentally handicapped people, in what would be classed by today's standards as primitive conditions. The staff who coped with them were real heroes.

However much the designation might have moved over the years from mongoloid, to mentally handicapped, or child with special needs, none of these capture the reality of the Irish vernacular, *páiste Dé*.[37] The two definitions are both right, but they are different. Over the years, there were little things about John which puzzled us, and occasioned a smile or a shake of the head.

One which is quite easily told relates to the death of my mother on a Sunday afternoon in March 1979. She had been ill for some time and from the day before had been in a comatose condition. After lunch we had gone over to see her and to find her very much the same as she had been overnight. It was the considered view of Anne and my sister Noreen, two experienced nurses, that she could possibly 'go another day.'

As we withdrew from the room, John, always a great favourite with my mother, moved to the door, opened it wide and motioned the four of us out, something he had never done before. He closed the door behind us and remained alone in the room for a couple of minutes. We waited on the landing until he appeared, descended the stairs and returned home. We were hardly through the door when the phone rang. It was my sister.

'Come quickly, Mammy has died,' was the message which I instantly repeated to Anne, Louise and John.

In the calmest tone imaginable, John announced, 'I know. I know.' He did not return with us.

Not only does John mystify us, at times he delights us. I go back to August 2001 when Anne was a patient in Daisy Hill Hospital in Newry. I was visiting her one afternoon when she told me that the lady in the bed opposite was the mother of Joe Kernan. Before I left, I chatted with her for a while but not about football or her son Joe, whose name and picture was on every media outlet. The week before, Joe had been offered the Armagh managership, and the question on the country's lips was, 'Is he going to take it?' In the evening I was back at the hospital and John was with me. We were there for a time when Joe came into the ward and I said to John, 'That's Joe Kernan, John.'

While I had met Joe a couple of times when he worked in Warrenpoint I didn't know him that well, but after a time I moved over to speak to him. It was firmly in my mind that I would not mention anything about football or the Armagh management situation. By the time I reached Joe, John was on my heels and I introduced him formally.

'This is my son, John Carr.'

'How are you, John?' says Joe, putting out his hand to John. As he took Joe's hand he put up the other hand to silence any further greeting from Joe and put the $64,000 question to him which I would not have dared ask, 'Joe, are you going to be the Armagh manager?' Joe, rocking with laughter, replied, 'John, you'll be the very first man I'll tell when I make up my mind.'

In his lifetime, John has been to Croke Park, Lansdowne Road, Dalymount Park, Highbury, Hampden Park and lesser venues for all brands of football. He has been to Dundalk, Leopardstown, Phoenix Park and even Dingle for the races.

---

37   Irish for a 'child of God'.

He has been to most of the theatres in Dublin, the National Concert Hall, the Point Depot, the Opera House, Belfast, the West End and many lesser venues for concerts, plays and what have you. He has enjoyed every outing as much as I did myself.

There is much more to John than sport and music. Sometime near the end of our never-ending troubles, we had a couple staying who were friends of our daughter, Louise, from her college days in England. Neither of them had ever been to Ireland and I was giving them a potted history of 'the problem,' during which time John had the newspaper spread out on the floor in front of him, his usual position for 'reading' the news. I had reached the point when I was listing the various Northern Secretaries of State who had passed through our hands, beginning with Willie Whitelaw and going through Humphrey Atkins, Merlyn Rees, Roy Mason. I knew there was another one, but his name eluded me. Neither Anne nor Louise could recall the name, either. I repeated the names a couple of times hoping the spark of memory would be ignited, but in vain, when, without lifting his head off the paper, John announced, 'Richard Pym,' the most forgettable of them all.

In the first part of this memoir I related my earliest excursions through to McAnultys, our backdoor neighbours. For many, many years John has followed in father's footsteps, not occasionally, but seven days a week. He keeps a pair of slippers there, for he has the run of the house and Mairead would claim he was a civilising influence on the lives of all her children and, indeed, her grandchildren. He had a beautiful relationship with Tarlach, the youngest of Mairead's children, who has battled with cystic fibrosis for all of his 30-odd years

Why should I be telling you about my son John in this memoir? There is a reason. In the year following the 2003 Special Olympics, a Dublin lady, well-known in literary and broadcasting circles, wrote:

'The mentally and physically handicapped lead hideous lives.'

There are many who lead much fuller lives than John and some, regrettably, not so full. Some parents have to make heroic sacrifices for their *páistí Dé,* but that's where love comes in. To love and to be loved is all that matters.

29—Mrs Ritchie

Sometime in the 70s, after I had resigned from the Down board, I was being driven home from somewhere by George Tinnelly, the former chairman. It was close to 2 A.M. when he dropped me at my home on Summerhill.

It was the brightest of nights and as I moved to the door with key in hand, I turned to watch the departing car; I also saw a woman walking slowly up the other side of the hill, possibly 60 yards from me. On the other side of Summerhill, my mother lived at number 37, my Aunt Kitty lived at 41, and my Uncle Hugh lived at 47 in the first of a terrace of five houses set well back from the road. Hugh's wife, Annie, had died a year or two before and he lived on his own. He was fond of a bottle of stout, and while he called regularly with my mother, and with us at 44, he would rarely call with Kitty. It was Kitty who worried most about him and it was she who would check that he was in and settled for the night. It was a regular occurrence to see her going up to or returning from his house, but never at two in the morning.

This was the thought which was uppermost in my mind as I put the key in the door and stole a glance across the street. I thought to myself, 'too slow and too measured a step to be Kitty.' I moved quickly though the door and into our sitting room overlooking the street. Our house has a bay window and, as I picked up this slow moving figure through the left window, I thought, 'definitely not Kitty, so who the hell is it?' As she moved slowly into my vision through the centre window I had a very clear picture of a woman in a dark coat and what seemed to be a wide, greyish scarf over her shoulders and wearing a hat.

'Where is that woman going at this hour of the morning?' I asked myself as I moved and turned my gaze through the window on the right expecting her to come into focus. But she didn't. I moved quickly to the window to scan the street but there was no one. I moved even more quickly out on to the street to find it completely deserted. I walked up to view Uncle Hugh's house and still there was no one.

Back into my own home I secured the front door and as I moved up the stairs I heard my wife's voice from the bedroom, 'Did you go out again, Barney?' I made no answer until I sat down on the bed beside her.

'I am either doting or I have just seen a ghost,' I started, before going on to tell her the whole episode. She had been awake, of course, and had heard George's car arriving and departing and had been wondering what had been keeping me. I told her that as a boy, my mother had spoken of a woman who had resided in the house across the street and had hanged herself the year before I was born. She recalled my eldest brother, John, who would have been six or seven at the time, being taken home by the scruff of the neck by one of the neighbours. He had been among a group of people who had gathered outside the house when the tragic event was known.

The house where the suicide had taken place was at this time the Commercial Club. The club had first been established in Duke Street in the thirties after a group, which included my father, had withdrawn from the Irish National Foresters.

My father was the first secretary of the new Commercial before it moved to Summerhill. I remembered the Nesbitt and Mackin families living there, and in my youth had spent many late nights playing cards there. While from time to time there would have been some humorous references to 'the ghost,' I had never heard of anyone seeing it. While there was no way of knowing that this was the spectre of the woman who had taken her own life, we prayed for her and decided to have a Mass offered for her eternal rest. This we did, though I also spoke to the Lord on the direct line, 'Lord you must have a reason for this experience.'

I have always had a problem dating that experience but I have no problem at all recalling the next time it became a subject of recollection. This was the occasion of the death of one of our neighbours on Summerhill, May McCabe. May, a comparatively young woman, wife of Desmond and mother of Desmond, Cathal and Eimear, and good friend of all the neighbours, died on 20 June 1982. Some of those friends and neighbours were gathered in her wake room the next evening and among them my youngest brother, Paddy, home on holiday from Chicago, and myself. It was not uncommon for 'ghosts' to come up as a subject for conversation at wakes in those days; I don't think he introduced the topic, but Paddy certainly startled me by announcing to the company, 'sure, that house we lived in at the top of Duke Street was haunted.' We lived there for just two years.

'For the love of God, Paddy, who told you that?' I laughed, 'the only thing which I remember about that house was the crickets in the kitchen and the cockroaches in the front room.' The crickets were not such a problem for we smoked them out from time to time with lit paper, even though my mother had reservations about such a practice. She had often heard it was unlucky to disturb the crickets but she had no such reservations about cockroaches. She openly encouraged us to go to the sitting room, switch on the light and massacre the participants on our front room lino in the weekly 'cricket *céilí*'. However, my brother proceeded with tales of noises and shadows on the stairs and he put the question to me, 'And why do you think we moved back to Summerhill so soon?' I could only answer, 'Because we loved Summerhill.'

It was in the nature of wakes that one story led to another, and one or two told their stories before my neighbour, Bernie Dinsmore, began, somewhat timidly, as if expecting to be laughed out of court, but I was immediately interested when she began, 'One night I was reading very late.' Billy, her husband, had gone to bed and eventually she decided to join him.

'As I put my foot on the first step of the stairs I glanced out of the window to see an elderly lady coming past Gus Carey's house.' She proceeded to describe in perfect detail how the woman was dressed and the questions which came into her mind, 'Who is that? Where is she going?' Even as she was posing the questions, the woman turned left to the door of the Commercial Club, as it then was, and dissolved through it. Bernie vanished just as quickly up the stairs, dived in beside the slumbering Billy and lay there for half an hour before getting out to undress. That, almost *verbatim*, is the story as told by Bernie.

Now when I witnessed the spectre, I was quite calm in my thinking and the notion of ghost did not occur to me until I sat down and put all the bits together.

Remember, I did not see the figure dissolve, for I'm sure I would have taken a heart attack if I had. But as Bernie told it so exactly, the shivers were going up and down my spine. When she finished it took me some seconds to clear my emotions.

I had been sitting back a little from the others and I finally got my voice back to ask, 'Bernie, have you a notion what year that might have been?' and she hadn't. I proceeded to verify everything that she had said and Bernie, being the woman she is, with gifts of observation way beyond mine, described the lady exactly as I had seen her. Some weeks later we went over the event again and we thought it probable that we experienced it on the same occasion.

Years before, when I had been going through the files of the *Newry Reporter* for information on the John Martin's team, I noted a reference to a woman's death on Summerhill. The thought struck me that this might be the woman who had taken her own life. So it was back to the *Reporter* where I eventually spotted a small legal notice to creditors 'of the estate of Anna Allen of 13 Summerhill, Warrenpoint, who died on 29 April 1922,' to forward their claims, *etc.* The notice also indicated that the executors of the will were Elizabeth Allen, whom I took to be her sister, and Charles Pedlow. Back I went in the files to April and May, but could find no reference to her death, though I did find a letter of acknowledgement from a Mrs Allen of Loughbrickland, thanking those who had sympathised with her on the death of her son who had been shot dead in Newry on 29 March 1922.

I turned the pages back to read the report of how 19-year-old David Allen, a member of the B Special Constabulary, was shot dead in an IRA ambush, about William Street in Newry. The funeral reports in both the *Newry Reporter* and *Banbridge Chronicle* listed among the relatives two younger sisters of David, Anna and Elizabeth—the same Christian names as the two ladies who lived, as I thought, at 13 Summerhill, Warrenpoint. I went to Loughbrickland and spoke with two elderly members of Allen families but there was no connection.

By another slight coincidence, when I went to the Public Records Office in Belfast and told part of my story to the member of staff who was dealing with me, he said, 'I am interested in this, as my name also is Allen.' He added, 'We'll see if she made a will.' He went to a shelf, selected a small book which showed that Anna Allen had indeed made a will. By the standards of the day she was well off. She left a sum in excess of eleven hundred pounds. It occurred to me that when someone dies by their own hand, a coroner's report normally ensues, so I asked Mr Allen about the availability of such reports. He advised that written application was essential for such information to be made available.

When I wrote to the office I furnished three names, and asked if coroners' reports existed for any of their deaths. The names I submitted were Anna Allen, Martha Callan, and Mrs Ritchie. The reason for the two additional names was that in searching the local papers of April 1922, I found that a Martha Callan of Hillside, Warrenpoint, had died. Mrs Ritchie was a familiar name from the past and is listed in the Ulster Streets Directory of 1918 and 1919 as a Summerhill resident, though house numbers were not included. I was advised that no coroner's reports existed for any of the three names. I cannot imagine my sighting of that elderly lady was an illusion, nor do I believe that Bernie Dinsmore's confirmation of the experience was just imagination, either. I have never heard of any other sightings and it is my earnest prayer that everyone who ever lived in that house is at rest.

More recently, my cousin, Eamon Carr, visited me and we were talking about the Commercial Club where his father (Uncle Jimmy) used to work. I recounted seeing 'this woman' all those years ago.

'Mrs Ritchie,' he exclaimed, and I realised it was in the course of my card playing days that the familiarity of the name Mrs Ritchie was cultivated. He reminded me that his late brother Brian, who had been secretary of the club for a lengthy period, had written a short history to mark its golden jubilee. I had the publication in the house but had forgotten about it. I soon put my hand on it and noted that in describing the purchase of the premises, Brian used the phrase, 'complete with resident poltergeist.' He also quoted some gems from the minutes over the years. On 7 July 1946, for instance, it was recorded that, 'Owing to the scarcity of drink it was decided on the proposal of Mr George Scarborough, seconded by Mr Johnnie Kelly, that no more new members be accepted until drink supplies improve.'

In October 2003, I went to see Bob Jones who, in his 95th year, was the oldest man alive to have lived on Summerhill. Bob finished his career as principal of Ballinahinch Further Education College. I met him occasionally when the Down Education Committee was in being and later when he retired to Newry. He was well known in the scouting world all his life, and was honoured with the OBE. I went to see him in a residential home in Kilkeel, where he was in for a short spell of respite care. Although he had forgotten my Christian name, he was as clear as a bell. We had a wonderful afternoon, and anyone who would have known him would be aware of the expansive character that he was. I was there for an hour before I mentioned the name 'Mrs Ritchie' to him. Yes, he remembered the name well, but he could not be sure of the house she lived in. Like myself, he remembered the Nesbitt and Mackin families living in what became the Commercial Club. He had no memory of the name Allen.

On a later occasion I was at the Public Records Office with my daughter, Louise, looking up another matter, when I suggested to her that I would like to have another look at Anna Allen's will. I expected her to come back with the small book I had seen on a previous occasion, but to my surprise she had an envelope which contained the actual will in copperplate handwriting. The first striking thing about the document was that it bore the date of 28 April 1922, the day before the lady died. The second was the signature of Anna Allen, which was indecipherable—a scrawled line which resembled nothing, and could have been made by the cat. There was nothing extraordinary about the contents. Some named jewellery was left to a friend and the remainder of her estate to her cousin Elizabeth (Betty) who resided on the Portadown Road, Armagh. The witnesses were Emily Lang, 4 Springfield Terrace, and B. McCartney Clayton of Inna-Neuke, Warrenpoint.

I cannot take the story of Annie Allen and Mrs Ritchie any further, though I have the feeling they were the same person. As for the significance of the event in my life, I can only claim that my neighbour Bernie Dinsmore's sighting on the same night is one more remarkable coincidence.

The Commercial Club, which once was 13 Summerhill, is now No. 45 and houses Summerhill Beauty Parlour. When I feel like it, I can drop over the road for St Tropez tanning, the Jessica nail system, Sothy's skin care, aromatherapy massage, Swedish massage, Anthony Braden make up, ear-piercing and waxing.

Is it any wonder people say to me, 'I have never seen you looking so well.'

30—The Most Dreadful Day

In 1979, the town of Warrenpoint was the centre of international focus for the most horrific of reasons. The British Army sustained the biggest number of casualties in any single operation of the northern troubles at Narrow Water when two massive bombs were exploded, killing 18 soldiers. It was the last Monday of August and it was the Bank Holiday weekend. Weather-wise it was one of the best days of the entire summer.

Even now, I can recall the air of contentment in the Carr household at the time, for my son, Hugh, was due to take up his first teaching job the next week while Louise, who was going into her final year at Our Lady's Grammar School in Newry, was in the last week of an extended stay with a French family near La Rochelle. Hugh was due to take his driving test a few days later and for added experience he drove Anne, John and myself to Newry. We had the radio on for the *RTÉ* news and were just passing Narrow Water when we heard of the shocking events at Mullaghmore in Co. Sligo where a bomb had exploded on a boat belonging to Lord Mountbatten.

Lord Louis Mountbatten had a home in the beautiful isolation of Mullaghmore and was a regular visitor to the area. He was in his 80th year and the other victims of the outrage were Nicholas Knatchbull, his 14-year-old grandson, an elderly lady of 83, Lady Doreen Brabourne and Paul Maxwell, a young Enniskillen boy of 15 who worked on the boat in his summer job.

We did not have these full details as we returned from Newry somewhat earlier than we had planned but we were glad to get home after listening to the unfolding story on the radio. Hugh parked the car, walked through the house and down the garden as, we assumed, to McAnulty's.

Minutes later, Anne and I were still looking at some of the items she had purchased when a massive explosion shook the windows and caused me to stop in my tracks.

'It must be the Barracks,' I exclaimed, as I headed out to the car. When I reached The Square I soon realised it wasn't the Barracks, for many of the townspeople were also there.

'It must be the Reed's factory,' was my next guess but when I got to the foot of Newry Street the plume of smoke still drifting upwards indicated the source of the explosion was further down the road. Traffic was still moving in the Newry direction but no further than the Gilbert-Ash entrance where police were turning it back. I parked the car and went on foot to join dozens of others. The events of the previous minutes were being pieced together to reveal that a load of hay on a trailer parked at the lay-by had been packed with explosives and detonated as the Army lorries were passing. Even as the story was unfolding a helicopter arrived from the Newry direction and landed at the scene. From ground level what was happening could not be seen, but from our vantage point we had a full view of the twirling rotors and could hear the engines which powered them. By this time Hugh joined me to tell me that the convoy had passed down Church Street as he emerged from Mary Savage's shop.

In minutes, the increased power signalled lift-off and as the heavy machine gained height, there was another explosion. It made the helicopter, barely one hundred feet off the ground, stagger. It survived the blast and headed for Daisy Hill Hospital.

When the full story emerged, it transpired that the last vehicle of the convoy took the full blast of the first explosion which was responsible for the deaths of six soldiers. Most of the others obviously sought cover at the gatehouse but a massive bomb had been placed there in anticipation of their reaction. Twelve soldiers lost their lives as we watched from our vantage point at the Gilbert-Ash entrance. The fuller picture of the casualty figures came out on the evening news when it was announced that eighteen soldiers had been killed. It was not until the following day that another casualty had been added to the list when it was revealed that an English holidaymaker, a bird watcher, across on the Co. Louth side of the water had been sighted viewing the events through his binoculars. He was mistakenly thought to be a participant and was shot dead, bringing the total death toll for the day to 19.

We had some concern for Louise hearing about the shocking events of the day from the French media so we rang the family with whom she was staying. Her hostess, Jocelyn, had picked up a news flash on television within an hour of the explosion happening; she had not told Louise who had left the house with some of the family members a short time before. When Louise returned she had the full story of the day in French and she has never forgotten it.

In the aftermath of the carnage, many of us who had passed that seemingly innocent trailer of hay within minutes of its eruption could only thank Providence that we were not part of the holocaust. I have to confess that on the day I had not even noticed the hay trailer either going or coming home, though I had a clear recollection of seeing it the previous day. Many people and families round the area had the same experience as we had and undoubtedly it has been recalled and retold many times since.

On the last Friday of May 1980, the entire family was returning from a performance of *Rose Marie,* staged by Newry Musical Society in Newry Town Hall. My wife, Anne, sat in the front passenger seat beside me. Hugh, John and Louise occupied the rear seat. At normal speed we passed the entrance to the castle where the gatehouse stood. Yards past the gatehouse something struck me and I asked, 'Am I imagining things, or was the castle entrance lit up?'

Hugh, from the rear seat answered, 'I was about to ask the same question myself. It appeared to be illuminated.'

Louise said, 'It was definitely lit up. I was looking to see where the source of the light was.'

My wife, who had her eyes closed saying her personal trimmings to the Rosary we had completed a mile or two back the road, saw nothing. As we approached the roundabout at the Mound Road I proposed, 'We'll go back and take another look' — a proposal which was turned down out of hand by my wife.

'You'll drive this car straight home,' she declared and I obeyed like the dutiful man I was and am.

When the double explosion occurred on 27 August 1979, it was the second one at the gatehouse which killed most of the 18 soldiers and did considerable damage to the gate lodge. It had not been repaired by this time but I am almost certain that my illuminated sighting revealed the lodge intact, as I had always known it.

Occasionally over the years we have spoken about that night and wondered if anyone else had shared our experience then or since.

On the last Friday of August 2009 I joined about 70 others in a commemoration service to mark the 30th anniversary of that most dreadful day. While we stood in driving rain I was disappointed that the occasion failed to reflect the enormity of the needless sacrifices which were made both at Narrow Water and Mullaghmore.

31—Ending the Ban

The only occasion in my life when I had any personal sanction imposed on me for infringements of 'the ban rule' was when I went to see my uncle, Hugh Tumilty, perform in John Thomas Bradley's Dalymount Park. I never felt that my three weeks' suspension changed or even lessened the attachment I had for soccer, my true love at the time. Nor, when I became a GAA playing member at the age of seventeen, did I lose any sleep over it. The rule was enforced by what was called a Vigilance Committee, which I believe was appointed by the county chairman and whose members were known only to him.

I was never aware of any vigilante activity and I well remember our long serving chairman, George Tinnelly, telling me that he would never ask any man to go and spy on another. If he got a report that a member was breaking the rule he was prepared to go and do the job himself. The notion that people climbed trees and hid behind ditches to spy on offenders was a bit of a fable put about by the Association's detractors. By and large, fellows turned to the games they preferred and I never experienced personal relations being damaged in the process. I had a great feeling for soccer and I didn't think it unpatriotic to play it or any of the other prohibited games. Cricket and hockey held no attraction for me when I was younger, though I had some interest in rugby; when I was older the attractions of both the other games became apparent. When I learned in later life that one of my good friends in the GAA, Sean McManus of Greencastle, went over to take in a test match or two on a regular basis, it didn't surprise me one little bit, for he is a man who shared my views on a variety of issues. His interest in cricket developed when he was a student in Manchester and he never lost it.

There were other aspects to the ban besides playing the forbidden games. One could not watch them, nor could a club organise a function at which there would be any type of dancing other than céilí dancing. When I came of age, and mature enough to represent Down at Congress, I invariably had proposals to ease the restrictions on watching games and to open up club functions to other types of dancing. As proposals on the ban rules were only taken every three years, it took a long time to get any movement.

One section of the ban which gained particular prominence in later years was the 'exclusion rule' which denied membership to members of the British armed forces and police. I cannot imagine that anyone in the Association 50 years before would ever have considered a proposal to change that section of the rule. Nor, indeed, was there any demand from the forces to take part in any GAA activities. But there was no denying that in the late 60s the ban on playing and watching other games was giving concern, so after a Congress debate in 1968, the Central Council set up a commission to consider the pros and cons of the matter and to make a recommendation.

The committee was chaired by Alf Murray, a distinguished Armagh and Ulster footballer who was also a past president of the Association. It produced its report in due course and the recommendation that the ban should stay. Curiously to my mind, and the minds of many others, the report made the case for doing away with the ban. In the debate that took place before the 1971 Congress, which was held in Belfast and ended the games ban, I was arguing for its retention. Not, might I add, because of any of the claims in the commission report, but rather, I argued, that if players moved from one game to another at will, soccer thinking would dominate the approach to Gaelic football. The rest is history and we now have a game which has elements of all three games served up in a basketball cocktail. I cringe at much of what passes for Gaelic football in the modern era.

It was 1971 when the ban on playing foreign games was repealed at the Congress in Queen's University in Belfast. That could well have been called the third year of The Troubles. It was almost 25 years later that the exclusion rule surfaced as one of the key issues of the peace process.

The momentum to have the exclusion rule repealed began, surprisingly, in Loughinisland, where one of the worst atrocities of The Troubles was perpetrated in June 1994. The massacre took place on a Saturday night; the locals were gathered in the O'Toole family bar watching a World Cup game in which Ireland was involved. A number of armed men entered the premises and in a frenzied attack left six men dead, one of them 87 years old Barney Green who had played football with the local club in his younger days. I went to some of the funerals for I had many contacts with people from the area over the years.

The IRA had called a ceasefire and the peace progress was edging precariously forward. About ten days before the Down Convention of 1995, the Loughinisland club had a proposal on the *clár*[38] to remove Rule 21, the exclusion rule. This came as a surprise to most people in the Association, for Down were the reigning All-Ireland Champions and in the celebration there was quite a bit of evidence that the GAA establishment was moving the reconciling process along quite nicely. It soon became evident, however, that whatever about the Loughinisland club, those behind the massive media campaign which exploded simultaneously were determined to stampede the Down Convention, if not the Association, into the removal mode.

After the weekend avalanche and the renewed media bombardment, I thought I should offer some words of advice to clubs who would be considering the motion in the days before the Convention, so I wrote the following letter to *The Irish Times* and *The Irish News,* the two papers I normally read and who seemed to be leaders of the crusade.

> *'It is obvious a highly orchestrated media campaign is being mounted to influence the discussion on the proposed deletion of the 'exclusion rule' at the coming Down Convention.*
> *Regrettably it is being mounted in circumstances which suggest that those who oppose it, even with sound and rational argument, are at best insensitive, and at worst, extremists and diehards. I do not suggest that this is the intention of the promoters of the motion, but this is the media message. Some of these promoters have indicated that they are prepared for a three- or four-year battle to get the necessary majority.*

---

38   Irish for 'agenda'

Most people in the Association are asking is such a campaign necessary, when the president, Jack Boothman, had indicated on a number of occasions since he took office that the Association would be quick to respond to any settlement in the North.

Why expose the Association to a drawn-out argument and a possible legacy of acrimony looking for a handful of votes, when the issue demands a noble and magnanimous conclusion? I am suggesting that at the appropriate time all the Ulster counties sponsor a deletion motion, and that it be accepted, not with debate, but with acclamation.

The exclusion rule is of long standing. It has been there in some shape or form for most of the Association's one hundred and ten years. It was there before the RUC came into existence. It has nothing to do with the performance of that force before or since 1968. Regrettably, some high level GAA minds have stated otherwise, from time to time. That stated however, we have to be realists and take account of what is happening around us. The chief constable himself, is seeking a Public Inquiry into policing in this part of the country. The Chairman of the police authority is asking for submissions on policing from every Tom, Dick and Harry in the country. If such realities emanate from the lips of the professional and lay police bodies do not suggest that the proposal is premature, what under heaven does?

The Irish citizenry and GAA members in particular, in this part of Ulster, are only too well aware of how essential it is for all sections of the community to support the police—and not only support them but to be part of them. Quite apart from the ethic of such a view, the fact that hundreds and maybe thousands of well paid jobs would be open to our young men and women is in itself desirable. I look forward to the day when the new policeman in the Barracks, will be a county player, expecting to turn out with the local club. This is the normality we must work for.

Hopefully, when the real peace progress gets under way, it will have as its aim the equalising of our two communities. The end product has to include a structure of policing to which all can give their support and which young men and women of Irish nationality can join, knowing they are serving their community and their country.

Jack Boothman has done well since he took office, in references to the "exclusion rule". Recently he was criticised in the Dublin Sunday "quality press". I faxed them some comments in defence of the president but my views did not get an airing even after a number of phone calls. Arguments are easily won if only one view is allowed to be expressed.

Over the years, the GAA has been subjected to media campaigns of all sorts, but to its eternal credit it has always made up its own mind in the light of what it felt was good for the Association and the country. I do not think it will be any different on this occasion. Already, the Association has shown its good faith by its invitation to the British Ministers to Croke Park Finals and by the acceptance of British hospitality at Hillsborough Castle.

A number of British officials were invited to the Down victory celebrations before Christmas, so no one can be in any doubt about our intent.

Jack Boothman will preside over three Congresses in his term of office and it is my fervent prayer that at one of these, possibly his last, he will have the honour of calling one of the Ulster Counties in the name of all the others to move the deletion of Rule 21. There is no doubt it will be accepted with acclamation.'

I faxed the letter to *The Irish News* and *The Irish Times* and later in the day rang *The Irish News* to check that it had been received. 'Yes, it had been received and would be published on Tuesday morning,' I was assured by a pleasant female voice. In the event, it did not appear in either *The Irish News* or *The Irish Times,* both of which for the rest of the week continued their concerted campaign.

It took another six years, until the Congress of 2001, before the rule was dropped and I have no doubt it was the premature proposal from Loughinisland which led to the extended period.

Before the 2001 Congress, I wrote again to *The Irish News* backing the deletion motion:

'I welcome the proposals and would encourage young men and women of Irish nationality who would wish to make a career in policing, to get into the new service.

I would not presume to advise Catholics on anything other than spreading 'the good news' of the Gospel message and living out their lives in conformity with it.

The 'exclusion rule' as it has come to be called, had to do with conquest and the non-acceptance of conquest. That conquest is over now and whatever British forces are left in the country are here with the agreement and consent of the Irish people.

I couldn't resist a last line which read:

'I trust that this letter will not meet with the same fate as my effort of 1995.'

Sadly, I have to report that it did.

Policing was and is the most sensitive of all the problems which beset us and one has to wonder if these staged events between teams of Irish and British soldiers or policemen are serving any purpose even in the guise of positive publicity. The problems will only begin to unravel when young policemen seek membership of their local GAA clubs or where the police organise their own clubs and play in competitions within the various counties. Some may well say, 'that will be the day,' but that's what normality is all about.

To finish this chapter on the exclusion rules I have to relate the true story of policemen playing Gaelic games, 'despite the bloody rule.'

Paddy Kelly, a tall athletic looking man in his younger days, was the RUC

Sergeant in Camlough, three miles outside Newry, County Armagh. He was a Galway man, born in one of the hurling areas of that county. He was an accomplished hurler when he joined the RUC. He was well past his best when he became the Sergeant in the South Armagh village but he was still a very competent hurler. The Bessbrook Geraldines Club held sway in the area in both hurling and football. It was more difficult for them to field the hurling team. Being the friendly man he was Paddy would go up to the field of an evening, out of uniform, of course, and enjoy a puck-about with the lads. In no time at all he was well established in the local community for he also liked a bet and kept a couple of running dogs. Such was the impression he created on the hurling field that some of the team mentors concluded that he could be an asset to the team. It was recognised, of course, that it would be impossible to play him in home games for he was too well known locally.

They decided to chance him in away games and Paddy was most enthusiastic. On these occasions the pre-match advice to him from the mentors was the same, 'Sergeant, should you get your bloody leg broken keep your mouth shut or that bloody accent of yours will get us all suspended.'

Paddy played a couple of games without incident but in the third outing he was faced with a very tough opponent who simply tortured him. In one joust both of them went down very heavily with Kelly coming off worst. He could contain himself no longer and shouted, 'Do you want to break my bloody leg?'

'Keep your bloody mouth shut, Kelly, or we'll both end up in the bloody river.' His opponent was another policeman.

Story as told by Bill O'Keefe, a great Tipperary man, who taught in Newry and Loughbrickland and who played in that game with Paddy Kelly. Bill also played both hurling and football in Armagh and Down, legally and illegally.

To complete Paddy Kelly's somewhat unorthodox police career, he married a local girl. Under police regulations this warranted a transfer. Paddy didn't transfer, he retired and ran his wife's family pub. He also ran a bookie's shop, kept more running dogs and reared six girls, all of whom turned out to be good camogie players. The family came to live in Warrenpoint, to the delight of the local Betsy Grays, and Paddy became a great supporter of both Betsy Grays and 'the Blues'.

The final chapter of the exclusion environment came when Croke Park was opened to the rugby and soccer fraternities, a move to normality which I fully supported. In return the Irish Rugby Football Union continues to offend the large majority of Irish people by its refusal to respect the national anthem on foreign fields.

32—The Political Files

The political furrow which I am opening at this stage is, if one excludes religious faith, the longest of my life. It dates from that early morning meeting with two policemen on our doorstep in search of my Uncle Tommy and the election of my father to the then Warrenpoint Urban Council a short time afterwards. My father's political career ended after one term on the Council but even before that term ended, it would seem that the National League had disappeared from the political landscape; it wasn't until I read Eamon Phoenix's account of 'northern nationalism' of that period that the full picture emerged.

But even as a young boy the political confusion of the period after the partitioning of the country was much apparent. As a ten-year-old, I had to reconcile the candidature of De Valera, as an abstentionist for the South Down seat, being opposed by a Republican candidate, who was supported by my Uncle Tommy. Fond of my uncle as I was, I have to confess that the magic of the De Valera name was sufficient for him to have my unregistered support. Dev's election as an abstentionist was a temporary and symbolic boost to northern nationalism but nothing more. By the time the next Stormont election came round whoever decided Nationalist policy maintained the abstentionist line and didn't even bother to nominate a candidate. This led to a Warrenpoint man, James Brown, being elected as an independent, but he was essentially a Unionist and a decent man to boot. He was editor and proprietor of the thrice-weekly *Newry Telegraph*.

All of the politicking of the time was going on to the accompaniment of a shocking sectarian campaign which introduced me to the word *pogrom* and applied to the situation in Belfast and elsewhere where Catholics were under every sort of threat. While I am sure we had a wireless at the time, I have no memory of ever hearing those riots mentioned. I vividly recall waiting on my father to come home with *The Irish News* every evening to get a picture of what was happening to those unfortunate victims. One also read of the goings-on in the Stormont Parliament where the most outrageous insults were being offered to Catholics, almost on a daily basis.

It was during the War in February 1944, however, that the grossest insult ever offered to our community was uttered in that august assembly: a member on the Unionist benches asked if it was true that Mass had been said in an Orange Hall in Portrush which was used as a billet by the American Army. The Minister of Home Affairs, Mr William Lowry, interjected to advise the questioner that such a happening had occurred, but went on to assure him that 'the hall has been fumigated since.' Naturally, there was a strenuous protest from the Nationalist side but the Speaker claimed not to have heard the remark. I think Mr Lowry later became Lord Chief Justice.

In the Nationalist politics of the day, some priests played an important role; the appearance of Newry priest, Fr Jim Burke, on a platform always ensured not only reasoned argument, but also a portion of humour which would now be labelled 'political satire' of the highest quality, and he was sure to have the audience in good tune. In those days there was no house-to-house canvassing, but rarely would there have been the plague of present day politics, 'a low turnout'.

In the disarray of local politics it was Canon McAllister who would have called the meeting to nominate the majority of the nationalist candidates for the council elections. Then, as now, Warrenpoint had two wards, East and West, now Seaview and Clonallon with the latter being regarded as the Nationalist ward. This ward returned seven councillors while the East, as the Unionist Ward, returned five. Neither side contested each other's territory until much later.

In due course, the Stormont seat returned to nationalism; its standard-bearer was Peter Murney who, along with some of his brothers, had been active in the Republican cause in the War of Independence. I was a comparatively young fellow and would not have been aware of or involved in the selection procedure by which he was chosen, but I was present in St Colman's Hall in Newry when he was deselected some years later. Admittedly, Peter was not the most articulate of public representatives but he was a 'sound man', though in the Stormont of the time, it hardly mattered what the quality of the opposition was, it counted for nothing. It could do little but protest against the humiliations which nationalists were subjected to in political, economic, religious and cultural terms.

I was aware of the selection meeting which was publicised by a simple statement in the local papers inviting those interested to attend, so I did just that. In the chair was Fr P.F. McCumiskey, the local administrator at Newry Cathedral. Early on, it became evident that Peter was coming to the end of his term, for while there was no direct criticism there was an undermining innuendo which did not bode well for him. Time came for nominations and Joe Connellan was proposed, seconded and supported by a number of people. I am not sure that Peter was even proposed, but I do remember the broken Peter speaking in his own defence, and probably more coherently than any of those present had ever heard him before. I had a degree of sympathy for Peter that night.

I relate this account of one of my early political meetings to illustrate the realities of what might be called 'constitutional nationalism' in those days. Often, over the years, I have heard, 'The Old Nationalist Party' being derided as if it was a collection of reactionaries rather than what it was—individual voices of a lost community. There was no party as we know party today. There was no membership. There was no organisation other than at election times when the people responded without any cajoling or promising. What could be promised?

In Newry, a well-organised group of nationalists emerged under the title, The Irish Citizens' Association (ICA); it became the strongest group on the Urban Council for over a decade. Some years ago, a Newry journalist, Fabian Boyle, writing in *The Irish News*, described the ICA as a party of 'big business-men.' Most of the members of the group were dead at the time so I wrote to the paper indicating 'the big business-men' who made up the party's councillors: Barney McShane and Jim McDonald were both dockers. Jack O'Hare was a bus driver. Jack Lallie, a motor mechanic who had a small garage, Micksey McMahon a barber who, with Owen McManus, acted as unpaid masseur for all Down teams on which I played. Quinn Bennett was office manager for a local building firm, and Mick Keogh was a journalist with *The Frontier Sentinel*. Big business-men how are ye!

The only reason I am going over this now is to indicate that *The Irish News* refused me space and did not publish my letter. More importantly, the service of honourable men, who gave local leadership when it was badly needed, needs to be recorded and remembered.

I note that in more recent times, Tom Kelly, also of Newry and also writing in *The Irish News,* repeats the canard of 'the big business' ICA, in relation to a Parliamentary election in which his grandfather, also Tom, was contesting as a Labour Party candidate. While I didn't vote for Tom's grandfather, I knew him well as a decent and honourable man which, of course, Tom is also.

Organised politics took off for the first time in Warrenpoint in the mid-40s, when a local group of trade unionists formed a branch of the Northern Ireland Labour Party (NILP) and made an impact on the local scene. In 1948, the NILP held its annual conference in Warrenpoint and in the spirit of the times it ended with the singing of the *Red Flag.* Probably because the anthem was associated to some degree with the Communist Party and the British Labour Party, some of the local members took exception to the choice of music. In due course, the branch withdrew from the NILP, as did the Newry Branch and affiliated with the Irish Labour Party in Dublin. I would imagine that Tom Kelly had something to do with that initiative for he, too, was a veteran of the War of Independence. The Irish Labour Party became an important part of the town's political and social life; it formed a very successful social club which served the community for a few generations.

History has shown that Warrenpoint Labour was light years ahead of its time, for it is only in recent years that the *Red Flag* has been under threat as the musical accompaniment to the annual conference of the British Labour Party, as orchestrated by its then leader, Tony Blair.

In the mid-60s, the Nationalist Party made an effort to reorganise itself properly. A Central Council had been formed with Eddie McAteer of Derry as its chairman and leader. It was given an injection by the return from England of the youthful Austin Curry; he took the East Tyrone seat at Stormont which Joe Stewart had held for some years. Austin's act of civil disobedience in occupying a council house in Caledon, in protest at the local council's housing allocations, was 'the first shot' in the civil rights campaign which was getting under way. By this time, I was chairman of the South Down Constituency Council of the Nationalist Party, and when Joe Connellan retired, it was suggested to me by a few members that I should seek to succeed him. At that time, I had no political ambitions.

While 1966, with its 50th commemoration of the 1916 Rising, demonstrated that Irish nationalism was still a very potent force, it also brought the first official public fusion with the other 'ism,' Unionism, in the Stormont meeting of Terence O'Neill and Sean Lemass. It was said at the time that 'nothing will ever be the same again' and nothing has. The civil rights campaign gathered its head of steam; the Unionists resisted change. People's Democracy emerged from Queen's University to make the Battles of Burntollet and The Bogside as famous as Waterloo.

In due course, violence erupted in Belfast with the awful house burnings making hundreds of families homeless and turning many Nationalist communities in the North into reception areas for 'the refugees'. In Warrenpoint, the Town Hall, the GAA Club and the Pantomime Club were all used as reception centres for those en route to the South though many returned to Belfast after a matter of days.

It went from one crisis to another, and while the Stormont election called by Terence O'Neill did nothing to stop the spiralling violence, it did bring some new names into that assembly. Among them were John Hume, Paddy O'Hanlon and Ivan Cooper all of whom had stood as independents with a strong civil rights background. Paddy Devlin, although an NILP Labour member, spoke with an independent voice. The only other organised group going at the time was the National Democrats and these, with the seasoned Gerry Fitt and Austin Curry, came together to form the Social Democratic and Labour Party (SDLP). It was a remarkable Warrenpoint man, John Duffy, who became the first secretary; doubtless his tact and diplomacy was sorely tried in those early days. Initially, it was a party of chiefs and no indians who saw the necessity of forming a united opposition to Unionism, and even though they represented a wide range of political ideologies, in what could be termed 'the original rainbow coalition,' it held together remarkably well.

I had continued in the Nationalist Party, which had held its two seats in South Down, for some months, but it soon became evident that events had overtaken it. It was obvious that the future was with the SDLP which I joined a short time later. I set about organising a branch in the town and it was up and running by the time 'The Dungiven Parliament' went into session.

For the next 29 years I held office of some kind in the branch but mainly as secretary and fundraiser. When the first assembly elections came in 1973, it was again suggested to me that I might let my name go forward at the selection Convention, but my political ambitions were still moribund. I had the feeling that whatever political structure came out of the election would not last too long. In the event it only lasted a matter of months and men like Paddy O'Donoghue, Frank Feeley and Seamus Mallon, who were members of the teaching profession and who had to resign on being elected, were left without jobs.

But the SDLP was a crusading party which proceeded to make the running in Local Government while the leadership made its mark on the national scene. Politics became a bit of a ritual, with the annual conference being the set piece of the year where personal friendships were renewed, and the party leader's address was the big public occasion.

Gerry Fitt was the leader for the first ten years of the party's existence and for the most part he was a very acceptable figure. He had moved the Northern problem on to the Westminster stage in a manner which had not been done before. At party conferences he could have spoken for an hour without a note and if most of it was run-of-the-mill stuff he would invariably have us 'rolling in the aisles' with jokes at Johnnie McQuade's expense. Johnnie was a Unionist representative from the Shankill Road with much the same background as Gerry, but not nearly as articulate or as fast on his political feet.

The 1978 conference was coming up and in seeking topics to debate someone at our branch had discovered we had no constitutional machinery for electing a leader. I can honestly say that there was not the slightest criticism of Gerry's leadership, but we thought it would be a good idea to have the machinery in place when it came to appointing his successor. All this was made clear when the proposal was presented at conference where it was duly passed and left for the Executive to consider.

The following year, 1979, was yet another watershed year for the North; for the party it brought another Westminster election, the Narrow Water massacre on the same day as the Mountbatten atrocity, and later the visit of the Pope.

The Westminster election brought a problem for the SDLP: it had to decide whether or not it should contest the Fermanagh-South Tyrone Constituency where there was an Independent Republican in the field, Frank Maguire. The Executive decided not to run a candidate but to the surprise of most in the party, Austin Curry resigned from the party to contest the election as an independent. It was even more surprising when the party leader announced he was backing the bold Austin who, unsurprisingly, was well beaten at the poll. Despite what most people thought was a severe hiccup, there did not appear to be any loss of confidence in the party leader when the annual conference came round the following November in Newcastle.

The Sunday morning session of conference is really the occasion when the serious business of party organisation is under scrutiny, and I was pretty critical of Gerry for undermining the Executive in publicly supporting Austin. I was somewhat amazed that the hall began to fill when the whisper went out that the leader was 'under attack'. Gerry turned my criticism into something of a joke, and I laughed myself at his comments. Before November was out, Gerry had resigned the leadership; I have read on a number of occasions since that Warrenpoint set the process in motion. I have never subscribed to such a theory because much that has been revealed over the years suggests that there were divisions at the top, unknown to the rank and file.

It was many years later that I met Gerry face to face again, on Royal Avenue, after he became a member of the House of Lords. He never knew my name, but his 'Ach, how are you big fella?' was warm and friendly. We chatted for five minutes without ever a mention of politics. When we parted, I felt all of us owed Gerry Fitt something for his contribution in putting the Northern problem on the bigger stage at Westminster and for his major contribution to the SDLP. That he and his family should have been put through the crucifixion and exile they endured at the hands of many of those he had tried to help, made for one of the sorriest chapters of The Troubles.

John Hume was the unanimous choice of the SDLP to succeed Gerry Fitt as party leader. In the course of the next 20 years he moved 'the Irish problem' on to the European and transatlantic platforms, while at the same time presiding over a party which was making great headway in representing the vast majority of Northern nationalists. In Local Government elections they were the dominant group and in South Down, when the Westminster seat of Enoch Powell was taken by Eddie McGrady, there was the enthusiasm of an All-Ireland Final day. Seamus

Mallon had already been elected in Armagh. All of this progress was being made to a continual background of atrocity which seemed to go from bad to worse, with no end in sight.

Eventually, it was Hume's persistence in engaging with Gerry Adams which brought the cessation, after a couple of false dawns, and led to the Good Friday Agreement. By this time, I was becoming a somewhat disillusioned member of the party. While Gerry Fitt and Paddy Devlin might have left the SDLP because it was not 'a socialist party,' others left because it was not a 'republican party,' and I left because I thought it was not a very 'democratic party'.

My problems began in 1996, when we had a special delegate conference to consider some proposed changes to the constitution. Among these was a proposal from the Executive to amend a clause which related to the anti-discrimination stance of the party, and which said, in effect, 'we oppose discrimination on grounds of religion, race or gender.' The Executive sought to extend this to include 'sexual orientation' which did not give me any real problem.

All the proposals had been circulated to the branches for perusal and amendments. When we considered them at the Warrenpoint branch, I moved a further amendment to the anti-discrimination clause to include 'unborn human life'. I was the branch secretary and I deliberately did not return the documentation until the very last minute. This did not prevent another branch having its name to an amendment which, if passed, had the effect of side-lining the Warrenpoint amendment. Obviously someone, or the group dealing with the conference agenda, felt that unborn human life was not as sacrosanct as 'sexual orientation' and did not merit constitutional inclusion, or even discussion. Need I state that it was passed and the Warrenpoint proposal never got an airing. Of course, I made a protest at the shafting of my proposal and had some sympathetic nods, but I had the feeling that they were mostly on grounds of my age—and I was only 73 at the time. I note with a degree of satisfaction that the SDLP has nailed its pro-life standard to the mast in more recent times.

In 1998, when the Good Friday Agreement was finally cobbled together, an air of euphoria descended on the Northern political scene and especially on the SDLP who could quite rightly take credit for its leading role over the years. In May the referendum took place, followed by the first Northern Ireland Assembly election in June. For this, the central election directorate decreed that in South Down four candidates should be nominated; this without any consultation with the local Constituency Committee. This might be all right in normal circumstances, but in the month of March a remarkable change came over the party in South Down, between the first and last days of March. A 'branch' which had one member registered on 1 March yet not a single member at all in 1996, was able to register 130 'members' on 31 March. Its neighbouring branch, a few miles up the road, which had 21 members on 1 March, and for a few years previously, ended the month with 150 'members'. A couple of other branches increased their numbers, but not on the scale of the two mentioned. By a stroke of good fortune a new branch with 70 members was registered just in time to qualify, and this after 25 years of the party's existence.

Representation at SDLP selection conventions at that time was two delegates per ten members so it can be seen that the two neighbouring branches had 56 delegates and this, added to the 14 votes of the newly registered branch, gave these three (or two) branches almost as many votes as all the other eight branches combined. In effect these three branches selected the team.

I give the background to the selection process because my son, Hugh, who had been active in the party from his student days, had Assembly ambitions. He had been a former chairman of the Constituency Executive and, with a few younger members, had spearheaded the campaign which ended Enoch Powell's tenure in the South Down seat at Westminster, with a majority of a few hundred votes for Eddie McGrady. Hugh had been leader of the SDLP group on the Newry and Mourne District Council for all his years on that body.

As the figures and the names of the likely candidates emerged I expressed some reservations to him about letting his name go forward. While I knew he would be chosen as a candidate, I knew there wasn't a hope that the party would win four seats. Indeed, the decision of the Party Executive to run four candidates is a story in itself. Into the bargain, I did not relish a contest with two locals fighting for a single seat, especially when one of them was PJ Bradley, a well-known local auctioneer and estate agent.

I understood Hugh's desire to get into the political fray, and he let his name go before the selection Convention. Both he and PJ were selected after the elimination of one other candidate. I will not say a word about the campaign which followed, only to record that PJ won well. I was disappointed for Hugh as I thought that he had something to offer the party and community in general.

In the early summer of 2000 the SDLP had what was described as 'a root and branch' look at itself in the shape of yet another special conference. In a proposal from the Warrenpoint branch, I sought to change the structure of selection conventions by putting a ceiling on the number of delegates a branch might have. When I read, with a degree of humour, the litany of 'improvements' the South Down branches had in a matter of weeks before the 1998 election, the room was in raptures. With it all, however, the Executive wanted to retain 'paper branches' and they got their way. With that, the SDLP and I parted company, and I have been an Independent ever since.

Of course, Hugh was a loyal party man and he continued his council role until his second son was born in 2003, when he felt the domestic scene required more of his time. While he told me of his intention, he did not tell me much more, for since I left the party we rarely discussed local branch affairs. It was from the papers that I learned that the Derrylecka and Rostrevor branches had decided that the Warrenpoint branch did not have the right to nominate a replacement for a Warrenpoint councillor. According to them, this was the responsibility of the Crotlieve selection convention which they called together. They had their own man nominated, and 'to hell with The Point.'

This was as much as Hugh could take, and he, too, resigned from the party, though he is not an Independent like I am. He still actively supports and has canvassed for the SDLP in all elections since. It is a matter of history that some level of authority in the SDLP reversed the decision of the Crotlieve executive, which forced a by-election at a cost of almost £10,000, and which returned the nominee of the Warrenpoint branch.

There were two big local issues which dominated the final decade of the last century in Warrenpoint: the sale of the Alexian Brothers and the proposal from the Warrenpoint Harbour Authority to extend the deep water quay and cargo handling area. They had a proposal which included the filling-in of the Town Dock, land reclamation, a future marina and a training wall on the foreshore, all of which would extend the harbour well into the town.

The townspeople did not have much of a say in the disposal of The Brothers, but the efforts on their behalf by the local district council, while initially seeming to be successful, had a disappointing outcome. On the other hand, when the townspeople organised to contest the proposals of the Harbour Authority they were able to stay 'the hand of progress.'

The Alexian Brothers came to Warrenpoint in 1923, to found what came to be known as Mount St Columb's, a nursing and residential home which provided a facility in the field of caring for over 70 years. In that time, many of the Brothers and quite a number of the residents were firm favourites with the townspeople. Not many of the present generation would remember Frances O'Farrell of the swinging arms, or the always exquisitely dressed Mr 'Death' O'Callaghan, so called, because of his ghostly pallid colouring.

Many will remember Harry Fitzsimons, the gentle Dubliner, who trekked into town every day, sometimes twice daily, regardless of the weather, complete with little portmanteau, invariably to the Post Office. Mostly he travelled via Springfield Road and Summerhill, and it was always a pleasure to chat with him. He was at his best after he had been down on holiday with his mother, but he loved to get back to The Brothers and The Point where he felt he had a fulfilling role. While it was never an obsession with him, there were very few about The Point who had not heard of his lineage, through his mother's side of the family, to Daniel O'Connell, always related with a gentle humour. Years before he died, he told me he was long enough in The Point to qualify for burial here, and when the end came his wishes were honoured. His headstone in St Peter's cemetery reflects his pride in the name, Henry O'Connell-Fitzsimons.

In its latter years, the Brothers' nursing home had an enhanced status because it became something of a satellite facility of the Downshire Hospital, Downpatrick, particularly for patients who were capable of living almost in the community. With the intensive usage of the facility, it soon became obvious that much of it needed updating to modern medical and structural requirements. The provision of a modern-day hospital was beyond the resources of the Brothers, and in due course, the Order had to announce closure.

Before 'the Brothers' officially came on the market, we were discussing its future at our SDLP Branch meetings, for it was a 40-acre site in a prime situation. It was the almost unanimous view that the Newry and Mourne District Council should attempt to purchase it for the community. In due course our council representatives were able to convince the council that 'the Brothers' would be a good community investment. Without being privy to any of the details, we were advised from time to time that negotiations were going ahead slowly.

Eventually, we were told that a deal had been done, and that it was only the formalities which had to be completed. It can be imagined, then, what the shock and disappointment was like when the branch members and townspeople at large learned that 'the Brothers' had been sold, not to the council, but to a developer.

Obviously, the Brothers were concerned with what the reaction in the town would be, so with the breaking of the news, they went to the press with a copy of a letter they had sent to the council, under a banner headline, 'Alexian Brothers Tell Their Side of the Story'. The country knew the contents of the letter before the council even had time to consider it.

The essence of Brother Moran's letter was that, in addition to the council's bid of £1.15 million, they had four other legitimate bids, the highest of which was £1.3 million, but because of their regard for the Warrenpoint community they were accepting the lower bid of the council. He went on to state that, at a later meeting on 7 March 1994, the council 'effectively withdrew its offer.' That essentially is the bones of the letter, but there were some minor matters mentioned.

In due course, the clerk of the council, Mr Kevin O'Neill, replied indicating that the council had never withdrawn its bid, but had approved the price and that the contract was sealed and forwarded through the council's own solicitor on 16 March. He went on to state that the council's solicitor had been advised five days later that 'a contract had been entered into with another party.' Mr O'Neill concluded, 'this was the first indication the council got that their bid had not been accepted. I feel it is my duty to let the public know the true facts of the council's involvement, so they may judge for themselves.'

I have no recollection of ever seeing Brother Moran's comments on the clerk's letter. I give this account of the correspondence between the council and the Brothers conducted in the local press not to apportion blame to either side, but merely to introduce the story as it has since developed, and underlining the fact that the highest figure mentioned in the correspondence is £1.3 million, one of the offers from a developer.

When the site opened up, there was a report in the local press that there would be 300 housing units on it, and that individual sites were going at £30,000. Locals began totting up and coming up with a total site value of £9 million, even before a spade was put in it. Some sites were £30,000, others were £125,000. Ten years on, the site is still developing and probably under 200 units have been built. A number of superior apartment blocks were built, and it would not surprise me if the penthouses were reserved for National Lottery winners. I wonder what Harry Fitzsimons would think of it all.

Nobody could blame the Alexian Brothers for wanting the best deal possible; I just hope and trust it was many times the £1.3 million which was originally on the table. If it wasn't, 'the Brothers' was the greatest 'steal' in development history.

The other great local issue to exercise the minds of The Point populace in the last 20 years has been the development plans of the Warrenpoint Harbour Authority, which envisaged the filling-in of what we call 'the Town Dock'. The first proposal came in the mid-80s, when the key element of its plan was to 'in fill the old Town Dock to provide hard standing area for containers, timber and parking'. As someone wrote in the local papers, 'gone would be the vista of the Cooley Mountains and sea, and replacing it would be a concrete parking area for stacks of containers, storage sheds and the likes.'

The business people in The Square and Dock Street came out strongly against the plan, with Maurice Murphy producing sketches of what the finished article might look like. Peter O'Hare, of the Glenmore, predicted that any such development would require a security fence of at least 12 feet in height from Jenkins' Shipping Office to the end of Dock Street and beyond. Jack Begg, of The Bakery, was of the view that, 'as well as containers and stacks of timber, we were sure to have heaps of scrap metal.' All three have passed to their eternal reward.

The local Conservation and Preservation Society, which was powered by Johnnie O'Hagan and his wife, Anne, made a strong case against the plan, part of which turned out to be prophetic. I quote, 'It is a very real fear that the fill-in of the Old Dock would only be the first stage of a development which would eventually extend as far as the Breakwater.' The Breakwater had been built by the Harbour Authority with the agreement of the Newry and Mourne District Council some ten years before. Some locals always viewed it as a Trojan horse.

Jim McCart, who was the council representative on the Harbour Authority at the time, expressed his disappointment that 'the Harbour Authority have decided to apply for planning permission to fill in the old Town Dock.' He stated, 'As a member of the Harbour Authority, I am conscious of the importance of the harbour to the town, but I feel there are other alternatives to that proposed.'

Eddie McGrady, the SDLP spokesman for the environment, weighed in with his support in opposition to the plan; he suggested that the old Town Dock could be developed as an environmental facility, and should be incorporated into the proposed seafront development plan.

The Conservation Society organised a protest collecting over 2,000 signatures opposing the plan—and such was the volume of opposition that the Harbour Authority did not go ahead with the project. That was all back in 1985.

Fourteen years later, with a new management in place, the Harbour Authority embarked on a massive campaign in support of proposals to change the face of the town. These included 'an extension to deep water quay; cargo handling area involving land reclamation; dredging of an area for future marina; and the filling in of the Town Dock. A training wall from the breakwater to an extended pier at the Town Dock would enclose the marina area, and provide berths for the unloading of ships.'

The Harbour Authority campaign, which is said to have cost in excess of £300,000, was conducted at local and national media levels; it included presentations to Newry and Mourne District Council, the local branch of the SDLP, and two public presentations for the local residents in the Town Hall, where they came under fire from many quarters because of the opposition of the vast majority of the town's people to the project. A new marina was the bait for the locals, even though there was no indication from the authority or the council as to who would actually provide it. The Harbour Authority would take responsibility for dredging the area and nothing more.

As secretary of the local SDLP, and after all the public presentations had been made, I invited a representative group of townspeople to a meeting in the Balmoral Hotel. Following a couple of lengthy sessions, a unified body emerged to take on the Harbour Authority under the banner *Save Our Seafront—SOS*. Calling the meeting was probably my only contribution to the campaign, for as things developed it became obvious that we had a mixture of enthusiasm and expertise which was reflected in the highly professional campaign we ran. The Harbour Authority made great efforts to get the backing of the Newry and Mourne District Council for the project, but my son Hugh, a member of that body and of SOS, did a remarkable job in keeping the council's mind open.

When the planning process got under way, SOS lodged hundreds of objections and a Public Inquiry into the application was ordered.

SOS had a couple of well-supported, successful public meetings in the Town Hall even as the nitty gritty of organising the campaign got under way. Money was a basic need, and SOS set themselves a target of £25,000; this was achieved in a comparatively short space of time. A succession of well-produced SOS news bulletins kept the locals informed of what was going on, while a skilled professional presentation was prepared for public bodies, and public representatives who had an interest.

Very early in the campaign, I sought some free legal aid from Ken McMahon, a Warrenpoint man and a well-known QC, whose father, Peter, had been chairman of the urban council during my father's membership of that body. Ken advised that the top man in the field of planning law was a chap called Reg Weir, QC. We had a lengthy discussion and I left him with the assurance of his full support, even to the extent of representing us if need be at the planning inquiry. Of course, Reg Weir's reputation was already well known to those members of SOS who were involved in various professions, and he was chosen to present our case.

The first time the full SOS group met Mr Weir was after the preliminary meeting of the commissioners in Warrenpoint Town Hall; he advised us that he had been retained by a Belfast shipping company to oppose the plans of the Harbour Authority. He went on to indicate that, while he was happy to continue with dual representation, if SOS preferred to seek another legal voice it would be acceptable to him. It did not take SOS too long to decide to stay with Reg Weir. He, in turn, thanked us for the vote of confidence and to our pleasure advised that our share of his fee would be the minor one.

In the preliminary meeting that night, the two female planning commissioners, Marie Campbell and Elaine Kingham, introduced themselves and laid down the ground rules for the arguments. A small number of other interests were represented.

When the battle was eventually joined in September 2000 in the Town Hall, the argument for the Harbour Authority team was spearheaded by Mr Donal Deeny, QC, and for the home team it was Reginald Weir, QC, known to everyone as 'Reg,' though in the confines of the battlefield itself, he was Mr Weir.

The inquiry lasted nearly three weeks and I must have been the only member of the public who sat through every single session. During one of the more tedious afternoon sessions, when things were very legalistic, Reg needed a bit of local information, a yes or no answer, and he turned round to his 'back-up team'. There I was, sitting on my own in the hall. The right man in the right place.

Regrettably, Reg was not available on the second Friday of the inquiry when members of the public were able to voice their objections or support. In his cross-examinations of expert witnesses Reg was in turn scathing, cynical, derisory and humorous, often drawing murmurs of approval and laughter from our side of the hall. He knew that he had an appreciative gallery.

So when Jim McCart, one of our local councillors and member of the Harbour Authority who had opposed that body's plan 15 years before, rose to support the new proposals, he got a comparatively easy passage from Reg Weir's understudy. Not so from the serried ranks of SOS members and supporters who were there in great numbers for the occasion. When Jim said that he agreed with the sentiments expressed in an anonymous letter to the *Newry Reporter* the week before that, 'the Town Dock was a dirty hole' we were ready to lynch him, for it was the Harbour Authority of which he was a member that had made it so. When our chairman, Liam Bradley, stood up to show a threatening clenched fist, he expressed all our outrage and the hapless Jim had to complain to the commissioners about the unveiled 'intimidation.'

But you couldn't fall out with Jim McCart, and he and I have laughed about that day many times since. When all was said and done, and the commissioners had heard all the arguments, they came down in favour of the townspeople. The Town Dock and the seafront were saved.

That judgement was given in the spring of 2001. Three years later, to the credit of the Harbour Authority, a new plan gave us a Town Dock which, besides providing first class harbour facilities, has transformed the town centre. The deep water, which was central to the original proposals, appears to have been found, for much bigger vessels are now using the port regularly.

The Harbour Authority has reason to thank SOS for its stance in opposing the initial proposals, which would have been a disaster for the town. It would not be out of place if a complimentary plaque recognising this fact was part of the civic furniture at that corner of the dock where the Famine commemorative tablet stands. The final thought on the seafront suggests that the matter of a marina must now come into focus. I leave it to the Newry and Mourne District Council to sort out the details.

While it would never have been considered a 'political issue,' the proposed Narrow Water Bridge is in the process of becoming a reality now that the politicians in both jurisdictions have taken it on board, and I am hopeful of seeing it in place before I take leave of Mother Earth. Bridge-building is an important exercise in the country at the minute, but the notion of a bridge at Narrow Water has been occupying the mind of one Warrenpoint man for much of 40 years. Donal O'Tierney, like his father before him, looked after the medical needs of a big part of the community until his retirement a few years ago. If any one man has to take credit for pursuing the cause of 'The Bridge' it has to be Donal. Since the latest announcement regarding the project, I sought to find out the full story of his involvement and make it part of this book.

It all began back in 1971 when he made a submission on the Newry Area Plan as produced by the Steering Committee at the Ministry of Development at Stormont. It was an extensive document for it made the case for a by-pass road and many proposals for the improvement of the town, some of which were prophetic. On the case for the bridge he had this to say:

> 'While I appreciate that the amount of money available for development is not unlimited, I feel that the case for a bridge at Narrow Water ought to be considered. Such a bridge would save expensive improvements to the Newry-Omeath road as traffic would use the dual carriageway on the North side of the estuary as far as Narrow Water.'

He went on to detail half a dozen advantages that would accrue for the area.

While the proposal did not merit inclusion in the area plan, Donal kept plugging away, and by 1979 he had convinced the Newry and Mourne District Council and the Louth County Council that it was worth examining. The two bodies jointly commissioned an engineering survey, carried out by consulting engineers Messrs Nicholas O'Dwyer, which showed that a bridge at Narrow Water presented no engineering problems. Even though the proposal was shelved by the two councils, on Donal's imitative the Warrenpoint-Cooley Bridge Action Group, with members from both sides of the lough, came into being in 1991.

Well-attended public meetings were held and presentations were made to a number of interested bodies over the years. With the changing political dispensation brought about by the Good Friday and St Andrew's Agreements, things began to happen. PJ Bradley, the local assembly member, arranged a meeting between representatives of The Bridge Action Group and Mr Noel Dempsey, the Minister of the Environment in Dublin. The outcome was a new feasibility study financed by the Louth County Council, Newry and Mourne District Council and the Department of the Environment. That was published back in 2002. Since then, things have moved slowly but surely and it was late in 2007 when Mr Dermot Ahearne announced that the Irish Government would fund the bridge—at which announcement cheers were heard all round the lough shores. A number of public presentations have been made on the progress of the concept and everything indicated the positive approach of the Irish Government. Whether or not the most recent financial down turn will delay the completion of the bridge is not clear at this time, but in the long term it seems assured.

When it does come to be a reality I have no idea what the bridge might be called other than The Narrow Water Bridge, but I think there should be a place on it somewhere for the name of Donal O'Tierney.

I revisit the wider political scene at a time when the main players are *Sinn Féin* and the Democratic Unionists, and to bewail the fact that the SDLP has lost its premier role in the process it initiated and led for so long. It is a moot point to argue that much of its failure has been of its own making and, dare I say it, at the higher levels of the organisation. Political leadership is a rather transient commodity in this television era when a good or bad 'performance' on the box can be the deciding factor, though this was not the problem with the SDLP.

My concerns about the SDLP leadership began as far back as 1996 when John Hume visited the South Down area during the European election campaign. I was in his company for part of that time, and it became obvious that he was not a well man. Others picked up the same signals, and the people much closer to him must have done likewise. That he completed his last two terms in the European Parliament was a tribute to his political instincts, rather than any display of the political sagacity which shaped his leadership of the party and which deservedly earned him his Nobel Peace Prize.

Most of those who have worked with John Hume, and who have written about him, have noted his inability to have confidants, not to speak of advisors. All his major initiatives appear to have been strategic solos; while this might be regarded by some as firm leadership, there are issues which require consultation and advice. For most people's money, such an issue would be a leader's retirement and the consideration of the best possible replacement.

I was not a member of the SDLP party in 2001 when John retired, but I was a totally committed supporter. Like most members and supporters, I was taking it for granted that his successor would be Seamus Mallon. Imagine the shock we all got the next day when Mallon announced his retirement from the Deputy Leader's post, and ruled himself out of the succession stakes. I did not know the mechanics of the dual decision which left us leaderless with one fell swoop, but I do know that I exclaimed to the family, as we watched and listened, 'Holy God, Hume has not discussed his retirement with him.'

If that was the case it borders on the unforgivable. If the two men discussed the issue and felt that it was in the best interests of the party that they should both forgo their leadership roles, it would have been unbelievable. But that was not the case, as I was later to learn. The leader did not discuss his retirement with his deputy, and the first Mallon heard of it was when he got a phoned enquiry for a comment from some of the political journalists.

None of this is to under-value the qualities of Mark Durkan, who in less than two years had to acquire the stature of leadership and attempt to contain the rising tide of *Sinn Féin* support. It may well be that things might not have been any better with Mallon's hand on the helm, but there can be no doubting the enormous stature of the man, not alone in the party but over the entire national spectrum. Now that the Derryman has retired from the leadership after eight years, the SDLP has a lot to think about, and one can only wish his successor, Margaret Ritchie, well. Politics is all about leadership in this day and age and the task facing the new leader is enormous.

The most important statement from a British Government Minister since the partitioning of the country was made by Peter Brooke in 1994, when he said, 'The British Government has no selfish, strategic or economic interest in remaining in Ireland.' The Prime Minister of the time, John Major, and all of his Government colleagues indicated their agreement by their silence. When I heard him speak it, I said aloud, 'The conquest is finally over.' It was left to a Labour administration to dot the *i's* and cross the *t's* and, with all its imperfections, 'the Agreement'— whether we call it Good Friday, Belfast or St Andrew's, as both Irish and British Governments indicate—is here to stay, though it has become obvious that some aspects require clarification.

If a section of the Unionist community cannot bring themselves to accept that the conquest is over, that reality must be more clearly defined. In this regard, it would be helpful if public broadcasting—and indeed commercial broadcasting— modified its British ethos and reflected a more balanced approach to both communities. A few Irish language programmes a week and a daily helping of Hugo Duncan are on their own hardly sufficient to create 'a sense of Ireland.' Neither does the Six County map, which introduces so many programmes, suggest that we are part of the Irish mainland.

Then there is 'the symbols thing'. I would never have been either a flag carrier or a flag waver and I would condemn out of hand the politicising of the national flag, which is the *Sinn Féin* saturation strategy of 'every pole a flagpole'. Our two emblems are entitled to the same degree of respect in the situation we are in, and I would hope that in due time, when things are being reviewed, the Irish dimension in the area of symbols will be attended to. I note the Stormont building has two flagpoles, though only one seems to be used. It will be a sign of our maturity and tolerance when the Irish flag occupies the other one.

A section of the Unionist people is claiming that they are now the down-trodden people, the people who suffer discrimination. Their culture is under attack, apparently, because they are prevented from marching at three or four locations round this part of the Province, where their cultural march is deemed by the locals as *conquistadorial*, as undoubtedly it is meant to be.

'Why can we march at Rossnowlagh (another part of the province) and we cannot march at Garvaghy Road, or the extra one hundred yards on the Springfield Road?' they ask. The simple answer is that the locals in Donegal do not see their march as 'conquistadorial,' and it isn't.

Now that *Sinn Féin* and the Democratic Unionists are in the driving seats, after accepting the policies they previously opposed, Unionism has to accept the fact that the conquest is over and that we live as real equals as British and Irish citizens, not goading each other, not taunting each other, but respecting and trusting each other. It does not help the agreement to get bedded down if *Sinn Féin* keep parroting the 'united Ireland in 15 years' theme. Either they accept the relevant provision in 'the Agreement' covering that eventuality, or they don't.

33 — The Price We Paid

In the aftermath of this horrible period those of us who have lived through it may well ask, 'Has the outcome been worth the price?' — and I am not talking about the billions which are still accumulating. I am talking about the lives which have been lost, almost 4,000 of them. It is in the nature of things that events like Omagh, Enniskillen, Bloody Friday and La Monde are the highlights of remembrance, while Warrenpoint will be remembered for the Narrow Water bombing. That event took the lives of 18 British soldiers who, for most of us, are anonymous names who will be remembered only by those who loved them most, their grieving families. Warrenpoint families have had to grieve, too, but the local victims of the violence are not anonymous names to us, nor are they forgotten. We meet their parents, brothers and sisters every day. They are victims, too, and I feel compelled to record the names of their loved ones, most of whom I knew, to give them a degree of permanence in the communal memory.

When Edmund and Anne Woolsey bought the Ulster Hotel in the late 60s, they came to Warrenpoint with high hopes for the future. They had two children and by 1972 their offspring had increased to four. In September of that year, Edmund had loaned his car to a friend who parked it in Dundalk where it was stolen. Sometime later, he was advised that it had shown up at Glassdrumman, near Crossmaglen, and could be collected. With his friend, he went to collect the car and in turning the ignition key he set off the booby trap bomb which caused his instant death. Edmund, an Armagh man, whom I met a few times in his short years in The Point, was aged 31, and the first Warrenpoint casualty of The Troubles.

Mattie Campbell was a young Burren man of 22, well known to me as 'young Campbell,' for I was at Carrick School with his father Pat, his Uncle Peter and his Aunt Mary. Like most young Burren men, Mattie was into sport and football in particular. On a Saturday night in April 1976, he was having a drink in the Ulster Hotel when a bomb exploded on the premises. He was severely injured and was taken to hospital in Belfast where he died three days later, 27 April. While most of the bombings were carried out by the IRA, this particular one was attributed to the Ulster Volunteer Force (UVF). Both his parents have passed to their eternal reward but the Campbell families are still grieving

Less than two months later, Liam Prince, a 27 year old teacher in St Mary's High School in Newry, was on his way to the Ballymascanlon Hotel when he was caught up in an incident in the Cloghogue area in which soldiers opened fire on his car and shot him dead. Apparently a bomb had gone off and there was a deal of confusion, but an innocent man lost his life and the lives of another family were shattered. Liam's mother was Lily Magee. I have good reason to recall her capacity for doing good, for she was a founding member of The Parents and Friends Association for the Mentally Handicapped in the Newry and Mourne area. Among the family who mourned Liam was his Down's syndrome sister, Carmel, on whom he doted and who died exactly nine months after his death. Jim Prince, his father, was an Englishman who was reared on the Royal Estate at Sandringham where his father was employed. He took early retirement from Reed's factory, where he was a very popular figure. He died only a few years into that retirement. Lily became confined to the house for the last few years of her long life. I used visit her occasionally and always found her to be an example of Christian goodness, fortitude and forgiveness. She died in May 2009.

Ivan Toombs was a part-time member of the Ulster Defence Association, in which he was a major. He worked as a customs officer and was in his office at Warrenpoint Docks when he was shot by the IRA. He was married with five children. I knew him from his earliest years; the Toombs children walked to school over Summerhill from Drumsesk Place where they lived. When he attended Newry High School he would often have travelled on my bus. It was there he developed his skill on the hockey pitch; his enthusiasm for the game as a stalwart of Newry Olympic lasted until he died at the age of 42 on 16 January 1981. I was 58 on the same day.

I have written about the Toombs family in an early chapter, and it is worth recording that they are probably the oldest family in Warrenpoint. Many years ago I got the present of a small booklet 'Oméith'—Its History—Ancient And Modern written by an tAthair Lorcán Ó Muireadhaigh, the famous Fr Larry, founder of the Irish College in Omeath in 1912. In its pages, it has the census lists of 1666 and 1766 for the townlands of Omeath. In the 1766 list for the townland of Dromula are Chris Toombs and George Toombs. The Point was still a green-field site then but in time came Toombs' Corner. Also on that same list is the name 'Jno' (sic) Bailey whose lineage must have included Johnny and his son, Charlie, who maintained the ferry service at Narrow Water for generations.

Richard McKee of Clermont Gardens was 27 and also a member of the Ulster Defence Regiment (UDR) when he met his death after the vehicle he was travelling in was ambushed near Castlewellan on 28 April 1981. His father, also Richard, was a Bessbrook native and his mother, Florence Irwin, a member of a well-known Warrenpoint family who lived originally at Hayes' Row, a quaint and lovely row of gardened cottages; but it was bulldozed into oblivion to make space for the Newry Road and the golf links. Florrie's father, Billy, was one of those milkmen of my early days; her mother, and indeed all the Irwin children, were regular travellers on my bus.

Richard had been in the Army for some years before transferring to the UDR. After his death the family moved to Banbridge where his father died some years ago. Florrie and her family are well remembered by her neighbours in Clermont Gardens.

William Gordon Wilson was a Sergeant in the RUC and serving in Armagh in February 1983. He was the victim of a bomb which exploded in one of the city streets on the day before his 30th birthday. He was married with one child. I did not know this family very well though people tell me I should remember his father, Billy, who was a native of the Ardarragh area, near Rathfriland, and who came to live at Ballydesland. Billy was a prisoner of war in the Japanese theatre of operations.

Brian McNally, a native of Rostrevor, was living in the town in 1984 when he was abducted by the IRA. His body was found in South Armagh near Meigh on

26 July 1984. I knew Brian only slightly, but I knew his parents well and they were the finest of people.

I have already written about a John (Johnnie) Dowd and the Dowd family who were our neighbours on Summerhill. I did not have a notion then that I would be writing about another John Dowd, grandson of that Johnny, to record his death in a mortar bomb attack on Newry RUC Barracks on the last day of February 1985, when eight other policemen lost their lives. John was 31 and married. He had served in one of the English county police forces before joining the RUC. It was by sheer chance that he was in Newry Barracks on that day, for he was a member of the drugs squad based elsewhere and had come to Newry to interview someone at the Barracks. I knew John well as a boy; he, too, travelled on my bus to and from Newry High School. From an early age, he was a member of the Warrenpoint Silver Band and was over Summerhill regularly on his way to band practice. Both on the bus and over the hill, it was always, 'Mr Carr'. His father, Jack, with whom I played regularly in my soccer playing days, died some years ago, while his mother, Lily, is in a retirement home in Banbridge.

I am very conscious of the one Warrenpoint female victim in the almost 30 years of strife, for I was over a year into retirement, and in my home on Summerhill on the fateful April morning in 1989, when the youngest of the Warrenpoint victims lost her life. A bomb was set off at the RUC Barracks in Charlotte Street. It did only minor damage to the Barracks but it wrecked the shop and office of Pete Morgan's building firm adjacent to it. Joanne Reilly worked in the office while Margaret, Pete's wife, looked after the shop. Margaret, who was in the shop at the front of the building, had severe injuries when the rescue team got to her, but she survived. The office at the rear, where Joanne worked, took the full force of the blast; before the rescue team got to her she had breathed her last. Just twenty, and the only daughter of Paul and Anne Reilly who live in Rossmara Park, Joanne was one of the few of the younger generation I would have known by name, for she regularly passed over Summerhill on her way to or from work.

After hearing the explosion I was at the scene within minutes to join scores of other locals in an atmosphere of concern and confusion. Think what it must have been like for her grandmother, who lived only two doors from the Barracks, and for Paul and Anne, her parents. Paul was at his work in St Mark's High School where he was caretaker, while Anne was doing the chores at their home in Rossmara when the bomb exploded. Think what the passing years have been like for them.

There were two other Warrenpoint related deaths and they were both members of the RUC Reserve who were based at Warrenpoint Barracks. On 20 February 1983, William Edward Magill, a young Belfast man of 20, left the Barracks to go to Imelda Connolly's corner shop across the road about lunchtime. A couple of gunmen emerged from nowhere and shot him dead.

William Fullerton was on his way home to Sheeptown after completing his duty on 10 January 1984, when he was shot dead in his car as he approached the Greenbank roundabout close to Newry. He left a wife and two sons.

As well as deciding who lived or died, accidently or otherwise, our 'liberators' were of the view that hotels were economic targets and for that reason the Ardmore in Newry, the Great Northern in Rostrevor and the Crown in Warrenpoint were legitimate targets, along with many others about the area.

It is the Crown Hotel, and its unique attraction for locals and visitors over my lifetime, about which I wish to write. While I never would have been much of 'a drinking man,' I was always conscious of the *bonhomie* which existed among patrons of both the front and the back bars. For them, the Crown was special—and it was. It was a landmark in The Square for almost 150 years and for more than half that period it was owned and run by the O'Neill family, latterly by Jim, the youngest son. There were too many sides to Jim's diverse and wonderful character to attempt to describe the man. It is sufficient to say that he was much loved. Both he and the Crown are sorely missed. In the last couple of years of his life he developed Alzheimers and spent them in a care home in Newry, where he died in March 2010. I often thought if he had been allowed to run his hotel he would have had a different ending to his life. But what's another victim.

34—Late Late Reviews

One night in the mid-seventies I was preparing for bed when the phone rang. It was my sister, Detta McCabe, from Chicago.

'You will never guess who I am watching on television, debating with Terence O'Neill, and wiping the floor with him,' and I never would have guessed if I had been trying for a month of Sundays.

'Denis Donoghue,' she continued, 'and he's powerful.'

The Irish use of the word 'powerful' is unique. We use it to describe weddings, funerals, wakes, weather, football matches, speeches and what have you. When my sister said 'powerful,' I knew exactly what she meant. When the English use the word 'powerful' they are describing something which is full of power and nothing else. It was a powerful surprise to learn that Denis Donoghue, above all people, would have been debating 'the Irish question' with the former prime minister of the Stormont Government.

My sister's memory of Denis would have been of a lengthy lad whose soprano voice had us half-way to heaven on Sunday mornings, and all the way at Christmas Mass with his *Silent Night*. She would hardly have been aware of his standing in the best literary and academic circles in the English-speaking world.

Denis Donoghue and his father have already been introduced in this book on an earlier page, a Kerryman, known to the locals as 'Steve' after the famous jockey, retired from the force in 1946. The family moved to Tullow in Co. Carlow, the home place of Mrs Donoghue. This was a bitter blow to Warrenpoint and Down football for the elder son, Tim, was a notable performer at club and county level. Admittedly, he suffered from a knee injury which gave him some trouble from time to time, but he continued to play with the local Tullow club, once he settled there. He and I kept a line of communication open over the years even though we never put pen to paper. On St Patrick's Day and All-Ireland Final days we went to the same spot on Hill 16, or on the odd occasion he would turn up at Down games, both when I was playing and later when I was managing.

Denis is the man under discussion, however, and it did not really surprise the Warrenpoint people who knew him that he would go far. I did not really appreciate just how far he had gone, until I had a chance meeting with Brother Newell, formerly my teacher at The Abbey, Newry, and at this time principal in CBS Grammar School in Armagh. This was in the late 50s and after the informal exchange of greetings, he queried, 'Do you ever have any contact with Tim Donoghue?,' and when I told him the nature of our odd meetings, he continued in a more serious vein, 'The next time you speak to him, would you ask him to ask his brother in UCD to stop demeaning the Brothers. Some of our students are refusing to go to his lectures and I am very disappointed in him.'

I expressed some surprise, and doubts, that a word from Tim would have had any effect—'Our fellow, will you lay-off the Brothers'—but as the years passed, the eminence of Denis grew as professor of Modern English and American Literature, and later Henry James professor of English and American letters at New York University. He delivered the prestigious Reith Lectures for the BBC, some of which I heard, and was suitably impressed. Some months later, when the late Fr Eamon McGivern was home on holidays from the diocese of Plymouth where he ministered, he told me how he had driven to the highest point in the parish to get the best possible reception for all the series. Eamon, a classmate of Denis at The Abbey confessed, 'There were a couple of times if I had been near him I would have kicked his arse.'

It was July 1983 before I met Denis in the flesh for the first time since he left The Point in 1946. The occasion was at the summer graduations in UCD where my daughter, Louise, was among those receiving their degrees. Our meeting took place at the post-ceremony refreshments and was of short duration. That did not bother me in the least, for I was conscious that he was involved officially, and there were many people there who would have had a call on him.

When Tim died rather suddenly in 1990 I was to meet Denis again, with his sisters May and Kathleen, neither of whom I had seen since they left The Point. Tim's wife Kitty, and Mary, his daughter, were long standing friends, so Louise drove me down to Tullow for the funeral.

Remembering his 'powerful' performance against Terence O'Neill on American television those years before, I had it in my mind to invite Denis to The Point the following year, which was the 75th Anniversary of the Easter Rising. While I knew it was going to be a low-key celebration and much different to the 50th in 1966, I thought he would be eminently suitable for a talk or two.

When I had the opportunity of speaking to him at the meal after the funeral, it was a much more leisurely exchange than our previous meeting in Dublin. He was genuinely and pleasantly surprised when I put the proposal to him.

'I would love to go up to The Point to speak, but I have to tell you that I have a book coming out soon and I might not be too popular in Warrenpoint when it does,' was his rejoinder.

There had been some indication earlier in the year that he was working on a book about his years in Warrenpoint, and that was in my thinking when my ideas were formulating about the invitation. When I dismissed the notion of any such concerns he finished that part of our chat with, 'We'll leave it until next year, and we'll see how things go.'

A couple of months later, my brother, Paddy, came on the phone from Chicago. 'I'm reading in the paper a review of a book by Denis Donoghue about The Point.'

I was surprised that it was coming out in America before Ireland or Britain, but I'm sure there was a reason for that. The brother thought the review was quite favourable and I asked him to send me a copy, for it seemed to me that it would be unlikely to be published at home before Christmas. He sent me two copies and I thought instantly that one of them would make a nice Christmas present for Bishop John Crawford, who had been home on holiday from the Solomon Islands a few months before. It should be said that I sent the book the day after receiving it from Chicago and without ever reading a line of my own copy. Had I done so, it is unlikely that I would have sent it to Bishop John.

Earlier I have written about the Chesterton Seminar at Maynooth in 2002.

I return to it now, to a conversation at dinner on the second evening, when Fr Oliver Rafferty, a Jesuit priest who was one of the contributors at the seminar, was sitting with me. When he learned I was from Warrenpoint his immediate reaction was, 'Did you know Denis Donoghue?' and when I answered in the affirmative, he followed with, 'What did the Warrenpoint people think of his book?'

'Most of us were disappointed, some were shocked, and some were deeply hurt,' I answered, and he responded with a sympathetic comment. I did not tell him that I had it in mind to respond to Denis in due course. *Warrenpoint* is the work of a master craftsman, as Denis undoubtedly is, but much of what he has written of his days spent in The Point is a fantasy, coloured by the events of the past 30 years. Nobody who lived in the Warrenpoint of his day recognised the place about which he wrote.

To paint a picture of Warrenpoint almost as a sectarian cesspool, even now, would be a travesty. To do it on the Warrenpoint of 70 years ago is an outrage.

'Who is my neighbour?'[39] Denis asks, and answers with the catechism definition, before asking again, 'Where, I neglected to ask, does that put Protestants?'[40] A couple of pages later he explains, 'When I say that I kept my distance from Protestants, I mean to say further, that I did this upon instinct.'[41]

Denis had already told us, 'the ability to tell a Protestant from a Catholic in Warrenpoint was a social necessity in those days, names were a help but not decisive.'[42]

Now the Protestants whom I lived with on Summerhill, the Taylors, the Hodges, the Dowds and many others, were our neighbours, in exactly the same way as were the other residents on the hill. If Gweny Dowd had lived longer on Summerhill I could possibly have married her, for she was my first love, when we were both under ten.

Protestants and Catholics lived side by side in every area of the town in complete harmony, but his father, 'wanted me to live as among aliens' with names like 'Newell and Chew designating Protestant.'[43] Denis has already told us that he could tell the Protestants instinctively. But Sydney Chew was a pillar of the Catholic Church, and was a regular collector both at the door, and round the church. It must have come as a surprise to Desmond, Eddie and Anne Marie Chew to learn that their father, Sydney, had been a Protestant, as designated by both Denis, with his surname, and Seamus Heaney, quoted by Denis, 'that Norman, Ken and Sydney signalled Prod.'[44]

'We were a Catholic family. That meant we bought our groceries at Catholic shops—Curran's mostly, and the butcher Fitzpatrick—and were on speaking terms only with Catholics. My mother was an exception: she was friends with Mrs Harper,

---

39   Denis Donoghue, *Warrenpoint,* London, Jonathon Cape, 1990, *p.* 49

40   *Ibid., p.* 49

41   *Ibid., p.* 53

42   *Ibid., p.* 47

43   *Ibid., p.* 48

44   Seamus Heaney, *North,* London, Faber and Faber, 1975, *p.* 59

wife of one of the policeman, a Protestant.'[45]

To claim, as Denis does, that his mother went to the Catholic butcher rather than the Protestant butcher is nonsense. To begin with, there was no butcher called Fitzpatrick. His mother went to Johnny Ward for her meat because it was only over the road from the Barracks. To go to the Protestant butcher, she would have had to go to the top of Church Street, to Jimmy Cumming, where many, many Catholics bought their meat, for both he and his wife, a Donegal woman, were friends of everyone in the town. Fitzpatrick's was a seven-day-week corner shop. And to suggest that his mother, in talking to Mrs Harper, the wife of a Protestant policeman, was an exception, is a fairy tale beyond belief. One year during the school holidays I was message boy for Joe Duffy, grocer, and famous for his pies, and I regularly brought 'an order' to Mrs Harper, who was a lovely woman and friendly with everyone in the town. Her husband, Joe, was never known to summons anybody.

Could I ask why Denis sought to dramatise 'the name thing' by announcing that the top man of The Shankill Butchers, Murphy, was 'Protestant,' when he could have referred to the chemist a few doors up the street from him. James Murphy and his family were real Protestants, who had the respect and friendship of everyone.

'The Marching Season' as described by Denis did not exist in the 30s and I am not sure that the 12th July was even a Bank Holiday. The 'Loyal Orders,' as they are now called, marched three times over the summer, and when the local lodge set off for the demonstration most of us would still be in bed. Scarva was, and is the magnet on the 13th, and then there was nothing until Black Saturday, the last Saturday in August. On those occasions when 'the twelfth' was held in The Point, I never was aware of any 'passions being aroused,' apart from my own indignation in 1938 when the tricolour was removed from the perches. But to illustrate just how much Denis has drawn on his imagination about 'the marching season,' the reality was the 'the twelfth' was not celebrated at all during the War years. There was no 'marching season' anywhere in the last six years of his life in Warrenpoint if he left before the 12th in 1946.

However critical I may seem to be of Denis, there are passages in *Warrenpoint* which engendered no small degree of sympathy for him when he referred to the girls, and particularly to Isobel Bridges, 'a girl who moved, at least on skates, like a queen. I wanted to dance with her, but it was out of the question, her father was a local manager of the railway and a Protestant.'[46]

Every fellow in the Town Hall wanted to skate with Isobel. She was a beautiful girl and, as Denis described her, 'the best skater among the girls.'[47] In fact, Billy Beattie, who acted as skating master, complete with whistle, always chose Isobel as partner to demonstrate new steps. Billy had more new steps than we needed.

Unlike Denis, I did not have any inhibitions about Protestants and I skated with her often, though not as often as I would have liked, for she was one of my Protestant neighbours on Summerhill. Not a mention from Denis about Isobel's

45   Denis Donoghue, *Warrenpoint*, p. 46

46   *Ibid., pp. 147–148*

47   *Ibid., p. 147*

younger sister, Roberta. She was an enthusiastic skater, too, though not in the classical mould of her sister. She was a heavier build of a girl who loved when 'fours' was called, when she would invariably be the girl on the outside, cornering at 40 mph. Many a time I was her partner in the foursomes, but once I was sitting just beneath the stage when the partner she had released his grip, and she landed on my lap at the speed of an express train. It took me an hour to recover. I have greater reason to remember Roberta than Isobel.

It strikes me that Denis, in confessing that the name, 'Isobel, to his cost and pain, was a Protestant name'[48], suggests a slight attraction which went beyond the skates, and it occurs to me that there could be another reason why he might not have skated with Isobel. In the summer of 1944 Denis was all of 16 years. I was 21, and Isobel was about the same age.

When Denis claims, as he did in his book, that he excelled among the boys in the skating scene, he is exaggerating slightly, for I can assure readers that long, lean lads do not look graceful on roller skates and he would never have been a suitable skating partner for Isobel. Despite his claim to excellence, it is my view that Denis on skates was not a pretty sight.

I have already mentioned my visit to Bob Jones, when I was anxious to tap into his memory bank. In the course of that wonderful afternoon, I asked if he had ever read Denis Donoghue's *Warrenpoint*.

'Indeed I did, wasn't it a dreadful concoction,' he replied dismissively.

I will give just one other example of how we got on with our Protestant neighbours in The Point, and it relates to a Mrs Hannah Watson, who would be remembered as caretaker at the old Technical School in St Peter's Street. She was a widow all my lifetime, and her only son, George, (who used to play football with me in Gilmore's garden,) lost his life while in the RAF during the War.

All her life she was very active in the British Legion and other charities. I was not aware she had gone to reside in a home in Kilkeel until I received a letter from a firm of solicitors with a cheque for £100. It was a donation for the GAA Band, of which I was the secretary, from Mrs Watson. This was the biggest single donation we had ever received at that time. I went to Kilkeel to thank her and she brushed my profuse thanks to silence with one sentence, 'I loved the band and your mother was my best chum when we grew up together in Meeting Street.' I knew that to be true, for my mother always spoke fondly of Hannah McCullough.

Bad as it was, the picture of sectarianism that Denis painted of the town did not cause as much hurt and embarrassment as did the pictures he drew of some of the inhabitants, even those of whom, it could be said, he was indebted.

Master Glancy never taught me, and I have long since forgiven him for the two whacks he gave me the day after the sea-plane landed on the lough, but I knew his family well when they lived in the town. His youngest son, Luke, was a classmate until I left St Peter's to go to Burren. He was one of my cronies when we were suspended for going to see my Uncle Hugh playing football. He followed a career in medicine and died about twenty years ago in Canada. Two other

---

48   *Ibid., p. 48*

brothers, Martin and Tom, who was also a lovely footballer, died many years before *Warrenpoint* was written. I understand that two sisters, one a Medical Missionary, were both alive when it was published. Warrenpoint people did not like that.

Master Glancy was an alcoholic before the definition was coined, and if he had other problems they would not have been known to his pupils. At any rate, Denis gave Mr Glancy a curt farewell: 'I don't remember if he was replaced, or who got the principal's job, because soon after, I went to school in Newry.'[49] I have already indicated that Mr Glancy was indeed replaced.

It was probably in his assessment of his teacher, Jack Crawford, that Denis caused most hurt and shock to the townspeople, not to speak of the Crawford family. While the following quote is neither hurtful nor shocking, I question its accuracy.

'He had strange hands. His nails were bitten down to the quick, and the palms of his hands were as soft as butter. He played the organ in the church, and I was in the choir.'[50]

Denis might have been in the choir, but Mr Crawford was not playing the organ. In an early chapter, I have described the circumstances of the choir's demise in 1931, and his 'retirement'. He did not resume at the organ until after the Donoghues had left in 1946. I have no doubt, however, that Denis (on the violin) was part of the Crawford ensemble at that time, and would have been aware of any defects in the master's make-up.

The assessment continues, 'He was a terrible teacher, except for stories and the talk of music. He, too, left the room as often as the coast was clear and Mr Glancy gone, but Mr Crawford only went for a walk. He had a peculiar manner of walking, always on the bias. If you walked straight along the street with him, he kept cutting across your path and crowding you off the pavement, as if he hated a straight line. His body was in some acute or oblique relation to his soul. Even if he intended to walk from his house at the west corner of The Square to go up Church Street, he always left the pavement and walked as if he were going to the school or the church, and then he would wheel back, tacking his way till he got to where he was going.'[51]

It would seem that Denis had some of his primary education with the Christian Brothers in Newry, so one has to assume that he had formed his judgement on Master Crawford's ability as a teacher by the age of 11. Possibly it wasn't formed until he scaled the heights at UCD, Cambridge or New York University. Of course, by that time, he had come to the conclusion that not only was he a terrible teacher, but a bit of a fool as well—the fool whose company and seat he shared, as well as his books; and Mrs Crawford was his mother's genuine friend and closest neighbour from the day she arrived until the day she left The Point. None of which counted, if a caricature of a man would raise a smile, sardonic or otherwise, on the faces of some literary buffs. It certainly caused hurt to those of us whom he taught, and who enjoyed his company and friendship for most of our

49 *Ibid., p.* 73

50 *Ibid., p.* 73

51 *Ibid., p.* 73

lives.

It is somewhat amazing that someone with the perceptive mind of the young Donoghue would not have appreciated the man Jack Crawford was—a blend of innocence, humour, irreverence, unworldliness, spirituality (a peculiar brand) and compassion. When the personality which evolved from such a mixture was steeped in musical expertise and musical appreciation, a unique character was formed and that was what 'Jackie' was, a unique character. But then Denis had no feeling for 'the character,' as most of us would know it, on the local scene. How could he have written a book about The Point without reference to Mary McCarthy, who lived next door to Crawfords and nearer the Barracks?

Mary is the third of the three flowers I introduced in an early chapter. The other two were Lilys, though I would always have addressed them both as 'Mrs'. Not so Mary. She was of a different nature to Jack Crawford, and was not as well disposed to Sergeant Donoghue, or any of the police, as were the Crawfords. She and her sister, Maggie, ran a fish, fruit and vegetable business, though I am not sure that the Donohues were among her customers. She had regular spats with the Sergeant and his men, most of which became part of 'Jackie's' humorous repertoire.

To give an idea of the quality of Mary's acerbic tongue, I relate the following incident which had nothing to do with either Jack Crawford or the police.

The occasion was a concert in St Mark's School, Warrenpoint, to celebrate the Golden Jubilee of Archdeacon Esler in the priesthood. Mary was sitting with her neighbour, Mrs Reilly. A local folk group came on to perform, all of them unknown to Mary. Mrs Reilly was filling her in on their identities.

'And who is that long fellow on the right?' she asked.

Mrs Reilly thought Mary should have known the fellow and replied, 'Ach, that's Hugh Carr, a son of Barney's.' This information prompted Mary to exclaim, 'Ah, wouldn't you know a Carr, two ends and no middle,' and this to the delight of all within earshot, including Cathal McAnulty. It was Cathal who relayed Mary's tribute to the Carrs and we haven't stopped laughing since.

While I have met members of the Crawford family regularly over the years, and have been in most of their homes from time to time, I had never discussed *Warrenpoint* with any of them, other than Bishop John, the year after the book was published.

In more recent times I indicated regularly to Master Jack Crawford's daughter, Madge Conway, 'I'll be round to see you some day,' until I finally fulfilled the notice. I wanted some information about her father and to let her know I was attempting a book on Warrenpoint. In the course of the conversation she left the room and returned with an envelope, which she handed to me saying, 'You might find something to help you in that.'

'Madge,' I said, 'I think I have written all I need to write about Denis' book.'

'Read it anyway,' she said, at which I queried, 'It's not personal, is it?'

'Some of it is, but you are free to use it, if you wish.'

A few days later I opened the envelope to find a quantity of newspaper cuttings, critiques of *Warrenpoint* and several pieces by Denis himself. There were also a number of letters Denis had written to her father, and herself, while he was living in Tullow and still at University in Dublin, most likely in the late 40s.

When I had read them, I thought to myself, 'Where the hell did Denis go wrong?' for in some of those letters is revealed the youthful idealism, the genius, the enthusiasm and the graciousness of a remarkable talent. Is it vanity or fame or intellectual snobbery that weakens the promptings of the heart?

This is Denis to his friend and former mentor:

'A Sheáin dílis, a chara chaoin,

Just a line to say 'go mbeannuigid Dia duit', *and to thank you very sincerely for all the trouble you took over my script. Well, you will be sorry to hear, they refused it.*

I suppose the sight of 2,500 words in their own language was too much for them.

I'd have had a better chance if it had been in Latin. I have sent it to Radio Éireann, but have received no answer. I have my suspicions about that crowd, but if they want it, they can have it. I know one thing—it's a good script and I'm perfectly satisfied with it. From the literary point of view, I will never feel ashamed of it, for it was written with all honesty and sincerity. But if Radio Éireann does not accept it, I will send it to my Irish professor as an axiomatic explanation of my decision not to take Irish in my degree. Yes, strange as it will seem, I am not taking my degree in Irish. You see, under the new regulations we may only take an honours degree in two subjects. Unless a miracle happens, my two subjects will be English and Latin. I shall not, however, give up writing in Irish; indeed I will probably flood the 32 counties with it, even if nobody buys it. For the delight of seeing a horrified look on the smug faces of our conceited prigs, I'd go a long way.

Thank Madge for helping my script on its way—it was very nice of her.

The post has just come in—another article returned. Well, it was no good anyway. I wrote a historical article 'With Swift in Kilroot' and sent it to The Irish Times. I hope they accept it, for I liked it well. (That's more than I can say for most of my stuff.)

I'm counting the days until I get back to good serious study. Hibernating in these 'hells of littleness and monotony' does not suit me at all.

I'll hardly see any of you before Christmas. I miss you all very much 'the roses' scent is bitterness to him that loves the rose.'

Mise, do chara go buan.

Denis

That is part of a letter which Denis sent to Jack Crawford on 25th. On none of the letters is there a month or a year, and in a *post scriptum*, he advises 'on the back of the page you'll find a few lines of doggerel I've just thrown together. It will give you a smile.'

Louis Trodden(Principal), Neoinín Uí Fhearáin
(Subbing for Ms McDonald) and Jack Crawford.

The doggerel is reproduced as written: *Inis Éimeir* was the name of Crawford's house and I supply a rough translation.

Inis Éimeir

'Inis Éimeir,' mór a cliú
Aoibhinn d'a bhfuil innti 'nois
Slán, follán ó'n gheimreadh fhuar
Grian an t-samhraidh is soillsiú fríd

Sult agus ceol agus gáire le'na gcois
An tae is milse blas in a dhiadh
Mairg a b'eigin imtheacht uaith
agus slán a sgaoil' le bean an toighe

Fuigheallach na nGaodhal tar éis na tuile
Grásta 's greann in a measg go h-oidche
Mai ag seinm is an ceol in a croidhe -sa
Fad saol is sogh díbh, 'uaisle Gaodhil.

Inis Éimeir, great is her fame
Everything that is in it now is lovely
Safe and healthy from the cold winter
The summer sun shining through it

Fun, music and laughter
And the tastiest tea afterwards
Too bad that I had to leave
And say good bye to the lady of the house

Those of the Irish left after the flood
Grace and happiness in their midst 'til night
Mae playing with music in her heart
Long life and happiness to you, noble Irish.

Three days later, the 28th, he wrote again:

> *'Radio Éireann has accepted my script, I don't know anything about it. —when they are going to do it, or (damnably important), how much of the old 'filthy lucre' I'll get for it. That script will always mean something to me, because I wrote it at your kind suggestion. Furthermore, I wrote it sincerely, and I like sincerity to be appreciated. I do not feel sore about the refusal of all the articles and short stories, but the script was different. It meant a lot of work, and a lot of thought, but I am glad I did it, for the script is (and I say this as objectively as I can), a good one, fit to go anywhere, in any company. That sounds egotistical but you can differentiate. Thanks for your delightful letter, which I received this morning. Kindness and that generosity which I love to believe our forefathers had, breathed through every line of it.*
>
> *Oineach is a very curious word in our language. It is untranslatable. It stands for that unique combination of character which we call Gaelic— generosity and charity in a sensitive person. The old saying, you know, goes: —*
>
> *Beo duine tar éis a anam. Ní bheo tar éis a oinigh.*[52]
>
> *I love to think that just as the American character is a sort of dynamic adolescence, and the English, sedate sensibility, so the old Irish character was synonymous with "oineach". A crime against generosity was a helluva lot more serious than high treason. This quality, this oineach, was the most attractive attribute of your family. I wish I could translate it, but I can't. The little poem I wrote for you was scribbled down in about two minutes, without the slightest respect for rhyme or any damn thing. It contained, however, the spirit I hold dearest in my life, you know what that means. Someday, when the words come, I'll try something better in that line, as a small token of thanks for the most pleasant memories of my youth. It will need to be good though. May and Kathleen, are going back tomorrow, so the house will be quiet. Solitude isn't such a pleasant thing despite Shelley, Keats and Hazlitt. I am beginning to hate it, and long for full happy hours again. I feel as if I am metaphorically treading on thin ice, so I'll finish!'*

With the introduction of *Letters from Denis,* I am very conscious of the improvement in the quality of writing in this book, but even more conscious of the esteem, regard and deep affection in which he held Jack Crawford and his family.

In a passage in Irish in the same letter he asks about 'Fr Alex' and sends a word of congratulations on his winning a boat race. This is a far cry from his reference in *Warrenpoint* to the same reverend gentleman, and even though it reflects his father's thinking, it drips with innuendo, 'The local priests, too, should be kept at a distance. One of them, Fr McMullan, was on familiar terms with the Crawford family and dropped into 'Innisaimer' several times a week for tea and a chat. My father thought this a regrettable matter. The Crawfords should be more careful and should not encourage informal relations between children and a

---

52   "A person is alive upon getting a soul. But not so, upon losing generosity and charity."

priest.'[53]

While Madge gave me *carte blanche* access to the correspondence, there is one item I felt I could not use: a photostat copy of a poem, also in Irish, by A. Ní Fhoghlugh, *Bláth mo chroíde*.[54] It is a poem which expresses terms of endearment as only the Irish language can.

In June 2003 at Queen's University, Belfast, the title Doctor of Literature was conferred on Professor Denis Donoghue.

In his citation, Professor Brian Caraher, of the school of English, said, 'His memoir *Warrenpoint,* about his coming of age as the son of the Sergeant-in-charge of the local RUC Barracks during the period 1928 to 1945, is a contemporary classic in the modern genre of memoir writing, and sets the origin of a brilliant academic career in the extraordinarily well-observed small-town life in Northern Ireland.'

As the man says, 'I'll say no more'—though I could say twice as much.

I will now shock readers by confessing that I wrote to Denis some time after the book came out, and offered my congratulations, though I have to explain the circumstances of such a paradox.

John Connolly was a classmate of mine in Carrick Primary School, and at The Abbey in Newry. I am not sure whether or not he left The Abbey before me but we maintained a friendship throughout our lives. He called with me in late February 1991 to tell me that he had the most vivid dream of his life; in it, he was back in The Abbey School, in a class being taught by the principal, Brother O'Donnell; (he was still alive and well, living in retirement at the Monastery in Newry.) John had it in his mind that Brother O'Donnell should be honoured in some way by his pupils of that era, and he felt I would be the right man to help him. 'No one outside Burren knows me, half the country knows you,' he suggested.

We floated the idea to a few others, and in no time we had a steering group with me as secretary and co-ordinator. We circularised nearly everyone in the country who had been at The Abbey in the 30s, and some others in various parts of the world. By this time, the steering group had grown a little and at a meeting weeks after the circulars had gone out, a newcomer asked, 'Did Denis Donoghue get an invitation?' and made some reference to his book, *Warrenpoint*.

Someone else said that Denis wasn't there in Brother O'Donnell's time, and there were a few inquiring eyes cast in my direction.

'I don't think Denis would come,' and I was not anxious to state my reasons for such a view.

'He should be asked anyway,' the questioner insisted, and without a great deal of discussion it was decided he should be asked. I thought the circular on its own, dated a few weeks before, might appear to be 'a second thoughts' invitation, so I wrote a short note offering my congratulations on the book, and offering the view that his opinion of his father's strict adherence to the rules was somewhat harsh.

We had no reply, but Denis could well have been in America at the time and unaware of the invitation. However, I have to record that I would have been

---

53   *Ibid., p.* 56

54   Irish for 'bloom/flower of my heart'

surprised if he had accepted.

The other work qualifying for inclusion in *Late Late Reviews* is Maurice Hayes' *Minority Verdict,* in which he relates in an early chapter his experience in the GAA. In it, he paints a picture of the Association which, for those of us who were part of it at the time, is completely at odds with the reality. Why Maurice chose *Minority Verdict* as a launch-pad for an attack on the GAA 34 years after he had left it, mystified myself and many others, and prompted me to put pen to paper.

To suggest, as Maurice does, that the GAA was in poor shape coming out of the Second World War indicates an acutely selective view of the historical impact of the Association on the Ireland created by the partitioning of the country. While its earliest units, in the shape of teams, rather than clubs, go back to 1888 in Down, there was still only a handful of teams active in the early 20s; these were weakened by the loss of members who had been involved in the War of Independence, and who had, of necessity, to take to the emigrant ships.

A decade later, in the 1930s it was a different story: clubs were increasing by the year and by the end of the Second World War had risen in numbers from 29 to 46. In 1939, St Patrick's Park, Newcastle, was purchased and Down had a home of its own for the first time. The high point of Down's football achievement at that time was reached in 1940, when they qualified for their first Ulster Senior Football Final, and for their second two years later. It was 1944 before they won their first senior trophy, the McKenna Cup, when its winning meant something. Another two years, and the first All Ireland honour came in the shape of the Junior Championship.

Far from emerging from the War in a weakened position, the GAA in Down was on the crest of a wave, and brimming with confidence. The fact that Championship success continued to elude Down in no way affected the enthusiasm in the county. With clubs like Bryansford, Clonduff, Newry Shamrocks, Castlewellan, Kilcoo and The Point, there was a lively club scene right through the decade. The level of attainment which was achieved was brought about by administrators who, according to Maurice:

> 'tend more often than not, to be the voice of the sporting establishment, to be more concerned with organisational and procedural matters, to regard themselves as the guardians of the purity of the tradition, to take themselves unduly seriously, to be generally conservative, older than the players, more committed than the followers. In the GAA this is a very dominant group, which shapes the widespread perception of the organisation as conservative, backward-looking and ultra-nationalistic,... whose main objective is the preservation of their own positions.' [55]

I wonder if he ascribes this description to Peadar Barry, his immediate predecessor, who had held the position of county secretary for 28 years, or to George Tinnelly, who was chairman of the County Board for 18 years, most of them

---

55   Maurice Hayes, *Minority Verdict*, Belfast, Blackstaff Press, 1995, *p.* 49.

in Maurice's era of influence.

A word about Peadar would not be out of place. He was a small farmer from Corrags, one of Burren's townlands, and had been active in the War of Independence. Long before I ever thought of joining the Association, his was a familiar name to me. He was renowned for his integrity and good judgement, and if Peadar pronounced something was right or wrong, his view would have been given precedence over that of any Bishop.

My first official contact with him came in the early '40s in the following circumstance: I was playing in a seven-a-side tournament in Mayobridge and I was sent off, after remonstrating with the referee, who had blown for a foul on me when I was clean through for a goal. A sending off meant an automatic month's suspension. In normal circumstances, I would not have had any problem with that, but for the fact that the Warrenpoint and Rostrevor clubs had a local league going. The team I captained was in the final play-off on the following Friday night.

The feeling in my team was that the rule would not apply in a local league, but I was advised to go out and see Peadar. Next day, I cycled out to Corrags where I was received most graciously by the county secretary, who listened to the exposition of my case with great courtesy, and, I thought, with a deal of sympathy. So much so, that my confidence in the outcome of the visit was beginning to rise. He reached to a shelf close behind him for the rule book, perused it for a short while, turning a few pages in the process, before finally handing the open book to me.

'Barney,' he said, 'read that No. 20 and tell me if you think you are not suspended for a month.'

I looked at the rule, took in its implications, and donned the robe of martyrdom. I appreciated Peadar's sympathetic smile as I drank the tea his sister had brought in.

As I headed back to The Point on my bike, I had serious reservations about the ability of my team to succeed without its captain and countyman. As things turned out on the Friday evening, I wasn't even missed, for my team won handsomely without me.

George Tinnelly was no less committed to the Association than was Peadar, though he would not have possessed some of the insights of the man from Corrags. He was a decent, honourable man in my experience, completely lacking in guile. It was significant that the year after he retired as chairman, Convention agreed to limit the term of the office to one of three years. In my view, not the best decision Convention ever made.

Another curse of the GAA, by Maurice's reckoning, was the fact that 'the committees were run by small men, national school teachers and country curates,'[56] and he remembers:

> 'seeing the serried ranks of the GAA's Central Council on television
> on the occasion of the organisation's centenary, and reflecting that they
> looked like the reviewing party on Lenin's tomb during the Moscow May Day
> parade. I further reflected that the GAA and the USSR's Komsomol, must

---

56   *Ibid., p. 50*

be the only youth organisations in the world to be run by a gerontocracy.'[57]

Might I add that among the serried ranks present on the occasion were every living past president and many distinguished hurlers and footballers. Had Maurice been appointed to succeed Paddy O'Keefe 30 years before, he would have been there, too.

On one occasion Maurice's heart warmed to Gerry Fitt, when at one stage in the development of the SDLP he complained about 'being up to his arse in country schoolteachers.' I have to confess it wasn't the country schoolteachers who led to my departure from the SDLP.

Anyone who has any knowledge of the GAA will know that it was the priests and teachers who dug the foundations for the organization which spans the country. There isn't a parish in the land where the local priest and teachers did not make a significant contribution in the formation and running of clubs, and, in many instances, as players. I could rattle off a litany of names which come to mind but it occurs to me that I should tell the story of a playing priest, the late Fr Austin Darragh, who lined out with Castlewellan when he ministered in that parish.

We were playing them at Moygannon, almost in the shadow of Slieve Foy on the other side of the lough, where Finn McCool is in repose. Fr Darragh, a big burly man weighing 15 or 16 stones and well known to everyone, was in goal. While I was playing full forward, I was in my football dotage, possibly slow thinking as well as slow moving. As I gathered a ball close to the square, or maybe in it, the weight of Fr Darragh landed on me, like the proverbial 'ton of bricks'. I was emptied of breath and unable to cry 'foul'. As I got to my feet, the referee arrived on the scene and with book in hand said to Austin, who was helping me to recover, 'What's your name? I'm booking you for that.'

Without even turning to him, the priest answered, 'Finn McCool.'

I collapsed again, this time in laughter, and when I glanced over at the mountain, Finn seemed to be enjoying the joke, too.

As for the country schoolteachers, alas, those of the masculine variety are becoming something of a dying breed, and it is not only the GAA which is beginning to miss their unique contribution to Irish life. Even before I joined the Association in 1940, many of their names were household words in Down. Two of them, George McKeown, an Antrim man, and Gerry O'Donoghue, a Kerryman, along with Peadar Barry, were regarded almost as the Blessed Trinity of the GAA. George McKeown was still an active member of the County Board when I joined it in 1958. Other teachers were Paddy O'Donoghue, Arthur Doran, Paddy McFlynn and, indeed, Maurice himself had his period in the classroom facing the boys. He was often called into question by George, whose 'little black book' might have carried a slightly different version of events. On the occasions when there was no record, 'the little black book' was deemed to be official. I have a feeling that 'the wee black book' was probably the source of Maurice's aversion to country schoolmasters.

Maurice identifies three members of the Association in his book, though

---

57   *Ibid., p.* 50

only one by name, Paddy O'Keefe, the General Secretary, whom he rightly lauds as a man of the highest ability, integrity and vision. He even describes him as his 'mentor'. The second is, 'one long-time supporter, a father of two players, complained to me that he was embarrassed, on behalf of his Protestant friends who had gone with him to support the team, by the singing of the Catholic hymn *Faith of our Fathers*, before the games at Croke Park.'[58]

That could only be Briany McCartan, the father of James and Dan, so I said to my long-time friend, Charlie Carr, who was a longer time friend of Briany's, and who regularly travelled to matches with him, 'Did you ever hear Briany McCartan complain about having to sing *Faith of our Fathers* in Croke Park?'

'Oh, not at all,' said Charlie, 'he and I used belt it out. It was the only hymn we both knew, and better still,' he continued, with tongue in cheek and twinkle in the eye, 'we never went to a match without the beads.'

He didn't stop for breath. 'The day that you played Kerry in the first final, at half-time Briany said to me, "We'll say a decade of the Rosary that they can keep it up," and we both got the beads out. When Johnnie Culloty dropped James' old soft shot and we got the goal, Briany hit the ceiling. When he landed in the seat again he turned to me and laughed, "By God Charlie, it's hard to beat the prayers."

And Maurice is wide of the mark in claiming that *Nearer my God to Thee* was equally inappropriate as the choice of music prior to the English Cup Final, 'which was also the practice at the time.'[59]

The first time I heard the broadcast of the English Cup Final in 1932, *Abide with Me* (not *Nearer My God to Thee*) came over loud, clear and moving. I sang it with great feeling when I was at Wembley in 1948, and it will come as a surprise to Maurice to know that it is still being sung at Football Association (FA) Cup Finals, and sung better than ever when the final moved to the Welsh National Stadium in Cardiff while Wembley was being rebuilt.

Much of what Maurice writes about the GAA appears to me as real Walter Mitty stuff, and, I would hazard a view, that Thurber's character may well have turned up in some of the succeeding chapters. The gem for me is the following:

> *'In the mid-1950s, a small group within the Down County Board, fed up being beaten year after year, disgusted by the defeatism of the majority, and determined to put Down's name on the map of Gaelic football, conceived the idea of trying to produce a team that would win an All-Ireland. We decided that it could be done, with careful planning and preparation, about five years hence, and we set about this, surreptitiously at first.'[60]*

There was no small group within the County Board before I joined it in 1958, nor in the following ten years of my membership of that body. As for a five-year plan, nobody told me about it. In any event, we did it in three. Any decisions which were taken in relation to the team and its management structure were taken by the County Committee, in the face of opposition from Maurice. I will not

---

58   *Ibid., p. 53*

59   *Ibid., p. 56*

60   *Ibid., p. 53*

repeat the parable of 'the crank,' though I should indicate that I approached Donal McCormack when he was county secretary of the Down Board, asking if I might view the minutes of County Board meetings of this historic period, to be told that no minutes of County Board meetings of that period exist.

For those who might not have read *Minority Verdict*, I am including this gem from Maurice for the benefit of prospective managers.

> '*I think I learned more about managing people from this group than from anything else I did: how to set objectives beyond the normal expectations of people, but achievable with effort and determination, how to motivate people. How to mobilise resources of training and support, how to support people in disappointment and defeat, how to put the activity in the context of a wider and more serious world, how to deal with interference, tensions and defeat within the group, how to cater for the special individual needs of a wide variety of people, how to dull the edge of disappointment, without blunting the thrust of ambition, how to bond people into a group with a single purpose, with a set of standards and with self discipline and how to re-motivate them to do it all again.*'[61]

Maurice's account of his departure from the Association, and this written 34 years after it happened, has to be nailed for the fantasy that it is. Fantasy though it be, in the opinion of many, it libelled an honourable man, probably the only one in the country who would not have sought a judicial ruling.

His farewell salvo reads:

> '*The zest of the action in Down had been dulled by the fact that many of those who had derided our early effort had now climbed on the bandwagon of success, and wanted to take control. What had previously been possible was now being questioned by nit pickers, decision making became cumbersome as Committees muscled in, and it felt as if we were having to push the stone the whole way up the hill again. It is also one of my weaknesses to lose interest in a subject when I know how to do it, or have acquired a certain competency...*
>
> *The GAA had for most of the previous 70 years maintained a ban on participation in, or even attendance at, cricket, soccer, rugby, and hockey matches, which were characterised in the cant of the times as "foreign games". Down had been trying to change this rule for a decade and a half without success, although the tide was turning, and the rule was to go within the next ten years. I found it less attractive to remain deeply involved in an organisation that required its members to be shackled by regulations characterised by meanness of spirit and lack of vision. My friend and mentor, Paddy O'Keefe, had died. I applied for his post as GAA General*

---

61   *Ibid., p. 54*

Secretary, not in any hope of success but only that I could say to myself that I had made my effort to change things. In the event, in a welter of canvassing in which I did not indulge, I received a derisory single vote (and that not from the Down delegate). I take a perverse pride in having been so rejected, and of having secured the vote of one of the few distinguished players in the room. In the end, my problem was solved for me by the Down County Convention which, in an orgy of vote rigging, having first replaced me as Central Council delegate, relegated me from Secretary to assistant Secretary. At this point I got the message—they wanted to drop the pilot— and I withdrew from active participation: without recrimination but not without some hurt and disappointment at a certain lack of grace in the transition.'[62]

This is not Walter Mitty. This is Maurice at his most perverse. Only he could weave a web of intrigue into a fabric which did not exist, but I will give, in some detail, the mechanics of that transition: at the Down Convention in 1964, Paddy McFlynn, who had been county treasurer for some years, stood for election as the Central Council delegate, a post held by Maurice since the retirement of Peadar Barry some seven or eight years previously. It was and is an influential post and McFlynn had contested it previously without success. To the surprise of the Convention, and I think of Paddy, himself, he beat Maurice and commenced what turned out to be a lengthy term in the top council of the Association, eventually becoming president.

Whether it was intentional or not, Maurice portrays the account of his 'demotion' to assistant secretary as happening on the same occasion, when in fact it did not happen until the following year, the 1965 Convention.

The full story of the period needs to be told, to put Maurice's disillusionment with the GAA into context, and chronological order. It began at the height of Down's success, when we took the second All-Ireland title and when it was confirmed that we were to do the comprehensive tour of America, about which I have already written.

The County Committee decided that we should organise a charter flight, which would accommodate the official party and a limited number of supporters. By Christmas nearly all the seats were booked, though the size of the official party had still to be decided. It was the general feeling that we would be going out on the national carrier, Aer Lingus, and what other way would the national champions travel. There was just one problem, we did not have a plane, nor did we have one as we approached Easter 1962. The County Committee decided that a sufficient number of seats should be reserved for the official party on a service flight, in case the whole operation fell through.

We were to open our tour in Boston on 18 May, and there we were, into April, without a plane. Can anyone not imagine the confusion and uncertainty which must have been caused to the hundred plus supporters, who would certainly have paid their deposits, if not the total cost of their flights? I do not wish to get

---

62   *Ibid., pp. 56–57*

into the nitty-gritty of the problem, but the County Committee decided that the chairman and secretary should travel to Dublin the very next day to meet the general secretary, Paddy O'Keefe, to see if he would use his good offices on our behalf. O'Keefe, an influential figure himself, took them to meet another high-ranking figure in the Department of Industry and Commerce, P.S. Lynch. Mr Lynch worked the oracle, but he had to get the Pakistani National Airline to do the job, and we had to travel to Shannon by bus to board the plane. No matter, the situation had been saved, and we experienced what was the greatest of any American tour.

Despite this, there was a residue of criticism levelled at Maurice for the near debacle by a number of East Down clubs, and I know that a couple of South Down members of the county board had been asked to stand against him as secretary at the 1963 Convention.

This was the background, then, to the contest with McFlynn in 1964, when a number of East Down clubs backed the Derryman. To suggest, as Maurice does, that there was 'an orgy of vote rigging,' is preposterous.

There is a much more involved story in Maurice's 'demotion' to the post of assistant secretary the following year, when he was the central player himself.

In 1962, he made the proposal that TP Murphy, who was assistant secretary, should become joint secretary, as recognition for his work in the county, and this was accepted by Convention. We move forward then to the end of August 1964, when the Central Council appointed a successor to Paddy O'Keefe, who had died somewhat unexpectedly. Maurice was among the six people who sought the post. Seán Ó Síocháin, the assistant secretary, and Kevin Heffernan, the well-known Dublin footballer, were also among the runners.

The Down Board had mandated Paddy McFlynn to support Maurice, and to use any influence he might have in Central Council to further his cause. It was no great surprise, however, when Seán Ó Síocháin, a Cork man, well-known balladeer and a country schoolmaster to boot, was chosen by the Council. There was surprise at the County Committee that Maurice only received one vote, but there was no credence given to the rumour that that vote was not cast by Paddy McFlynn. It was McFlynn himself who raised the issue, when the County Committee came to discuss it, and he also advised that Maurice got two votes.

Maurice never appeared at the County Committee again.

What follows is an excerpt from Síle Nic an Ultaigh's (Sheila McAnulty's), O Shíol go Bláth. The GAA Story.

> 'In October 1964, Maurice Hayes, who was Town Clerk of Downpatrick UDC[63] had written to the County Committee pointing out that, owing to the death of the council chairman, considerable additional duties would fall on him, and he asked to be excused from all secretarial duties for the next few months. In January 1965, he had not resumed; a letter was read from him apologising for non-attendance at the Convention, but the Joint Secretaries' Report was presented as before.
>
> It may well be that this situation prompted George Tinnelly in his address to Convention, to express concern about the working of the

---

63   Urban and District Council

County Committee during the year. He said he found the position of Joint Secretaryship unworkable:

> *'In plain language there must be some one person responsible. As the Joint Secretaryship was set up by simple declaration, I have no hesitation in declaring it dissolved on your ballot paper today. You can vote for Secretary and Assistant Secretary.'[64]*

Síle (Sheila) continued,

> *'The Chairman's declaration came as something of a surprise to the delegates. While it was true that the Joint Secretaryship had come about by a simple declaration, a number of delegates, including TP Murphy, pointed out that the clubs had been requested to nominate Joint Secretaries. Other speakers supported the Chairman's view that it was in order to revert to the pre-1962 procedure, that this was correct as stipulated in the Official Guide, and that any departure from that procedure would require a two-thirds majority. On the issue being put to Convention, the necessary two-thirds majority was not obtained, and the Convention went on to elect TP Murphy as Secretary, and Maurice Hayes as Assistant Secretary.'[65]*

Síle (Sheila) has it as it happened, and any suggestion that there was 'an orgy of vote rigging' is groundless.

I return again to *Minority Verdict* and the third man Maurice identified in his chapter relating to the GAA, Paddy McFlynn, who, if Maurice is to be believed, did not cast the vote Maurice received in his bid to succeed Paddy O'Keefe. He attributed his single vote to 'one of the few distinguished players in the room' whose identity has been an open secret from the day the council met. I refer to Leo McAlinden, an Armagh man, who had been at the heart of Leitrim and Connacht football for most of his life and who, as a long-time member of the Central Council, was one of the 1984 'gerontocracy' so despised by Maurice. Not only would I put him in the Top Twenty of All-Time Greats, but he was the most companionable man one could meet. I have had that pleasure many times over the years.

A couple of months after I read *Minority Verdict,* I met Leo at a funeral in Rostrevor, and after we had caught up on each other's well-being, he told me he had come to retire in the Newry area, where his brother, Jack, was a well-known veterinary practitioner.

Felicitations finished, my first question to him, 'Did you read Maurice's book?,' and even as he answered in the affirmative, I was back with an incredulous, 'but you didn't vote for him!' question and statement.

Leo smiled, 'I didn't get the chance,' and he went on to explain how the Leitrim County Chairman had mandated him to support a candidate from Connacht, who had no chance, and was bound to be eliminated at the first vote. Leo, and most of those at the meeting, felt there would be more than one vote, but the reality was that Seán Ó Síocháin had a decisive overall majority after the first

---

64   Síle Nic an Ultaigh, *Ó Shíol go Bláth*, 1989, pp. 340–341

65   *Ibid., p.* 341

count. There was no other vote required.

I can now declare that Leo McAlinden did not vote for Maurice in that decisive contest to succeed Paddy O'Keefe in 1964, and that one of the two votes Maurice got that day came from the Down delegate, Paddy McFlynn.

That meeting with Leo in Rostrevor took place in January of 1997. We had occasional meetings after that, all of them pleasant. In October 2004, my neighbour, Eileen McPolin, who had been taken into hospital suddenly a few days before, came over to tell me that while there, she met a very nice man, Leo McAlinden. When he learned she was from Warrenpoint, and knew Barney Carr well, she carried his good wishes home to me. Eileen's bulletin on his well-being was, 'He is in great form and expects to go home in a day or two.'

I went up to see him in the afternoon, and his condition was exactly as Eileen described. We had a wonderful hour, during which I indicated that I was attempting to write a book, and that he would be featuring in it. He was delighted, and laughingly declared, 'Well, that is one book I will be looking forward to reading.'

He was discharged the following day and went to convalesce with his daughter in Drogheda. Two weeks later he suddenly took ill, and died in hospital in Dublin.

His death was recorded in the obituary column of the two daily papers I read, but to my surprise I did not read one word of tribute to one of the great football talents of my lifetime, and a gentleman to boot.

In bringing this chapter to a close, I have to reflect that Paddy McFlynn served the Down County Board, the Ulster Council, and the Central Council at the highest levels, and the entire Association for his presidential term. I have found it somewhat disturbing that from none of these areas of officialdom was there one word of refutation of the jaundiced view of the GAA expressed in *Minority Verdict,* not to mention the slur on the personal integrity of the former president.

35—The Quality of Justice

In an early chapter I wrote of Rory Duffy, whom I described as one of the unforgettable characters of my boyhood years on the boats. It is the story of his son I now seek to record. He was christened William John, but from his earliest days he was known as 'Sonny'. I have already noted that he lived at Dromore Terrace whose frontal green was among my early football pitches. Sonny, a quiet lad even then, was not much into football, though he played. Through his primary school days he was part of the local scene, and while he would have been down with his father at the boats from time to time, he was not as interested in the boats as I was. He spent only a short part of his life in Warrenpoint for the simple reason that when he was in his teens he was sent to the training school in Belfast for some minor misdemeanour. While there, he had a nervous breakdown and was transferred to the Downshire Hospital in Downpatrick, in whose care he remained for the rest of his life. At least, that was my memory of his early life, until in the course of writing this book I learned a fuller story.

Bob Heaton was unmarried and after his mother died he lived on his own in Clermont Gardens for many years. He had three great enthusiasms for much of his life. He was an accomplished golfer, a keen angler and he had a great interest in bands. He played in the INF band and in the GAA Band which succeeded it. While I would have known him from an early age it was in this latter period that we became quite good friends. When he retired from the band he still came to the odd band practice when we had some good chats about past times. On one occasion, shortly after Sonny Duffy's death, he recounted how Sonny jumped the Park railing, and I expressed amazement and even unbelief. But he assured me it happened, and added, 'someday I'll tell you the story of Sonny.'

When Bob stopped coming to the band I did not see him so much, but I met him on one occasion in the Post Office since this memoir began. I said to him, and without any thought of memoir, that I had never heard the story of Sonny Duffy that he had promised to tell me 'some day'.

'Well, I'll tell you the story of Sonny,' he began, and proceeded to recount a day in his own life, which impacted on Sonny's life, too. We were speaking about something which had happened over 60 years before, and we must have been ten minutes talking, when I interrupted him.

'Stop, Bob,' I said—we were still by the Post Office. 'I am appalled. I can't let you tell me this on the street—I'll go down to see you some day next week.' We parted, and I retraced my steps homeward with a burning sense of injustice at what I had heard.

This is the story Bob told me, when I called with him a week or two later. Bob was 13 years of age at the time, the last Tuesday in March, 1941. He left home for school as usual, but with no exercise done, he decided he would mitch. The Park was the favourite haunt for mitchers, and that was where he put in his morning. When the lunch bell went at the school across the road, he joined the group heading for Charlotte Street, where he lived. After dinner it was back to the Park for the afternoon, during which time he noticed a 'pitch and toss' school at the small lane behind the seafront houses. He had two pennies and he joined in, turning them into two shillings of pennies. When the bell sounded the end of the school day, he headed for home full of the joys of spring, and a pocket full of pennies.

A couple of boys, both from Charlotte Street, joined him, and one of them gave him a number of tickets, which it transpired had been stolen from the local cinema. Bob gave one each to two other boys, took one himself, and threw the remainder over the railing which protected the basement of Nellie Caulfield's house in Church Street. That night he went to the pictures; those of us who would ever have patronised the Garden Cinema will remember the covered open passage which overlooked the tennis courts and bowling green of the Balmoral Hotel. As he walked up the passage to where Gerry Boyle was taking the tickets, Bob noted that Gerry was examining every ticket number so he decided just to take a 'look in,' a very common practice in those days. He returned to the ticket office, bought a ticket and in he went.

Before the performance began, there was a bit of excitement when Constable Slevin entered the cinema and removed two boys from the bench seats. Bob breathed a sigh of relief, and felt he had had a very lucky escape—that was, until the following day, shortly after he returned home from school, when a policeman called at his home and took him to the Barracks just up the street. In all, about eight boys were questioned that Wednesday and all were released. Again, Bob thought he was in the clear, but when he returned home from school on Thursday, a policeman called within minutes, and he was again taken to the Barracks. There were three other boys there when he arrived—Sonny Duffy and the two boys who had given him the cinema tickets two days before. All four were held in the Barracks that night and on through Friday, Saturday and Sunday, and this despite the protests of their parents who had a pad beaten to the Barrack doors. Over the four nights, they slept on improvised 'mattresses' on the floor of the day room, and in the company of the constable who was on duty. Mrs Donoghue, the Sergeant's wife, brought them in breakfast and their tea in the evening, while their parents brought in their mid-day meal.

On one of the nights the youthful quartet was in custody, the constable on duty, thinking his charges were settled for the night, climbed on to the large table which was the main piece of furniture in the room, lay down, and in no time at all was snoring his head off. Anyone who has ever been in the dayroom in the Barracks will recall there were a few rifles and a couple of revolvers on the walls. Some of the lads, according to Bob, had these weapons in their hands as the constable lay asleep. Might I say that I knew the constable well, as would most of my generation, and he was a decent man. On Monday morning, the four boys were taken by train to Belfast by two policemen, and deposited in St Patrick's Training School. They remained there until the last Friday of April, when they were taken back to Warrenpoint for trial. They were there for the whole month of April in 1941, a significant period in the history of wartime Belfast: German planes bombed the city, doing tremendous damage and killing hundreds of people. High on the rising ground of West Belfast, 'The Warrenpoint Four' viewed the horrific happenings from the dormitory windows, until staff marshalled all to the ground floor. Bob Heaton, the only one of the four boys still alive, had reason to remember 11 April 1941.

At Warrenpoint Petty Sessions, on the last Friday of April, the four boys appeared before Major McCallum, RM. He found them guilty of breaking into the local cinema but discharged them. The RM was of the opinion that they had been punished sufficiently. They were represented by Mr H. Rutherford, a Warrenpoint solicitor. Bob did not give me the details of the court appearance; I read them in the *Newry Telegraph* of that week.

The admission to the Garden Cinema at the time was sixpence. If six boys who used stolen tickets had paid their way in, the cinema takings for the evening would have been enhanced by three shillings—15 pence in today's currency. Neither of the two boys who gave Bob the tickets went to the cinema themselves. The sophistication of the crime, in which known numbered tickets could be detected at a glance, says something for the ingenuity of the robbers.

Sonny's story did not end with that discharge; in fact, the real story of his life was only beginning, for according to Bob Heaton, Sonny was ever after sure to be called in for questioning if anything happened about the town. In Bob's words, 'the police tortured him.'

Bob went on to tell me that a few years later, Sonny appeared before the court on a charge of breaking and entering a small shop on the Grinan Road near Newry, and how he was found guilty—though Bob would swear he had neither act not part in it. Guilty or not, he got a custodial sentence in what Bob thought was the training school. While there, he had a nervous breakdown, and was transferred to the Downshire Mental Hospital. It could be said he spent the rest of his life in its care, though when the Alexian Brothers' Nursing Home at Warrenpoint became a satellite of the Downshire, he was among the patients who arrived there sometime in the late 70s.

At this time, I was a member of the local St Vincent de Paul Society whose members visited the home every week, and at our Monday night meeting some of the members asked me if I had been talking to Sonny the day before. This was the first time I was aware that he was domiciled at the Brothers, and I had not been talking to him.

On my next visit I scanned the large common room, to see if I could pick him out, but I couldn't. I asked one of the nursing staff, 'Is Sonny Duffy in this room?' He looked round the room and directed me to 'the man up in the corner wearing the cap.'

I was surprised to find that Sonny knew me, and he said that he had seen me on a previous occasion when we were visiting. He was somewhat reserved, spoke quietly and neither of us made any reference to the past. Deep inside, I was apologising to him for the hurt our society had heaped on him. I met him occasionally on the Rostrevor Road when he had the notion to taking a walk. He rarely came into the town as some of the residents did, but that was understandable.

Before the Alexian Brothers finally closed their doors in the 90s, there was another dispersal of the residents. Sonny could have moved into another care facility in the town, but he chose not to. Instead, he elected to move to a home in another area of the county. I suppose it was completely understandable, for his memories of his hometown could not have been happy ones. He died in May 1993, aged 66, and was buried at Killyleagh on 'the other side of the county'. Whether or not that was his expressed wish I know not, but it would be understandable. Since then I have come to know a fuller story and I cannot help feeling that we let Sonny down badly.

When Bob Heaton told me the story initially in his home in Clermont Gardens, I said to him, 'Bob, would you mind if I write about what you have told me, with permission to use your name'? Bob readily assented saying, 'No man got a rawer deal than Sonny Duffy.'

I relate the sad story of Sonny Duffy's life for the sole purpose of drawing a comparison with two other boys of his age, whose criminal behaviour was much more serious than his. On an earlier page, I described the destruction of a railway carriage compartment by two boys who turned out to be the sons of policemen. In money terms, the damage done to the carriage could well have been close to £50, a lot of money in those days. The cinema owners in Warrenpoint would have lost about three shillings if six boys had got in without paying. Those four boys slept under the same roof as Denis Donoghue—who lived in the Barracks with his family at the time—for four nights in March 1941. Despite the horrid description of his own 'urine smelling mattress' in *Warrenpoint* I'll bet he was much more comfortable than the boys who lay on the floor of the day room below him for four nights, and for four weeks of nights in the dormitory in St Patrick's Training School.

In more recent times I have inquired into the circumstances which led to Sonny's placement in Downshire Hospital. There was no information available from the hospital. The Data Protection legislation apparently precludes any such disclosure. The Public Records Office however, was able to provide me with the information that:

> 'On 15th January 1946, William John Duffy of Warrenpoint, appeared before Newry Hilary Quarter Sessions and was found guilty of the following charge: that between 10.30 P.M. on the 18th and 1P.M. on the 19th days of July 1945, he feloniously did break and enter the lock-up shop of one Catherine McAteer, situate at Grinan, Newry in this county with intent to steal, and then in the said lock up shop, three gross of Joker Safety Blades of the value of £4.10.0, ten ounces of War Horse Tobacco of the value of £1.4.2, and the sum of £1.10.0 in coppers to the total value of £7.4.2, of the moneys goods and chattels of the said Catherine McAteer in said lock up shop he feloniously did steal.
>
> He was sentenced to three years in a Borstal Institution.'

I read the report of the court proceedings in the *Newry Reporter* of a couple of days later, and learned that the case had been first heard at the Petty Sessions Court some time before and the same evidence had again been presented. The account given to me by Bob Heaton was not entirely correct, in that the only razor blades relating to Sonny were in the words of a police witness 'a thorough search of the defendant's home was made and all the razor blades of the 'Joker' type were two old used blades and some of an American type were found in the bathroom.' The crucial evidence was given by a Sergeant McCord from the finger print branch in Belfast; he said he found 'five-finger prints on a pane of glass taken from Mrs McAteer's window, and these were identical with the finger prints taken from Duffy by Sergeant Small.'

Under cross-examination by Mr Dan O'Hare for Sonny, the witness said there were other prints which bore a resemblance to each other but no two finger prints were absolutely identical. Sonny's aunt, with whom he lived, and who I knew well, gave evidence that 'early in July the defendant was signing on at the Labour Exchange. She never saw him with any money except what he got in the house. She never saw him with any tobacco or razor blades.'

In evidence, Sonny denied the charge, and said that he did not even know where Mrs McAteer's shop was.

The jury returned a verdict of guilty and in sentencing him the judge said he had been well represented by Mr O'Hare. In the judge's words, Sonny, unlike other boys who appeared before him, had a good home, but that he had to protect the community and, seeing he had previous convictions, he sentenced him to three years Borstal treatment.

Other than the cinema ticket experience which was four years before, I do not know what Sonny's criminal record was, nor do I know how long he was exposed to 'the Borstal treatment' before being moved to the Downshire Hospital in whose care he spent the remainder of his life.

In even more recent days, June 2006, I have heard the celebrated lawyer, Mike Mansfield, a central figure in the Birmingham Six and Guilford Four cases, make a comment after the successful appeal of a conviction which had depended on finger print evidence. He said, 'Finger printing is not an exact science. It is an art which is open to interpretation.' If finger printing was not an exact science in 2006, it was even less so in 1946, and if Mike Mansfield had been advising Dan O'Hare I doubt if there would have been a conviction. My generation of Warrenpoint inhabitants will have no difficulty recalling the hard-done-by Sonny Duffy, and while I do not imagine that he needs our prayers he is entitled to our fond remembrance.

I have included Sonny's story in this memoir with the permission of his family.

Bob Heaton died in 2006.

36—Síle/Sheila

When I was born on Summerhill, these 80 years ago
No Rices, no McPolins, no O'Hares, I'll have you know.
Of Dinsmores and O'Hanlons, there was neither sight nor track,
But Sheila was a big girl, who lived somewhere down our back.

The Sheila to whom I am referring, in that opening verse of a song I wrote for my 80th birthday celebration, is Sheila McAnulty whose book[66] I have already introduced as having the authority of Down GAA Scripture, [Síle Nic an Ultaigh's, *O Shíol go Bláth, The GAA Story*] and who came to live out her retirement on Summerhill. On that occasion, she sat at my left hand and enjoyed the night as much as I did myself. She was coming to the end of her 86th year then, and sadly she died in July 2004 weeks after passing the 88th milestone of an eventful life.

Life stories are invariably told from the beginning, but in Sheila's case, it is much easier and more rewarding to begin at the end, which was as fruitful as any period of her long life. Her arrival on Summerhill came as result of one of the fastest property deals in the local annals. It was a November Sunday evening in the early 80s when we learned from some of the neighbours that the Sands family intended leaving 52, Summerhill. That snippet of news did not ring any bells with me, but my wife, Anne, picked up on it immediately. 'That would be the right house for Sheila,' she said, and all present agreed. Sheila, at the time, was still living in Dublin sorting out her affairs after her retirement, but came home to The Point every weekend, as she had done all her working life. Her Sunday evening routine was well known to us, so we rang her sister-in-law, Mairead, to learn that she had already left for Dublin, but was likely to be in McCormack's, her sister Moya's home. She was, and when I asked if she would like to retire to Summerhill, she was partial to the notion. When I explained the location of the house she knew it well.

Sheila was never in a hurry going back to Dublin on a Sunday night, so I suggested I would contact the Sands family to see if she could view the house within the next hour. 'No problem,' said Claire. Within the hour, Sheila had viewed the house, liked it, and the deal was done. She drove back to Dublin a very contented lady that night.

It took her a couple of years to wind up her affairs in Dublin, but once installed and settled on Summerhill, she proceeded to achieve two of the great ambitions of her life. The first was to write the Down GAA History, and the second was to study for a degree in Social Studies at Queen's University, Belfast, which was awarded to her in 1984. This, after a working life spent mostly in Dublin as the representative of an international engineering concern allied to the motor industry. It would be more exact to say she was based in Dublin, but travelled the country.

In terms of Gaelic games, it was camogie which had her interest from her earliest days in The Point, where she played with the local Betsy Grays. I was a very young boy at the time and while I can remember her enthusiasm, I will betray

66   Síle Nic an Ultaigh, O Shíol go Bláth, The GAA Story

my Summerhill bias by declaring that she lacked the capabilities of Lily Savage and Maureen Gribben, each of whom lived a few doors from me, and who were the real dynamos of the team. Lily (Pettigrew) has long since passed to her eternal reward, but Maureen (Fitzpatrick) still looks capable of wielding a *camán*[67] or a golf club. She married Paddy Fitzpatrick in 1938. He had been the Down full back of the 1934 junior team and later captained Ballymartin when they won the Down Senior Championship. One other survivor of that Betsy Gray team is Maureen Yorke (Kelly), who has already been introduced in these pages.

Camogie was over for these girls when they finished playing, whereas Sheila's involvement was just getting into its stride. Long before she went to work in Dublin, she was heavily involved in camogie administration in Down and Ulster, and even after moving to the capital she was chairman of the Ulster Council for a three-year period. Then followed a four-year term as president of the Association, after which she became *Ard Rúnaí* for a period of 22 years. Until her death, she was also a trustee of the Association.

So far, I have not indicated that she also acted as a referee on occasions, and I do so now, to recount a tale from her refereeing experiences. The Betsy Grays were playing Ballyvarley at the latter venue. The referee did not turn up and it was agreed that Sheila would take charge of the game. The linesmen were Paddy Kelly from The Point and Jack McGrath from Ballyvarley. Four of Paddy Kelly's six daughters lined out for the visitors, while three daughters of Jack McGrath, represented the home side. Before ten minutes had elapsed Sheila realised she had a problem with her linesmen. Another ten minutes and she realised if she did not do something about her problem the game would never finish. She stopped the match, gave both linesmen their marching orders, and insisted that new officials were brought in. I have no idea who won the game.

There were many sides to Sheila, and, despite her deep involvement in sport, she had a great interest in the theatre. Her assessment of a play was always worth listening to. It was 1966, however, when her creative talents were apparent to me. That year, the 50th Anniversary of The Easter Rising, was widely celebrated and the GAA centrepiece was a pageant in Croke Park written by Bryan McMahon, the Kerry author. It was a spectacular offering, involving a cast of hundreds and was very well received. Sheila came up with a proposal that we should stage a version of the pageant in the Warrenpoint Town Hall. She adapted McMahon's script for the stage, producing and directing the show herself. It was a huge success, running for three nights.

Sheila was born in 1916, and no one was more conscious of the importance of that year in Irish history than herself. Her uncle, Paddy McGivern, was another of the local men who was involved in the War of Independence and was later chairman of the Down GAA Board, so it is understandable that she was steeped in the nationalist and republican tradition from her earliest years.

She had the most remarkable memory of anyone I have known in my life, a facility she retained right to the end of her days. She was in her 80s when she related an incident to me which occurred when she was six; she was returning

---

67   Irish for hurley stick

from a match at Moygannon where Clonduff had beaten the John Martins, the Warrenpoint team of the time. Nellie and Harriet Ryan were in charge of the McAnulty children on the day, the youngest of whom was in the pram. A couple of tenders of Black and Tans were passing and one of the occupants shouted something at the Ryan girls which drew a retort from Nellie, the older of the two. The tender stopped and a couple of the auxiliaries approached, one of them an officer. Sheila related every word of the ensuing exchanges, which ended with Nellie being placed under arrest and driven off in the tender. Then there was the uproar in the McAnulty household when they arrived home, the subsequent efforts of her father to trace Nellie, and the events which led to her release the next day. All in all, a remarkable story.

In the early 60s, when she was well settled in Dublin, a voluntary group was set up to promote the historical significance of Kilmainham Jail; it had lain almost derelict since it was closed a couple of years after the Irish state came into being. Sheila was a member of that group which initiated public opening and limited tours of the prison. She trained as a guide herself and often arranged groups from home to visit and be guided by her. Now Kilmainham Jail is a national museum of great significance.

For the uninitiated, *Scór* is an off-the-field GAA activity which is organised on the same basis as the National Football and Hurling Championships, in that it is contested at club, county, provincial and national levels. It comprises competitions in music, dancing, recitation, *etc.,* as well as a quiz, through which vehicle Sheila became famous to a wider GAA family. I was instrumental in introducing her to the competition the first time it was held in Warrenpoint Town Hall. I had been given the responsibility of getting three members for the quiz team but I could only field two, Mickey Devlin and myself. I had already advised my 16-year old son, Hugh, that he would have to make his debut—a parental direction he accepted under strenuous protest. The proceedings were about to get under way when I spied Sheila coming through the door and taking a seat well down the hall. The thought, 'there's my girl' struck me instantly, and I was at her side before she had settled. She turned me down point blank, but I persisted until she finally asked, 'Who have you?'

'Myself, Michael Devlin and Hugh, if you refuse me,' I replied.

'You wouldn't put the child on the stage,' she came back with a note of disgust in her voice and I knew I had her. That was the introduction of Sheila to *Scór.* In time, Michael Devlin retired and later I called it a day, too. Sheila persevered and eventually won an All-Ireland medal with Matt Durkin and Hugh, the child, as teammates. Her expertise in a wide range of cultural pursuits and her in-depth knowledge and feeling for the Association not only made her a remarkable contestant but it was also at the disposal of the Central Council when it set up the GAA museum in Croke Park, and they readily availed of it.

The last occasion she saw Down play was at Breffni Park in June 2004 when Cavan and Down replayed the game which had ended in a draw at Casement Park a couple of weeks before, and which she also witnessed. She watched both games from a wheelchair and those outings took a toll on her resistance. She died on 7

July of the same year.

I have no doubt that Sheila, in her lifetime, saw more Down games than any other person, living or dead. Nor do I have any doubt that she qualifies for the *Guinness Book of Records* as the person who has seen more All-Ireland Finals than any other. She attended every football and hurling final from 1930 until 2003, with only one exception, the Armagh-Kerry meeting in 2002, when Armagh collected the Sam Maguire Cup for the first time. Sheila viewed the game in Daisy Hill Hospital, Newry, and had the pleasure of congratulating Joe Kernan a couple of days later, when he visited the hospital with the cup.

While she was largely an establishment voice in the Association she had serious reservations about the advent of Ladies' football, and not merely because of the long-term undermining of the camogie code that it is likely to bring about. In her final days in hospital, the Ulster Council took the decision to stage the Ulster Final in Croke Park and, weak as she was, she wanted to know my reaction which I may say was very critical as I was very much against it. Not for the first time she and I differed, as she defended the decision, though I felt not with her usual conviction.

Something she said to me on one occasion suggested there had been romance in the early part of her life which never came to full blossom, but Sheila, being the woman she was, took it in her stride. Certainly there was a man in her life in the declining years in the person of Tommy Rice, her neighbour directly across the road. In his retirement, Tommy was part of the Summerhill furniture as he held court with the passing world over his garden wall. He had a key to Sheila's house, as we had, and was something of a full-time caretaker, making sure windows and doors were locked and unlocked night and morn. Tommy, himself, has since passed to join Sheila in eternity.

She will be long remembered.

37—Reflections

Sixty-five years of GAA membership as player, referee, delegate, commentator, administrator and spectator gives me some small degree of competence to comment on the changing face of the Association over that lengthy period. One can only contrast the blanket media coverage that is accorded to it, day and daily, with the unobtrusive reporting and comment of earlier years.

Alas, everything is directed to commenting and reporting on games, and little or nothing is directed at the game itself. I am specifically referring to football, where the rate of minor rule changing is causing greater confusion while the major changes, which might improve the game, are not being looked at. Hurling seems to have an in-built capacity for renewing itself without any detriment to the basic skills of the game, which make it the great spectacle that it is.

Those who write and comment on football simply do not seem to be aware of the dreadful spectacle that Gaelic football has become. Before anyone can say 'old fogey' or even 'purist,' I concede that some of it is exciting, which is all the public wants at this stage of our development. But our pundits are, for the most part, only concerned with what happens on the Inter-County playing fields and with the excitements of the hour; they appear blissfully unaware of the thousands of games around the country, from the under eights up, in which the players and their coaches are all trying to emulate the skills they see at the highest levels. With the avalanche of coaching and training which we are experiencing one must ask how can natural talent emerge. Will we ever see another Doherty or O'Neill?

I have a clear recollection of my earliest association as manager with the Down team putting forth the view that, under the rules of the game, it should be possible to coach a team to retain possession almost indefinitely, but that it would be a dreadful game to watch. Many are of the view that we are now in the era of that dreadful game. Now, we have a game in which all 15 players, goalkeeper included, are required to be ball carriers, producing pace that varies from slow bicycle race to 100 yards sprint, and all this in a game in which there is no legitimate tackle.

Of course, there is harassment, shoulder charging and blocking, the combination of all three, almost defying consistent interpretation by referees, and producing injuries on a scale that was unheard of even 25 years ago. Is it beyond the wit of our legislators to devise a tackle which can be clearly defined and executed?

The simple fact is that it is too easy today for a team to retain possession in Gaelic football. Therefore, it may be that the time has come to examine those elements of the game which tend to make Gaelic football resemble what might be called, 'vigorous basketball'. I refer to the solo run and the hand (fist) pass. In the present climate their unrestricted use is detrimental to the game.

About 50 years ago I, along with some others, were proposing that some experimentation should be done with the 13-a-side game. Eventually it was decided to try it out in one of the subsidiary competitions in Ulster. It was a total flop. The urge to run with the ball was given even freer rein. Seven-a-side competition went the same way. There seems to be no end of subsidiary competitions at the present time, so I suggest that one of them might be used to experiment with a game with a restricted use of the hand pass, or one in which the man in possession is restricted to limited toe taps. Alternatively, the introduction of a tackle on the Australian model should be considered, as indeed should a couple of other rules from the Australian game.

Recalling the most recent Australian debacle of 2006, one would have thought that the case for discontinuing the series had been made, but apparently not so as we had the resumption of hostilities in 2010. The 2006 visit of the Australians to Ireland should have been the watershed that brought the series to an end; this after a marketing campaign which exploited all the excesses of the Melbourne meeting the previous year. The marketing campaign was a success, for it resulted in the biggest attendance ever to watch the Australians. The game, however, was a fiasco displaying all the unruly scenes which had been part of the performance of the previous year. But the 'internationalisation' of the Association goes on, and to what purpose? Hong Kong, Singapore, Dubai and wherever next. While one is conscious of the role the GAA has in sharing the national ideal with the Irish *diaspora,* some thought has to be given to the club scene at home. Now that 'the back door' has been opened, the club scene has been almost completely side-lined. Here in Down, the leagues, and even the County Championship, operate on week nights, though the Senior Championship is awarded a Sunday final.

Is it any wonder that a Club Forum held in Killarney in November 2005 attracted 1,400 representatives from all over the country? Obviously, it seems to be the same story all over the place, when leagues which commence in March or April are still unfinished in December. Worse still, games are played at the most awkward days and times, but rarely, if ever, on a Sunday, and generally before the minimum of spectators. I do not know how 'the Club Forum' came about, but I do hope that it has not gone into oblivion. It has never been more needed.

It is most apposite that one of our 'quality' scribes should be telling us, 'the GAA must move away from the past,' when all the evidence is that our past has made us what we are. As a nation, we have struggled over centuries to preserve a culture that said something of what we are. Now, we are being advised to dump it and embrace the new multi-culturalism spawned by globalisation and economic forces. It is in those areas, where we have moved away from the past, that demean us.

Our great finals are becoming tawdry in the manner that they have been taken over by the commercial and drinking cultures. Some of our members have recourse to law in circumstances that undermine the best interests of the Association. Worse still, we have a Co. Antrim Board flouting the ruling of Central Council in relation to the use of Casement Park. Not only is it a disturbing development, it is also a sinister development, and one to which serious consideration must be given. Are we to be held hostage to fortune for evermore? No County Committee would defy the Central Authority unless it sensed implications, which most outside the Northern province might not appreciate.

I had always assumed the GAA was the body that controlled its members in the most democratic manner possible, but that is no longer the case. Now we have a small body of members who are attempting to change the very nature of the Association. Our Gaelic Players' Association, true to the spirit of the age, reflects the price of everything but the value of very little: €127 (per week, or per match, I know not,) was the value it put on the services of its select group of members when it first came into existence some years ago. Then it became player grants from Government funds. The credit crunch seems to have closed that avenue of enrichment, so now it is seeking a percentage of the Association's annual income; unbelievably, the powers that be have caved into their demands. This is a serious breach in the amateur status of the GAA movement and stems from the appalling lack of leadership at the highest levels in recent years. We have seen the Cork county players take on the Cork County Committee and, with the help of the media, rub officialdom's nose in the mud. Is this to be the pattern of the relationship between these select groups of playing members over the whole country in the coming days? I have no objection to any group founding a professional Gaelic sports body but I strongly object to any group turning the GAA into such a body.

I do not know how many of our GPA members have read Con Short's *The Ulster GAA Story*. In it, he includes a message from Cardinal Tomás Ó Fiach to mark the centenary of the Association in 1984. I will quote a few sentences from it:

> 'For a centenarian, the GAA is surprisingly young at heart. No organisation has made a greater contribution to Irish life and to the national revival. Its members are sprightly, noisy, unselfish and idealistic. I hope they never become silent, materialistic, soft or self-centred.
>
> In the North, the GAA is now our strongest link with the rest of Ireland. For GAA men, Ulster has still nine counties and Ireland 32. Clones, Breffni Park, and Ballybofey are as well known to us as Armagh, Newry and Dungannon. There are still bridges to be built with people with the tradition of McCracken and Munroe, Mitchel and Casement. A great task lies ahead during the coming century.'

It is only recently that I have heard myself introduced as Gaelic football's first manager and, while I do not lay claim to that distinction, there were not many of the breed about in 1959. If it is true, I will stake a claim to be the man responsible for introducing the role, for I have already indicated I made the proposal to appoint a Down manager. At this stage in our development, managers have become the lynch-pin of the game, and the media portray the games as contests between the respective managers, rather than between the teams. If success is not achieved in the specified time, either the manager commits hari-kari or gets the chop. This might be all right in professional soccer or rugby, where the pool of players is a global one, and where millions of pounds are available to the competing managers seeking to fill the weak spots in their teams. Even with that, the pile of ex-managers gets higher by the year.

Contrast this to the GAA scene, where residence or birthplace are the deciding factors, and the pool of players is a limited one. Clubs and counties have to grow their own. This is what makes the GAA so different to other sporting organisations, and this is why success comes in cycles for most counties and, indeed, for most clubs. It is this 'sense of place' which makes it impossible to 'forget the past', as we have been advised to. With these thoughts in mind, is it any wonder I was shocked by the treatment accorded to Paddy O'Rourke, who had managed the Down team for a four-year period? That he should have had to defend his performance before a meeting of club delegates, as a prelude to his dismissal, was beyond belief. In taking on the Armagh managerial role, Paddy must feel he has something to prove. I wish him all the luck in the world.

His successor, Ross Carr, got his marching orders, too, in much the same fashion, though he was spared Paddy O'Rourke's final humiliating experience before the club delegates. Ross, however, felt the need to have it out with the county executive, but I doubt if their meeting resolved anything. The process of appointing a successor to Ross seems to have been a very involved operation, but it ended in renewing the McCartan family link to Down football at the highest level. That can't be a bad thing, though it was unfortunate that Peter McGrath should have felt aggrieved in the process.

I recall Peter's period as manager, when one of the players saw fit to criticise him publicly. I wrote a short letter to *The Irish News* which they published and awarded me £10 for 'best letter of the week'. Down went on to win two All-Irelands under Peter, but my reward from *The Irish News* must have gone astray in the post for I never received it. In my time, County Boards took responsibility for appointing managers and selectors and took the blame if things did not turn out well. Now it seems a convention of clubs takes these decisions, and nobody can be blamed.

I could not leave the management scene without contrasting my own approach to the job with the style of some of the modern breed. I have in mind the manager with one of the Armagh clubs who featured in a television series shown by the BBC a few years ago. I only viewed one episode, after which I felt he should have been suspended for life for bringing the Association into disrepute.

In more recent times, the pile of ex-county team managers grows by the year and one wonders what the end of the story will be. Take Dublin for instance, they have won five Leinster titles in a row, and have gone through at least three managers in the process. Their failure against Kerry in 2007 and subsequent failures underlined the lack of real leadership on the field, which has characterised Dublin teams of the past decade. I watched that game with Kerry and when that demoralising goal was scored in the opening seconds I thought of the Down-Offaly final of 1961 when the Leinster men scored two goals in the opening five minutes. I have described that game as Down's finest hour. It had nothing to do with the management of the team. It had everything to do with the quality of leadership on the field.

It is unfortunate that Dublin have not been able to make the breakthrough in their long spell of Leinster dominance, but the notion of a Kerry melt-down has to be seen for the mirage (cooked up by most of our pundits) it turned out to be. It was disappointing that Tyrone failed to renew their final rivalry with Kerry in 2009, but they were well beaten by a Cork side which seemed capable of repeating their Munster Championship success over The Kingdom. But Kerry is still Kerry, whether they get in by the back door or the front door. They certainly left Croke Park with a smile which almost had the suggestion of a smirk in it.

I have to confess that I left 'the field of dreams' with a bit of a smiling face myself, but the smile quickly changed to a frown when Hugh and Louise simultaneously announced, 'We're clamped' as we came in sight of the car. I had to put my hands up at once to plead guilty, for I had insisted that my invalid badge would be acceptable on the yellow line. It wasn't, and over the phone we paid our €80, but still had to wait an hour before we were unclamped. The fourth member of our party was my grandson, Eoin, who thought it was a great, if long lasting adventure. In the course of our enforced stay a young member of the Gardaí on a bicycle stopped to sympathise with us on our plight. I drew his attention to my invalid badge on display and he advised me to write to the authority enclosing a copy of my badge. Louise did as advised and, in a couple of weeks, we had our €80 returned complete with an expression of regret for any inconvenience caused. So I give a public 'thank you' from the Carrs.

We are all conscious of the changing face of Ireland, much of which is to be welcomed, but few will deny that the virus of affluence is undermining many of the values we thought were in-built. In its lifetime, the GAA has been conscious of its role in helping to shape the nation, sometimes to good effect and sometimes to no effect, but always with the best of intentions. One must ask if the present obsession with 'marketing' the games reflects the values which made the Association what it is. To read the reported grovelling apologies offered to the sponsors of the National Leagues for the poor attendances at the 2006 finals was stomach churning.

Again, we had the Ulster Council playing the Provincial Final in Croke Park because of the possibility of an additional 25,000 spectators. Using the same accounting logic, the Munster Hurling Final, with its 52,000 gate, would be a sell-out in Croke Park. Is Thurles such a different place from Clones? Is it so much easier for people from all over Munster to get to Thurles than it is for people from all over Ulster to get to Clones? It is to be hoped the new Casement Park will be the Ulster showpiece capable of taking any Ulster Final crowd.

And what of the National League Final of 2008? Then, less than 10,000 people viewed the proceedings at Parnell Park, where Derry just shaded Kerry in a lustreless encounter. Contrast that with the Down–Cavan final of 1960 which attracted over 50,000 without any marketing at all.

38—Deeper Reflections

It had been my intention to finish this memoir with a reference to the pastoral letter issued by Dr John McAreavey, Bishop of Dromore, a few years ago, *A Time of Scarcity. A Time of Opportunity.* It dealt with the falling numbers of priests in the diocese and the scarcity of priestly vocations. Serious as these problems are for thinking and believing Catholics, they have almost been side-lined by the awful disclosures of *The Ferns Report* on the sexual abuse of children and young people by some clerics in that diocese. More recently, we have had *The Ryan Report* which examined the abuses in schools, homes and orphanages run by some of the religious orders. And even more recently we have had the report on the Dublin Archdiocese which more than fulfilled the predicted horror story we had been warned to expect.

Add to these the various other cases which have come to light in different parts of the country, and we get the impression that the Church is crumbling at its very foundations. Indeed, Maynooth itself, and those who were responsible for the directing of that establishment, must share a heavy responsibility for its failure to realise what was happening, even under its own roof, over a period. That was back in the 70s. Had the whistleblower been heeded we might have been spared much of what was to come later. Probably we all share the responsibility, for in all our lives 'the man who has the name of early rising, can sleep to dinner time.' Seldom is he caught out. Even when he was caught out the measures taken to deter and sideline him beggar belief, and this after the whistle blower had been banished— but then it is easy talking from hindsight.

It is hard to imagine that any man would offer himself to the priesthood of Christ for any other reason than to serve God and the Church, but obviously some have failed to understand the true meaning of their vocations. The wonder and the reality is that the overwhelming majority of our priests and religious are untainted by the tidal wave of distorted and disordered sexuality which has built up around the world, particularly in the last few decades, creating a tsunami of immorality and degradation that will have even more devastating effects than those which shocked the world on St Stephen's Day 2004.

Of course, the critics and the enemies of the Church are on their high horse. 'God is dead, the Church is finished,' is what they shout, not realising that over the centuries, because of its human face, the Church has always had to contend with corruption in some shape or form. If Christ had not been at its heart, the Church would have been extinct centuries ago.

Christ is not called the Eternal Priest for nothing. Uniquely, He is the backbone of a priesthood which has spanned two thousand years. Every man who has had the defining hands laid on him is part of the mystical body that has Christ as its spinal cord, and through which flows the power to renew Christ in the Eucharist, and dispense Christ's forgiveness in the confessional. He is in effect another Christ. I repeat Newman's warning to those who feel called to receive the sacrament of Holy Orders:

> *'So again they who enter Holy Orders promise they know not what,*

engage themselves they know not how deeply, debar themselves of the world's ways they know not how intimately, find perchance they must cut off from them the right hand, sacrifice the desire of their eyes and the stirring of their hearts at the foot of the Cross, while they thought in their simplicity they were choosing the easy life of quiet plain men dwelling in tents.'

One hundred years after Newman, the Lutheran theologian Dietrich Bonhoeffer, who was hanged by the Nazi Government in Germany in 1945, was more succinct when he wrote, 'when Christ calls a man, He bids him come and die.'

To suggest, as the new enlightenment does, with the approval of some bishops and priests, that celibacy is at the heart of the abuse problem, is in my view to misunderstand the relationship between Christ, the priesthood and the Eucharist. Not only does the priest enact the sacrifice, he is part of the sacrifice. He is a man apart from others. The fact that some former Anglican married clergy have been ordained to the priesthood is often paraded as double-speak by the Church, when in reality, it is the Church exercising both its power and its humanity. By the same token, the ordination of women to the priesthood is unlikely ever to be a runner, not for any desire to discriminate but rather to maintain and sustain the spinal cord of Christ's Mystical Body. The Church 'distinguishes between the equal dignity of men and women on the one hand and the differentiation of the two sexes.'

Some reading this might imagine that I regard myself as having some expertise in the theology of the priesthood, but I can assure them such is not the case. I would claim, however, a degree of expertise in the centrality and uniqueness of the spinal cord, as we shall see.

In his pastoral letter of September 2005, Dr John McAreavey painted a picture of the dearth of priestly vocations in the diocese, which would reflect the situation in every part of the country. Not only are there fewer priests, there are fewer of 'the faithful' attending Sunday Mass or, indeed, taking part in religious observance of any kind. In the climate of a 24 hours a day, 7 days a week economy, there is little time for God after the excesses and frivolity of our lives are indulged. Nothing that I could write is likely to change the trend, but I am compelled to repeat the relevant words of Christ for those inhabitants of Capernaum who rejected his teaching, despite the number of miracles he performed in that area. Ireland, which has been sustained by the Christian message over the centuries, is in danger of dispensing with it, too. Hell-fire sermons are out of fashion these days, but according to Matthew's gospel 11: 23-24, this is what He said:

> 'You shall be thrown down to hell, for if the miracles done in you, had been done in Sodom, it would have been standing yet. And still, I tell you it will not go as hard with the land of Sodom on Judgement day as with you.'

I have no notion of the nature of hell, but I have had the slightest insight of the all-consuming joy of heaven. It would be hell for me not to experience that joy in eternity.

In 1997, we had 53 priests working in the diocese of Dromore and of those, two were over the retirement age of 75 years; it was much the same picture over the entire country. In 2005 we had 41 priests, and one young man studying for the priesthood. What will the picture be like in 2029 when, even today, we have parishes in the diocese without a priest? I use the particular year, marking two centuries of 'emancipation,' to ask and wonder if a return to the penal days would be good for us? It goes without saying that we should continually be praying for vocations, but we need to do more. Bishops ordain priests, they cannot make and fashion them—that process, up until recently, was the preserve in nearly all cases of the Catholic home where the faith was a living reality. While there is an impression around that vocations in the past were plentiful, they were hardly adequate to sustain the home and foreign mission. In my lifetime, three or four homes in the old parish of Clonallon supplied half the priestly vocations between them. I refer to the Carvill–Treanor connection, and the Boyle and McGivern families, most of whom touched my life to good effect.

There is a notion, too, that in earlier times the paucity of employment opportunities spurred vocations, but I have not the slightest doubt that any of those who sought to follow Christ would have been equally successful in any path they chose.

Believing Catholics have to sit up and take stock of the world we live in today. Our families are the seedbeds of vocations and we must ensure that every seedling is nurtured with its ultimate end in view: being with, and in Christ. It is unlikely that the vocations' crisis in Ireland will be solved in the short-term, but every encouragement must be given to our young people. The emphasis in our education system is all about success, as indeed it is in every aspect of living, reflecting 'the spirit of the times'. Chesterton, as relevant today as ever, says:

> *'If you marry the spirit of the times, you will soon become a widower.*
> *If you seek and find and communicate "the permanent things", you are*
> *permanently relevant.'*

On Saturday, 9 April 2005, I was at morning Mass in St Peter's Church, Warrenpoint, at the end of which Fr Peter McNeill asked for a few volunteers to finish off a distribution of envelopes, which is an annual chore in the parish. I had almost completed the area I had been allocated the previous day but I volunteered to take another helping.

After Mass, I proceeded to deliver the three boxes I had from the previous day on the Upper Dromore Road. First call was Pat Longridge and as I got to the top of the short but sharp incline to his house I felt a strange sensation just at the back of the knee joints in both legs. It passed in a second and I dropped the package through the letterbox, completed the delivery and went home to my lunch. It was Grand National day, so John, Louise and I made our selections. I made my annual pilgrimage to Frank Hughes' betting emporium in Newry Street, where I was accorded the courtesy shown to regular punters by Kevin Farrell.

All bets laid, and off I headed for Rowallon and Rathgannon to deliver the boxes I had got that morning. Plenty of time for the delivery and then home to watch the race. I had about four boxes left when I realised that something was happening to me and I struggled to get back to my car. With some difficulty, I managed to drive back to Summerhill, but when I opened the car door and put my feet on the ground I was powerless. I could not get out of the car. I called a passer-by, a complete stranger, asked him if he would ring my doorbell and if he would mind waiting to assist me out of the car. There was no response to the doorbell, but fortunately one of my youthful neighbours, Paul Mackin, came on the scene and realised I had a problem.

Paul and the Good Samaritan got me out of the car and into my front room just as Louise came in from the garden. She contacted the emergency doctor services which operate at weekends while I sat powerless but without the slightest pain. It occurred to me that it was getting close to Grand National starting time, but the television was in the middle room. I slid onto the floor, pushed myself in and viewed the race sitting on the floor cheering Hedgehunter, one of Louise's choices, over the finishing line. She already had established that my son, Hugh, was in Belfast, so she rang McAnulty's to look for assistance to get me off the floor. When I heard from her conversation with Mairead that Tarlach would come up, I shouted, 'No, don't let Tarlach come up,' for Tarlach suffered from cystic fibrosis. Louise put the phone down and said, 'Mairead says that when he's well that he is as strong as a horse, and he's well today.' In a matter of seconds Tarlach appeared at the back door and they had me on the settee without a bother.

It was a couple of hours before the doctor came. After examining me he expressed the view that it might be a mild stroke—a view I did not share, though without giving expression to it. The ambulance he ordered arrived in little more than half an hour to convey me to Daisy Hill Hospital. In the next couple of hours, and after every test in the book, it was confirmed that I did not have a stroke. One of the resident consultants saw me the next day, Sunday, after which she advised, 'Dr Craig, a consultant neurologist from the Royal, will see you when he comes on Wednesday.'

On Monday morning, a youthful physiotherapist came to speak to me about my condition. In the afternoon he came back with a senior colleague. With their assistance I was able to stand and take a step or two. On Tuesday, with support, I was able to move slowly round the bed. On Wednesday, Dr Craig came. We talked for a few minutes and he did the routine tests which the other medics had done, after which he said, 'I am aware you were on your feet yesterday, so you are improving, and I will not need to see you again unless you disimprove.' Happily that is the last I have seen of Dr Craig.

I was in the hospital for one day short of three weeks and during that time I was able to observe at first-hand how a hospital works. Despite all the complaints, we have a unique Health Service. Leaving the hospital I had a greatly reduced ability to walk, and a walking stick, which has earned me a great deal of respect from motorists and other pedestrians ever since.

When I was called to a clinic on 7 July, I expected to see Dr McDowell whom I had been under during my stay in hospital, but it was a colleague standing in for her who introduced herself warmly with, 'So you are Mr Carr, the mystery man.'

'Mystery man?' I queried in an exaggerated tone.

'Yes,' she continued, 'you have had a very rare condition and we are at a loss to know how a man of your age of 82 could have contracted it.'

She told me the name of the condition, though beyond knowing that it was an *'itis'* of some kind, it did not register. We talked about it at some length, and I took my leave of her in the knowledge that I would be seen again in October. By that time, I was doing remarkably well and had managed the hurling and football finals in Croke Park, with the aid of a couple of minders and the lift. Come October, it was the same lady whom I had seen in July. She commented favourably on the manner I had walked through the door, and before we really got talking I put my open diary in front of her, and asked, 'Would you mind writing down the name of the condition that I have?' This she did commenting, 'This is my very best handwriting.' She wrote, *'transverse myelitis'*.

When Louise came home from school I showed her what the doctor had written; an hour later she showed me a six page document she had taken off the Internet, *'Transverse myelitis—Symptoms, Causes and Diagnosis,'* over the name of a Joanne Lynn, MD. Therein lies all of my expertise on the spinal cord and I could only marvel at the precise detail of the descriptions of the symptoms. It was reassuring to read that 'most patients with TM show good to fair recovery' if the healing process commenced within three months. I had started to improve within a couple of days. The brain and spinal cord is the most complex computer of them all. Imagine, ten million nerves running along that narrow channel conveying never- ending messages to every part of the body and using billions of neurons in the process.

Even before I read all the information off the Internet, I had a fair degree of reassurance from the doctor at Daisy Hill, for the second question I put to her was, 'Do you think I'll walk naturally again?'

As she sat back in her chair, she answered, 'Oh, I think you will, but it will be slow process. It will take four or five years at least.'

'Do you mean to say I have another five years in me?' and this with a note of humorous incredulity.

'It will not surprise me if you do another ten,' she laughed.

Driving home from that appointment at Daisy Hill I was considering an important decision I had to make before the end of October; the doctor's confidence made up my mind for me. I have already mentioned that I was at the hurling and football finals in 2005. I did not intimate that these were the last finals of my ten-year ticket. The decision I had to make was whether or not I should be in for another ten years. I decided, yes. My first errand next morning was to the bank to see if the balance would stretch to €5,000—for me and my minder—a lot of money. It didn't, but Credit Union came to my rescue and, for the next ten years, if I have not reached the celestial level, I will be on a lower level to that from which I viewed for the past decade. I'll be 93 then.

I had a couple of valid reasons for delaying the publication of this memoir, which could well have been (or still be) a posthumous publication. In the early spring of 2007, my doctor referred me to a clinic in Daisy Hill Hospital for examination into what we both thought was a not too serious condition.

In the course of the examination, the youthful doctor picked up something else which required investigation, an abdominal aneurysm. In due course, I was called back to Daisy Hill for a full-scale discussion on the implications, and the news that I would be going to the vascular surgery unit in the City Hospital, Belfast. The investigation into my original complaint would be hurried, and it was. On 16 May I received a letter from Belfast City Hospital to contact them to discuss an appointment on 20 June. I rang them at 7.45 P.M. and confirmed the appointment.

I watched the *RTÉ* News at 9.00 P.M. and settled to watch the election debate which was to follow. I never heard a word of it. A searing pain in stomach and back made me call my daughter's name before losing consciousness. This I recovered as an ambulance team was getting me on to a stretcher and thence to Daisy Hill Hospital, from where I was dispatched to the Royal Infirmary in Belfast. I was completely aware of everything that was happening. But I was totally unaware that the doctor in Daisy Hill had advised my son and daughter that I had a three-in-ten chance of surviving the journey, and hardly a 50–50 chance of surviving the operation if I did.

There are not as many bends on the road to Belfast now as there were when I drove and conducted buses on it, but I was acutely aware of each of the roundabouts which were the milestones for me. A team of doctors and nurses awaited my arrival and the quiet confidence they exuded, combined with the reassurance they conveyed, could have suggested I was having a few minor procedures carried out, rather than the three-plus hours life-saving operation they completed. Next morning, a number of them came in to see me in the recovery ward. They were amazed to see me sitting up in bed after having a cup of tea.

'What age are you, Mr Carr?' one of them asked, and when I admitted to 84 years past and expressed an expectation that I would get to 85, there was a mild ripple of laughter in which I joined. Later that day, a nurse came to tell me that the doctor who had seen me at Daisy Hill the previous night had phoned to ask if I had survived, and conveyed his best wishes for a full recovery.

I was discharged after nine days, progressing from recovery, to high dependency, to a single bed ward where time passed at a much slower rate, providing ample time for reflection. The constant theme of that reflection was prompted by a party piece of the late Fr Tom McConville, one of the great priests of the Dromore Diocese in my life time. No night of jollification was complete without 'The Touch of the Master's Hand' from Fr Tom, and this embellished with his interlude on the violin, which instrument is central to the story of the poem.

Fr Tom varied his tune regularly, but it was always a slow air—*Home sweet home, Just a song at twilight, An Cualann* or the like, all giving effect to the touch of the Master. I have long been conscious of the touch of the Master's hand in my own life but never has the experience been so dramatic as in this life-preserving surgery, a miracle in timing, in efficiency and in medical skill for which I am truly grateful. Some will say coincidence, but Chesterton and I know better.

When I arrived home, visiting was somewhat restricted for the first week.

Andy Tohill called in due course, giving voice to the shock he and his wife, Aveen, experienced when they heard I had been prayed for at Mass and was unlikely to survive. In a concerned tone of voice he added, 'I hope you will not be offended at this, but I have to tell you, I considered what the band would play at your funeral.' We chatted for a time, but as he was leaving I said to him, 'About the music for my funeral, Andy; I don't know what you were going to play, but I'll tell you what I would like,' and I mentioned the name of a piece of music. 'We'll need a week's notice of your death to get that ready,' he laughed, 'but we'll do our best.'

I was back at The Royal on 4 September when the doctor was very pleased with my recovery. He had been a member of the team involved in my operation and he knew how ill I had been. In the course of our conversation, I told him I had not resumed driving and asked if it would be in order for me to do so. When he indicated that there was nothing to stop me from driving, I said to him, 'I'm good for a year or two, then,' in the form of a question. He gave me the same answer as the doctor in Daisy Hill Hospital, 30 months earlier, 'Mr Carr, you could do another ten years.'

Over many years, two of my September Sundays have normally seen me at the hurling and football finals at Croke Park, but that year, 2007, I decided I would be very charitable to a fervent Kilkenny supporter in The Point, my eldest grandson, Eoin, all of seven years, who did not have a ticket. He was delighted when I offered him mine, and even more delighted with the result of what was, for most people, a rather disappointing game. Limerick just did not perform. Like the football final between Kerry and Cork at which I was present, it exposed the deficiency in the backdoor system. It was the same story as far as the football was concerned in 2006 when Mayo folded against Kerry. Both could be classed as entirely missable events.

One event in September 2007, which I would not liked to have missed, was Joe Boylan's funeral. Joe, two years my senior, was the friendliest fellow, boy and man, whom one could have ever met. The story told by Canon Kearney of the Boylan family's arrival in The Point was as clear to me as if it had happened the previous day, and it was more than 75 years before. Joe's father, James Boylan, was a sea captain whose wife had died shortly before he came to live at Irene Terrace with his five children and an outstanding housekeeper, Minnie Kennedy.

While the Canon continued speaking, I was mentally sorting out the Fisher fleet of boats, all named after trees, and decided that Captain Boylan skippered the *Poplar*. I recalled, too, the Boylan children coming down to the pier head to wave to their father as he passed through the perches on his way to or from Newry, and his recognising blast on the ship's horn. I even recalled the Mullan family greeting and saying 'goodbye' to their father, who was the master of the *Dundalk* and getting the same blast of recognition.

The highlights of Joe's long life were remembered with some humour before the Canon paused, and advised the congregation, 'You know, Joe had a party piece.' Many would have known Joe's favourite, but the Canon, completely in the context of the sermon, took a breath and in perfect pitch intoned....

> *South of the border, down Mexico way*
> *That's where I fell in love when stars above, came out to play.*
> *And now as I wander my thoughts ever stray,*
> *South of the border down Mexico way.*

There was a silence, and the congregation wondered if there was more to come, but when it was realised that the song had ended, there was an outburst of feeling, a heart warming ovation the like of which Bing Crosby or the first of the singing cowboys, Gene Autry, at their best never experienced. When it was finished, the Canon continued his eulogy of Joe, still in complete context. Joe Boylan and his funeral will be long remembered in The Point.

Canon Kearney's arrival in Warrenpoint as administrator of St Peter's, Clonallon, caused an older generation to sit up and take notice. All our lives we had been used to older men—in my own case beginning with Canon McAllister and continuing with Canon Fitzpatrick, Canon Hugh Esler and Canon Hamill. To illustrate the youthfulness of Canon Kearney, I recall that on one of Down's returns with the Sam Maguire cup in the 90s he and I were standing with thousands of others waiting to welcome them home. In the course of our stand he said to me, 'One of my abiding memories is the return of the Down team in 1960. I was a boarder above in St Colman's and we were allowed out for two hours. I will never forget you leading the singing of *The dear little town in the old County Down*. Lord, you were singing from the heart that night.'

I have to note that since Joe's passing in 2007, I have followed the funerals of many whose names and deeds have been part of this memoir, for the period has seen the passing of Liam Bradley, Moya McCormack, and Joe Lambe; Charlie Carr, Liam O'Hare, and Tarlach McAnulty; Des Slevin, Pat Finnison, and Lily Prince; Maurice Murphy, Kevin Farrell, my neighbours Kay O'Hare and Vera O'Neill. Vera died in an accident on her way to see her husband, Jim, who was still alive and well in his Newry residential home. I feel compelled to expand on the lives of three of those names whose friendship was a bit special.

Even though Charlie Carr spent half his long life as a Warrenpoint citizen, he was forever 'a Bridge man' and would never have anyone think otherwise. In his years of retirement, however, he was very much a part of The Point community; there, his good humour and his good sense were enjoyed and appreciated by a wide circle of friends.

Charlie's university was the 'University of Life' and he graduated to his own quarry and roads operations after serving his time at the Paddy Fitzpatrick establishments at Mount Panther and Dundrum. Aughnagun and Charlie Carr became synonymous with the roads business once he got into his stride.

Business aside, he was a sportsman from his earliest years when he lined out with Mayobridge, and he was in his element when Down came to the fore in the late 50s and 60s. By that time, his sporting interests had widened considerably, for besides having running dogs he also had jumping horses whose jockeys sported the red and black of Down at venues round the country.

Despite Down's preponderance over Cavan in those days, he named his house *Breffni* in tribute to his wife Finola, a native of that county and she, with their daughter Orla, made it a happy and welcoming home to the end of his days.

As well as running dogs, Charlie had an affinity with 'lame dogs', most of whom he helped over stiles with a hidden hand. One man at his funeral said, 'Charlie never changed. He was a decent man all his life.' He was indeed, for he always walked close to the Lord in whom he now exists.

Our beloved 'Toots', whom I accompanied to Charlie's funeral, passed to his Eternal Home within weeks of Charlie's demise; we can only offer a communal thanks to the Lord for the gift of this great man, who has touched so many lives in so many ways over his lengthy life-span. I was his senior by a few months, so I have had the privilege of sharing his friendship from our earliest days in school, and it strikes me that I might have been better employed writing his story rather than my own these last few years.

By any standard Liam O'Hare was unique, for he suffered his share of sorrow in his lifetime. His father, John, principal at Carrick School and by all accounts a remarkable teacher, died before Liam had reached his seventh birthday. His brother, Brian, died in 1937 at the early age of 16. His son, Seamus, died at the age of 21 in the late 70s. Every seeming reverse deepened his faith, leaving him in complete uniformity with God's will. His successful business career never seemed to be a priority in his life for he always made time for the Lord and the Lord's work. The Mass was central to his life and it must be said if there was no choir, he provided his own. How wonderful it was to have the hymns he loved sung and played by the band at his funeral Mass.

With his commitments to the Lord, to the parish, to his family and to his business, one wonders how he got time for the GAA to which he had a lifetime attachment, first as a player and later as long-time chairman of St Peter's Club. He was a remarkable talent, playing for Down in their second-ever Ulster Final against Cavan in 1942, a few weeks after his nineteenth birthday, and later winning three Down Championships with St Peter's. His tenure as chairman saw the club make some remarkable advances with the provision of the clubrooms in Mary Street and its playing field at Moygannon. Later, he turned his energies to the promotion of *Scór* and the revival of hurling, achieving a remarkable degree of success in both activities.

After his funeral, Dickie McGuigan observed, 'There you are, Toots is the first of "The Big Three" to go,' and he left it at that. The other components of "The Big Three," as we were called in the club, were Ted Bradley and myself. We were both honoured guests at Moygannon on the occasion of the naming of the ground *Páirc Liam Uí Ír* in September 2009, an honour which he fully deserved. It was the most memorable day in the history of the GAA in Warrenpoint and a deserved tribute to this wonderful man who made such a contribution to the Warrenpoint community. I have no doubt, however, that the locals will be calling it "Toots' field".

Tarlach McAnulty did not enjoy the length of days accorded to Charlie Carr or Liam O'Hare. His life lasted just 36 years. His father, Terry, died at the early age of 47, the year after he was born. Soon after birth, Tarlach was diagnosed as a cystic fibrosis sufferer; most of us know the implications of that condition for both the patient and the family. From his earliest years, he had to cope with the restrictive binds of his illness, but he took them all in his stride, never once complaining. He carved out a lifestyle for his periods of well-being which would have done justice to any healthy man. He missed out on the comradeship of the classroom and the school yard but no one had more genuine friends. He never did more than kick a ball as a child, yet he was an avid follower of Warrenpoint and Down teams and, let it be said, could make valid judgements on individual and team performances. He was on the top of the world in 1991 and 1994 when Down took their last two All-Irelands, witnessing most of the games in both campaigns. He had hoped for a third during his life time but that ambition was not fulfilled. Golf was the game he really got into, for he could play it at his own pace, and if he holed a few good putts in a round that was an achievement in which he took great pleasure.

Music was a wonderful outlet for his artistic talent. While concert going was a big thing for him, it was as drummer in his brother Cathal's band that provided the main outlet for his enthusiasm. The gentle humour with which he related some of the escapades with the band was always evident in the telling, as indeed it was of his travels to America and the continental holidays. He could find humour in very simple things. Despite its brevity and its restrictions, Tarlach had a wonderful life.

It would be true to say that he had an even more wonderful death; I am sure the McAnulty family will not mind me intruding on their memories of those special hours when the wills of Tarlach and the Lord were in complete conformity. I was made aware of the hospital situation when the phone rang and I found myself talking to Tarlach's brother, Hugh. He described in some detail how Tarlach had said his farewells to all the family, speaking to them individually and as a family. He was consoling them and was completely in control. When he was finished he said to his mother, 'I would love to see my pal, John, before I go,' hence Hugh's phone call to us. I said I would leave with John in minutes, but he insisted, 'No no, don't rush down tonight, come early in the morning, he will go another day.' It was 8.30 P.M. on a Friday.

Our John's barometer on Tarlach's well-being over the years had just two markers. When he would come up from Macs (McAnulty), and we asked, 'How is Tarlach?' the answer was either 'great' or 'not too bad.' When I advised him that we would be going to see Tarlach early the following morning he punched the air with clenched fist and exclaimed, 'Great.' He thought Tarlach was on the recovery mode.

I was awakened by a ringing phone before 7 A.M. on Saturday morning and at once I thought, 'Tarlach has died.' It was his mother, Mairead, confirming he had passed away minutes before. I think the Lord wished John to have only happy memories of Tarlach.

In writing of Tarlach McAnulty's death I am deeply conscious of the other families in the town whose beautiful children were victims of the cystic fibrosis scourge, and who did not have the length of his days. They are all remembered.

I am also conscious that writing about the deaths of so many of my friends and neighbours might be thought by some to be a sad ending to this book. Death itself is not sad. It is the partings which make it so, and it is for that reason I write now about my two oldest and dearest living friends, who have shared some wonderful chapters of my long life and who are preparing themselves for the Lord's call. Both are younger men than me and, while I could be called at short notice, I have the feeling I will outlive them.

Eugene McKay was one of the boys who shared the road to Carrick School with me in the mid-thirties. Even in those early days he displayed the gentle humour which became an integral part of his personality. Our paths divided for a few years as we sought an education, but we came together again as part of the great Point side of the 40s, and, indeed, a good Down team of the period. He had a unique dummy, the slowest action imaginable, so slow at times we thought it wasn't going to happen. He settled in Armagh, married, reared his family there, and is as highly thought of as he is in the home parish. We shared a few wonderful holidays, one of which came back into focus when I read one of the books I got on Russell Trodden's book shelves, *Three men in a boat*. It sent me back to 1952 when Eugene, Toots and I went on a camping tour of the country which commenced at the Ulster football final between Cavan and Monaghan, and ended a week later at the All-Ireland semi-final in Croke Park. Had I read Jerome's classic earlier in my life I'm sure I would have attempted a *Three Men in a Tent* saga. He and I have relived those days in more recent times, when his frailty has not completely concealed his sense of humour. I pray for a gentle and peaceful end to his wonderful life.

Ted Bradley has figured in the early pages of this memoir as the hard-done-by schoolboy wrongly blamed, so it is entirely fitting that the story of his life should be briefly recorded in this last chapter. We did not share any early school experiences because he grew up in Clontifleece, where his father was school principal, and I had left The Abbey before he started there. His eldest brother, Arthur, was one of the youthful group who came to the fore in St Peter's first senior success, and all the Bradley boys played as they came of age. Both Liam and Ted were later to become club secretaries.

Like most of his family, Ted entered the teaching profession and after a period working in Belfast he was appointed to the staff of St Peter's Boys Primary School, of which he later became principal. His tenure there was a happy and rewarding one; parents, pupils and staff all recognised a man of remarkable integrity. I was fortunate to have had a rewarding professional relationship with him for much of my time in the Education Welfare Service. While he contributed much to the Warrenpoint community in his teaching career, the GAA fraternity will remember him much more for the central role he played, first as player and then as long-time secretary in St Peter's Club. Even with his central role in the club, he made time for his other great interest, sailing boats. He loved the sea and the challenges it presents. Now he is coming to the end of his great life voyage, with all sails set for the home port called eternity. I can only marvel at the composure of this man, who takes every day as it comes with the clear-cut discernment that was the feature of his life. In irregular episodes, I have read most of this book to him for our mutual enjoyment, not in the merits of the writing but in some fuller pictures we both recalled about individuals or incidents.

One great moment in these sessions, which we both will cherish for our remaining days, was supplied by Ted's granddaughter Aoife, shortly before her fifth birthday. She would have been used to my presence in the house and would have known me as 'Barney,' but had never been at a reading session until this particular day. She had a small drawing book and pencil and appeared to be engrossed in her work. As I read, I was conscious that she came to sit close to me on the couch. I finished the chapter, and as Ted and I exchanged some views she held up her book and began to read. We stopped to listen to the most enthralling story either of us had ever heard. It lasted for at least six or seven minutes during which I looked at the blank page from which she was 'reading'. We both applauded as she finished and she was pleased. I feel Aoife will read this book in years to come, so it is in order for me to thank her for the pleasure she gave Granda and Barney with her reading from the imagination.

The first week of March 2010 is one I will never forget. I attended the funeral of Eugene McKay in Armagh Cathedral on Monday. On Tuesday I was in Newry Cathedral for the funeral of Sean Toal, a well known and much loved Armagh zealot. Wednesday saw me in my home church, St Peter's, for the funeral of Siona Carey, only daughter of Gus and Rose, for years my neighbours on Summerhill. On Thursday I was in Clonallon Parish Church for the funeral service of Jimmy Cumming, butcher and gentleman, whose father and mother I have written of in an early page. Friday saw me back in St Peter's for the obsequies of Ted Bradley, and the band played for Ted as it did for Toots.

The next day I was in Massforth for the funeral of Susan Rodgers, my classmate in Carrick School and later my neighbour on Summerhill for many years. I finished the week on Sunday at the commanding height of Barr Church, with most of Down's 1960 team, to pay tribute to Seamus Kennedy of Glenn, a popular and valued member of the panel whose death took us all by surprise. I had to be represented by a family member at two other funerals in the course of those seven days. Harry Lambe, whose father and grandfather I have written about, died in New York; his funeral took place in Warrenpoint as I attended the McKay funeral in Armagh. Finally, Joe Smith, who was the friend of everyone in the town, and who always looked so well, slipped away quietly and was buried as I attended at Barr. I was surprised to learn that the dapper Joe had reached the 90 mark.

Before March ended the name of Jim O'Neill was added to the list of the dead, thereby bringing The Crown Hotel-O'Neill story to an end, and a sad end at that, being the last remaining link of that O'Neill family with The Point. Finally, March also brought the death of Patsy O'Hagan, one of our stalwarts of the 1960 era. I was unable to travel to Galway for his funeral, but I was present in Cabra Church a few nights later when Down Gaeldom gathered to pay him a massive tribute. Kevin Bradley, younger brother of Ted, died in August.

With such a litany of deaths one would imagine that we were on our knees for most of the year but, even as we mourned, the locals were in celebration mode, recalling and commemorating Down's historic win in the famous final with Kerry 50 years before, our very first Championship win over The Kingdom. In truth, I think we celebrated more than we did in the eventful 1960 year itself.

In mid February the BBC made a documentary, bringing the 1960 team survivors and family representatives of those deceased down to Croke Park for a re-run of the great day. Next was the wonderful Congress celebration at Newcastle, where we were hosted by the GAA Central Council and the Down County Board. Then came the Stormont Assembly, the Ulster Council, and the Irish Sportswriters' Association tributes, followed by the Castlewellan Festival, and the very personal event in my home town at The First and Last picture gallery in The Point, and finally the Down Supporters' Club event. Such was the pace of celebrations I could not keep up with it all, and had to miss some of them. While all these activities were going on, and after disappointing us in failing to Tyrone in the Ulster Championship, Down went through the magical back door and emerged as potential champions after beating Longford, Offaly, Sligo, Kerry and Kildare, showing improvement with every outing.

The final with Cork took on added significance. It was an unbelievable turnabout in a matter of months. The atmosphere in Down was as frenetic as it was in 1960. The Down and Kerry teams of that first Championship meeting were guests of the Association on the day with the Downmen taking a bow in the pre-match presentations. The hand of history may have pressed heavily on Down shoulders but our standard bearers lost nothing in defeat. They have revived Down fortunes with displays which showed the quality which might be termed typical Down. James McCartan and his team have set us back on the path of optimism.

Even in the midst of such a joyful period we were brought to earth by the death of a young Warrenpoint man, Patrick Dinsmore; he collapsed and died during a minor game with Rostrevor in Pettit Park a week before the Down-Kildare game. When I heard the shocking news I immediately recalled the night I was told of the death of Brian McGreevy 53 years before. I thought of his parents, Barney and Deirdre, and his grandparents, my neighbours, Billy and Bernie, and the anguish which they and the wider Dinsmore family would experience for the rest of their lives. Over his early years, I would have known Patrick as a young Dinsmore who was always very respectful to 'Mr Carr'.

When he was a second year student in St Colman's College, he called with me one day and asked if he could speak to me. I invited him in, and he explained that his class had been given a project. Each boy had to interview a famous person in their locality. He continued, 'I asked Granny were there any famous people in The Point, and she told me to come down and speak to you, for you were the first manager of the Down team.' Patrick and I talked for 40 minutes in which questions and answers were interspersed with laughter. It was a beautiful experience for me, because I recognised the natural innocence which the Lord bestows on His chosen. At the time, I was very pleased to have been interviewed by Patrick, now I feel privileged.

I can think of no better way of closing this memoir than by introducing another little coincidence. It concerns a man called Bertie Bain, who worked at the Southern Education and Library Board's headquarters in Armagh where I was based for the last years of my working life. Bertie acted as a security officer cum commissionaire in the entrance hall. Every morning he greeted me as 'Mr Carr', and on leaving in the evening his farewell was the same, 'Mr Carr'. Any other time of the day it was 'Barney'.

When I was leaving the building for the last time as an official of the Board, he was dealing with a member of the public remote from the door; I waved over to him, but he called, 'Mr Carr, could I speak to you for one minute.' He came over to me and apologised for not being able to attend my official farewell which had taken place a couple of days before. He shook my hand as he took a small box from his pocket saying, 'Mr Carr, this is small gift I would like to give you but it is very precious. It is a copy of the Scripture and I have written an inscription which I hope you will like.' I thanked him profusely and took the lid off the small box to reveal 'The Salvation Testament', the first page of which bore the inscription:

'To: Mr B. Carr From: Bertie Bain (27th January 1988)

With sincere best wishes, for a long, happy and healthy retirement.
AND
May the blessing of the Lord, that maketh rich and addeth no sorrow with it, be your daily portion.'

In red ink and underlined was the instruction:
Please read, St Matthew 6:33

When I got to my car I opened the little testament and read the familiar verse,
'But seek ye first the kingdom of God and his righteousness; and all these things shall be added on to you.'
It is over 23 years since Bertie Bain blessed me. In that time, I have been enriched and without sorrow.

The End

The Summerhill Croquet Club
Back row left to right : Tom O Hare, Mick Barry, John Carr, Brother John Carr, Kevin O Callaghan
Front row left to right : Jimmy Morgan, Paddy Carr, Philly Carr, Mickey Savage

Barney Carr with Peter McDermott at Jubilee celebrations 2010

At a wedding
John Carr and Tarlach McAnulty

Barney with grandsons Eoin, Éanna and Iarlaith

It's the way I tell them
Barney with Seamus Mallon

Cruising with the Canon
Left to right : Seamas McNulty, Barney Carr, Jim O Hanlon, Joe Powderly, Canon John Kearney, Betty McNulty,
Kate Powderly, Florrie O Hanlon, Bernadette Barry, Maureen Burns and Kay McParlan

Wedding 1951
Barney, Chris & Cynthia O Boyle, Sally Stanley

Liam O Hare's Wedding 1956
Anne & Barney Carr, Tom & Maggie Byrne(Née O Brien).

Boston 1962
The Down party meets Archbishop Cushing

Left to right: TP Murphy, Barney Carr, Brian Morgan, Bobby Langan, George Tinnelly,
George Lavery, Dan McCartan, Kevin Mussen, extreme right Jarleth Carey

Index

Y

Pictures from the Past

Warrenpoint National Flute Band 1921

Back row left to right: Joe 'Blossom' McAnulty, Jack Hanna, Jimmy Caulfield, Paddy O Hagan, Barney Carr, Pat Cunningham, Pat Durkin, James Burns.
Middle row left to right: Harry Smyth, Jack Moore, Paddy McCaughey, Hugh Carr, J. Clarke, John Clarke, Matt Doran, Harry O Prey, Barney Gallagher, J.Burns, Jim Caulfield, Harry McCormack.
Front row seated left to right: Jimmy Carr, Joe McGuigan, P. McAnulty, C. Caulfield, Joe Burns, Dan Caulfield.
Front line on ground: F. Smyth, M. Durkin, Billy Burns, B. Hanna, Paddy Mackrell, H. McGuigan.

Production of The Colleen Bawn 1920s

Back row left to right: Harry O Prey, Edward Grant, Kathleen McGivern, unidentified ,unidentified, , Paddy McCaughey, Tommy Boyle, Hugh Carr, Hugh White, Harry Peers, Paddy McGivern, unidentified, Tom McGivern, Mick Boyle.
Middle row left to right: May Hoy, Vincent Crawford, Rose Mehegan, George Donaldson, Rose Crawford, Mick Trainor, Kate McAnulty.
Front row left to right: unidentified, Harry Smyth, Sarah O Hagan, Mary Boyle, Jack Campbell.

New York Celtic Football Team circa 1922
3rd from left Jimmy Watters from Warrenpoint

Down Team 1940
*Back row left to right: Tom Hannity (Bryansford), Mickey King (Bryansford), John O Hare
(Warrenpoint), Jimmy McLoughlin (Newry), Johnnie Carr (Warrenpoint), Dan Morgan (Annaclone),
Danny Doran (Annaclone), Brian Denvir (Kilief).
Front row left to right: Joe Kane (Kilcoo), John McClorey (Warrenpoint), Gerry Carr (Warrenpoint), Terry
McCormack (Warrenpoint), Tom McCann(Bryansford), Bro. Mick Lynch (Downpatrick),
Charlie McConville (Kilkeel).
Charlie is the sole survivor aged 97.*

The Commercial Club – Retirement of Jack Moran as Secretary
Back row left to right: Harry Lynch, Hugh Carr, Pat Trainor, Joe Boylan, Bill O Reilly, Pat McShane,
Jim Cunningham, James O Hare, Colin Slater, Stewart Lawson, Bob Matthews.
Front Row left to right: Charlie Burns, Isaac Coffey, Kitty Moran, Jack Moran, Eugene O Hagan,
Seán Smyth.

Uncle Jimmy Carr on O Connell St.